WHAT YOU DON'T KNOW ABOUT THE
100
MOST IMPORTANT EVENTS IN
CHURCH HISTORY

CASEY PAUL GRIFFITHS • SUSAN EASTON BLACK • MARY JANE WOODGER

DESERET
BOOK

SALT LAKE CITY, UTAH

Library of Congress Cataloging-in-Publication Data
Names: Griffiths, Casey Paul, author. | Black, Susan Easton, author. | Woodger, Mary Jane, author.
Title: What you don't know about the 100 most important events in church history / Casey Paul Griffiths, Susan Easton Black, Mary Jane Woodger.
Description: Salt Lake City, Utah : Deseret Book, [2017] | Includes bibliographical references.
Identifiers: LCCN 2016048595 | ISBN 9781629722467 (paperbound)
Subjects: LCSH: The Church of Jesus Christ of Latter-day Saints—History. | Mormon Church—History.
Classification: LCC BX8611 .G75 2017 | DDC 289.3/3209—dc23
LC record available at https://lccn.loc.gov/2016048595

Printed in the United States of America
Edwards Brothers Malloy, Ann Arbor, MI

10 9 8 7 6 5 4 3 2 1

For Elizabeth, Acacia, Joshua, and Emmeline
—*CPG*

For George
—*SEB*

For Chris
—*MJW*

Contents

Preface

We live in an era when "top ten" lists seem to be multiplying at an exponential rate. Often such lists present an excuse for sensationalized writing and shallow analysis. At the same time, the mental exercise of creating a list of the most important events in any span of time can impel a person to think critically about events, stories, and people. This book project began when Casey Griffiths read a book called *The 100 Most Important Events in Christian History* and thought about what events a similar list from the history of the Latter-day Saints would include. After accepting an invitation to become a visiting professor at Brigham Young University, he began to create his list.

Recognizing that the task might be beyond his individual expertise, he invited a distinguished colleague, Mary Jane Woodger, to join in formulating the final list of 100 events. Her skill as a writer and her insights into the history of Latter-day Saint women added to Casey's focus on the development of the global Church. Mary Jane in turn reached out to Susan Easton Black, whose wide-ranging knowledge of nineteenth-century Church history proved an invaluable addition to the project. All three of us likewise received generous assistance from colleagues in the Department of Church History and Doctrine at Brigham Young University. From them we gained expert insights into early, modern, and global Latter-day Saint history.

We also used the most current scholarship and sources available to us. In many instances, this means we have cited the Joseph Smith Papers and other documents at josephsmith papers.org. Spelling, capitalization, and punctuation in such quotations has been modernized for ease in reading.

With a history and records that span nearly 190 years, the story of the Latter-day Saints is a vital and lively topic for historians, critics, and members alike. As teachers of Church history, we see the inherent worth of providing readers with a series of brief essays on the top 100 events that have shaped the Latter-day Saints as a people.

Nonetheless, it was not our intention to create a definitive list of such events. We have made no attempt to list these 100 events in order of importance or prominence—we have simply listed them chronologically. It is our hope to start a conversation about well-known events and introduce a few lesser-known ones that have played a key role in shaping the beliefs and practices of Latter-day Saints worldwide.

Our approach toward the well-known events, such as the First Vision, has been to provide a brief overview of the complexities that surround the defining historical moments. For instance, most Latter-day Saints are familiar with the story of the First Vision as presented in the Pearl of Great Price but are less familiar with other accounts that Joseph Smith and his contemporaries shared about that pivotal, sacred event.

Our approach to lesser-known events has been to tell the event in context and then show why we think the event is significant enough to be included in the list. For instance, most Latter-day Saints likely know the basics of Brigham Young's epic trek to the Great Basin in 1847 but know little of the last months of his life thirty years later when the aging leader initiated a sweeping series of reforms that created the modern ward and branch structure of the Church.

Ever-present was our realization that from small things proceeds that which is great, from the organization of the Church with only a handful of members to the creation of such worldwide programs as Humanitarian Services and the Perpetual Education Fund, and from President Spencer W. Kimball's announcement that all worthy males could receive the priesthood to the fulfillment of President Gordon B. Hinckley's vision to build smaller temples around the world and have a hundred operating temples before the end of the twentieth century. Selecting events from the most recent years of Church history was thus a particular challenge, as in many cases not enough time has passed to show clearly which events should be included.

More important, however, is our recognition that the history of the Church is continuing and that the greatest events are still to come. Yet as this generation moves toward the millennial day, it is important to pause to reflect upon the events of the past that shape our future. With that in mind, we are proud to present *What You Don't Know about the 100 Most Important Events in Church History.*

Acknowledgments

We gratefully acknowledge the faculty and staff of Religious Education at Brigham Young University, many of whom contributed to this work and assisted in its preparation. Robert L. Millet and Richard E. Bennett provided encouragment and suggestions when the project was just an idea. As the work progressed, Gerrit Dirkmaat, J. B. Haws, Kenneth L. Alford, Craig K. Manscill, and Scott C. Esplin read portions of the manuscript and offered suggestions. Alexander L. Baugh, Andrew H. Hedges, Michael Hubbard MacKay, and Greg Wilkinson were also consulted. We are grateful for their expertise in early LDS Church history and their valuable guidance. We also thank the Religious Education staff, led by Patty Smith and Beverly Yellowhorse, for their help in preparing the manuscript. It is a blessing to work with such talented and generous people.

We were fortunate also to have the assistance of a number of hardworking and diligent BYU students who assisted in researching and editing the manuscript. The project would not have been possible without the assistance of Jillie Orth, Anne Katherine Toronto, Elijah "Kaika" Cole, Charlotte Searle, Tyler Smith, Kalli K. Searle, and Carli Hanson.

We likewise express thanks to the staff at the Church History Library, Harold B. Lee Library, J. Willard Marriott Library, Merrill-Cazier Library, and other archival repositories. We express special appreciation to Cindy Brightenburg, who assisted in securing several images used in the book. We appreciate the assistance of Brent L. Top, dean of Religious Education at BYU, because many of the photographs featured in this book were taken during a tour for new faculty that Dean Top arranged. We thank him and others in the dean's office, including Robert L. Freeman and Dana Pike, for their support of Religious Education.

We thank the wonderful staff of Deseret Book for their fine work and encouragement. We are indebted to Lisa Roper, who tirelessly shepherded the project through each stage. It was a delight to work with Suzanne Brady, Heather Ward, Malina Grigg, and Rachael Ward, who completed their work with grace and courtesy.

Finally, we express appreciation to our families, who offered encouragement and moral support. It can be difficult to live with a family member who resides in the twenty-first century but spends most of the day wandering around in an earlier one. We thank them for their love and patience.

1
The First Vision

The Sacred Grove, site of the First Vision.

1820

The First Vision—the appearance of God the Father and his Son, Jesus Christ, to young Joseph Smith—is the founding event in the history of The Church of Jesus Christ of Latter-day Saints. In a few moments in the woods near his home in Manchester, New York, Joseph Smith saw in vision Heavenly Beings. The vision cut through thousands of years of debates, councils, theological writings, and guesses about the nature of God. The experience of Joseph Smith in the grove confirmed the existence of God, and the reality of the resurrection and mission of Jesus Christ.

Although members of the Church today are most familiar with the 1838 description of the First Vision found in the Pearl of Great Price, the Prophet also gave several other accounts of the event. The earliest known account of the First Vision, the only one in Joseph Smith's own handwriting, dates to the summer of 1832.[1] It reads, in part: "A pillar of light above the brightness of the sun at noon day came down from above and rested upon me. I was filled with the Spirit of God and the Lord opened the heavens upon me, and I saw the Lord. He spake unto me saying, 'Joseph, my son, thy sins are forgiven thee.'"[2]

The next account of the First Vision was recorded by a scribe on November 9–11, 1835: "A personage appeared in the midst of this pillar of flame which was spread all around, and yet nothing consumed. Another personage soon appeared like unto the first, he said unto me, 'Thy sins are forgiven thee,' he testified unto me that Jesus Christ is the Son of God; . . . I saw many angels in this vision."[3]

A third account, recorded a few days later, adds, "[I] received the first visitation of Angels . . . when I was about 14 years old."[4]

The 1838 account in the Pearl of Great Price has long been regarded by Latter-day Saints as holy writ. Joseph Smith said that this account was written "to disabuse the public mind, and put all enquirers after truth into possession of the facts, as they have transpired, in relation both to myself and the Church."

The account emphasizes Joseph's search for the true Church, the appearance of God the Father, and the introduction of Jesus Christ. It records that the Savior advised Joseph Smith not to join any of the churches, "for they were all wrong" and "all their creeds were an abomination in his sight." The account concludes with Joseph's words, "Many other things did he say unto me, which I cannot write at this time" (Joseph Smith–History 1:1, 19–20).

Another account of the First Vision is contained in an 1841 letter Joseph Smith addressed to John Wentworth, editor of the Chicago *Democrat.* Wentworth had inquired of the vision on behalf of George Barstow, who was writing a history of New Hampshire. A published version of Joseph's letter to John Wentworth first appeared in the *Times and Seasons* under the heading "Church History."[5]

Joseph also addressed a word-for-word copy of the Wentworth letter to Israel Daniel Rupp, a historian from Pennsylvania, who was documenting the history of religious denominations within the United States. Joseph said of his vision, "My mind was taken away from the objects with which I was surrounded, and I was enwrapped in a heavenly vision and saw two glorious personages who exactly resembled each other in features and likeness, surrounded with a brilliant light which eclipsed the sun at noon day." He wrote of learning that none of the churches of his day "was acknowledged of God as his Church and Kingdom" and that he received "a promise that the fulness of the gospel should at some future time be made known unto me."[6]

A few of Joseph's associates also published accounts of hearing from Joseph Smith about the First Vision. Orson Pratt's 1840 account tells of Joseph seeing a pillar of light at a "considerable distance" and "as it drew nearer, it increased in brightness and magnitude." Elder Pratt concluded that Joseph "expected to have seen the leaves and boughs of the trees consumed, as soon as the light came in contact with them; but, perceiving that it did not produce that effect, he was encouraged with the hopes of being able to endure its presence."[7]

Orson Hyde's 1842 account says that the adversary filled Joseph's "mind with doubts and brought to mind all manner of inappropriate images to prevent him from obtaining the object of his endeavors."[8]

Other Latter-day Saints, including David Nye White and Alexander Neibaur, wrote of Joseph Smith telling them of the First Vision. White wrote that Joseph told him that he "went out into the woods where my father had a clearing, and went to the stump where I had stuck my axe."[9] Brother Neibaur wrote of "a personage in the fire [with] light complexion, blue eyes, [and] a piece of white cloth drawn over his shoulders. His right arm [was] bare." Neibaur added, "After a while another person came to the side of the first."[10]

In recent years more reports of the vision have come to light. In his diary John Walker recorded a testimony meeting in which Elder John Alger reported hearing Joseph Smith speak of the First Vision. Walker penned, "God touched his [Joseph's] eyes with his finger and said, 'Joseph, this is my Beloved Son, hear Him.' As soon as the Lord had touched his eyes with his finger he immediately saw the Savior." Walker also wrote, "Joseph while speaking of it put his finger to his right eye, suiting the

DID YOU KNOW?

- The earliest known account of the First Vision, the only one in Joseph Smith's own handwriting, dates to the summer of 1832.

- In one account of the First Vision, the first words spoken to Joseph Smith were that his sins were forgiven.

action with the words so as to illustrate and at the same time to impress the occurrence on the minds of those unto whom he was speaking."[11] This account was recorded in 1893, nearly fifty years after the event Walker wrote about, but it does provide interesting details about the deeply personal nature of the First Vision.

These additional contemporary accounts of the First Vision give us further insights into the founding event of the Restoration. It should be noted, however, that the details are less significant than the central message of the reality of God the Father and his Son Jesus Christ and of the Savior's infinite atonement. President Henry B. Eyring said that the First Vision "represents that moment when Joseph learned there was a way for the power of the Atonement of Jesus Christ to be unlocked fully. Because of what Joseph saw and what began at this moment, the Savior was able, through this great and valiant servant and through others that He sent, to restore power and privilege. That power and privilege allows us, and all who will live, to have the benefit of Jesus Christ's Atonement work in our lives."[12]

NOTES

1. History, ca. Summer 1832, source note, joseph smithpapers.org.
2. Davidson et al., *Histories,* 1:12–13, or History, ca. Summer 1832, 3, josephsmithpapers.org.
3. Jessee et al., *Journals,* 1:88, or josephsmithpapers.org.
4. Jessee et al., *Journals,* 1:100, or josephsmith papers.org.
5. "Church History," *Times and Seasons,* Mar. 1, 1842, 706–7, josephsmithpapers.org.
6. History, 1838–1856, vol. E-1 [1 July 1843–30 April 1844], josephsmithpapers.org; "Church History," *Times and Seasons,* Mar. 1, 1842, 706–10.
7. Pratt, *Interesting Account of Several Remarkable Visions,* 3–5.
8. Hyde, *Ein Ruf aus der Wuste* [A cry out of the wilderness], 14–15; English translation at joseph smithpapers.org.
9. White, "The Prairies, Joe Smith, the Temple, the Mormons &c.," *Pittsburgh Weekly Gazette,* Sept. 15, 1843.
10. Alexander Neibaur, Journal, May 24, 1844, 23, josephsmithpapers.org.
11. John Alger, in McConkie, *Remembering Joseph,* 312–13.
12. Eyring, unveiling of *The Vision* (statue), Brigham Young University, Provo, Utah, Oct. 17, 1997.

2
The Angel Moroni Visits Joseph Smith

1823

Monument at Hill Cumorah depicting the angel Moroni.

The visitations of the angel Moroni to seventeen-year-old Joseph Smith in September 1823 are the most detailed descriptions of an angelic appearance in all of holy writ. On Sunday evening of September 21, in Manchester, New York, young Joseph supplicated the Lord "for forgiveness of all my sins and follies, and also for a manifestation to me, that I might know of my state and standing before him." While calling upon the Lord,

Joseph said, "I discovered a light appearing in my room, which continued to increase until the room was lighter than at noonday, when immediately a personage appeared at my bedside, standing in the air, for his feet did not touch the floor." The angelic being "called me by name, and said unto me that he was a messenger sent from the presence of God to me, and that his name was Moroni." The angel informed Joseph Smith that "God had a work for me to do; and that my name should be had for good and evil among all nations, kindreds, and tongues, or that it should be both good and evil spoken of among all people." The conflicting reputation would center on a book written on gold plates and a Urim and Thummim prepared "for the purpose of translating the book" (Joseph Smith–History 1:29–30, 33, 35).

According to an account written in 1835 by Oliver Cowdery, the angel quoted more than two dozen biblical passages to Joseph during the course of their visit. The general theme of those passages centered on the work and mission of Joseph Smith, as foretold by God's ancient prophets and apostles, and spoke both of the Lord's desire to gather the righteous and of the prophesied destructions before the Savior's second coming.[1]

Using those passages, Moroni informed Joseph of "a marvellous work and a wonder" about to take place and that "God hath chosen the foolish things of the world to confound the wise" (Isaiah 29:14; 1 Corinthians 1:27). Oliver's witness of the event was secondhand, but given his close relationship to the Prophet, there are compelling reasons to accept his more detailed descriptions of Moroni's message.[2]

After this recitation of the scriptures, the angel turned to more immediate matters. During their conversation, Joseph later noted, "the place [the hill] where the plates were deposited" was shown him in vision. When the vision closed, "the room was again left dark," and Joseph was left alone to reflect on the message. Before dawn, the messenger appeared two more times to converse with him again, his visitations occupying "the whole of that night" (Joseph Smith–History 1:42–43, 47).

The next morning, September 22, 1823, Joseph arose from his bed and went about the "necessary labors of the day" in harvesting the fields of his father's farm. In so doing, he discovered "my strength so exhausted as to render me entirely unable." While Joseph was returning home, the angel Moroni appeared again and "related unto me all that he had related to me the previous night, and commanded me to go to my father and tell him of the vision and commandments which I had received." Obediently, Joseph retraced his steps to the field and told his father of the angel and his message. Father Smith assured his young son of the divine nature of the visitations: "It was of God" (Joseph Smith–History 1:48–50).

Recovering somewhat, Joseph then walked to the place shown him in vision the night before: "a hill of considerable size, and the most elevated of any in the neighborhood," about three miles southeast of Joseph Smith Sr.'s farm. There, "under a stone of considerable size, lay the plates, deposited in a stone box." Joseph's attempt to take the plates out of the box was "forbidden by the messenger" (Joseph Smith–History 1:51, 53). In his 1832 history, Joseph Smith admitted he was tempted to take the plates, writing that he "straightway made three attempts to get them [the plates] . . .

therefore I cried unto the Lord in the agony of my soul, Why can I not obtain them?" The angel appeared to Joseph again, telling him, "'You cannot now obtain them' . . . for now I had been tempted of the adversary and sought the plates to obtain riches and kept not the commandment that I should have an eye single to the glory of God."[3]

Four years passed before Joseph, by then twenty-one, was given the plates and the Urim and Thummim. His mother, Lucy Mack Smith, later recorded that during the interim, Joseph shared with his family a description of "the ancient inhabitants of this continent; their dress, mode of travelling, and the animals upon which they rode; their cities, and their buildings, with every particular; . . . their mode of warfare, as also their religious worship." Mother Smith recorded that "this he would do with as much ease, seemingly, as if he had spent his whole life with them." She added, "I presume we presented an aspect as singular as any family that ever lived upon the face of the Earth: all seated in a circle, father, mother, sons, and daughters, and giving the most profound attention to a boy."[4]

Joseph's brother William was asked years later, "Did you not doubt Joseph's testimony sometimes?" He replied, "No. We all had implicit confidence in what he said. He was a truthful boy. Father and Mother believed him; why should not the children?"[5]

The Smiths were "convinced that God was

DID YOU KNOW?

- After the First Vision, three years passed before Joseph Smith received another heavenly visitor.

- According to Oliver Cowdery, the angel Moroni quoted nearly two dozen biblical passages during his visit to Joseph Smith, most of them centering on events of the last days.

about to bring to light something that we might stay our minds upon, something that we could get a more definite idea of than anything which had been taught us heretofore." Their conviction of forthcoming truth led Mother Smith to write, "Peace and tranquillity reigned in our midst."[6]

During the four years before he received the plates, Joseph met and conversed annually with Moroni on the hill in Palmyra. Joseph also had other encounters with the angelic messenger. His mother wrote of Joseph returning home one evening later than expected in the spring of 1827. When his father asked about his lateness, "Presently [Joseph] smiled, and said in a calm tone, 'I have taken the severest chastisement that I have ever had in my life.'" Father Smith was "quite angry" with what he assumed was the action of some man in town. "'Stop, father, stop,' said Joseph, 'it was the angel of the Lord: as I passed by the hill of Cumorah, where the plates are, the angel met me, and said that I had not been engaged enough in the work of the Lord; that the time had come for the record to be brought forth; and that I must be up and doing, and set myself about the things which God had commanded me to do.'"[7]

Near midnight on September 22, 1827, Joseph climbed the hill where the plates were deposited and, he recorded, the angel Moroni "delivered [the plates] up to me." Joseph Smith translated the plates into what is now entitled the Book of Mormon: Another Testament of Jesus Christ. It is one of the most widely distributed books in the world, with more than 150 million copies published in 110 languages.

As for the whereabouts of the gold plates and the Urim and Thummim, Joseph wrote, "When, according to arrangement, the messenger [Moroni] called for them, I delivered them up to him; and he has them in his charge until this day" (Joseph Smith–History 1:59–60).[8]

NOTES

1. "Letter IV. To W. W. Phelps, Esq.," *Latter Day Saints' Messenger and Advocate,* Feb. 1835, 77–80; see also "Letter VI. To W. W. Phelps, Esq.," *Messenger and Advocate,* Apr. 1835, 108–12.

2. "Letter IV. To W. W. Phelps, Esq.," *Messenger and Advocate,* Feb. 1835, 77–80; *Messenger and Advocate,* Apr. 1835, 109; see Kent P. Jackson, "The Appearance of Moroni to Joseph Smith," in Millet and Jackson, *Pearl of Great Price,* 348–59.

3. History, circa Summer 1832, 4–5, josephsmith papers.org.

4. Lucy Mack Smith, History, 1845, 87, 86, joseph smithpapers.org.

5. "Another Testimony. Statement of William Smith, Concerning Joseph, the Prophet," *Deseret Evening News,* Jan. 20, 1894, 11; Journal History of the Church, Jan. 20, 1894, Church History Library, The Church of Jesus Christ of Latter-day Saints, Salt Lake City, Utah; Barrett, *Young Joseph,* 73.

6. Lucy Mack Smith, History, 1844–1845, bk. 4, p. 1, josephsmithpapers.org.

7. Smith, *History of Joseph Smith by His Mother,* 100; Peterson, *Moroni,* 110.

8. History, 1838–1856, vol. A-1 [23 December 1805–30 August 1834], 8; josephsmithpapers .org.

3
Joseph Smith Receives the Plates

A representation of the plates and the Urim and Thummim, an instrument used in translating the Book of Mormon.

1827

anticipated that he would receive the ancient plates. Joseph recorded how agonizing it was for him to fail to obtain them: "I cried unto the Lord in the agony of my soul, Why can I not obtain them? Behold the angel appeared unto me again and said unto me, You have not kept the commandments of the Lord which I gave unto you therefore you cannot now obtain them for the time is not yet fulfilled; therefore, thou wast left unto temptation that thou mightest be made acquainted with the power of the adversary; therefore, repent and call on the Lord. Thou shalt be forgiven and in his own due time thou shalt obtain them. For now I had been tempted of the adversary and sought the plates to obtain riches and kept not the commandment that I should have an eye single to the Glory of God; therefore, I was chastened and sought diligently to obtain the plates."[2]

Joseph's mother recorded that they "doubled [their] diligence in prayer that Joseph might be more fully instructed and preserved from all the wiles and machination of him who lieth in wait to deceive."[3]

The following year Joseph and his father traveled to Harmony (near what is now Oakdale, Susquehanna County), Pennsylvania, to work for a man named Josiah Stowell. During that time, Joseph boarded at the farmhouse of Isaac Hale. He later recorded that there "I first saw my wife . . . Emma Hale." The happiness of meeting Emma was tempered by the cold attitude of her father toward him. Joseph explained, "Owing to my still continuing to assert that I had seen a vision,

Of all his family, it was Alvin, Joseph Smith's oldest brother, who "showed the most intense interest" in Joseph's angelic visitations. On November 15, 1823, after a short illness, Alvin said, "Joseph, I am going to die now. . . . I want you to be a good boy, and do everything that lays in your power to obtain the record—Be faithful in receiving instruction, and in keeping every commandment that is given you."[1] Nearly a year later, when Joseph was again visited by the angel Moroni in September 1824, his family anxiously persecution still followed me, and my wife's father's family were very much opposed."[4]

When the employment ended, he stayed in the vicinity and courted Emma for a time before returning to his family in New York. There Joseph harvested wheat for his father and, according to Joseph Knight Sr., learned what he needed to do to receive the treasure in the nearby hill. Joseph had confided to Knight that the angel Moroni had told him he could receive the treasure the following September if he brought with him the "right person." Joseph looked into the seer stone and discovered the right person to be "Emma Hale."[5]

Joseph Smith and Emma Hale were married a short time before Joseph was to receive the plates. Because of the disapproval of Emma's father, the couple chose to elope and were married on January 18, 1827. Emma wrote later: "I was married at South Bainbridge, New York; at the house of Squire Tarbell. . . . I was visiting at Mr. Stowell's . . . and saw [Joseph] there. I had no intention of marrying when I left home; but, during my visit at Mr. Stowell's [Joseph] . . . urged me to marry him, and preferring to marry him to any other man I knew, I consented."[6]

After the ceremony, the newlyweds journeyed 130 miles to the Smith farmhouse, where Lucy Mack Smith had worked "to put [her] house in order, for the reception of [her] son's bride."[7]

Near midnight on September 22, 1827, nine months after their marriage, Joseph and Emma drove in a wagon to what has become known as the Hill Cumorah.[8]

While Emma waited in the wagon, Joseph climbed the hill to the place where the plates were deposited. There he was met by Moroni, who "delivered them [the plates] up to me with this charge: that I should be responsible for them; that if I should let them go carelessly, or through any neglect of mine, I should be cut off; but that if I would use all my endeavors to preserve them, until he, the messenger, should call for them, they should be protected" (Joseph Smith–History 1:59).[9]

Knowing the determination of his adversaries in Palmyra, Joseph hid the plates in sundry places on the Smith farm. Cash and property were offered for a glimpse of the plates, but when Joseph Smith refused, his adversaries contrived schemes to steal his treasure. Joseph wrote, "Several times I was shot at, and very narrowly escaped, and every device was made use of to get the plates away from me."[10]

To safeguard the plates, Joseph and Emma left Palmyra. They lived in the Hale home in Harmony, Pennsylvania, until Emma's father learned that he was not allowed to see the sacred objects Joseph possessed. Joseph and Emma soon purchased a home nearby from Emma's brother Jesse. There Joseph began to translate the Book of Mormon. In the east end of an upstairs room of what today we call the Joseph Smith Jr. farmhouse in Susquehanna County, Pennsylvania, Martin Harris scribed while Joseph translated the book of Lehi, the first book inscribed on the gold plates. Joseph may have used a blanket to shield the plates and the interpreters from onlookers who were anxious to observe him while he was translating.[11]

Emma Smith also served as a scribe. She testified, "I am satisfied that no man could have dictated the writing of the manuscripts unless he was inspired." In explaining the translation

DID YOU KNOW?

- Emma Smith went with Joseph the night he was given the plates by the angel Moroni.

- Joseph Smith used several different instruments, often called interpreters, during the process of translating the plates.

process, Emma said, "When [I was] acting as his scribe, [he] would dictate to me hour after hour; and when returning after meals, or after interruptions, [Joseph] would at once begin where he had left off, without either seeing the manuscript or having any portion of it read to him." Emma affirmed, "This was a usual thing for him to do. It would have been improbable that a learned man could do this; and, for one so ignorant and unlearned as he was, it was simply impossible."[12]

Of the several individuals who served as scribes to Joseph during the translation of the Book of Mormon, Oliver Cowdery was the most extensively involved. He later testified, "I wrote with my own pen the entire Book of Mormon (save a few pages) as it fell from the lips of the Prophet Joseph Smith, as he translated it by the gift and power of God, by the means of the Urim and Thummim, or, as it is called by that book, 'holy interpreters.' I beheld with my eyes, and handled with my hands the gold plates from which it was translated. I also saw with my eyes and handled with my hands the 'holy interpreters.' That book is true. Sidney Rigdon did not write it; Mr [Solomon] Spaulding did not write it; I wrote it myself as it fell from the lips of the Prophet. It contains the Everlasting Gospel . . . to preach to every nation, kindred, tongue and people. It contains principles of salvation; and if you, my hearers, will walk by its light, and obey its precepts, you will be saved with an everlasting salvation in the kingdom of God on high."[13]

Oliver declared, "These were days never to be forgotten—to sit under the sound of a voice dictated by the inspiration of heaven, awakened the utmost gratitude of this bosom. . . . to write from his mouth, as he translated, with the Urim and Thummim . . . the history, or record, called 'The book of Mormon.'"[14]

From the accounts of various witnesses of the translation, it appears that Joseph Smith used several different instruments during the process, including a seer stone he had procured sometime earlier.[15] Decades after he left the Church, David Whitmer recalled that "Joseph Smith would put the seer stone into a hat, and put his face in the hat, drawing it closely around his face to exclude the light; and in the darkness the spiritual light would shine. A piece of something resembling parchment would appear, and on that appeared the writing. One character at a time would appear, and under it was the interpretation in English. Brother Joseph would read off the English to Oliver Cowdery, who was his principal scribe, and when it was written down and repeated to Brother Joseph to see if it was correct, then it would disappear, and another character with the interpretation would appear."[16]

Early accounts of the translation process refer to the instruments given to Joseph by Moroni as "spectacles." The Book of Mormon itself refers to these instruments, indicating that their function was to "translate all records that are of ancient date; and it is a gift from God" (Mosiah 8:13). Martin Harris described the spectacles as follows: "The two stones set in a bow of silver were about two inches in diameter, perfectly round. . . . The stones were white, like polished marble, with a few gray streaks." Joseph Smith also described them as "two transparent stones." The precise amount of time Joseph used the "spectacles" or the seer stone is not known, and both instruments were at times referred to as "interpreters." In later recollections, Emma Smith often used the biblical term "Urim and Thummim," which became the phrase commonly used in the Church to describe the spectacles. In 2015 the Church published photographs of a stone that is believed to be one of the instruments Joseph used in the translation process.[17]

A most significant testimony of the Book of Mormon translation process is found in a letter Joseph Smith wrote November 13, 1843, to James Arlington Bennett. Joseph said: "By the power of God I translated the Book of Mormon from hieroglyphics; the knowledge of which was lost to the world: in which wonderful event I stood alone, an unlearned youth, to combat the worldly wisdom, and multiplied ignorance of eighteen centuries, with a new revelation; which, (if they would receive the everlasting gospel,) would open the eyes of [the world], and make plain the old paths, wherein if a man walk in all the ordinances of God blameless, he shall inherit eternal life."[18]

Latter-day Saint scholar Terryl L. Givens wrote: "When Joseph dated the commencement of his labors in the great cause of the Restoration, he would not refer back to his first vision, or even the visit of the angel Moroni. September of 1827, he told the church, was the month of his enlistment."[19] And with that enlistment, Joseph Smith began to translate the Book of Mormon, the beginning of a "marvellous work and a wonder" long prophesied by the Lord's servants (Isaiah 29:14; 2 Nephi 29:1).

Notes

1. Lucy Mack Smith, History, 1845, 91, josephsmith papers.org.
2. History, ca. Summer 1832, 4–6, josephsmith papers.org.
3. Lucy Mack Smith, History, 1845, 89, josephsmith papers.org.
4. History, 1838–1856, vol. A-1 [23 December 1805–30 August 1834], 8, josephsmithpapers.org.
5. Lucy Mack Smith, History, 1845, 105, joseph smithpapers.org; Dean C. Jessee, "Joseph Knight's Recollection of Early Mormon History," *BYU Studies* 17, no. 1 (Autumn 1976): 1, 31.
6. Emma Smith, in Backman, *Eyewitness Accounts,* 54.
7. Lucy Mack Smith, History, 1845, 97, josephsmith papers.org.
8. Lucy Mack Smith, History, 1845, 105, josephsmith papers.org
9. History, 1838–1856, vol. A-1 [23 December 1805–30 August 1834], 8, josephsmithpapers.org.
10. *Joseph Smith* [manual], 441.
11. Richard E. Turley Jr., Robin S. Jensen, and Mark Ashurst-McGee, "Joseph the Seer," *Ensign,* Oct. 2015, 56, give a brief analysis of the translation process, including the use of a seer stone in the possession of the Church.
12. *Saints' Herald,* Oct. 1, 1879, 290; "Last Testimony of Sister Emma," in Bushman, *Beginnings of Mormonism,* 96.
13. Reuben Miller, Journal, Oct. 21, 1848, in *Deseret News,* Apr. 1859, 8; *Millennial Star,* May 4, 1891, 275.
14. *Latter Day Saints' Messenger and Advocate,* Oct. 1834, 14.
15. Turley et al., "Joseph the Seer," 52.
16. Whitmer, *Address to All Believers in Christ, Part 1,* 12.
17. Skousen and Jensen, *Revelations and Translations,* 3:ix–xxiii, or josephsmithpapers.org.
18. Smith, "Reply to Jas Arlington Bennet," *Times and Seasons,* Nov. 1, 1843, 373.
19. Givens, *By the Hand of Mormon,* 21.

4
The Lost Manuscript

1828

Martin Harris, scribe for Joseph Smith until the 116 pages were lost.

With the sacred record in his care, Joseph Smith began translating in earnest. He began with the record he called the book of Lehi.[1] Martin Harris served as scribe. At some point during the first two months of the translation process, Martin asked Joseph to show him the plates. Joseph refused. Martin continued to act as scribe as Joseph dictated, but he was not placated. He again broached the subject with Joseph and asked for "liberty to carry the writings home and shew them" to his wife, Lucy, and others. Joseph said, "[He] desired of me that I would enquire of the Lord, through the Urim and Thummim, if he might not do so. I did enquire, and the answer was that he must not."[2]

Disappointed, Martin left Harmony (now Oakdale, Susquehanna County), Pennsylvania, and returned to his home in Palmyra, New York, where he told Lucy, his wife, he had been denied the privilege of showing her the translation. She insisted that he ask again. Upon returning to the Smith home in Harmony, Martin continued to serve as a scribe. Then, "after much solicitation" on Martin's part, Joseph "again inquired of the Lord." This time "permission was granted him to have the writings on certain conditions; which were, that he show them only to his brother, Preserved Harris, his own wife, his father and his mother [Nathan and Rhoda Harris], and a Mrs. [Polly Harris] Cobb, a sister to his wife."[3]

Martin agreed to the conditions and entered into a written covenant with Joseph "that he would not do otherwise than had been directed." He then "took the writings and went his way" on June 14, 1828.[4]

Martin had the manuscript in his possession for three weeks or until about July 7, 1828.[5] During that time, he showed the manuscript to his wife. It is assumed that Martin showed the manuscript to the named family members, but nothing is written on the subject. It is known, however, that Martin showed the manuscript to others:

"A very particular friend made him a visit, to whom he related all that he knew concerning the record. The man's curiosity was much excited, and he earnestly desired to see the transcript. Martin was anxious to gratify his friend although it was contrary to his obligation, but he went to seek for it. He found that the key could not be found but he resolved to carry his design into execution and to do this he picked the lock."[6]

As the days passed, Martin showed the manuscript to anyone who called or as Joseph Smith wrote, "Notwithstanding . . . the great restrictions which he had been laid under, and the solemnity of the covenant which he had made with me, he did shew them to others."[7]

When Martin "had been absent nearly three weeks, and Joseph had received no intelligence whatever from him; which was altogether aside of the arrangement when they separated," Joseph journeyed to Palmyra to recover the manuscript.[8] His visit there had been delayed nearly three weeks because of the birth of his and Emma's first child, a son they named Alvin. The baby lived only a few hours. Emma's health was precarious, and Joseph stayed by her side, nursing her back to health. As soon as she began to recover, Emma urged her husband to go to Palmyra to discover the fate of the manuscript.[9]

Lucy Mack Smith reported that as soon as Joseph arrived at the Smith farmhouse, he asked that Martin be summoned at once. Anticipating that Martin would arrive shortly, Mother Smith set out food at 8 A.M. The

Smiths "waited till 9 o'clock, and [Martin] came not—till 10. And he was not there—till 11. Still he did not make his appearance." It was not until "half-past 12" that Martin was seen "walking with a slow and measured tread towards the house—his eyes fixed thoughtfully upon the ground." When he reached the gate in the yard, "instead of passing through, he stopped short and mounted the fence; and sat some time with his hat drawn over his eyes."[10]

Finally entering the house, he sat down at the table next to those already seated. "He took up his knife and fork, as if he were going to use them; but immediately dropped them." Seeing this, Hyrum Smith asked, "Martin, why do you not eat? are you sick?"

Martin pressed "his temples with his hands, [and] cried out in a tone of deep anguish, 'Oh, I have lost my soul! I have lost my soul!'"

Joseph, who was seated at the table, jumped to his feet and asked, "Martin, have you lost that manuscript? Have you broken your oath and brought down condemnation upon my head, as well as your own?"

"'Yes, it is gone,' replied Martin, 'and I know not where.'

"'Oh, my God!' said Joseph, clinching his hands; 'All is lost! all is lost! what shall I do? I have sinned; it is I who tempted the wrath of God; for I should have been satisfied with the first answer, which I received from the Lord— for he told me that it was not safe to let the writing go out of my possession.'"

At length Joseph asked Martin to go back to his house and search again for the manuscript.

"'No,' said Martin, 'it is all in vain: I have ripped open beds and pillows; and I know it is not there.'"[11]

What happened to the lost manuscript? The answer is still unknown today.

According to Lucy Mack Smith, when Martin Harris arrived home in Palymyra his wife, Lucy, "seemed highly pleased with what she heard and entered into the spirit of it so much that she gave her husband the privilege of locking it up in a set of drawers which she had never permitted him to look into."[12] A few days later Martin broke the lock in order to show the manuscript to a friend. Lucy Smith believed that this action so enraged Lucy Harris that she hid the manuscript from Martin.[13]

If Lucy Harris did take the manuscript, what she did with it remains unknown. Years after the incident, rumors circulated through Palmyra that Lucy had destroyed the manuscript. One local resident recounted that he heard Lucy Harris "say she burned the papers. She was pretty high on combativeness." He continued, "She says she burned them up. And there was no mistake, but she did. They were never found; never came to light."[14] Another former resident claimed that Lucy Harris stole the manuscript and passed it off to "a certain Dr. Seymour" for an unknown purpose.[15]

Joseph Smith received a stern rebuke from the Lord, who told him, "You should not have feared man more than God. Although men set at naught the counsels of God, and despise his words—yet you should have been faithful" (D&C 3:7).[16] A later revelation warned Joseph not to translate again the portion he had completed: "For behold, if you should bring forth the same words, they would say that you have lied; that you have pretended to translate, but that you have contradicted your words; and behold they would publish this, and Satan would harden the hearts of the people, to stir them up to anger against you, that they might not believe my words."[17] The young prophet was devastated by the loss of the manuscript, and for a season he also lost his gift to translate and the privilege of keeping the plates. By March 1829, he had received the plates again and resumed translating.[18]

The loss of the manuscript remains one of the most dramatic and emotional episodes in the story of the coming forth of the Book of Mormon. It highlights the inexperience and poor judgment of Joseph Smith but also his sincerity and humility. The events of the episode are themselves a testament of the reality of the translation process.

Elder Jeffrey R. Holland commented on the incident, calling it "an elaborate little side story—which makes absolutely no sense at all unless, of course, there really were plates, and there really was a translation process going on, and there really had been a solemn covenant made with the Lord, and there really was an enemy who did not want that book to 'come forth in this generation' (D&C 10:33)." Elder Holland continued, "Which is only to say what so many have said before: that if Joseph Smith—or anyone else, for that matter—created the Book of Mormon out of whole cloth, that, to me, is a *far* greater miracle than the proposition that he translated it from an ancient record by an endowment of divine power."[19]

NOTES
1. Preface to the Book of Mormon, ca. Aug. 1829, iii, josephsmithpapers.org.
2. History, 1838–1856, vol. A-1 [23 December 1805–30 August 1834], 9, josephsmithpapers.org.
3. History, 1838–1856, vol. A-1 [23 December 1805–30 August 1834], 9, josephsmithpapers.org; William Pilkington, Autobiography, 15–16, Church History Library, The Church of Jesus Christ of Latter-day Saints, Salt Lake City, Utah; James C. Bennett, "Mormonism," *Hillsborough [Ohio] Gazette*, Oct. 29, 1831, 1.
4. Lucy Mack Smith, History, 1845, 127, josephsmithpapers.org.
5. Lucy Mack Smith, History, 1845, 127, josephsmithpapers.org.
6. Lucy Mack Smith, History, 1845, bk. 7, p. 7, josephsmithpapers.org.

7. *Times and Seasons,* May 16, 1842, 786; History, 1838–1856, vol. A-1 [23 December 1805–30 August 1834], 10, josephsmithpapers.org.

8. Lucy Mack Smith, History, 1845, 127, josephsmithpapers.org.

9. Lucy Mack Smith, History, 1845, 127–28, josephsmithpapers.org.

10. Lucy Mack Smith, History, 1845, 130, josephsmithpapers.org.

11. Lucy Mack Smith, History, 1845, 130–31, josephsmithpapers.org.

12. Lucy Mack Smith, History, 1844–1845, bk. 7, p. 7, josephsmithpapers.org; MacKay and Dirkmaat, *From Darkness unto Light,* 95.

13. Lucy Mack Smith, History, 1844–1845, bk. 7, p. 8, josephsmithpapers.org.

14. Lorenzo Saunders, interview by E. L. Kelley, Nov. 12, 1884, in MacKay and Dirkmaat, *From Darkness unto Light,* 95.

15. Arthur Denning, *Naked Truths about Mormonism,* 2, in MacKay and Dirkmaat, *From Darkness unto Light,* 95.

16. Revelation, July 1828 [D&C 3], 1, josephsmithpapers.org.

17. Revelation, Spring 1829 [D&C 10], 24, josephsmithpapers.org.

18. Historical Introduction, Revelation, Spring 1829 [D&C 10], 24, josephsmithpapers.org; MacKay and Dirkmaat, *From Darkness unto Light,* 105.

19. Holland, "'A Standard unto My People,'" Church Educational System Symposium on the Book of Mormon, Aug. 9, 1994, 6, byu.edu.

5
The Restoration of the Aaronic Priesthood

Monument commemorating the restoration of the Aaronic Priesthood, Susquehanna County, Pennsylvania.

1829

The Aaronic Priesthood is "an appendage to the greater, or the Melchizedek Priesthood" (D&C 107:14). It is often called the preparatory priesthood. John the Baptist—a descendant of Aaron through his priestly father, Zacharias, and his mother, Elisabeth, one of the "daughters of Aaron"—held the keys of the Aaronic Priesthood, which priesthood embraces the "gospel of repentance and of baptism, and the remission of sins, and

the law of carnal commandments" (Luke 1:5; D&C 84:27). John the Baptist conferred the Aaronic Priesthood upon Joseph Smith and Oliver Cowdery on May 15, 1829 on the banks of the Susquehanna River near Harmony (now Oakdale, Susquehanna County), Pennsylvania.[1]

As Joseph and his scribe Oliver were engaged in translating the Book of Mormon, they came upon a passage about baptism for the remission of sins.[2] They were concerned enough about the matter that on May 15, 1829, they "went into the woods" near the Susquehanna River "to pray and inquire of the Lord respecting baptism for the remission of sins as we found mentioned in the translation of the plates."[3]

Joseph recorded, "While we were thus employed praying and calling upon the Lord, a messenger from heaven descended in a cloud of light." The angel then "ordained us, saying unto us, 'Upon you my fellow servants in the name of Messiah I confer the priesthood of Aaron, which holds the keys of the ministering of angels and of the gospel of repentance, and of baptism by immersion for the remission of sins, and this shall never be taken again from the earth, until the sons of Levi do offer again an offering unto the Lord in righteousness.'"[4]

The messenger then informed them that "his name was John, the same that is called John the Baptist in the New Testament, and that he acted under the direction of Peter, James, and John, who held the keys of the priesthood of Melchizedek, which priesthood he said should in due time be conferred on us."[5]

John the Baptist commanded Joseph and Oliver "to go and be baptized" (Joseph Smith–History 1:70). Joseph recorded: "I baptized [Oliver] first, and afterwards he baptized me, after which I laid my hands upon his head and ordained him to the Aaronic Priesthood, and afterward he laid his hands on me and ordained me to the same priesthood, for so we were commanded. . . . No sooner had I baptized Oliver Cowdery than the Holy Ghost fell upon him, and he stood up and prophesied many things which should shortly come to pass. . . . We were filled with the Holy Ghost, and rejoiced in the God of our salvation."[6]

Oliver Cowdery, in near poetic form, recorded his response to receiving the Aaronic Priesthood: "What joy! what wonder! what amazement! While the world were racked and distracted—while millions were groping as the blind for the wall, and while all men were resting upon uncertainty, as a general mass, our eyes beheld, our ears heard. As in the 'blaze of day;' yes, more—above the glitter of the May sunbeam, which then shed its brilliancy over the face of nature! Then his voice, though mild, pierced to the centre, and his words, 'I am thy fellow-servant,' dispelled every fear. We listened, we gazed, we admired! 'Twas the voice of the angel from glory, 'twas a message from the Most High! and as we heard we rejoiced, while his love enkindled upon our souls, and we were wrapt in the vision of the Almighty! Where was room for doubt? No where; uncertainty had fled, doubt had sunk no more to rise, while fiction and deception had fled forever!"[7]

The angel also took the first steps in restoring the Church hierarchy by designating Joseph Smith as the first elder of the Church and Oliver Cowdery as the second.[8] The priesthood keys Joseph Smith and Oliver Cowdery received on May 15, 1829, gave them the right to administer in the Church and kingdom of God. These same keys were once held by Aaron and his descendants.[9]

The role of the Aaronic Priesthood in the Church has grown and changed throughout the years. Joseph Smith spoke of the role of "the Levitical [Aaronic] Priesthood, consisting of priests to administer in outward ordinance."[10] The Prophet received a later revelation explaining that the Aaronic Priesthood is "called the lesser priesthood . . . because it is an appendage to the greater, or Melchizedek priesthood, and has power in administering outward ordinances."[11] The appearance of John the Baptist opened the door for the ordinances of the gospel of repentance to be administered again in our day, but there was greater power of the priesthood yet to be revealed.

DID YOU KNOW?

- The restoration of the Aaronic Priesthood came about because of questions Joseph Smith and Oliver Cowdery came to have while translating the manuscript of the Book of Mormon.

- John the Baptist stated that he was acting under the direction of Peter, James, and John in conferring the Aaronic Priesthood upon Joseph Smith and Oliver Cowdery.

NOTES

1. History, 1838–1856, vol. A-1 [23 December 1805–30 August 1834], 17, josephsmithpapers.org.
2. History, 1838–1856, vol. A-1 [23 December 1805–30 August 1834], 17, josephsmithpapers.org.
3. History, ca. June 1839–ca. 1841 [Draft 2], 17, josephsmithpapers.org.
4. History, ca. June 1839–ca. 1841 [Draft 2], 17, josephsmithpapers.org.
5. History, ca. June 1839–ca. 1841 [Draft 2], 17; History, 1838–1856, vol. A-1 [23 December 1805–30 August 1834], 18, josephsmithpapers.org.

6. History, 1838–1856, vol. A-1 [23 December 1805–30 August 1834], 18, josephsmith papers.org.

7. "O. Cowdery's First Letter to W. W. Phelps," *Millennial Star,* Jan. 1843, 153.

8. History, ca. June 1839–ca. 1841 [Draft 2], 18, josephsmithpapers.org.

9. See Robinson and Garrett, *Commentary on the Doctrine and Covenants,* 1:91.

10. *Joseph Smith* [manual], 109.

11. Instruction on Priesthood, between ca. 1 Mar. and ca. 4 May 1835 [D&C 107], 83, josephsmith papers.org.

6
The Restoration of the Melchizedek Priesthood

1829

Tribute to the restoration of the Melchizedek Priesthood, Susquehanna County, Pennsylvania.

Although the exact date and relative location of the restoration of the Aaronic Priesthood are well known, determining the same information for the appearance of Peter, James, and John is more difficult. Neither Joseph Smith nor Oliver Cowdery ever recorded an exact date, though both bore a fervent witness of the restoration of the Melchizedek Priesthood through angelic messengers.[1]

Joseph recorded that he and Oliver were "forced to keep secret the circumstances of having received the Priesthood, . . . owing to a spirit of persecution which had already manifested itself."[2] No other close associate from the time recorded the date, either.

Though the exact date of the visitation of Peter, James, and John is unknown, there is no ambiguity in the revelations of Joseph Smith about the reality of the visitation or its importance in the work of restoring the gospel.[3]

In a revelation given in August 1830, the Lord spoke of "Peter, and James, and John, whom I have sent unto you, by whom I have ordained you and confirmed you to be apostles and especial witnesses of my name."[4] Speaking of this event in 1839, Joseph Smith testified, "How have we come at the Priesthood in the last days? It came down, down in regular succession. Peter, James, and John had it given to them and they gave it up."[5]

In 1846, after leaving and then returning to the Church, Oliver Cowdery declared he had "stood in the presence of John, with our departed brother Joseph, to receive the Lesser Priesthood—and in the presence of Peter, to receive the Greater."[6] On another occasion Oliver testified, "I was also present with Joseph when the Melchizedek priesthood was conferred by the holy angels of God."[7]

Understanding precisely when the Melchizedek Priesthood was restored is made more difficult because Joseph and others had an evolving understanding of the priesthood, learning more as they received more revelatory instruction, line upon line and precept upon precept. For instance, in Joseph Smith's own 1839 account, he references the Melchizedek Priesthood restoration simply in terms of having the ability to give the gift of the Holy Ghost, rather than connecting it directly to Peter, James, and John.

In his 1839 history, the Prophet recorded, "We now became anxious to have that promise realized to us, which the angel that conferred upon us the Aaronic Priesthood had given us, viz, that provided we continued faithful, we should also have the Melchizedek Priesthood, which holds the authority of the laying on of hands for the gift of the Holy Ghost."[8]

The Prophet further records, "We had for some time made this a subject of humble prayer, and at length we got together in the Chamber of Mr. [Peter] Whitmer's house in order to more particularly seek of the Lord information." In response to their pleas, "the Word of the Lord came unto us, . . . commanding us, that I should ordain Oliver Cowdery to be an Elder in the Church of Jesus Christ, and that he also should ordain me to the same." They also received further instruction to "defer our ordination until we had called together our brethren and had their sanction, and been accepted by them as their teachers."[9]

When the Church was organized in April 1830, the articles and covenants accepted for Church governance spoke of "Joseph Smith, Jun. who was called of God and ordained an apostle of Jesus Christ, an elder of the church, and also to Oliver Cowdery, who was also called of God an apostle of Jesus Christ, an elder of the church, and ordained under his hand, according to the grace of God the Father and our Lord Jesus Christ."[10]

Joseph Smith's history records that in compliance with the early directions given at the home of Father Whitmer, "we proceeded, (according to solemn commandment) to call on

our brethren to know whether they accepted us as their teachers in the things of the Kingdom of God, and whether they were satisfied that we should proceed and be organized as a Church according to said commandment which we had received. To these they consented by a unanimous vote." With the Church now officially organized Joseph recorded, "I then laid my hands upon Oliver Cowdery and ordained him an Elder of the 'Church of Jesus Christ of Latter Day Saints.' After which he ordained me also to the office of an elder of said Church."[11]

These events marked the beginning of the restoration of priesthood keys and ordinances necessary to ensure the proper governance and saving power of the Lord's kingdom. Soon other men were ordained to the priesthood. Among them was Samuel Smith, a younger brother of the Prophet, who was ordained an elder on June 9, 1830.

At a conference of the Church a year later in Kirtland, Ohio, in early June 1831, Joseph Smith recorded that he "conferred [the high priesthood] for the first time, upon several of the elders. It was clearly evident that the Lord gave us power in proportion to the work to be done and strength according to the race set before us; and grace and help as our needs required. Great harmony prevailed. Several were ordained; faith was strengthened; and humility, so necessary for the blessing of God to follow prayer, characterized the Saints."[12]

Joseph Smith remarked that "those holding

DID YOU KNOW?

• The exact date of the visitation of Peter, James, and John is unknown.

• The visitation of these ancient apostles marked the beginning of the restoration of the Melchizedek Priesthood, with later angelic ministers bringing other keys of the Melchizedek Priesthood.

the fullness of the Melchizedek Priesthood are kings and priests of the Most High God, holding the keys of power and blessings. In fact, that priesthood is a perfect law of theocracy, and stands as God to give laws to the people, administering endless lives to the sons and daughters of Adam."[13]

Later, other keys of the Melchizedek Priesthood were restored by Moses, Elias, and Elijah (D&C 110), and the powers of the priesthood continued to be unfolded throughout the early years of the Restoration.[14]

With this link between apostles of days past and apostles called anew in our own time, the critical foundation of priesthood authority was now in place.

Notes

1. See Jae R. Ballif, "Melchizedek Priesthood: Restoration of the Melchizedek Priesthood," in Ludlow, *Encyclopedia of Mormonism*, 885–86.
2. History, 1838–1856, vol. A-1 [23 December 1805–30 August 1834], 18, josephsmithpapers.org.
3. Some documents support a time for the visitation of Peter, James, and John between May 15 and May 29, 1829. These documents include the reminiscences of Addison Everett, given in 1881, and Erastus Snow, given in 1882. Although these accounts provide interesting background, neither is firsthand, both having been recorded decades after the events took place. For a thoughtful consideration of these sources and others, see Larry C. Porter, "The Restoration of the Aaronic and Melchizedek Priesthood," *Ensign*, Dec. 1996; Bushman, *Rough Stone Rolling*, 118.
4. Revelation, ca. Aug. 1835 [D&C 27], 180, josephsmithpapers.org. This revelation was later combined with a revelation given in August 1830 to form section 27 of the present edition of the Doctrine and Covenants.
5. Report of Instructions, between 26 June and 4 Aug. 1839–A, as reported by Willard Richards, 65, josephsmithpapers.org.
6. Oliver Cowdery to Phineas Young, Mar. 23, 1846, Tiffin, Seneca County, Ohio, in Welch, *Opening the Heavens,* 244.
7. Reuben Miller, Journal, Oct. 21, 1848, in Welch, *Opening the Heavens,* 244.
8. History, ca. June–Oct. 1839 [Draft 1], 7, josephsmithpapers.org.
9. History, ca. June–Oct. 1839 [Draft 1], 8, josephsmithpapers.org; MacKay et al., *Documents,* 1:xxxviii.
10. Articles and Covenants, ca. Apr. 1830 [D&C 20], 4, josephsmithpapers.org.
11. History, ca. June 1839–ca. 1841 [Draft 2], 37, josephsmithpapers.org; MacKay et al., *Documents,* 1:xxxvii–xxxix.
12. History, 1838–1856, vol. A-1 [23 December 1805–30 August 1834], 118, josephsmithpapers.org.
13. *Joseph Smith* [manual], 109.
14. Revelation, Apr. 3, 1836 [D&C 110], 192, josephsmithpapers.org.

7
The Witnesses of the Book of Mormon

THE EIGHT WITNESSES

1829

Monument to the Eight Witnesses of the Book of Mormon, Liberty, Missouri.

"The Testimony of Three Witnesses" and "The Testimony of Eight Witnesses" appear in every copy of the Book of Mormon. These testimonies were placed at the end of the first edition of the Book of Mormon.[1] In all subsequent editions, however, their testimonies have been placed at the beginning of the book, after the title page.

Late in June 1829, the Three Witnesses were shown the plates near the log home of Peter Whitmer Sr. in Fayette, New York. The day before this sacred event, David Whitmer, Oliver Cowdery, and Martin Harris read passages from the Book of Mormon manuscript and "rejoiced exceedingly," believing that the "greatest difficulty was then surmounted."[2]

They spoke of witnesses testifying of the truthfulness of the gold plates and wondered aloud if they might be the chosen witnesses. After all, they had received a conditional promise that if they relied upon the word of God, they "shall have a view of the plates, and also of the breastplate, the sword of Laban, the Urim and Thummim" (D&C 17:1).

Joseph Smith was asked to "inquire of the Lord" if Oliver, David, and Martin might have their witness. Joseph said, "They became so very solicitous, and urged me so much to inquire that at length I complied, and through the Urim and Thummim" received an answer: "This generation shall have my word through you; and in addition to your testimony, the testimony of three of my servants, whom I shall call and ordain, unto whom I will show these things. . . . Yea, they shall know of a surety that these things are true, for from heaven will I declare it unto them" (D&C 5:11–12).

The next morning Joseph Smith said to Martin Harris, "You have got to humble yourself before your God this day, that you may obtain a forgiveness of your sins: if you do, it is the will of God that you should look upon the plates in company with Oliver Cowdery and David Whitmer."[3]

As the morning progressed, Joseph and Oliver brought David from the field, where he was plowing, and in company with Martin ventured into a nearby "piece of woods" to "try to obtain by fervent and humble prayer, the fulfillment of the promises given"—that of viewing the plates. They knelt down and Joseph prayed aloud. He was followed "by each of the rest in succession," yet no manifestation came. They "again observed the same order of prayer, each calling on, and praying fervently to God in rotation." The result was as before. Fearing he was impeding the process, Martin "proposed that he would withdraw himself from us, believing as he expressed himself that his presence was the cause of our not obtaining what we wished for."[4] Accordingly, he walked away.

Joseph, Oliver, and David "knelt down again, and had not been many minutes engaged in prayer," when an angel appeared.[5]

David Whitmer recalled: "The angel stood before us. He was dressed in white, and spoke and called me by name and said 'Blessed is he that keepeth His commandments.' This is all that I heard the angel say. A table was set before us, and on it the records were placed. The records of the Nephites, from which the Book of Mormon was translated, the brass plates, the Ball of Directors, the sword of Laban and other plates. While we were viewing them the voice of God spoke out of heaven saying that the Book was true and the translation correct."[6]

After this manifestation, Joseph "went in search of Martin Harris." He found him "at a distance earnestly engaged in prayer." Joseph "joined with him." In answer to their prayers,

Joseph recorded, "[We] immediately obtained a view of the plates and [Martin Harris] cried out in an ecstasy of joy, ''Tis enough 'tis enough mine eyes have beheld mine eyes have beheld' and jumping up, shouted Hosanna and rejoiced exceedingly."[7]

When Joseph Smith returned to the Whitmer home, he exclaimed, "Father, mother, you do not know how happy I am; the Lord has now caused the plates to be shown to three more besides myself. . . . I feel as if I was relieved of a burden which was almost too heavy for me to bear, and it rejoices my soul, that I am not any longer to be entirely alone in the world." As Martin entered the Whitmer home, he said, "I have now seen an angel from Heaven who has of a surety testified of the truth of all that I have heard concerning the record and my eyes have beheld him. I have also looked upon the plates and handled them with my hands and can testify of the same to the whole world."[8]

Eight other men—Christian Whitmer, Jacob Whitmer, Peter Whitmer Jr., John Whitmer, Hiram Page, Joseph Smith Sr., Hyrum Smith, and Samuel H. Smith—were shown the plates by Joseph Smith near Joseph Smith Sr.'s log home in Manchester, New York.[9] They "did handle with [their] hands" the plates and examined the engravings "of curious workmanship."[10]

Of the eleven official witnesses of the Book of Mormon, not one ever denied his testimony.[11]

All of the Three Witnesses became disaffected from the Church in 1838. Oliver Cowdery returned to fellowship on October 21, 1848. He addressed a congregation of Latter-day Saints in Kanesville, Iowa: "Friends and Brethren,—My name is Cowdery, Oliver Cowdery. . . . I wrote, with my own pen, the entire book of Mormon (save a few pages) as it fell from the lips of the Prophet Joseph Smith. . . . That Book is true."[12]

Martin Harris journeyed west at age eighty-eight and was rebaptized. At seeing Salt Lake City, he exclaimed, "Who would have thought that the Book of Mormon would have done all this?"[13]

David Whitmer defended the Book of Mormon and his witness of it, but he did not return to the Church.

Of the Eight Witnesses, five remained in the Church until their deaths: Christian Whitmer, Peter Whitmer Jr., Joseph Smith Sr., Hyrum Smith, and Samuel H. Smith. Three of the eight left the Church in 1838 and did not return: John Whitmer, Jacob Whitmer, and Hiram Page.

In addition to the official witnesses of the Book of Mormon, Mary Musselman Whitmer (1778–1856)—wife of Peter Whitmer Sr. and mother of witnesses Christian, Peter Jr., Jacob, and John Whitmer—was also shown the plates, according to an 1878 interview David Whitmer gave to Orson Pratt and Joseph F. Smith.

Apparently, while the final stages of the translation were taking place in her home, Mary Whitmer became overwhelmed at the amount of work necessary to take care of her family and their guests. While on her way to milk the family cow, she was met by an "old man" who told her in a calm, friendly tone, "You have been very faithful and diligent in your labors, but you are tired because of the increase of your toil, it is proper therefore that you should receive a witness that your faith may be strengthened." According to another account, provided by Mary's grandson John C. Whitmer, the stranger then "untied his knapsack and showed her a bundle of plates, which in size and appearance corresponded with description subsequently given by the witnesses of the Book of Mormon. . . . He told her to be patient and faithful in bearing her burden a little longer." According to John C. Whitmer, Mary

was "a strong believer in the Book of Mormon until the day of her death."[14]

The experiences of the Three Witnesses and the Eight Witnesses, combined with the accounts of Joseph Smith and Mary Whitmer, form a total of thirteen different witnesses of the reality of the gold plates. More important, not one of these witnesses ever denied his testimony.

Throughout the remainder of their lives, the witnesses often received questions about their experience. John Corrill, an early Church member wrote, "After getting acquainted with them, I was unable to impeach their testimony, and consequently thought that it was as consistent to give credit to them as to credit the writings of the New Testament, when I had never seen the authors nor the original copy."

Before his death, Hyrum Smith bore his testimony of the Book of Mormon, saying, "I felt a determination to die, rather than deny the things which my eyes had seen, which my hands had handled, and which I had borne testimony to, wherever my lot had been cast."[15]

Notes

1. Appendix 4, Testimony of Three Witnesses, late June 1829, 589, josephsmithpapers.org.
2. Lucy Mack Smith, History, 1845, 153, joseph smithpapers.org.
3. Lucy Mack Smith, History, 1845, 153, joseph smithpapers.org.
4. "History of Joseph Smith," *Times and Seasons,* Sept. 1, 1842, 897–98.
5. "History of Joseph Smith," *Times and Seasons,* Sept. 1, 1842, 898.
6. "Letter from Elder W. H. Kelley," *Saints' Herald,* Mar. 1, 1882, 68.
7. History, 1838–1856, vol. A-1 [23 December 1805–30 August 1834], [fair copy], 25, joseph smithpapers.org; "History of Joseph Smith," *Times and Seasons,* Sept. 1, 1842, 898.
8. Lucy Mack Smith, History, 1844–1845, bk. 9, p. 1, josephsmithpapers.org.

9. Lucy Mack Smith, History, 1844–1845, bk. 9, p. 2, josephsmithpapers.org.

10. History, 1838–1856, vol. A-1 [23 December 1805–30 August 1834], 26, josephsmithpapers.org.

11. Richard Lloyd Anderson, "Witnesses of the Book of Mormon," in Largey, *Book of Mormon Reference Companion,* 787–92.

12. Jenson, *L.D.S. Biographical Encyclopedia,* 1:249.

13. Journal History of the Church, June 1, 1877, Church History Library, The Church of Jesus Christ of Latter-day Saints, Salt Lake City, Utah.

14. Royal Skousen, "Another Account of Mary Whitmer's Viewing of the Golden Plates," *Interpreter* 10 (2014): 35–44, mormoninterpreter.com.

15. Appendix, Testimony of Eight Witnesses, late June, 1829, Source Note, josephsmithpapers.org.

8
The Book of Mormon Is Published

The Grandin Building, Palmyra, New York, where the Book of Mormon was first printed.

1830

Joseph Smith negotiated with Egbert B. Grandin, a Palmyra printer, bookseller, and publisher of the *Wayne Sentinel,* to print the Book of Mormon manuscript. Grandin declined at first, "believing the whole affair to be a wicked imposture and a scheme to defraud Mr. [Martin] Harris."[1]

The response was the same when Joseph Smith met with Thurlow Weed, former publisher of the *Rochester Daily Telegraph* and then editor of the Rochester *Anti-Masonic Enquirer.* Joseph and Martin Harris called on Elihu F. Marshall, a book publisher in Rochester, New York. He was willing to publish the manuscript, but the price was exorbitant.

Seeing no other alternative, Joseph asked Martin Harris to guarantee payment for the publication. Martin considered his request and agreed. Joseph and Martin approached publisher E. B. Grandin again, hoping he would reconsider. Grandin took "the advice of several discreet, fair-minded neighbors," who assured him that his connection with the book would be nothing more than a business matter. Their advice and Martin's willingness to enter a contract to guarantee payment for the printing led Grandin to reconsider his stance and agree to publish the book.[2]

On August 25, 1829, Martin entered into an agreement with Grandin, guaranteeing that before the expiration of eighteen months from August 1829, he would pay $3,000 to cover the costs of publication. If sales of the book were insufficient to meet those costs, Martin agreed he would sell a little over 150 acres of his farm to pay Grandin.[3]

With the agreement in place, Grandin proceeded. The Book of Mormon was printed on a Smith Patented Improved Press manufactured by Robert Hoe & Company of New York City.[4] The printing of some 296,000 pages of text was slow. One reason was that additional type ordered for the job did not arrive from Albany, New York, until late November 1829. Other reasons were rumors suggesting that Martin

Harris would refuse to sell his mortgaged acreage or pay the full cost of printing.

Adding to Grandin's growing concerns, citizens of Palmyra passed a resolution calling on all residents to boycott purchase of the Book of Mormon and to use their influence to prevent others from buying the book. Several residents of Palmyra called on Grandin to express their opposition. Grandin was persuaded by their arguments and suspended printing the Book of Mormon in January 1830.[5]

On January 16, 1830, Martin Harris and Joseph Smith agreed to sell the Book of Mormon until sufficient copies had been sold to pay the publishing costs. The agreement was as follows: "I hereby agree that Martin Harris shall have an equal privilege with me & my friends of selling the Book of Mormon of the Edition now printing by Egbert B Grandin until enough of them shall be sold to pay for the printing of the same or until such times as the said Grandin shall be paid for the printing the aforesaid Books or copies. Joseph Smith Jr, Manchester January the 16th 1830, Witness, Oliver H P Cowdery."[6]

Convinced that Martin Harris would make good on their contractual agreement, a relieved Egbert B. Grandin resumed printing the Book of Mormon. On March 19, 1830, through the *Wayne Sentinel*, a Palmyra newspaper, Grandin announced, "The 'Book of Mormon' will be ready for sale in the course of next week." On March 26, 1830 he advertised, "First Public Sale of the Book of Mormon: the above work, containing about 600 pages, large Deuodecimo, is now for sale, wholesale and retail, at the Palmyra Bookstore, by E. B. Grandin."[7]

The price of the Book of Mormon was equivalent to about two days' wages of an adult laborer. The price ranged from $1.25 to $1.75 per book.[8]

Joseph Smith was not in Palmyra when Martin Harris gave the first printed copy of the Book of Mormon to his brother Emer Harris on March 26, 1830. When Joseph arrived in town a few days later, he was surprised to find Martin Harris crossing the road ahead with "a Bunch of morman Books." Martin greeted him by saying, "The Book will not sell for no Body wants them." Joseph replied, "I think they will sell well."[9]

Yet nearly eighteen months had elapsed since Martin contracted with E. B. Grandin to pay for the printing of the Book of Mormon, and it was apparent that sales of the book would not cover Martin's obligation. To solve the problem and quiet rumors that he would default, Martin entered an arrangement with entrepreneur Thomas Lakey, a property owner in Palmyra who also bought and sold properties.[10]

On April 1, 1831, Martin agreed to sell to Lakey 150 acres for twenty dollars per acre. The deed, or indenture, for the acreage was signed by Martin Harris and Thomas Lakey at Lyons, New York, on April 7, 1831.[11]

Lakey, who was essentially a broker in this arrangement, looked for a buyer. After some nine months, he found such a buyer in Englishman John Graves, who had journeyed to Walworth, New York (north of Palmyra), with his wife, Jane, and their daughter, Mrs. Christina Graves Grainger, a widow with four children. Christina had $3,000 worth of gold, which she had kept in a belt fastened about her waist as she voyaged to America. She willingly

---

DID YOU KNOW?

- E. B. Grandin refused at first to publish the Book of Mormon.

- The first copies of the Book of Mormon sold for $1.25 to $1.75 each, or about two days' wages for an adult laborer.

gave the gold to her father to purchase just over 150 acres of Martin Harris's farm. Lakey, who added an extra $300 for his services, received from Graves $3,300 on January 28, 1832.[12] Lakey in turn gave $3,000 to Martin, who paid Grandin and satisfied the debt.

Was the cost to Martin Harris worth the price? President Ezra Taft Benson said, "The Book of Mormon is the instrument that God designed to 'sweep the earth as with a flood, to gather out [His] elect' (Moses 7:62). This sacred volume of scripture needs to become more central in our preaching, our teaching, and our missionary work.

". . . We need to read daily from the pages of the book that will get a man 'nearer to God by abiding by its precepts, than by any other book.' (*History of the Church*, 4:461.)"[13]

Notes

1. Tucker, *Origin, Rise, and Progress of Mormonism*, 51.
2. Tucker, *Origin, Rise, and Progress of Mormonism*, 52; Nibley, *Witnesses of the Book of Mormon*, 48–49.
3. Tucker, *Origin, Rise, and Progress of Mormonism*, 52–53.
4. In 1906, Church President Joseph F. Smith purchased the very press used to print the first copies of the Book of Mormon. Today the press is on exhibit at the Museum of Church History and Art in Salt Lake City. See Sterne, *Catalogue of Nineteenth-Century Printing Presses*.
5. See Joseph Smith to Oliver Cowdery, Oct. 22, 1829, josephsmithpapers.org.
6. Agreement, Manchester [New York] 16 Jan.

1830, MS 822, josephsmithpapers.org; Joseph Smith, Agreement, 1830, MS 929, josephsmith papers.org.
7. "Large duodecimo" is the traditional description of a book 5–1/2 inches by 7–1/2 inches. Grandin, "First Public Sale . . . ," *Wayne Sentinel*, Mar. 26, 1830; "The 'Book of Mormon' will be ready . . . ," *Wayne Sentinel*, Mar. 19, 1830. See Egbert Bratt Grandin, Diary, Jan. 1, 1831, and Feb. 2, 1841, New York State Library microfilm.
8. O'Driscoll, *Hyrum Smith*, 64; Hyrum Smith, Diaries, 1831–1833, May 29, 1832, Vault MSS 774, vol. 1, L. Tom Perry Special Collections, Harold B. Lee Library, Brigham Young University, Provo, Utah.
9. Joseph Knight, Reminiscences, MS 3470, 6, Church History Library, The Church of Jesus Christ of Latter-day Saints, Salt Lake City, Utah; Dean C. Jessee, "Joseph Knight's Recollection of Early Mormon History," *BYU Studies* 17, no. 1 (Autumn 1976): 36–37.
10. Martin Harris gave Thomas Lakey a copy of the Book of Mormon. See Willard Bean to Joseph F. Smith, 30 Nov. 1934, Church History Library.
11. Martin Harris Deeds, MS 3417, Church History Library.
12. Descendants claim that the gold used in the transaction went to Grandin for the printing of the Book of Mormon. See Minor T. Patton, "How It Was My Great-Grandmother's Gold Paid for the Printing of the First Edition of the Book of Mormon," MSS 9852, Church History Library; Thomas Lakey to John Graves, 28 Jan. 1832, Wayne County, New York, Property Deeds, Books 10:515–16; 11:128–29, in Susan Easton Black and Larry C. Porter, "For the Sum of Three Thousand Dollars," *Journal of Book of Mormon Studies* 14, no. 2 (2005): 4–11, 66–67.
13. Benson, "Flooding the Earth with the Book of Mormon," *Ensign*, Nov. 1988, 4.

9
The Church Is Organized

1830

The reconstructed home of Peter Whitmer Sr. in Fayette, New York, where the Church was organized.

Believers in the Book of Mormon looked forward to the day when the Lord would fulfill his promise: "If this generation harden not their hearts, I will establish my church among them" (D&C 10:53). Joseph Smith received by the spirit of prophecy and revelation "the precise day"—April 6, 1830—"we should proceed to organize his Church once again, here upon the earth."[1]

About sixty believers met on Tuesday, April 6, 1830, in the log home of Peter Whitmer Sr. in Fayette, New York, for the first meeting of what would become The Church of Jesus Christ of Latter-day Saints.[2] David Whitmer recalled that "on the 6th of April 1830, 6 Elders were at Peter Whitmer's[.] David's Father's [two] Rooms were filled with members, about 20 from Colesville, 15 from Manchester Church, and about 20 from around about Father Whitmer's. About 50 members & the 6 Elders were present."[3]

The six elders were Joseph Smith Jr., Oliver Cowdery, Hyrum Smith, Peter Whitmer Jr., Samuel H. Smith, and David Whitmer.[4]

The foundational meeting opened with a "solemn prayer to our heavenly Father." After the prayer, the assembled persons were asked "whether they accepted us [Joseph Smith and Oliver Cowdery] as their teachers in the things of the Kingdom of God, and whether they were satisfied that we should proceed and be organized as a Church according to said commandment which we had received." A unanimous affirming vote was received. Joseph Smith then laid his hands upon the head of Oliver Cowdery and ordained him an elder. Oliver, in turn, ordained Joseph to the same priesthood office. Joseph and Oliver then "took bread, blessed it, and brake it with them, also wine, blessed it, and drank it with them." After partaking of the Lord's Supper, those who had been previously baptized received the gift of the Holy Ghost and were confirmed members of the Church of Christ. This was followed by the Holy Ghost being "poured out upon us to a very great degree. Some prophesied, whilst we all praised the Lord, and rejoiced exceedingly."[5]

In front of those present, Joseph Smith received a revelation in which he was named "a seer, a translator, a prophet, an apostle of Jesus Christ, an elder of the church through the will of God the Father, and the grace of your Lord Jesus Christ" (D&C 21:1). A few other men were then ordained to priesthood offices.

Joseph summarized the meeting with this observation: "After a happy time spent in witnessing and feeling for ourselves the powers and the blessings of the Holy Ghost, through the grace of God bestowed upon us, we dismissed with the pleasing knowledge that we were now individually, members of, and acknowledged of God, 'The Church of Jesus Christ,' organized in accordance with commandments and revelations, given by Him to ourselves, in these last days, as well as according to the order of the Church as recorded in the New Testament."[6]

Note that on April 6, 1830, the name of the newly organized church was the Church of Christ.[7] It was known by that name from 1830 to 1834 (D&C 20:1). From 1834 to 1838, it was known as the Church of the Latter Day Saints. It was commonly but unofficially known as the Mormon Church. The name "The Church of Jesus Christ of Latter-day Saints" was given by revelation on April 26, 1838 (D&C 115:4).[8]

At the conclusion of the foundational meeting, Joseph Smith Sr. and others requested baptism. After witnessing from the water's edge the baptism of his father, Joseph exclaimed, "Praise to my God! that I lived to see my own father baptized into the true Church of Jesus Christ!"[9]

The Prophet witnessed other baptisms that day and in the days to come, for the church established in Fayette was "like to a grain of mustard seed, which a man took, and sowed in his field: . . . when it is grown, it is the greatest among herbs" (Matthew 13:31–32).

Today, there are approximately 16 million members of The Church of Jesus Christ of Latter-day Saints throughout the world.

DID YOU KNOW?

- Joseph Smith received by the Spirit the precise date, April 6, 1830, that the Church should be organized.

- The name originally given to the Church was the Church of Christ.

NOTES

1. History, 1838–1856, vol. A-1 [23 December 1805–30 August 1834], 29, josephsmith papers.org.
2. History, 1838–1856, vol. A-1 [23 December 1805–30 August 1834], 37, josephsmith papers.org.
3. Edward Stevenson Collection, Jan. 2, 1887, Church History Library, The Church of Jesus Christ of Latter-day Saints, Salt Lake City, Utah.
4. Richard Lloyd Anderson, "Who Were the Six Who Organized the Church on 6 April 1830?" *Ensign,* June 1980, 44.
5. History, 1838–1856, vol. A-1 [23 December 1805–30 August 1834], 36, josephsmith papers.org.
6. History, 1838–1856, vol. A-1 [23 December 1805–30 August 1834], 38, josephsmith papers.org.
7. Articles and Covenants, ca. Apr. 1830 [D&C 20], 4, josephsmithpapers.org.
8. Susan Easton Black, "Name of the Church," in Ludlow, *Encyclopedia of Mormonism,* 3:979.
9. Lucy Mack Smith, History, 1845, 169, josephsmith papers.org.

10
Hiram Page and His Seer Stone

Oliver Cowdery, who supported Hiram Page's revelations until he was corrected by the Lord.

1830

In a religion in which every person is entitled, even commanded, to seek revelation from God, the question may arise about who is entitled to receive revelation for whom. Without an understanding of the structure of stewardship and Church hierarchy, a few of the early Saints claimed to have received revelations that were contrary to the revelations received by the Prophet Joseph Smith.

The first signs of confusion appeared in the summer of 1830 when a dispute arose between Joseph Smith and Oliver Cowdery over phraseology in the articles and covenants of the Church (D&C 20). Oliver was displeased with the directive that baptismal candidates "truly manifest by their works that they have received of the Spirit of Christ unto the remission of their sins" (D&C 20:37). The phrase had not been included in an earlier draft of the articles and covenants produced by Oliver, nor was it found in the Book of Mormon. Oliver wrote to Joseph, calling the addition "erroneous" and adding, "I command you in the name of God to erase those words, that no priestcraft be amongst us."[1]

Joseph's written response asked Oliver "by what authority he took upon him to command me to alter, or erase, or add to or diminish from a revelation or commandment from Almighty God."[2] Joseph then journeyed to the Whitmer home in Fayette, New York, to meet with Oliver about the issue.

In the discussion that ensued with Oliver and the entire Whitmer family, all but Christian Whitmer took Oliver's side. With Christian's help, Joseph was able to persuade others in the Whitmer family and Oliver of the correctness of the change. Joseph concluded this disturbing episode on a hopeful note, by writing, "Thus was the error rooted out, which having its rise in presumption and rash judgment, was the more particularly calculated (when once fairly understood) to teach each and all of us the necessity of humility, and meekness before the Lord."[3]

In the months that followed, the question of who had the right to receive revelations for the Church did not subside. In September 1830 Hiram Page "got in his possession, a certain stone, by which he had obtained to certain revelations." Page, one of the Eight Witnesses of the Book of Mormon, claimed to have received "certain revelations, concerning the up-building of Zion and the order of the Church." Joseph knew that instructions given through Page's stone were "entirely at variance with the order of God's house, as laid down in the New Testament, as well as in our late revelations."[4]

Yet many false instructions or revelations continued to come forth. Newell Knight wrote that Hiram Page "had quite a roll of papers full of these revelations, and many in the church were led astray by them."[5] George A. Smith later described Page's revelations as being received "through the medium of a black stone, [with] certain characters appearing on that stone which he wrote down."[6] Beyond these statements, nothing is known about the contents of the alleged revelations or how the stone was used to receive them.

Nevertheless, Page's claim to revelations created a crisis in Church governance, for "many of the brethren (especially the Whitmer family and Oliver Cowdery) were believing much in the things set forth by this stone."[7]

At issue was the question: If it was possible for anyone to receive personal revelation, was it also possible for anyone to receive revelation for the entire Church? Joseph hesitated to confront the difficult situation, intending to wait until a forthcoming conference to discuss the issue. He concluded, however, that it was "best to enquire of the Lord concerning so important a matter."[8]

The revelation received in response to Joseph's inquiry lays out the basic principles of Church government: "Verily, verily I say unto you, no one shall be appointed to receive commandments & Revelations in this Church excepting my Servant Joseph, for he Receiveth them even as Moses, & thou shalt be obedient unto the things which I shall give unto him." In the same revelation, the Lord directed Oliver Cowdery to take Hiram Page "between him & thee alone & tell him that those things which he hath written from that Stone are not of me & that Satan deceiveth him."[9]

There was to be no public humiliation or shaming of Page, just a private conversation to correct a well-meaning but misled brother.

A number of other important items came forth in this revelation, including the first mention of the location of the city of Zion: "No man knoweth where the City shall be built But it shall be given hereafter . . . it shall be built among the Lamanites." Oliver Cowdery was directed to "go unto the Lamanites & Preach my Gospel unto them & cause my Church to be established among them."[10]

Subsequent revelations called John Whitmer, Parley P. Pratt, and Ziba Peterson to accompany Oliver on his mission and for David Whitmer to repent of his involvement in the Page seer stone affair: "Thou hast not given heed unto my Spirit & to those who were set over thee But hast been persuaded by those whom I have not commanded."[11]

The incident with Hiram Page was not the last time a question of authority to receive

DID YOU KNOW?

- Oliver Cowdery rebuked the Prophet Joseph Smith over certain phrases he found offensive in the articles and covenants of the Church.

- Oliver Cowdery was later asked by the Prophet to teach Hiram Page that "Satan deceiveth him" and that his claimed revelations were not from God.

revelation for the entire Church was raised. A few months later, after Joseph Smith and the New York Saints had relocated to Kirtland, Ohio, a certain "Mrs. Hubble" (likely Laura Hubbell, a thirty-two-year-old mother of three), claimed to have received revelations on behalf of the Church. Once again the Lord declared, "There is none other appointed unto you to receive commandments & Revelations until he [Joseph Smith] be taken. . . . Verily, Verily I say unto you that none else shall be appointed unto this gift except it be through him."[12]

Other revelations of the Lord to his prophet, Joseph Smith, laid the groundwork for the principle of stewardship and the hierarchy of revelation in the Church today (D&C 28; 48). These revelations clearly established that the Lord's house is a house of order and that revelations for the entire Church come through proper channels—"him whom I have appointed" (D&C 43:7).

NOTES

1. History, 1838–1856, vol. A-1 [23 December 1805–30 August 1834], 51, josephsmith papers.org.
2. Davidson et al., *Histories,* 1:426, or josephsmith papers.org.
3. Davidson et al., *Histories,* 1:426–28, or joseph smithpapers.org.
4. History, ca. June 1839–ca. 1841 [Draft 2], 54, josephsmithpapers.org.
5. Revelation, Sept. 1830-B [D&C 28], in Davidson et al., *Histories* 1:184n351, or josephsmith papers.org.
6. George A. Smith, in *Journal of Discourses,* 11:2.
7. Davidson et al., *Histories,* 1:438, or josephsmith papers.org.
8. Davidson et al., *Histories,* 1:438, or josephsmith papers.org.
9. Revelation, Sept. 1830-B, in McKay et al., *Documents,* 1:186, or josephsmithpapers.org.
10. Revelation, Sept. 1830-B, in McKay et al., *Documents,* 1:185, or josephsmithpapers.org.
11. Revelation, Sept. 1830-C (D&C 30:1–4), in McKay et al., *Documents,* 1:187–88, or joseph smithpapers.org.
12. Revelation, Feb. 1831–A (D&C 43), in *Documents,* 1:258, or josephsmithpapers.org.

11
Mission to the Lamanites

Parley P. Pratt, who served as a missionary to the Lamanites.

1830

The answer came in revelations directing Oliver Cowdery, Peter Whitmer Jr., Ziba Peterson, and Parley P. Pratt to journey to the borders of the Lamanites—a phrase understood to mean the line between Missouri and the Indian territory—and preach the gospel to the Native Americans (D&C 28:8–9).

"As soon as this revelation was received," wrote Lucy Mack Smith, "Emma Smith, and several other sisters, began to make preparations to furnish those, who were set apart for this mission, with the necessary clothing."[2] Other Saints provided the newly called missionaries with food, and Martin Harris gave them copies of the Book of Mormon. "Before departing, the missionaries bound themselves in writing to give 'heed unto all words and advice' of Oliver Cowdery" and pledged to preach the "'fulness of the Gospel' to their brethren, the Lamanites."[3]

On October 18, 1830, the missionaries to the Lamanites began a 1,500-mile journey to the western borders of the United States.[4] They traveled first to Buffalo, New York, where they met with a tribe of Seneca Indians on the Cattaraugus Reservation. "We were kindly received, and much interest was manifested by them on hearing this news," Pratt recorded.[5] These were the first American Indians to hear of the restored gospel in this dispensation.

The missionaries traveled on to Mentor, Ohio, where they visited with Sidney Rigdon, a prominent minister and a former teacher of Parley P. Pratt.[6] After listening to their message about the Book of Mormon, Rigdon said, "I

The ancient Book of Mormon prophet Alma declared, "At some period of time they [the Lamanites] will be brought to believe in [God's] word, and to know of the incorrectness of the traditions of their fathers; and many of them will be saved" (Alma 9:17). By 1830 Joseph Smith and his followers believed they were on the cusp of fulfilling the ancient promise. In October 1830 the Lord recognized the great interest and desires of the elders respecting the Lamanites and their desire to know whether elders should be sent at that time to the Indian tribes in the West.[1]

will read your book and see what claims it has upon my faith, and endeavour to ascertain, whether it be a revelation from God or not."

At a meeting of his parishioners, "Rigdon arose and stated to the congregation that the information they had that evening received was of an extraordinary character, and certainly demanded their most severe consideration, and as the Apostle advised his brethren 'to prove all things and hold fast that which was good' [see 1 Thessalonians 5:21]."[7]

Within days, Sidney Rigdon and many of his congregation sought baptism, as did numerous others. Parley P. Pratt wrote: "The news of our coming was soon noised abroad, and the news of the discovery of the Book of Mormon and the marvelous events connected with it. . . . The people thronged us night and day, insomuch that we had no time for rest and retirement. Meetings were convened in different neighborhoods, and multitudes came together soliciting our attendance; while thousands flocked about us daily; some to be taught, some for curiosity, some to obey the gospel, and some to dispute or resist it."[8]

In about three weeks, an estimated 127 persons were baptized in the greater Kirtland area of Ohio. Among them was John Murdock, who penned, "I came out of the water rejoicing and singing praises to God, and the Lamb."[9] Convert Philo Dibble wrote, "When I came out of the water, I knew that I had been born of

water and of the spirit, for my mind was illuminated with the Holy Ghost."[10]

The missionaries took an affectionate leave of the Saints in Ohio. Then, in company with Frederick G. Williams, a new convert who asked to join them, they headed to the borders of Indian territory. Fifty miles west of Kirtland, they visited in the Simeon Carter home. When a warrant on a frivolous charge was served against Parley P. Pratt in the Carter home, Ziba Peterson accompanied him to the courtroom. Near midnight Parley invited Ziba to sing with him in the courtroom the hymn "Oh How Happy Are They." The exasperated judge detained Pratt in a public inn, and Ziba rejoined his fellow missionaries.

"After sitting awhile by the fire in charge of the officer," Pratt wrote, "I requested to step out. I walked into the public square accompanied by him. Said I, 'Mr. Peabody, are you good at a race?' 'No,' said he, 'but my big bull dog is, and he has been trained to assist me in my office these several years; he will take any man down at my bidding.'" Despite the warning, Pratt bade farewell to the officer and started to run. The officer sent his dog to catch Pratt. When the dog "came close on my footsteps with all his fury," Pratt pointed his finger in the direction of a forest "and shouted in imitation of the officer. The dog hastened past me with redoubled speed towards the forest."[11]

After Pratt joined his companions, they preached in small settlements along the way as they continued to journey toward the borders of the Lamanites. "Some wished to learn and obey the fulness of the gospel," Pratt wrote. "Others were filled with envy, rage and lying." When they stopped at Sandusky, Ohio, the missionaries preached to the Wyandot Indians. Pratt wrote of the Wyandots' response to their message, "They rejoiced in the tiding, bid us God speed, and desired us to write to them in relation to our success among the tribes further west."[12]

The missionaries left Sandusky in the winter of 1830–31 and faced "a dreadful storm of rain and snow, which lasted for a week or more" as they trekked westward, sometimes in knee-deep snow. Ice that choked the Ohio River ended their plans to travel by boat to St. Louis. As for food, Pratt wrote, "the bread would be so frozen that we could not bite or penetrate any part of it but the outside crust."[13] Yet the missionaries pressed on toward the western frontier. They arrived on January 13, 1831, in Independence, Missouri, the westernmost settlement in the United States at that time.

While they waited for the weather to become more moderate, the missionaries stayed at the home of Colonel Robert Patterson. As Whitmer and Peterson were setting up a tailor shop, Cowdery, Pratt, and Williams crossed over the United States border to meet with the Delaware Indians. An aged chief of the Delaware tribe, William Anderson, invited the elders to preach to about forty tribal leaders in his lodge. On that occasion, Cowdery said, "Thousands of moons ago, when the red men's forefathers dwelt in peace and possessed this whole land, the Great Spirit talked with them, and revealed His law and His will, and much knowledge to their wise men and prophets." Placing his hand over his heart, Chief Anderson responded to Cowdery's words by saying, "It makes us glad in here."[14] For several days the missionaries taught the chief and his tribe.

Their preaching came to an abrupt halt, however, when Indian agents discovered the missionaries had failed to obtain a permit to preach in the Indian Territory. One government agent told them to desist until they had secured permission from General William Clark, Superintendent of Indian Affairs in St. Louis. Pratt saw the issue as having more to do with

their success among the Indians, which "stirred up the jealousy and envy of the Indian agents and sectarian missionaries to that degree that we were soon ordered out of the Indian country as disturbers of the peace; and even threatened with the military in case of non-compliance."[15]

Although it could be truthfully said that the mission to the Lamanites failed in its aim of proselyting Native Americans, it was significant to the history of the Church. The mission introduced the gospel to some Native Americans, heightened awareness of Church members about the importance of the Lamanites in the eyes of the Lord, brought into the waters of baptism a large number of converts in Ohio, and provided the missionaries with firsthand knowledge of what would become the center city of Zion (D&C 28:9).

NOTES

1. Historical Introduction, Revelation, Sept. 1830–B [D&C 28], 40, and Historical Introduction, Revelation, Sept. 1830–D [D&C 30:5–8], joseph smithpapers.org.
2. Lucy Mack Smith, History, 1845, 189–90, josephsmithpapers.org.
3. Letter dated Oct. 17, 1830, in *Ohio Star,* Dec. 8, 1831, 1, in *Church History in the Fulness of Times,* 88.
4. See Richard Dilworth Rust, "A Mission to the Lamanites," history.lds.org.
5. *Autobiography of Parley P. Pratt,* 49.
6. *Autobiography of Parley P. Pratt,* 49.
7. History, 1838–1856, vol. A-1 [23 December 1805–30 August 1834], 73, josephsmith papers.org; *Autobiography of Parley P. Pratt,* 49; "History of Joseph Smith," *Times and Seasons,* Aug. 15, 1843, 289–90.
8. *Autobiography of Parley P. Pratt,* 52.
9. "An Abridged Record of the Life of John Murdock Taken from His Journals by Himself," 16, in *Church History in the Fulness of Times,* 81.
10. "Philo Dibble's Narrative," in *Early Scenes in Church History,* 76.

11. *Autobiography of Parley P. Pratt*, 55–57.

12. *Autobiography of Parley P. Pratt*, 52.

13. *Autobiography of Parley P. Pratt*, 58.

14. *Autobiography of Parley P. Pratt*, 63–65.

15. *Autobiography of Parley P. Pratt*, 66.

12
The Commandment to Gather to the Ohio

1830

The restored Newel K. Whitney Store, Kirtland, Ohio.

The Lord declared, "I give unto you a sign . . . that I shall gather in, from their long dispersion, my people, O house of Israel, and shall establish again among them my Zion" (3 Nephi 21:1).

Of the doctrine of gathering, Joseph Smith said, "All the prophets that have written, from the days of righteous Abel down to the last man, that has left any testimony on record, for our consideration, in speaking of the salvation of Israel in the last days, goes directly to show,

that it consists in the work of the gathering" (Deuteronomy 30:3–4; 3 Nephi 20:22; Ether 13:3–11).[1]

According to Joseph Smith, one purpose of gathering the elect from among the unrepentant is to "build unto the Lord a house whereby he could reveal unto his people the ordinances of his house and the glories of his kingdom, and teach the people the way of Salvation."[2]

Another purpose is to prepare the elect for the Second Coming of the Savior, for "the signs of the coming of the Son of Man are already commenced,—One pestilence will desolate after another—we shall soon have War and Bloodshed. The moon will be turned to Blood—I testify of these things and that the coming of the Son of Man is nigh even at your doors."[3]

The historical setting for the doctrine of gathering was in Kirtland, Ohio. Missionary Parley P. Pratt wrote, "The people thronged us night and day, insomuch that we had no time for rest and retirement."[4]

Most notable in the throng was a preacher named Sidney Rigdon. He advised those who listened to Elder Pratt and his missionary companions to "prove all things and hold fast that which is good."[5] More than a hundred entered the waters of baptism and became Latter-day Saints.

Joseph and his New York followers received a revelation commanding them to "assemble together at the Ohio," the first gathering place of the Church (D&C 37:3). Although the January 2, 1831 entry in the Journal History of the Church reads, "The Saints manifested unshaken confidence in the great work [in] which they were engaged, and all rejoiced under the blessings of the gospel," the doctrine of gathering led to divisions among the New York Saints.[6] Some accepted the doctrine as the word of God; others refused to acknowledge the heavenly origin of the directive.

The Whitmers, Knights, and other families obediently left their homes in the state of New York. Peter Whitmer Sr. sold his Fayette farm and farmhouse for $2,200. Not everyone received such a favorable price. "As might be expected, we were obliged to make great sacrifices of our property," wroted Newel Knight.[7]

But to some the words of Phoebe Carter were representative of their real sacrifice: "When the time came for my departure I dared not trust myself to say farewell; so I wrote my good-byes to each, and leaving them on my table, ran downstairs and jumped into the carriage. Thus I left the beloved home of my childhood to link my life with the saints of God."[8]

The New York Saints began arriving in Ohio as early as February 1831. Among them were the Prophet Joseph and his wife, Emma. When they arrived at the N. K. Whitney and Company store in Kirtland, Joseph asked storekeeper Newel K. Whitney, "You've prayed me here, now what do you want of me?"[9] Whitney, a recent convert, became one of the Prophet's closest associates.

The Prophet immediately tackled the task of setting the Church in order. He needed to teach the Ohio Saints about discerning the Spirit, the workings of the priesthood, and keeping the commandments of God.

The editor of the *Painesville Telegraph* expressed discomfort at seeing "about two hundred men, women and children, of the deluded followers of Jo Smith's Bible speculation, have arrived on our coast . . . from New York." He feared, "If the growth of the Church were not soon halted, inhabitants of Kirtland would be governed by the revelations of the Mormon Prophet."[10]

Other Ohioans noted with some concern that the new movement attracted the destitute to their doorsteps. Brigham Young recalled: "When we arrived in Kirtland, if any man that ever did gather with the Saints was any poorer than I was—it was because he had nothing. . . . I had two children to take care of—that was all. I was a widower. 'Brother Brigham, had you any shoes?' No; not a shoe to my foot, except a pair of borrowed boots."[11] Whatever their economic circumstances, neither poverty nor discomfort stopped the flow of faithful Latter-day Saints to Ohio.

Most unusual about these first converts in Ohio was their refusal to discard a belief in the "gifts of the spirit" present in their former religions.[12] At Latter-day Saint meetings, the newly baptized clamored for a chance to show off their "god-given" abilities—questionable revelations and unusual physical movements. Some would "swoon away, and make unseemly gestures, and be drawn or disfigured in their countenances. Others would fall into ecstasies, and be drawn into contortions, cramps, fits, etc. Others would seem to have visions and revelations, which were not edifying, and which were not congenial to the doctrine and spirit of the gospel. In short, a false and lying spirit seemed to be creeping into the Church."[13]

Failure to discern between the "strange notions and false spirits" led to differences of opinion and widespread doctrinal confusion within the Latter-day Saint congregation in northeastern Ohio.[14]

So widespread had the confusion become that converts expressed their belief that only the Prophet Joseph Smith could set the Church in order. In May 1831, Joseph received a revelation informing the Saints that "there are many spirits which are false spirits which have gone forth in the Earth deceiving the world & also Satan hath sought to deceive you that he might overthrow you." The Lord carefully reasoned with the Saints "even as a man reasoneth one with another," explaining, "that which doth not edify is not of God & is darkness [and] that which is of God is light."[15]

Parley P. Pratt directly observed Joseph receiving the revelation and later recorded, "Each sentence was uttered slowly and very distinctly, and with a pause between each, sufficiently long for it to be recorded, by an ordinary writer, in long hand . . . was never any hesitation, reviewing, or reading back, in order to keep the run of the subject . . . he dictated them so they stood, so far as I have witnessed; and I was present to witness the dictation of several communications of several passages each."[16]

The gathering was a sacrifice for the early Saints but it also afforded them direct access to the Prophet and the revelations of God. Over time the doctrine of the gathering has continued in different forms. For a season, Kirtland, Ohio, served as a gathering place for the elect. In 1837–38 faithful Latter-day

Saints fled from religious persecution in Ohio to Far West, Missouri. There would be other gathering places, such as Nauvoo, Salt Lake City, and hundreds of settlements in the Rocky Mountains. Today, missionaries are gathering the elect to the wards and stakes of Zion located throughout the world, fulfilling the Lord's admonition to his disciples to "gather together, and stand in holy places" (D&C 101:22).

Notes

1. History, 1838–1856, vol. B-1 [Sept. 1834–2 Nov. 1838, 622, josephsmithpapers.org.
2. History, 1838–1856, vol. D-1 [Aug. 1842–1 July 1843] 1572, josephsmithpapers.org.
3. History, 1838–1856 vol. C-1 [Nov. 1838–31 July 1842], 12, josephsmithpapers.org.
4. *Autobiography of Parley P. Pratt,* 52.
5. History, 1838–1856, vol. A-1 [23 December 1805–30 August 1834], 73, josephsmith papers.org.
6. Journal History of the Church, Jan. 2, 1831, Church History Library, The Church of Jesus Christ of Latter-day Saints, Salt Lake City, Utah.
7. "Newel Knight's Journal," *Scraps of Biography,* 10:68.
8. Anderson, *Joseph Smith's Kirtland,* 13.
9. Orson F. Whitney, "Newel K. Whitney," *Contributor,* Jan. 1885, 125, in *Joseph Smith* [manual], 159–60.
10. *Painesville [Ohio] Telegraph,* May 17, 1831; Apr. 17, 1835.
11. Brigham Young, in *Journal of Discourses,* 11:295.
12. Historical Introduction, Revelation, May 9, 1831 [D&C 50], josephsmithpapers.org.
13. *Autobiography of Parley P. Pratt,* 70–72.
14. History, 1838–1856, vol. A-1 [23 December 1805–30 August 1834], 93, josephsmith papers.org.
15. Revelation, May 9, 1831 [D&C 50], 83, joseph smithpapers.org.
16. *Autobiography of Parley P. Pratt,* 72.

13
Joseph Smith's Translation of the Bible

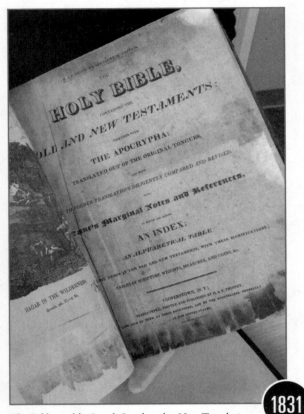

The Bible used by Joseph Smith in his New Translation.

1831

"I believe the Bible as it read when it came from the pen of the original writers," Joseph Smith professed. "Ignorant translators, careless transcribers, or designing and corrupt priests have committed many errors. . . . Many points touching the salvation of men, [have] been taken from the Bible, or lost before it was compiled."[1]

Joseph's followers concur: "We believe the Bible to be the word of God as far as it is translated correctly" (Article of Faith 8). "Translated correctly" is a recognition that biblical text has been altered by "editors, copyists, and revisionists through centuries of transmission."[2]

The purpose of Joseph Smith's translation of the Bible was to restore plain and precious truths that had been lost through the ages. The word *translation* in the context of Joseph Smith's work refers to "copying, editing, adding to, taking from, rephrasing, and interpreting" the Bible, not translating from one language to another.[3] Translating the scriptures proved an important part of the education of the young prophet and a significant part of Joseph Smith's prophetic calling from 1831 to 1833.

In the translation process Joseph used a large edition of the King James Version of the Bible printed in 1828 by H. & E. Phinney Company of Cooperstown, New York. This Bible, purchased on October 8, 1829, at Egbert B. Grandin's bookstore in Palmyra, New York, for $3.75, contained the Apocrypha. Joseph did not translate the Apocrypha after he was told by revelation that it was "mostly translated correctly" and the errors in the text were "interpolations by the hands of men" (D&C 91:1–2). Joseph's writings on the pages of the Cooperstown Bible, consisting primarily of hundreds of notations in the form of checks and crosses, often beg for an explanation.

Joseph Smith commenced the work of translation in June 1830 with Oliver Cowdery serving as his first scribe. Oliver scribed as Joseph read from and dictated revisions of the Old Testament until October 1830. John Whitmer served as the scribe from October to

December 1830. When Whitmer accepted a missionary call to preach the gospel in Ohio, the Lord commanded Sidney Rigdon to assist as scribe in the translation (D&C 35). In December 1830 Rigdon scribed the words of Enoch, which compose Moses 7 in the Pearl of Great Price.[4] Sidney continued to serve as scribe for Joseph until the translation was mostly completed in 1833. Even after he recorded its completion, the Prophet continued to work on what he called the New Translation intermittently throughout the remainder of his life, though he did make plans to publish a version of it while he was living in Nauvoo.[5]

Joseph began his translation in Genesis, completing through Genesis 19:35 before a revelation received on March 7, 1831, directed him to translate the New Testament (D&C 45:60–61). His work on the New Testament began the next day, March 8, with the first chapter of the Gospel of Matthew. During the month of March, Joseph worked on Matthew and Genesis concurrently. In early April, his translation of the Old Testament ended for a brief period. As to the New Testament translation, Joseph wrote, "I completed the translation and review of the New Testament, on the 2nd of February, 1833, and sealed it up." He then turned back to translating the Old Testament. On July 2, 1833, Joseph wrote, "We [Joseph and Sidney] this day finished the translating of the Scriptures, for which we returned gratitude to our heavenly Father."[6]

When finished, the New Translation manuscript totaled 477 pages. Although some suggest that Joseph Smith's translation of the Bible was finished in its entirety, this was the completion of a preliminary work. When "the manuscript was later reviewed and prepared for publication, further revisions, refinements, and alterations were made."[7]

The statistical results of Joseph's inspired changes in the Bible are as follows: "A total of 3,410 verses in the printed Joseph Smith Translation differ in textual construction from the King James Bible. Of this number 25 verses compose the visions of Moses (Moses 1), 1,289 changes are in the Old Testament, and 2,096 in the New Testament."[8]

While translating biblical text, Joseph received great knowledge of ancient prophets and people and his understanding of doctrines and gospel principles was heightened. Revelations now recorded in the Doctrine and Covenants were received—a few being a direct result of questions asked about doctrinal and organization issues (D&C 76–77; 84; 86; 91; 107; 113; 132; and possibly others).

As to publication, excerpts of Joseph Smith's New Translation were published in Latter-day Saint newspapers. The entire text, titled *Holy Scriptures* (1867), was first published by the Reorganized Church of Jesus Christ of Latter Day Saints.[9] This edition of Joseph Smith's translation of the scriptures was followed by several publications that were "amended to correct typographical and judgment errors in the 1867 edition."[10]

The Church of Jesus Christ of Latter-day Saints has not published all of Joseph Smith's New Translation, or what we today call the Joseph Smith Translation. But in 1979 the Church published the Latter-day Saint edition of the King James Version with hundreds of footnotes and a seventeen-page appendix

DID YOU KNOW?

- Joseph Smith's translation of the Bible resulted in 3,410 inspired revisions in the Old and New Testaments.

- Except for excerpts from the book of Moses, the Joseph Smith Translation did not appear as an official part of Latter-day Saint scriptures until 1979.

from the Joseph Smith Translation.[11] When the Church published an updated edition of the scriptures in 2013, numerous Joseph Smith Translation entries were "added or adjusted."[12]

As to the importance of Joseph Smith's translation of biblical text, Elder Bruce R. McConkie said, "It is the crowning part of the doctrinal restoration," for it opened "the doors of our understanding to the marvelous reality that Christ and his gospel, with all its gifts, powers, and graces, has been had among men, in divers dispensations, from the days of Adam to this present hour."[13]

NOTES

1. *Joseph Smith* [manual], 207, 217.
2. Robert J. Matthews, "Joseph Smith Translation of the Bible (JST)," in Ludlow, *Encyclopedia of Mormonism,* 2:764.
3. Matthews, "Joseph Smith Translation of the Bible," 2:764.
4. See Cannon, *Life of Joseph Smith the Prophet,* 103–4.
5. Matthews, *"Plainer Translation,"* 41–48.
6. History, 1838–1856, vol. A-1 [23 December 1805–30 August 1834], 316, josephsmith papers.org.
7. Matthews, "Joseph Smith Translation of the Bible," 2:766.
8. Millet and Jackson, *Doctrine and Covenants,* 136.
9. Matthews, *"Plainer Translation,"* 52.
10. Matthews, "Joseph Smith Translation of the Bible," 2:766.
11. Matthews, "Joseph Smith Translation of the Bible," 2:766.
12. "2013 Edition of the LDS Scriptures," lds.org.
13. Bruce R. McConkie, "The Doctrinal Restoration," in Nyman and Millet, *Joseph Smith Translation,* 21–22.

14
The Law of Consecration Is Revealed

1831

Isaac Morley's farm, Kirtland, Ohio.

When the missionaries to the Lamanites—Oliver Cowdery, Parley P. Pratt, Peter Whitmer Jr,. and Ziba Peterson—arrived in Kirtland, Ohio, they found a number of enthusiastic Christians living an economic order patterned after the disciples in the New Testament. Kirtland resident "Isaac Morley had contended that in order to restore the ancient order of things in the Church of Christ, it was necessary that there should be a community of goods among the brethren," observed contemporary Josiah Jones, "and accordingly a number of them removed to his house and farm, and built houses and worked and lived together, and composed what is here called the 'Big Family,' which at this time consisted of 50 or 60, old and young."[1] Most of "the family,"

including Morley, converted to the new faith of the restored gospel through the efforts of the missionaries to the Lamanites. But an intriguing question remained—should "the family" continue to live together like the disciples in the New Testament, having all things in common? (Acts 4:32).

When John Whitmer, newly arrived in Kirtland from New York, saw the operations of "the family," he was less than impressed. He wrote, "The disciples had all things in common, and were going to destruction very fast as to temporal things: for they considered from reading the scripture that what belonged to a brother belonged to any of the brethren, therefore they would take each other's clothes and other property and use it without leave, which brought on confusion."[2]

When Joseph Smith arrived in Kirtland in February 1831, converts were anxious to know the will of the Lord concerning the practice of communal living on the Isaac Morley farm. In answer to their queries, Joseph sought the Lord in prayer. He received a revelation in February 1831 concerning a new economic order known as "the Law" or "the Law of Consecration." Under this law, faithful Saints were expected to consecrate their property to the bishop, who, in turn, assigned them a stewardship, deemed "as much as is sufficient for himself and family" (D&C 42:32). Surplus received by the bishop was to be kept in a storehouse until administered "to the poor and the needy" (D&C 42:34). A May 1831 revelation commanded Edward Partridge, the "bishop unto the Church," to appoint stewardships to every man according to "his circumstances and his wants and needs" (D&C 41:9; 51:3).

Faithful Saints in Ohio and Missouri struggled to live the law of consecration. As difficulties arose, application of the law was changed according to circumstances, but the principles of the law remained intact. A mistaken impression is that the law of tithing received by the Prophet Joseph Smith in 1838 replaced the law of consecration. Revelations indicate otherwise (see D&C 70; 78; 82–83; 85; 90; 92; 96; 104). The revelation outlining the law of tithing instructs Latter-day Saints to offer a surplus to the Church (D&C 119). Some suggest that the law of tithing requires a greater sacrifice than the law of consecration, for consecration required the Saints to give of their surplus *after* their needs were satisfied, whereas tithing requires ten percent *before* their needs are met. However, the requirement to give a surplus did not end with the law of tithing. Brigham Young asked, "Who shall be the judge of what is surplus property?" The Prophet Joseph Smith replied, "Let them be the judge for themselves."[3]

Recently, evidence has emerged that Joseph Smith tried again to implement the law of consecration during the Nauvoo period. In 2011, several historians published twenty affidavits of consecration dated from June through July 1842. During the same time Brigham Young preached a sermon "on [the law of] consecration or union of action in building up the city & providing labor & food for the poor."[4] This promising start did not result in a full implementation of the law, though a covenant to live the law of consecration was a vital part of the temple ordinances revealed in Nauvoo.

The martyrdom of Joseph Smith in 1844 did not change the Latter-day Saints' determination to live the law of consecration. In many respects, the Mormon trek to the Salt Lake Valley was a consecrated effort. As early as October 1845, Brigham Young proposed that the Saints make a covenant: "We take all the saints with us to the extent of our ability, that is, our influence and property."[5]

A few months later, a revelation given to Brigham Young, titled the "Word and Will of the Lord," directed the Saints to "let each company bear an equal proportion, according to the dividend of their property, in taking the poor, the widows, [and] the fatherless" on the westward journey (D&C 136:8).

Concerted efforts to live the law of consecration continued after the pioneer trek. In small Mormon settlements in the Rockies, Brigham Young launched a number of efforts to encourage the Saints to live the principles of the law. In an 1854 address, Brigham declared, "The Latter-day Saints will never be prepared to enter into Zion, or into the Celestial Kingdom of our Father and God until they attend to the first thing required of them after they have received the remission of sins . . . named for them to become of one heart, and of one mind in things that pertain to this life, in things that are before them every day, in business transactions, in the avocations of life, and in all things that are naturally understood."[6]

Unfortunately, living the law of consecration proved difficult during the unrest that surrounded the Utah War and other events.

DID YOU KNOW?

• The Saints have made several attempts to implement the principles of the law of consecration throughout their history in such diverse places as Ohio, Missouri, Illinois, Utah, and Idaho.

• The current system of Church welfare is based on the principles of the law of consecration.

After the war, many Saints again attempted to have all things in common. For those who hesitated, in 1872 George Q. Cannon of the First Presidency said, "The time must come when we must obey that which has been revealed to us as the Order of Enoch, when there shall be no rich and no poor among the Latter-day Saints; when wealth will not be a temptation; when every man will love his neighbor as he does himself."[7]

Before long, new united orders sprang up throughout the Intermountain West. Success varied among the orders, but most ended the practice when federal laws against plural marriage took center stage.

A worldwide economic catastrophe in the twentieth century brought about a new application of the principles of the law of consecration. In the darkest days of the Great Depression, Harold B. Lee, president of the Pioneer Stake in Salt Lake City, launched an innovative series of programs to provide work and support for struggling members of his stake. President Lee gave oversight to the building of a storehouse where food and commodities could be brought and then distributed to the needy. Under his direction, warehouses, a farm, and other enterprises were established so that brethren in his stake had opportunities to work for products received from the storehouse. Church leaders, observing the success of President Lee's programs, called him to launch what has become the much-touted Church welfare system.

Noting the similarity between the Church welfare system and the law of consecration, President J. Reuben Clark said in 1942, "We have all said that the Welfare Plan is not the United Order and was not intended to be. However, I should like to suggest to you that perhaps, after all, when the Welfare Plan gets thoroughly into operation—it is not so yet—we shall not be so very far from carrying out the great fundamentals of the United Order."[8] President Marion G. Romney said in 1975, "The procedural method for teaching Church Welfare has now changed, but the objectives of the program remain the same. Its principles are eternal. It is the gospel in its perfection—the united order, toward which we move."[9]

Consecration is not a past practice of the Church. Its implementation has evolved over time, but it remains an eternal and essential part of Latter-day Saint belief.

NOTES

1. Josiah Jones, "History of the Mormonites," *Evangelist*, June 1, 1831, 132, in Staker, *Hearken, O Ye People*, 45.
2. Davidson et al., *Histories*, 2:22–23, or josephsmith papers.org.
3. Van Wagoner, *Complete Discourses of Brigham Young*, 970.
4. Jessee, *Papers of Joseph Smith*, 2:391–93, in Mitchell K. Schaefer and Sherilyn Farnes, "Myself . . . I Consecrate to the God of Heaven," *BYU Studies* 50, no. 3 (2011): 104.
5. Van Wagoner, *Complete Discourses of Brigham Young*, 102; Arrington, Fox, and May, *Building the City of God*, 42.
6. Van Wagoner, *Complete Discourses of Brigham Young*, 778–79.
7. Cannon, in *Journal of Discourses*, 15:207.
8. Clark, in Conference Report, Oct. 1942, 57.
9. Romney, in Arrington, Fox, and May, *Building the City of God*, 361.

15
Locating the Land of Zion

1831

Independence, Jackson County, Missouri, 1868.

W hen will Zion be built up in her glory, and where will thy Temple stand unto which all nations shall come in the last days?" Joseph Smith asked God, just as ancient prophets had done in an earlier age (Isaiah 2:2–3; Psalm 87:1–3).[1]

Joseph recorded the divine answer to his query: "[I] received, by a heavenly vision, a commandment in June [1831] following, to take my journey to the western boundaries of the State of Missouri, and there designate the very spot, which was to be the central spot, for the commencement of the gathering together of those who embrace the fulness of the everlasting gospel."[2]

On June 7, 1831, the day following a general conference of the Church in Kirtland, Ohio, Joseph Smith announced that the next conference would convene in Missouri "upon the land, which I [the Lord] have appointed and consecrated for the gathering of my saints" (D&C 57:1). Twenty-eight pairs of traveling elders and members of the branch of the Church in Colesville, New York, were told by the Lord to attend the conference in "the land of Missouri, unto the borders of the Lamanites" (D&C 54:8). This was the area from which, between 1825 and 1840, the United States government forced the removal of "Indians from east of this line and assign[ed] them to reservations on the Great Plains."[3]

On June 19, 1831, Joseph Smith and others left Kirtland to begin their journey to the borders of the Lamanites. They traveled by wagon, canal boat, and stagecoach to Cincinnati, Ohio, where they boarded a steamer bound for Louisville, Kentucky. From Louisville, they traveled to St. Louis, Missouri. From that point, Joseph and a few other men then crossed the state on foot. After traveling 240 miles, they arrived in Independence, Missouri, on July 14, 1831.[4] The remainder of their party arrived at Independence Landing on July 25, 1831, aboard the steamboat *Chieftain* under command of Captain Shalcross.[5]

During their stay in Independence, the

Lord declared to the Prophet Joseph Smith that Missouri was "the land of promise, and the place for the city of Zion" (D&C 57:2). The Lord further revealed, "Behold, the place which is now called Independence is the center place; and the spot for the temple is lying westward, upon a lot which is not far from the courthouse" (D&C 57:3). The Lord told Joseph that one reason for their coming to Independence was so that "you might be honored in laying the foundation and in bearing record of the land upon which the Zion of God shall stand" (D&C 57:8).

On August 2, 1831, Sidney Rigdon, in accordance with the commandment "let my servant Sidney Rigdon consecrate and dedicate this land," dedicated the ground where the community of Zion was to be established (D&C 58:57). During the dedicatory service, Rigdon asked those present:

"Do you receive this land for the land of your inheritance with thankful hearts from the Lord?

"Answer from all, We do.

"Do you pledge yourselves to keep the laws of God on this land, which you never have kept in your own land?

"We do.

"Do you pledge yourselves to see that others of your brethren, who shall come hither do keep the laws of God?

"We do."

After offering the dedicatory prayer, Sidney Rigdon said, "I now pronounce this land consecrated and dedicated unto the Lord for a possession and inheritance for the Saints. . . . And for all the faithful Servants of the Lord to the remotest ages of time. Amen."[6]

At that point in the service, Joseph Smith stepped forward and "laid a stone at the Northeast corner of the contemplated Temple in the name of the Lord Jesus of Nazareth." Of this sacred event, Joseph recorded, "I proceeded to dedicate the spot for the Temple, a little west of Independence." The Eighty-seventh Psalm was then read to the assembled, including the verses "The Lord loveth the gates of Zion more than all the dwellings of Jacob. Glorious things are spoken of thee, O city of God" (Psalm 87:2–3).

To Joseph, "it was a season of joy to those present, and afforded a glimpse of the future, which time will yet unfold to the satisfaction of the faithful."[7]

On August 4, 1831, the first Church conference was held in the land of Zion. During and after the conference, Joseph received revelations promising blessings to those "whose feet stand upon the land of Zion, who have obeyed my gospel" (D&C 59:3). By way of revelation, Sidney Rigdon was commanded to write a description of the land of Zion.

In accordance with the command, Rigdon wrote, "[The country is] unlike the timbered states in the east. . . . As far as the eye can glance the beautiful rolling prairies lay spread around like a sea of meadows . . . [and are] decorated with a growth of flowers as gorgeous grand as [to] exceed description. . . . Turkeys, geese, swans, ducks, yea a variety of the feathered race, are among the rich abundance that graces the delightful regions of this goodly land of the heritage of the children of God. Nothing is more fruitful, or a richer stockholder in the blooming prairie, than the honey bee."[8]

DID YOU KNOW?

- Joseph Smith was commanded to travel to Missouri so that the spot where the City of Zion would be built could be revealed to him.

- After the arrival of Joseph Smith in Missouri, the Lord designated a lot in Independence, Missouri, as the site for a temple and the future location of the City of Zion.

Rigdon also wrote of some disadvantages: "Lack of mills and schools, together with the natural privations and inconveniences."

But Rigdon's description pales in comparison to the words of holy prophets concerning Zion in the last days: "How the glory of Lebanon is to come upon her, the fir tree, the pine tree, and the box together, to beautify the place of his sanctuary, that he may make the place of his feet glorious: where, for brass he will bring gold, and for iron he will bring silver, and for wood, brass, and for stones, iron:—and where the feast of fat things will be given to the just; yea when the splendor of the Lord, is brought to our consideration for the good of his people, the calculations of men and the vain glory of the world vanishes, and we exclaim; God will shine the perfection of beauty out of Zion."[9]

For a brief time, Zion arose in Independence, Missouri. The early Saints received lands of inheritance and were called to live sacred doctrines, the law of tithing and the law of consecration. But the Zion-like society of about 1,200 Latter-day Saints was short-lived.[10]

In 1833 an angry spirit of prejudice and hatred from the other settlers forced Saints to abandon personal property and lands of inheritance and flee across the Missouri River to Clay County, Missouri. Yet Zion has "not be[en] moved out of her place" (D&C 101:17). In the future a New Jerusalem will again be established, the Saints will assemble "upon the land of Zion" and "receive an inheritance" (D&C 62:4; 63:48).

But until that time, Latter-day Saints are invited to gather to the stakes of Zion throughout the world.

Notes

1. History, 1838–1856, vol. A-1 [23 December 1805–30 August 1834], 127, josephsmith papers.org.
2. History, 1838–1856, vol. B-1 [1 September 1834–2 November 1838], 606–7, josephsmith papers.org.
3. Cowan, *Doctrine and Covenants*, 95.
4. Smith, Manuscript History of the Church, Book A-1, josephsmithpapers.org; letter of W. W. Phelps, *Ontario [New York] Phoenix*, Sept. 7, 1831, in Richard Lloyd Anderson, "Jackson County in Early Mormon Descriptions," *Missouri Historical Review* 65, no. 3 (Apr. 1971): 274.
5. Larry C. Porter, "The Colesville Branch in Kaw Township, Jackson County, Missouri, 1831 to 1833," in Garr and Johnson, *Missouri*, 286, 307n22.
6. John Whitmer, History, 1831–ca. 1847, 32, joseph smithpapers.org.
7. History, 1838–1856, vol. A-1 [23 December 1805–30 August 1834], 137, josephsmith papers.org; *Times and Seasons*, Mar. 1, 1844, 450.
8. History, 1838–1856, vol. A-1 [23 December 1805–30 August 1834], 137–38, josephsmith papers.org.
9. History, 1838–1856, vol. A-1 [23 December 1805–30 August 1834], 139, josephsmith papers.org.
10. Revelation, 20 July 1831 [D&C 57], 89, joseph smithpapers.org.

16
The First Presidency and the Call of the Twelve

Joseph Smith Jr., Sidney Rigdon, and Frederick G. Williams.

1832

The Quorum of the First Presidency is the highest council, or governing body, of The Church of Jesus Christ of Latter-day Saints. The First Presidency consists of the President of the Church and two counselors. Members of the Presidency are called and sustained as prophets, seers, and revelators. They are special witnesses of Jesus Christ, whom the Lord has called to teach and testify of the Savior Jesus Christ throughout the world. This governing body holds the "keys of the kingdom," presides in council, and sets in order the affairs of the Church (D&C 81:2; 90:16). The "Presidency of the High Priesthood," that is, the First Presidency, "has power and authority over all the offices in the church in all ages of the world" and makes the "final decision upon controversies in spiritual matters" (D&C 107:9, 80).

The first First Presidency of the Church in this dispensation began to be formed on January 24, 1832, at a conference in Amherst, Ohio, when Joseph Smith was named "President of the High Priesthood." Less than two months later, on March 8, 1832, Joseph "chose this day and ordained brother Jesse Gause and Brother Sidney [Rigdon] to be my counsellor[s] of the ministry of the presidency of the high Priesthood."[1]

Both men were called "counselors," but if the ordering principle used later with the first Quorum of the Twelve was used in this case, Jesse Gause might have been the first counselor. He was eight years older than Sidney Rigdon and twenty years older than the Prophet Joseph Smith. A week after Gause was called as a counselor, a revelation was given to Joseph Smith "explaining the dignity of the appointment" (D&C 81, headnote).

Gause functioned as a counselor for only six months. In August 1832 he went east to serve a mission and then abandoned his calling. He was excommunicated in December 1832, and his whereabouts thereafter are unknown. On March 18, 1833, the First Presidency was reorganized with Frederick G. Williams as a counselor in the place of Gause.[2] Sidney Rigdon remained as counselor for the remainder of Joseph's life.

The second highest governing body of the Church is the Quorum of the Twelve Apostles. Apostles, like members of the First Presidency, are called and sustained as prophets, seers, and revelators. They too are special witnesses of Jesus Christ who teach and testify of the resurrected Lord throughout the world. Under the direction of the First Presidency, they are given charge over the affairs of the Church.

In June 1829 the Lord made known to Joseph Smith, Oliver Cowdery, and David Whitmer that twelve disciples were to be called as special witnesses of Jesus Christ "to go into all the world to preach my gospel unto every creature" (D&C 18:28). Oliver and David were commanded to "search out the Twelve" (D&C 18:37). More than four years later, on February 14, 1835, at a schoolhouse in Kirtland, Ohio, these men, together with Martin Harris, named the members of the first Quorum of the Twelve Apostles in this dispensation. The occasion was a meeting of those who had journeyed to Missouri with Zion's Camp.

Joseph called the meeting to order and after reading from the fifteenth chapter of the Gospel of John asked that all present "endeavor to solemnize our mind that we may receive a blessing by calling upon the Lord & said let us pray." After the prayer, Joseph requested that those who had marched with Zion's Camp sit together. Joseph then related some of the harrowing experiences the camp had experienced during their march to Missouri. He explained that "those who went to Zion, with a determination to lay down their lives, if necessary, it was the will of God that they should be ordained, to the ministry, and go forth to prune the vineyard for the last time."[3]

Joseph asked the members of Zion's Camp if they were in agreement with what he had said and to signify it by rising to their feet. All arose. He then called upon the congregation to signify by raising their right hands if they sanctioned what had been said. All hands were raised. The congregation then sang "Hark, Listen to the Trumpeters." After a prayer was offered by Hyrum Smith, those present were dismissed for an hour.

When the meeting reconvened, Joseph Smith said that the "first business of the meeting was, for the Three Witnesses of the Book of Mormon, to pray, each one, and then proceed to choose twelve men from the Church, as Apostles, to go to all nations, kindred[s], tongues, and people." The Three Witnesses (Oliver Cowdery, David Whitmer, and Martin Harris) united in prayer before the First Presidency (Joseph Smith Jr., Sidney Rigdon, and Frederick G. Williams). The Presidency then laid their hands upon the heads of the Witnesses and set them apart to select and ordain twelve men to be special witnesses, or Apostles, of the Lord Jesus Christ.

After having sat in counsel with the First Presidency, the Three Witnesses named (1) Lyman E. Johnson, (2) Brigham Young, (3) Heber C. Kimball, (4) Orson Hyde, (5) David W. Patten, (6) Luke S. Johnson, (7) William E. McLellin, (8) John F. Boynton, (9) Orson Pratt,

DID YOU KNOW?

- Jesse Gause, a figure now virtually unknown, was called to serve in the original First Presidency but was replaced by Frederick G. Williams.

- Since all the members of the original Quorum of the Twelve in this dispensation received their call at the same time, seniority in the quorum was determined by age.

(10) William Smith, (11) Thomas B. Marsh, and (12) Parley P. Pratt. Nine of the twelve men called were at the meeting. Because all the quorum members were called at the same time, seniority was determined by age.[4]

Joseph Smith told them, "It will be the duty of the twelve when in council to take their Seats according to their ages. The oldest to be seated at the head, and president in the first council, the next oldest in the Second, and so on until the youngest has presided." Thomas B. Marsh was presumed to be the oldest in the group, though he could not remember if his birth year was 1799 or 1800. He became the presiding officer of the quorum. Later investigations of census records have determined that David W. Patten, the next in line, was in fact the oldest.[5] Today seniority is determined by the length of time an apostle has served as a member of the Quorum.[6]

These men were given an opportunity to express their feelings. Then Lyman E. Johnson, Brigham Young, and Heber C. Kimball stepped forward to receive their ordinations from the Three Witnesses. Heber C. Kimball's blessing, recorded "in substance" on that occasion, reads:

"He shall be made like unto those who have been blessed before him and be favored with the same blessings. That he might receive visions, the ministration of angels and hear their voices & even come into the presence of God. That many millions may be converted by his instrumentality. That Angels may waft him from place to place and that he may stand unto the coming of our Lord and receive a crown in the kingdom of our Lord, that he be made acquainted with the day when Christ shall come, that he shall be made perfect in faith and that the deaf shall hear, the lame shall walk, the blind shall see, and greater things than these may he do, that he shall have boldness of speech before the nations and great power &c."[7]

The First Presidency also laid their hands on those who had been ordained and spoke at length regarding the sacred callings bestowed that day. The other men who had been called but were not ordained on that day would subsequently receive the same ordination and bestowal of keys.

The following day, February 15, 1835, Oliver Cowdery gave a "General Charge to the Twelve." In his remarks, Cowdery said, "Our minds have been on a constant stretch, to find who these Twelve were: when the time should come, we could not tell, but we sought the Lord by fasting and prayer, to have our lives prolonged to see this day, to see you."[8]

The two governing bodies—the First Presidency and the Quorum of the Twelve—continue to lead and guide the affairs of The Church of Jesus Christ of Latter-day Saints throughout the world. They are special witnesses of Jesus Christ and are sustained as prophets, seers, and revelators by faithful members worldwide.

NOTES

1. Kirtland Revelation Book, 10–11, josephsmithpapers.org.
2. Historical Introduction, Revelation, 15 Mar. 1832 [D&C 81], josephsmithpapers.org.
3. History, 1838–1856, vol. B-1 [1 September 1834–2 November 1838], 564, josephsmithpapers.org.
4. Brent L. Top and Lawrence R. Flake, "The Kingdom of God Will Roll On: Succession in the Presidency," *Ensign,* Aug. 1996, 29, 31–34.
5. Shepard and Marquardt, *Lost Apostles,* 85.
6. Top and Flake, "Kingdom of God Will Roll On," 29, 31–34.
7. Kirtland Council Minute Book, Feb. 14, 1835, 146, josephsmithpapers.org.
8. Minute Book 1, Feb. 21, 1835, 158–59, josephsmithpapers.org.

17
The Visions of the Degrees of Glory

1832

The vision of the degrees of glory was received by Joseph Smith and Sidney Rigdon in this room in John Johnson's home, Hiram, Ohio.

Doctrine and Covenants 76, referred to as the vision of the degrees of glory and, simply, the vision, presents a detailed view of the afterlife and provides the basic outline for the Latter-day Saint understanding of the plan of salvation. Joseph Smith called the revelation "a transcript from the records of the eternal world." He said, "The sublimity of the ideas, the purity of the language . . . the rewards for faithfulness & the punishment for sins, are so much beyond the narrow mindedness of men,

that every honest man is constrained to exclaim, *It came from God.*"[1]

The vision was one of several revelations Joseph Smith received in conjunction with preparing what became known as the Joseph Smith Translation. Of his translation of holy writ, Joseph wrote, "From sundry revelations which had been received, it was apparent that many important points, touching the Salvation of man, had been taken from the Bible, or lost before it was compiled." He continued, "It appeared self-evident from what truths were left, that if God rewarded every one according to the deeds done in the body, the term 'heaven' as intended for the Saints' eternal home, must include more kingdoms than one."[2]

The vision was received while Joseph Smith and Sidney Rigdon were pondering John 5:29, which speaks of a "resurrection of life" for the faithful and a "resurrection of damnation" for the wicked.[3] According to Philo Dibble, several of the brethren were present at the John Johnson farmhouse in Hiram, Ohio, when Joseph and Sidney received the vision there.[4] They heard Joseph ask Sidney, "What do I see?" followed by a description of the scene. They heard Sidney reply, "I see the same." According to Dibble, when the vision closed, "Joseph appeared as strong as a lion but Sidney seemed weak as water, and Joseph noticing his condition smiled and said: 'Brother Sidney is not as used to it as I am.'"[5]

The vision was actually a series of six visions: the Father and the Son (D&C 76:19–24); the fall of Lucifer, son of the morning

(D&C 76:25–29); the eternal fate of the sons of perdition (D&C 76:30–38, 43–49); celestial glory (D&C 76:50–70, 92–96); terrestrial glory (D&C 76:71–80, 87, 91, 97); and telestial glory (D&C 76:81–86, 88–90, 98–107, 109–12).

The Prophet Joseph Smith immediately embraced the teachings of this vision. Unfortunately, other Church members grappled with the universalist nature of the vision and its generous terms of salvation for all but the most hardened of sinners.[6] Brigham Young recalled, "Some apostatized because God was not going to send to everlasting punishment heathens and infants, but had a place of salvation, in due time, for all and would bless the honest and virtuous and truthful whether they belonged to any church or not. It was a new doctrine to this generation, and many stumbled at it."[7]

Brigham's younger brother Joseph Young was troubled: "When I came to read the visions of the different glories of the eternal world, and of the sufferings of the wicked, I could not believe it at first. . . . Why the Lord was going to save everybody!"[8]

Orson Pratt and John Murdock both recorded that a member of the Church declared the revelation was from Satan and "believed it no more than he believed the devil was crucified." The man exclaimed "he would not have the vision taught in the church for $1000."[9] Elders Pratt and Murdock tried unsuccessfully to help the brother understand the restored doctrine of the eternities.

Joseph Smith acknowledged the theology of this revelation might be overwhelming for new converts who had been raised in the heaven and hell teachings of other Christian faiths. He instructed missionaries in England "to adhere closely to the first principles of the Gospel, and remain silent concerning the gathering, the vision, and the Book of Doctrine and Covenants, until such time as the work was fully established, and it should be clearly made manifest by the Spirit [to do otherwise]."[10]

Although the doctrine taught in this series of revelatory visions ran contrary to the theology of traditional Christianity, Joseph Smith was not the first man to embrace the idea of multiple heavens. Alexander Campbell, a former associate of Sidney Rigdon, wrote of a system of salvation that had three degrees—"the kingdom of Law, the Kingdom of Favor, and the Kingdom of Glory."[11] Emanuel Swedenborg, a Swedish philosopher and mystic in the mid-1700s, wrote of an afterlife with three realms—celestial, spiritual, and natural. There is some evidence that Joseph Smith may have encountered Swedenborg's writings before Doctrine and Covenants 76 was revealed but not enough to establish a definite conclusion. Joseph Smith never cited Campbell or Swedenborg as influences on the visions, and when examined closely, we find the theology presented by Campbell and Swedenborg is fundamentally dissimilar.

Over time, the vision became the most distinctive and important of Joseph Smith's revelations in constructing the framework of the Latter-day Saint understanding of the plan of salvation. The vision became generally accepted among the faithful by 1834. However, through

DID YOU KNOW?

- Joseph Smith and Sidney Rigdon together experienced the vision of the degrees of glory while in the presence of twelve other men at the John Johnson home in Hiram, Ohio.

- Many early Church members, raised with the traditional philosophy of heaven and hell, were at first uncomfortable with the vision and its expansive teachings on salvation.

the 1830s and early 1840s, it was rarely mentioned in Church publications or in private writings of Latter-day Saints. During the last eighteen months of Joseph's life, the doctrine of the eternities moved to the forefront of his teachings. In 1843 the entire revelation was rewritten by W. W. Phelps as an epic poem and published in the Church newspaper, the *Times and Seasons*. On April 7, 1844, as Joseph presented what became known as the King Follett discourse, he announced, "*I have no fear of hell fire, that doesn't exist,* but the torment and disappointment of the mind of man is as exquisite as a lake burning with fire and brimstone."[12]

Several important sermons from this time forward provide the foundation for revelations received about temple covenants and eternal marriage (D&C 131–32).

The vision is a key document in understanding the true nature of God and his kindness towards his children. Brigham Young summarized that eternal message by saying, "[The Lord] is compassionate to all the works of His hands, the plan of His redemption, and salvation, and mercy, is stretched out over all; and His plans are to gather up, and bring together, and save all the inhabitants of the earth, with the exception of those who have received the Holy Ghost, and sinned against it. With this exception, all the world besides shall be saved."[13]

NOTES

1. History, 1838–1856, vol. A-1 [23 December 1805–30 August 1834], 192, josephsmith papers.org.
2. History, 1838–1856, vol. A-1 [23 December 1805–30 August 1834], 183, josephsmith papers.org.
3. Godfrey et al., *Documents,* 2:180, or josephsmith papers.org.
4. Historical Introduction, Vision, 16 Feb. 1832 [D&C 76], josephsmithpapers.org.
5. "Philo Dibble's Narrative," in *Early Scenes in Church History,* 80–81.
6. See Casey Paul Griffiths, "Universalism and the Revelations of Joseph Smith," in Hedges et al., *Doctrine and Covenants,* 168–87.
7. Van Wagoner, *Complete Discourses of Brigham Young,* 296.
8. *Deseret News,* Mar. 18, 1857, 11.
9. John Murdock, Diary (1830–59), 27–29, and Orson Pratt, Journal (1833–34), in Robert J. Woodford, "The Historical Development of the Doctrine and Covenants," doctoral dissertation, Brigham Young University (1974), 2:930–31.
10. History, 1838–1856, vol. B-1 [1 September 1834–2 November 1838], 762, josephsmith papers.org.
11. See McGavin, *Historical Background of the Doctrine and Covenants,* 197–200.
12. Stan Larson, "The King Follett Discourse: A Newly Amalgamated Text," *BYU Studies* 18, no. 2 (Winter 1978): 205; emphasis added.
13. Van Wagoner, *Complete Discourses of Brigham Young,* 558–59.

18
A Mob Attacks at the John Johnson Farm

1832

John Johnson's farmhouse, Hiram, Ohio.

Twenty-five-year-old Joseph Smith was well acquainted with verbal abuse and threats. He wrote, "They were persecuting me, reviling me, and speaking all manner of evil against me falsely" (Joseph Smith–History 1:25). One of the most brutal attacks on the Prophet and his associates came in 1832 in Hiram, Ohio, when a mob introduced to Joseph a new depth of hostile fury, anger, and rage. Joseph's hope of Hiram becoming a continuing refuge for pondering the scriptures and translating the Bible ended abruptly on March 24, 1832, when a mob sought to do him bodily harm and even to

kill him. It is ironic that this barbaric action occurred in a Christian farming community. This seeming contradiction between upright and vicious prevailed because Hiram shared with other American communities the English tradition of "appropriate" mob rule. The practice of tarring and feathering was considered a right and even a responsibility of citizens under certain circumstances. Southern abolitionists, wife beaters, government agents, immoral persons, and a prophet of God were its victims.

John Johnson had invited Joseph and his family and Sidney Rigdon and his family to be guests at his farm in Hiram. Joseph recorded, "On the 12th of September I removed with my family to the township of Hiram, and commenced living with John Johnson."[1]

The Prophet's seven months in the home of Johnson were vital to the spiritual growth and definition of the Church. Joseph received at the home sixteen of the most important revelations on the development of the Church. Among these revelations was section 76 on the three degrees of glory. Other significant events that happened while the Smiths were living in the Johnson home included a decision to compile and publish the Book of Commandments, the convening of five Church conferences, and the translation of portions of the Bible.

These months of uninterrupted spiritual outpourings came to an abrupt end on the night of March 24, when violence ended the sense of peace for Joseph Smith and Sidney Rigdon and their families. On March 24, 1832, Joseph and Emma were taking turns caring for their eleven-month-old twins, ill from the effects of measles. As the night hours waned, Joseph slept beside young Joseph while Emma comforted Julia.

Suddenly, a dozen men with blackened faces broke into their bedroom. The intruders grabbed at Joseph's "shirt, drawers and limbs." His struggle to free himself brought threats of death from the lawless men in his room. "[This] quieted me," Joseph said.[2]

Joseph was taken from the farmhouse to a nearby meadow. As the mob carried him to the meadow, Joseph saw the bloodied body of Sidney Rigdon lying on the frozen ground. Sidney had been attacked, tarred and feathered, and mercilessly dragged along the ground.

At the sight of Sidney, Joseph fully understood his own peril. He pleaded with his captors, "You will have mercy and spare my life, I hope."

The profane response was, "Call on yer God for help. We'll show ye no mercy." The mob proceeded a short distance past Sidney Rigdon to the meadow. They then proposed to "pound and scratch me well, tear off my shirt and drawers and leave me naked," Joseph said.[3]

One member of the mob, referred to as Dr. Dennison, tried to force a vial of nitric acid into Joseph's mouth.[4]

Then Dennison proposed to emasculate Joseph, whose clothes were torn off in the attempt. An unnamed mobber "like a mad cat [fell on Joseph], . . . muttered out: 'God dam ye, that's the way the Holy Ghost falls on folks.'"[5]

DID YOU KNOW?

- During the attack on Joseph Smith, one assailant tried to force a vial filled with nitric acid into the Prophet's mouth.

- The day after being tarred and feathered, Joseph appeared at a church service "all scarified and defaced."

Dennison, however, seeing Joseph's body stretched on a plank, declined to operate.

The refusal seemed to spur on the shouts and assaults by other mobbers. "'Simonds, Simonds, where's the tar bucket?' 'I don't know' answered one, 'where 'tis, Eli's left it.'" When the tar was fetched, the mob tried to force the tar paddle into Joseph's mouth, but Joseph twisted his head so they could not. An angry mobber cried, "God dam ye, hold up yer head and let us give ye some tar."[6]

Finally, they forced tar into his mouth, which all but smothered him. They covered his scratched and beaten body with the hot substance. Joseph lost consciousness. As the final touch to this barbarity, in mockery they dumped feathers on him.

The mob fled to the old brickyard in Hiram to wash themselves and bury their clothes, hoping their participation in the deed would be hidden.

Joseph was left alone. When he regained consciousness, he struggled to rid the tar from his mouth in order to breathe more freely. He attempted to rise but failed. In a moment, he made a second effort and saw two lights in the distance. "I made my way towards one of them, and found it was father Johnson's."[7]

When Joseph neared the farmhouse, he called from the shadows to Emma. Already highly stressed, Emma saw Joseph covered with what she assumed was blood. Concluding that he was "all mashed to pieces," she fainted.[8]

Neighbors ministering to Emma gave Joseph a blanket. Wrapping it around himself, he staggered into the farmhouse. Throughout the remainder of the night his friends scraped and washed his wounded body in an attempt to remove the tar.

The local press decried the vicious attack as "a base transaction, an unlawful act, a work of darkness, a diabolical trick." Nevertheless, the press hinted at widespread sympathy: "But bad as it is, it proves . . . that Satan hath more power than pretended prophets of Mormonism."[9]

Although Joseph was not safe in Hiram, the next morning, March 25, he appeared in a public church service "all scarified and defaced."[10] On March 26, he went to the log cabin across the road from the farmhouse to comfort Sidney Rigdon. On March 29, Joseph buried his eleven-month-old son, Joseph Murdock Smith. Already weakened by measles, young baby Joseph had died of a severe cold brought on by the mob's invading the farmhouse.

The sorrowing father left Hiram for Missouri on April 1, 1832, leaving Emma and baby Julia behind, but he was pursued by mobbers from as far as Cincinnati. He instructed Emma by letter to move back to Kirtland to stay with the Newel K. Whitney family.

Hiram, Ohio, was Joseph Smith's introductory experience to physical brutality. In this community he saw former friends plotting his destruction, faithful friends murmuring, and the effects of unleashed anger and vengeance. This introduction to fury was the beginning of the mob violence that continued throughout his life and culminated in his murder on June 27, 1844, in Carthage, Illinois.

NOTES

1. History, 1838–1856, vol. A-1 [23 December 1805–30 August 1834], 153, josephsmithpapers.org.
2. History, 1838–1856, vol. A-1 [23 December 1805–30 August 1834], 205, josephsmithpapers.org.
3. History, 1838–1856, vol. A-1 [23 December 1805–30 August 1834], 206, josephsmithpapers.org.
4. Staker, *Hearken, O Ye People*, 351–52.
5. History, 1838–1856, vol. A-1 [23 December 1805–30 August 1834], 207, josephsmithpapers.org.
6. History, 1838–1856, vol. A-1 [23 December 1805–30 August 1834], 206–7, josephsmithpapers.org.
7. History, 1838–1856, vol. A-1 [23 December 1805–30 August 1834], 207, josephsmithpapers.org.
8. History, 1838–1856, vol. A-1 [23 December 1805–30 August 1834], 207, josephsmithpapers.org.
9. *Warren News-Letter and Trumbull County Republican,* Apr. 10, 1832, in Max H. Parkin, "Conflict at Kirtland: A Study of the Nature and Causes of External and Internal Conflict of the Mormons in Ohio between 1830 and 1838," master's thesis, Brigham Young University (1966), 204.
10. History, 1838–1856, vol. A-1 [23 December 1805–30 August 1834], 208, josephsmithpapers.org.

19
The Word of Wisdom

1833

Reconstructed room where the School of the Prophets was held in Newel K. Whitney's store, Kirtland, Ohio.

The School of the Prophets met in a small room on the upper floor of Newel K. Whitney's store in Kirtland, Ohio. In that room, brethren gathered together to be instructed by Joseph Smith and other leaders. Brigham Young remembered the meetings: "When they assembled together in this room after breakfast, the first thing they did was to light their pipes, and while smoking, talk about the great things of the kingdom and spit all over the room, and as soon as the pipe was out of their mouths a large chew of tobacco would then be taken." He indicated that the distraction of smoke "and the complaints of his wife [Emma] made the Prophet think upon the matter, and he inquired of the Lord relating to the conduct of the Elders in using tobacco."[1] When Joseph inquired of the Lord on February 27, 1833, he received a revelation today known as the Word of Wisdom.

From the beginning, the interpretation and implementation of the Word of Wisdom was complex. The opening line in the revelation stated: "To be sent by greeting; not by commandment or constraint."

That wording led to debates about whether the revelation was a commandment or a guideline.[2] A number of other questions also arose, including the meaning of "hot drinks" (D&C 89:9).

Joseph Smith believed strongly in the truths presented in the Word of Wisdom, though he favored a more relaxed interpretation than later Church leaders. Entries in Joseph Smith's journal tell of his consuming tea and wine in times of stress. In Carthage Jail, for example, he and his friends felt "unusually dull or languid" and requested that wine be brought to the jail. Nevertheless, Joseph strongly opposed the abuse of alcohol and drunkenness in any form. After hearing of a man freezing to death while under the influence of spirits, he lamented in his journal, "O my God how long will this monster intemperance find its victims on the earth."[3] On another occasion, he counseled,

"There is no excuse for any man to drink and get drunk in the church of Christ."[4]

The Word of Wisdom received less attention after the martyrdom of Joseph Smith in June 1844. During the exodus from Nauvoo in 1845, a list of suggested supplies for the westward journey was printed in the *Nauvoo Neighbor*. The list included one pound of tea and coffee and one gallon of alcohol per family.

In Winter Quarters, Brigham Young tried to curb the use of alcohol. A sweep at Winter Quarters uncovered five barrels of moonshine in a single day.[5]

After the Saints' arrival in the Salt Lake Valley and the hardships of pioneering began to recede, Brigham Young made additional attempts to persuade Latter-day Saints to follow the Word of Wisdom. At a September 1851 conference, Brigham Young moved that "all the sisters who will leave off the use of tea, coffee, etc., to manifest it by raising the right hand." He then moved that "all the boys who were under ninety years of age who would covenant to leave off the use of tobacco, whisky, and all things mentioned in the Word of Wisdom, to manifest it in the same manner." According to conference minutes, the motions were carried unanimously. During the same conference, President Young threatened to "cut off from the Church" those who "will not keep the Word of Wisdom."[6]

At the same time, Brigham was reluctant to impose penalties for failing to obey the commandment. Additionally, he struggled with his own use of tobacco, taken partly to deal with unbearable tooth pain. By 1860 President Young had ended his personal use of alcohol, tobacco, tea, or coffee, except for medicinal or sacramental purposes.[7]

Renewed efforts by Church Presidents John Taylor, Wilford Woodruff, and Lorenzo Snow moved the Latter-day Saints toward total abstinence from the harmful substances. By 1900 evidence suggests that most Church leaders were living the Word of Wisdom. A landmark event came in 1902 when President Joseph F. Smith instructed stake presidents to refuse a temple recommend to "flagrant violators" of the Word of Wisdom. For the first time, violation of the Word of Wisdom led to restrictions in Church privileges.[8]

This trend continued under Heber J. Grant. President Grant was a fierce advocate of Prohibition and a strict interpretation of the Word of Wisdom. In 1921 observance of the Word of Wisdom became a requirement for admission to the temple. President Grant clearly taught the revelation as a commandment, not as a guideline or a suggestion. On one occasion he wrote, "I have met any number of people who have said the Word of Wisdom is not a command from the Lord, that it is not given by the way of commandment. But the Word of Wisdom is the will of the Lord."[9]

By the 1940s and 1950s, the question was not *if* the Latter-day Saints would live the Word of Wisdom but how far they would go in their zeal to follow its precepts. In 1945 Elder Joseph F. Merrill preached a fiery sermon against excessive use of meat. Elder John A. Widtsoe and his wife,

DID YOU KNOW?

- The Word of Wisdom was originally intended "to be sent by greeting; not by commandment or constraint," and its implementation as a Church standard took place gradually over nearly a century.

- Penalties were not imposed for violating the Word of Wisdom until 1902, when President Joseph F. Smith instructed a bishop in Farmington, Utah, to refuse a temple recommend to blatant violators of the Word of Wisdom.

Leah, wrote a book on the principles of the Word and Wisdom and gave as their opinion, "The expectant mother who uses caffeine-containing beverages is laying the foundation for failure in life for the unborn child."[10]

Other Church leaders advocated a more measured approach. When a theater employee apologized for giving President David O. McKay a cup with the Coca-Cola logo on the outside, President McKay quipped, "I don't care what it says *on* the cup, as long as there is a Coke *in* the cup."[11] While individual interpretations have varied since the days of Presidents Heber J. Grant and David O. McKay, most faithful Latter-day Saints settle on the common ground of abstaining from alcohol, tobacco, coffee, tea, and harmful drugs.

Why was there such a gradual approach to accepting the Word of Wisdom as a commandment? President Joseph F. Smith offered the following opinion: "The reason undoubtedly why the Word of Wisdom was given—as not by 'commandment or constraint' was that at that time, at least, if it had been given as a commandment it would have brought every man, addicted to the use of these noxious things, under condemnation; so the Lord was merciful and gave them a chance to overcome, before He brought them under the law."[12]

The Word of Wisdom has become one of the key measures of Latter-day Saint faithfulness and is a signature practice in the Church.

NOTES

1. Van Wagoner, *Complete Discourses of Brigham Young,* 2:2532.
2. See Alexander, *Mormonism in Transition,* 258–72; Paul H. Peterson and Ronald W. Walker, "Brigham Young's Word of Wisdom Legacy," *BYU Studies* 42, nos. 3–4 (2003): 29–64.
3. Jessee et al., *Journals,* 1:196, or josephsmith papers.org.
4. Dirkmaat et al., *Documents,* 3:17 [D&C 89], or josephsmithpapers.org. These instances are recorded in Joseph Smith's journal for Mar. 11, 1843, and May 3, 1843, josephsmithpapers.org.
5. Peterson and Walker, "Brigham Young's Word of Wisdom Legacy," 34.
6. Van Wagoner, *Complete Discourses of Brigham Young,* 1:453.
7. Peterson and Walker, "Brigham Young's Word of Wisdom Legacy," 46–47.
8. Thomas G. Alexander, "The Word of Wisdom: From Principle to Requirement," *Dialogue* 14 (Fall 1981), 79.
9. Clark, *Messages of the First Presidency,* vol. 5, 301.
10. Widtsoe and Widtsoe, *Word of Wisdom,* 96.
11. Prince and Wright, *David O. McKay,* 23.
12. Smith, in Conference Report, Oct. 1913, 14.

20
Expulsion from Jackson County

Pioneer life in Missouri in 1820.

1833

including a school for the elders patterned after the School of the Prophets in Kirtland, were underway. There was a growing spirit of optimism among the Saints, despite some jealousy and envy. The worst problem faced in Zion, however, was hostilities that surfaced between the Saints and the original Missouri settlers.

By the summer of 1833 old settlers claimed that the faith of the Latter-day Saints was a strange and threatening religion and sought occasion to ridicule and intimidate the Saints living among them. A few of the Saints confronted their neighbors with boasts that they could drive the naysayers out of the county. Joseph Smith counseled his followers to rise above retaliation and resolve to build New Jerusalem, a Zion-like community, despite outward challenges. Encouraged by his words and with resolute determination, his followers clutched hammers, shovels, and spades and resolved anew to build the prophesied community. But these efforts were hampered on every side. Surprisingly, mobs formed in the frontier settlement, a town whose very name, Independence, connotes the sacred nature of the inalienable rights of mankind.

As flames of hatred erupted on July 20, 1833, about four hundred to five hundred citizens of Jackson County gathered near the Independence courthouse to devise a plan to rid their county of Mormons. They concluded: "No Mormon shall in the future move to or settle in this county, that those now here, who shall give a definite pledge of their intention, within a reasonable time, to remove out of

The designation of Independence, Missouri, as the center place and Jackson County as a consecrated land for the gathering of a Zion people in 1831, opened the gate to the migration of hundreds of Saints. By 1833 an estimated 1,200 Mormons had established themselves in small settlements throughout the county. They had built homes, shops, mills, ferries, bridges, and more. Algernon Sidney Gilbert had established a Church storehouse, and W. W. Phelps, a printing office. Schools, the county, shall be allowed to remain unmolested."[1]

Within minutes violence broke out. The printing press owned and operated by William W. Phelps was destroyed, Saints were driven from their homes, and Church leaders Charles Allen and Edward Partridge were tarred and feathered at the town square. Partridge wrote, "I bore my abuse with so much resignation and meekness, that it appeared to astound the multitude, who permitted me to retire in silence, many looking very solemn, their sympathies having been touched."[2]

The third day after these horrific events, "some five hundred, again came dashing to Independence bearing a red flag, and armed with rifles, pistols, dirks, whips and clubs. . . . [They shouted,] 'We will rid Jackson County of the "Mormons," peaceably if we can, forcibly if we must.'" The hostile men were only slightly appeased when the leading elders "resolved to offer themselves as a ransom for the Church."[3]

Although these Church leaders signed an agreement to leave Jackson County, other Saints refused to agree. They sought redress for their wrongs through local government and received sympathy but nothing more.

In the meantime, Joseph Smith received a revelation counseling his followers in Jackson County to "bear it patiently and revile not against them, neither seek revenge" (D&C 98:23). Consistent with an earlier revelation

that told the Saints they needed to buy all the land they could near Jackson County (D&C 57:4–5), in the midst of being forced to leave, Joseph penned, "I would inform you that it is not the will of the Lord for you to sell your lands in Zion, if means can possibly be procured for your sustenance without. Every exertion should be made to maintain the cause you have espoused."[4]

He added: "Let your sufferings be what they may; it is better, in the eyes of God, that you should die, than that you should give up the land of Zion; the inheritances which you have purchased with your moneys; for every man that giveth not up his inheritances, though he should die, yet when the Lord shall come, he shall stand upon it, and, with Job, in his flesh he shall see God. Therefore this is my counsel that you retain your land; even unto the uttermost."[5]

To sell their land before the Second Coming seemed to the Saints "a very sore and grievous sin" in the eyes of God (D&C 101:98). On October 20, 1833, the Saints publicly announced that "as a people they intended to defend their lands and homes."[6]

Two weeks later, on November 5, well-armed men from all parts of the county journeyed to Independence and forced the Saints to surrender their arms and flee for safety. "All my property was scattered to the four winds, tools and all for pretended claims, where I owed not one cent justly," wrote Levi Hancock.[7]

Joseph Knight attempted to preserve his property from pillage and destruction: "We calmly submitted to the numerous indignities *heaped* upon us . . . [and] made many concessions to the mob in hope of pacifying them, but it was useless."[8]

Parley P. Pratt wrote, "My house was . . . burned, and my fruit trees and improvements destroyed or plundered. In short, every

DID YOU KNOW?

• The Christlike example of Edward Partridge, the first bishop in the Church, in enduring mob persecution briefly deterred further mob action against the Saints.

• Parley P. Pratt rode more than 1,000 miles to Kirtland to inform Joseph Smith of the persecutions in Jackson County.

member of the society was driven from the county, and fields of corn were ravaged and destroyed; stacks of wheat burned, household goods plundered, and improvements and every kind of property destroyed." The Saints fled from the angry mobs and armed militia across the Missouri River to Clay County where they were received "with some degree of kindness."[9]

While dwelling in Clay County, the exiles petitioned the courts and the governor to reinstate them on their lands in Jackson County but to no avail. In early January 1834, Elders Parley P. Pratt and Lyman Wight journeyed to Kirtland to apprise Joseph Smith of their situation and seek his assistance in rectifying the injustice against the Saints. Elder Pratt recalled, "On the first of February we mounted our horses, and started in good cheer to ride one thousand or fifteen hundred miles through a wilderness country. We had not one cent of money in our pockets on starting."[10]

When Pratt and Wight arrived in Kirtland, they reported the fall of Zion to Joseph Smith. The Prophet wrote to his friends sheltering on the banks of the Missouri River, "When we learn your sufferings it awakens every sympathy of our hearts, it weighs us down; we cannot refrain from tears, yet, we are not able to realize, only in part, your sufferings."[11]

Although the lawless and despicable actions of the mob who drove the Saints from their lands in Zion are inexcusable, the Lord himself said the Latter-day Saints in Jackson County were in part to blame "because of their transgressions" (D&C 101:2) of his holy laws that all who are to live in Zion must obey. Among the Saints "were jarrings, and contentions, and envyings, and strifes, and lustful and covetous desires," and because of these things "they

polluted their inheritances" (D&C 101:6). If and when we as Latter-day Saints are to be blessed to build up the center place of the city of Zion, the Lord tells us, "My law shall be kept on this land" (D&C 58:19).

Efforts were made to redeem Zion, but the New Jerusalem envisioned by the early Saints is still a future dream. Brigham Young assured the Latter-day Saints that Zion would yet be built in Jackson County: "Are we going back to Jackson County? Yes. When? As soon as the way opens up. Are we all going? O no! of course not. The country is not large enough to hold our present numbers."[12] He also said, "A portion of the Priesthood will go and redeem and build up the centre Stake of Zion."[13]

NOTES

1. Roberts, *Missouri Persecutions,* 67.
2. History, 1838–1856, vol. A-1 [23 December 1805–30 August 1834], 327, josephsmith papers.org.
3. Roberts, *Missouri Persecutions,* 71.
4. History, 1838–1856, vol. A-1 [23 December 1805–30 August 1834], 394–95, josephsmith papers.org.
5. History, 1838–1856, vol. A-1 [23 December 1805–30 August 1834], 395, josephsmith papers.org.
6. Roberts, *Missouri Persecutions,* 77.
7. Autobiography of Levi Ward Hancock, typescript, 50, Church History Library, The Church of Jesus Christ of Latter-day Saints, Salt Lake City, Utah.
8. "Newell Knight's Journal," *Classic Experiences and Adventures,* 97.
9. *Autobiography of Parley P. Pratt,* 122.
10. *Autobiography of Parley P. Pratt,* 133.
11. History, 1838–1856, vol. A-1 [23 December 1805–30 August 1834], 394, josephsmith papers.org.
12. Young, in *Journal of Discourses,* 18:356.
13. Young, in *Journal of Discourses,* 11:16.

21
The March of Zion's Camp

The march of Zion's Camp.

1834

By November 1833 persecuted Mormons in Jackson County, Missouri, had fled from mobs across the Missouri River to Clay County. Without adequate shelter and food, many of the outcasts became ill. Others were more fortunate. Nonetheless, "the situation of the Saints as scattered is dubious and affords a gloomy prospect," wrote William W. Phelps to Joseph Smith. "The Governor is willing to restore us, but as the Constitution gives him no power to guard us, when back, we are not willing to go. The mob swore, if we come *we shall die!*"[1]

Upon receiving word of the distressing circumstances of the Missouri Saints, Joseph was "overwhelmed with grief; he burst into tears, and sobbed aloud: 'Oh my brethren! my brethren! . . . Would that I had been with you to have shared your fate—Oh my God, what shall I do in such a trial as this.'"[2]

Joseph was told in answer to his pleas, "I, the Lord, have suffered the affliction to come upon them, wherewith they have been afflicted, in consequence of their transgressions. . . . Therefore, they must needs be chastened and tried, even as Abraham" (D&C 101:2–4).

The revelation included a parable of a vineyard that had been destroyed because of neglectful servants. In the parable, the owner of the vineyard called upon his servants to "go and gather together the residue of my servants and take all the strength of mine house which are my warriors" to reclaim the vineyard.[3]

After receiving this revelation, Joseph made plans to reclaim the vineyard, for he knew that Zion had not "forfeited her claim to a celestial crown notwithstanding the Lord has caused her to be thus afflicted" and that "Zion shall not be moved out of her place notwithstanding her children are scattered."[4]

At a Kirtland High Council meeting in February 1834, Joseph was appointed "Commander in Chief of the Armies of Israel and the leader of those who volunteered to go and assist in the redemption of Zion."[5] Joseph rallied the strength of the Ohio Saints to form a quasi-military force called Zion's Camp.

As the camp journeyed from Ohio to Missouri, Joseph counseled the men to keep the commandments of God and be united in faith, promising deliverance from their enemies by obedience. If unfaithful, the men were warned that the Lord "would visit them in his wrath" as he had the children of Israel and "vex them in his sore displeasure."[6]

There were two divisions in Zion's Camp, one led by Joseph Smith from Kirtland, Ohio, and the other led by Hyrum Smith from Pontiac, Michigan. The assembled force ranged in age from ten-year-old Bradford Elliott and George Fordham to the oldest, Noah Johnson, seventy-one. The average age was twenty-nine. At its maximum numerical strength, Zion's Camp had 207 men, 11 women, and 11 children.[7]

The march afforded those in Zion's Camp opportunities to be taught by the Prophet. For instance, when Joseph learned that the men were about to kill three rattlesnakes, he intervened, saying, "Let them alone, don't hurt them. How will the serpent ever lose its venom, while the servants of God possess the same disposition?"[8]

On another occasion, Parley P. Pratt, riding to near exhaustion to catch up with the camp, dismounted and collapsed into a deep sleep. "I had only slept a few moments," he recalled, "when a voice, more loud and shrill than I had ever before heard, fell on my ear." The voice commanded him to rise and continue his journey. "I sprang to my feet so suddenly that I could not recollect where I was or what was before me to perform."[9]

When Elder Pratt reached the camp, he related the experience to Joseph, who told him the voice was an angel of the Lord. Joseph later wrote, "God was with us and his angels went before us, and the faith of our little band was unwavering. We know that angels were our companions, for we saw them."[10]

At times, however, the men grumbled and complained, for the journey was long and many were unprepared for the hardships. Joseph Smith wrote, "I told them they would meet with misfortunes, difficulties and hindrances . . . and [exhorted] them to . . . become united, that they might not be scourged."[11]

The closest Zion's Camp came to battle was in late June, as the group encamped near Fishing River in Missouri. Several men rode into their camp, issuing threats and claiming three hundred men were coming to attack the Saints. According to Wilford Woodruff, "soon the whole heavens over our heads were lined with a cloud as black as ink." The storm struck with such violence the men of Zion's Camp scrambled for cover, some seeking shelter in a nearby Baptist church. Wilford Woodruff recalled, "The Prophet Joseph came in shaking the water from his hat and clothing [and] said, 'Boys there is some meaning to this. God is in this storm.'"[12]

The opposing force was battered by the storm and unable to cross Fishing River as it swelled from the massive rains. Joseph Smith later noted that "one of their men was killed by lightning, and that another had his hand torn off by his horse . . . they declared 'that if that was the way God fought for the . . . Mormons, they might as well go home about their business.'"[13]

On June 22, 1834, Joseph received a revelation informing him that the camp should disband and "in consequence of the transgressions of my people, it is expedient in me that mine elders should wait for a little season for the redemption of Zion" (D&C 105:9). The revelation commanded the Saints to "lift up an ensign of peace" (D&C 105:39).

Two days later, on June 24, an attack of

DID YOU KNOW?

- There were 207 men, 11 women, and 11 children in Zion's Camp.

- Nine members of the original Quorum of the Twelve, all seven presidents of the First Council of the Seventy, and sixty-three members of the original First Quorum of the Seventy were called from among those who served in Zion's Camp.

infectious cholera erupted in camp. "The brethren were so violently attacked that it seemed impossible to render them any assistance," said Joseph. "The Heavens seemed sealed against us and every power that could render us any assistance shut within its gates."[14]

He continued, "The moment I attempted to rebuke the disease, I was attacked, it seized upon me like the talons of a hawk, . . . and had I not desisted I must have saved the life of a brother, by the sacrifice of my own."[15] Seventy members of the camp were stricken with cholera, and thirteen died, including one woman, Betsy Parrish.

When Joseph Smith returned to Kirtland in August 1834, the *Painesville Telegraph* labeled his march to Zion as "one of the wildest 'goose chases' in history."[16] Yet, in the months that followed, a deeper purpose behind the journey began to unfold. In February 1835 Joseph told of a vision of those who had died on the march, saying, "If I get a mansion as bright as theirs, I ask no more." On February 14, Joseph told an assembly of the veterans of Zion's Camp, "God did not want you to fight. He could not organize His kingdom with twelve men to open the Gospel door to the nations of the earth, and with seventy men under their direction to follow in their tracks, unless He took them from a body of men who had offered their lives, and who made as great a sacrifice as did Abraham." Nine members of the original Quorum of the Twelve, all seven presidents of First Council of the Seventies, and all members of the First Quorum of the Seventy served with Zion's Camp.[17]

As a training ground for future Church leaders, Zion's Camp is unparalleled in the history of the Church. When asked about his experience in the camp, Wilford Woodruff stated, "We gained an experience we never could have gained in any other way. We had the privilege . . . of traveling a thousand miles with him [the Prophet] and seeing the workings of the Spirit of God with him, and the revelations of Jesus Christ unto him."[18]

Notes

1. Letter from William W. Phelps, Dec. 15, 1833, josephsmithpapers.org; see Dirkmaat et al., *Documents,* 3:384.
2. Lucy Mack Smith, History, 1845, 221, josephsmithpapers.org.
3. Revelation, December 16–17, 1833 [D&C 101], in Dirkmaat et al., *Documents,* 3:393–94, or josephsmithpapers.org.
4. Letter to Edward Partridge and others, Dec. 10, 1833, in Dirkmaat et al., *Documents,* 3:376, or josephsmithpapers.org; Revelation, Dec. 16–17, 1833 [D&C 101], in Dirkmaat et al., *Documents,* 3:390, or josephsmithpapers.org.
5. Minutes, Feb. 24, 1834, in Dirkmaat et al., *Documents,* 3:456–57, or josephsmithpapers.org.
6. "Sketch of the Auto-biography of George Albert Smith," *Millennial Star,* July 15, 1865, 439.
7. Backman, *Heavens Resound,* 185; Andrea G. Radke, "We Also Marched: The Women and Children of Zion's Camp, 1834," *BYU Studies* 39, no. 1 (2000): 147–65.
8. History, 1838–1856, vol. A-1 [23 December 1805–30 August 1834], 8 [addenda], josephsmithpapers.org.
9. Andrew Jenson, *Historical Record,* July 1866, 580.
10. History, 1838–1856, vol. A-1 [23 December 1805–30 August 1834], 481, josephsmithpapers.org.
11. History, 1838–1856, vol. A-1 [23 December 1805–30 August 1834], 4, [addenda], josephsmithpapers.org.
12. *Wilford Woodruff* [manual], 137.
13. History, 1838–1856, vol. A-1 [23 December 1805–30 August 1834], 16 [addenda], josephsmithpapers.org.
14. Lucy Mack Smith, History, 1844–1845, page [13], bk. 13, josephsmithpapers.org.
15. History, 1838–1856, vol. A-1 [23 December 1805–30 August 1834], 505, josephsmithpapers.org.
16. *Painesville [Ohio] Telegraph,* in Backman, *Heavens Resound,* 196.
17. Backman, *Heavens Resound,* 199.
18. Wilford Woodruff, in *Journal of Discourses,* 13:158.

22
The Publication of the Doctrine and Covenants

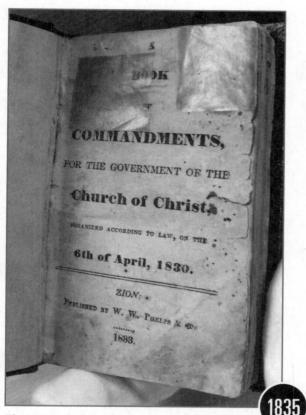

1835

The 1833 Book of Commandments owned by Joseph Smith, now in the possession of the Community of Christ.

Of the Doctrine and Covenants, the Prophet Joseph Smith said, "[It is] the foundation of the Church in these last days, and a benefit to the world, showing that the keys of the mysteries of the kingdom of our Savior are again entrusted to man" (D&C 70, headnote).

The history of the publication of the Doctrine and Covenants began in July 1830 when Joseph Smith began arranging and making copies of the revelations he had received

from God. Between 1830 and 1831, the process of arranging and copying went forward at an uneven pace with the assistance of Oliver Cowdery and John Whitmer. By the fall of 1831, about sixty revelations were prepared for printing in book format. Of these revelations, Elder Orson Pratt said, "So highly were they esteemed by us, that we committed some to memory; and a few we copied for the purpose of reference in our absence on missions, and also to read them to the saints for their edification."[1] The manuscript copies created by Orson Pratt and others inevitably contained errors, such as misspelled words and incomplete phrases.

In November 1831 at a "conference of high priests" in Hiram, Ohio, the decision was made to publish the revelations in a "Book of Commandments" or "Covenants and Commandments," with ten thousand copies to be printed by W. W. Phelps. In mid-November 1831 Oliver Cowdery and John Whitmer left Kirtland, Ohio, with the printer's copy of the revelations and headed to Independence, Missouri. On January 5, 1832, they arrived in Independence and presented the manuscript to W. W. Phelps, editor of *The Evening and the Morning Star,* a newspaper "devoted to unfolding the meaning of the revelations of God from the earliest times to the present."[2]

Starting in June 1832, Phelps published several of the revelations in the *Star.* Due to limited resources and possibly a shortage of paper, by April 1832 the decision was made to publish only three thousand copies of the Book of Commandments. Proceeds from the sale of the book were to compensate members of the Literary Firm—Joseph Smith, Oliver Cowdery, Sidney Rigdon, John Whitmer, and Martin Harris—for the "diligence of our brethren . . . in bringing to light by grace of God these sacred things."[3]

By February 1833, the copyright of the Book of Commandments had been secured from the United States District Court for Missouri, introductory headnotes were written for a few revelations, and printer's proofs were sent to Joseph Smith for approval. Three months later, in May 1833, the *Star* announced that the Book of Commandments would be "published in the course of the present year, at from 25, to 50 cents a copy."

W. W. Phelps and his staff were close to binding the book by mid-summer when a letter by Sidney Rigdon July 2, 1833, advised Phelps to ship the work to N. K. Whitney & Co. in Kirtland. By mid-July "five large forms, each containing thirty-two pages—hence a total of 160 pages in all—had been printed" along with the title page: "A Book of Commandments for the Government of the Church of Christ, Organized According to Law, on the 6th of April, 1830. Zion: Published by W. W. Phelps & Co. 1833." The text of the printed sheets ended at what today is the midpoint of Doctrine and Covenants 64:36.

On July 20, 1833, a mob broke into the printing establishment of W. W. Phelps and destroyed his office and most of the printed sheets of the Book of Commandments. During the mob attack, fifteen-year-old Mary Elizabeth Rollins and her thirteen-year-old sister, Caroline, saw mobbers carrying large printed sheets of the Book of Commandments out of the print shop and dumping them in the road.

"When they spoke about them being the commandments," Mary recorded, "I was determined to have some of them. So while their backs were turned, prying out the gable end of the house, we ran and gathered up all we could carry in our arms." Mary and Caroline ran away from the mob and hid in a nearby cornfield.

Later, Oliver Cowdery bound together some of the sheets the young girls had saved and gave Mary her own copy of the book. Others besides the Rollins sisters also rescued pages of the Book of Commandments, and some two and a half dozen copies of the book are known to exist today.[4] Because of its rarity, it has become one of the most desired and expensive books in American history. Originally intended by its printers to sell for 25 to 50 cents a copy, by the early twenty-first century, a copy of the Book of Commandments was worth over $1.7 million.[5]

Nine days after the mob attack, Phelps wrote to Church leaders in Kirtland: "Although the enemy has accomplished his design in demolishing the printing establishment they cannot demolish the design of our God, for his decree will stand & his purposes must be accomplished."[6] Plans to publish the Book of Commandments were abandoned, but Church leaders retained their resolve to print the revelations.

On April 19, 1834, Sidney Rigdon and Oliver Cowdery were set apart to assist each other "in publishing . . . the Book of Covenants," which was to include the sixty-five revelations planned for the Book of Commandments, in addition to other revelations received

DID YOU KNOW?

- Originally titled the Book of Commandments, the first version of the Doctrine and Covenants is considered to be one of the most rare American books, and by the twenty-first century, an original copy was valued at over $1.7 million.

- The most recent additions to the Doctrine and Covenants were made in 1981.

by the Prophet Joseph Smith after November 1831.[7] On September 24, 1834, the Kirtland high council appointed "a committee [Joseph Smith Jr., Oliver Cowdery, Sidney Rigdon, and Frederick G. Williams] to arrange the items of the doctrine of Jesus Christ, for the government of the church."[8]

The committee labored for a year arranging and preparing the revelations for publication. In the meantime, the Saints were asked "[to] donate and loan us all the means or money you can that we may be enable[d] to accomplish the work as a great means towards the salvation of Men."[9]

It was decided that the first part of the book would contain the seven Lectures on Faith delivered to the School of the Prophets—or the theology "on the doctrine" of the Church, as it explained. The second part of the book was to contain the "covenants or commandments of the Lord" to Joseph Smith—his revelations. Thus, the title of the book was changed from Book of Commandments to Doctrine and Covenants.[10]

Those in attendance at the August 17, 1835, conference voted to accept the revelations as scripture and to print the revelations. Approval was also given to include with the revelations the Lectures on Faith, a preface, and articles on marriage and governments, and the publication moved forward with few problems. Bound copies were available for purchase by mid-September 1835 at a dollar per book.

Eight sections were added in the 1844 edition of the Doctrine and Covenants.

In 1876 Elder Orson Pratt oversaw the creation of a new edition of the Doctrine and Covenants: twenty-six revelations were added, and the article on marriage by Oliver Cowdery was omitted. The revelations were placed in chronological order, divided into verses, and footnotes were added.[11]

President George Q. Cannon said of that edition at the October 1880 general conference, "I hold in my hand the Book of Doctrine and Covenants. . . . As there have been additions made to it . . . which were not contained in the original edition, it has been deemed wise to submit these books with their contents to the conference, to see whether the conference will vote to accept the books and their contents as from God."[12] The vote was unanimous.

In the 1921 edition of the Doctrine and Covenants, changes were made to the footnotes, the introductory statements were enlarged, the text was divided into double columns, and the Lectures on Faith were omitted.

In the 1981 edition of the Doctrine and Covenants, sections 137 and 138 and Official Declarations 1 and 2 were added. New footnotes, cross-referencing, section headings, maps, a topical guide, and an index were also added.[13]

The Prophet Joseph Smith said the Doctrine and Covenants is "the foundation of the Church in these last days, and a benefit to the world, showing that the keys of the mysteries of the kingdom of our Savior are again entrusted to man" (D&C 70, headnote).

President Ezra Taft Benson said, "The Book of Mormon is the 'keystone' of our religion, and the Doctrine and Covenants is the capstone, with continuing latter-day revelation. The Lord has placed His stamp of approval on both the keystone and the capstone."[14]

NOTES

1. Orson Pratt, "Explanation of Substituted Names in the Covenants," in *The Seer,* Mar. 1854, 228, in Robert J. Woodford, "The Story of the Doctrine and Covenants," *Ensign,* Dec. 1984, 32.
2. See *Evening and Morning Star* 1, no. 1 (June 1832): 1:259, contentdm.lib.byu.edu. 1:259.
3. Cannon and Cook, *Far West Record,* 32.

4. Turley and Slaughter, *How We Got the Doctrine and Covenants,* 35.

5. Turley and Slaughter, *How We Got the Doctrine and Covenants,* 35–36.

6. Letter from John Whitmer and William W. Phelps, July 29, 1833, josephsmithpapers.org.

7. Joseph Smith, Journal 1832–1834, April 18–19, 1834, 77–78, josephsmithpapers.org

8. Minutes, Sept 24, 1834, josephsmithpapers.org

9. Letter to Church brethren, June 15, 1835, josephsmithpapers.org.

10. Turley and Slaughter, *How We Got the Doctrine and Covenants,* 101–8.

11. Staker, *Hearken, O Ye People,* 23.

12. Cannon, "Fiftieth Semi-Annual Conference," *Millennial Star,* Nov. 15, 1880, 724.

13. Turley and Slaughter, *How We Got the Doctrine and Covenants,* 114–15.

14. Benson, "The Book of Mormon and the Doctrine and Covenants," *Ensign,* May 1987, 83.

23
Emma Smith's Hymnbook

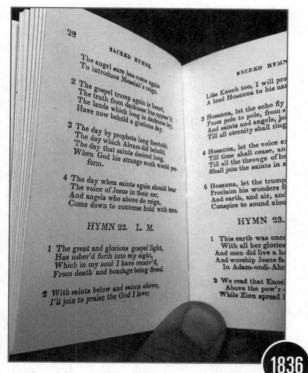

A replica of the original hymnbook compiled for the Church by Emma Smith.

1836

An essential component of worship services in The Church of Jesus Christ of Latter-day Saints is the singing of praises unto God. Such singing can be traced back to the early days of the Church. The first Latter-day Saint hymnbook had its origin in a divine command given to Emma Smith in July 1830:

"And it shall be given thee, also, to make a selection of sacred hymns, as it shall be given thee, which is pleasing unto me, to be had in my church. For my soul delighteth in the song of the heart; yea, the song of the righteous is a

prayer unto me, and it shall be answered with a blessing upon their heads" (D&C 25:11–12).

Note the word *selection* in verse 11. Emma was instructed not to compose or commission the creation of hymns but to select hymns from those that were sung in other churches of the day and were familiar to early converts to the Church. Her guide in the selection process was to choose the "song of the heart," which suggests that sacred music is akin to worship.

Within eighteen months of receiving this divine directive, Emma Smith had chosen a few hymns, as evidenced by the mention of hymns sung in conferences between August and October 1831. In April 1832, her selection process was well underway, for it was determined that hymns already selected were to be edited by W. W. Phelps.

Figuring out where Emma's selection ended and Phelps's editing began is problematic. It is known that Phelps changed wording and added his own verses to well-known Protestant hymns that Emma selected. In the June 1832 issue of *The Evening and the Morning Star,* Phelps printed the first of the edited "hymns, selected and prepared for the Church of Christ, in these last days." By February 1833 Phelps had begun printing in the *Star* hymns of his own composition.

At a meeting of the Presidency of the Church and the Kirtland high council on September 14, 1835, it was "decided that Sister Emma Smith [should] proceed to make a selection of sacred hymns, according to the revelation, and that President W. W. Phelps be appointed to revise and arrange them for printing."[1]

Emma Smith, with the assistance of Phelps, soon compiled enough hymns to fill a pocket-sized hymnbook titled *A Collection of Sacred Hymns for the Church of the Latter Day Saints, Selected by Emma Smith*. The hymnal was printed in Kirtland, Ohio, by Frederick W. Williams and Company, in early 1836 (though the date on the title page of the hymnal reads 1835).[2] All ninety hymns were printed in stanzas but without music.

The 128-page hymnal was published in "hexadecimal" form, measuring about 3 inches by 4½ inches. It was the least expensive size for bound books at that time.

The hymnal began with this preface: "In order to sing by the Spirit, and with the understanding, it is necessary that the church of the Latter Day Saints should have a collection of 'SACRED HYMNS,' adapted to their faith and belief in the gospel, and, as far as can be, holding forth the promises made to the fathers who died in the precious faith of a glorious resurrection, and a thousand years' reign on earth with the Son of Man in his glory. Notwithstanding the church, as it were, is still in its infancy, yet, as the song of the righteous is a prayer unto God, it is sincerely hoped that the following collection, selected with an eye single to his glory, may answer every purpose till more are composed, or till we are blessed with a copious variety of the songs of Zion."[3]

Twenty-seven of the hymns had been published in *The Evening and the Morning Star* by W. W. Phelps. They were included in Emma's published hymnal as a group, mostly in the same order in which they had been printed. Eleven additional hymns had been published in the *Latter Day Saints' Messenger and Advocate* between December 1834 and January 1836. A tune for each hymn was suggested in its original publication in the newspaper but not in the hymnal itself.

"At least fifty hymns in the new collection were overtly borrowed and rewritten Protestant hymns" composed by such renowned authors as Isaac Watts and Reginald Heber.[4] Thirty-four others were written by early Latter-day Saint converts, Phelps contributing twenty-six. The first hymn was "Know Then That Ev'ry Soul Is Free," a well-known Christian standard dating back to 1805, and the last, "The Spirit of God," was a new composition by W. W. Phelps.[5] Original copies of Emma's hymnal are extremely rare—only a dozen are extant.

On October 27, 1839, "the High Council of Nauvoo voted . . . that Sister Emma Smith select and publish a [second] hymn Book for the use of the Church."[6] In accordance with this decision, Emma compiled another hymnal in 1841 that included 304 hymns with suggested tempos. This hymnal, like the 1835 hymnal, had a words-only format. Original editions of the 1841 hymnal are also very rare.

Emma Smith was not involved in the selection of hymns for the 1840 words-only hymnal referred to as the Manchester Hymnal, or Small Hymnal, nor was she involved in the 1844 unofficial hymnal published by G. B. Gardner and Jesse C. Little in Bellows Falls, Vermont. It should be noted, however, that both these later hymnals included hymns from her 1835 compilation.

Since that time, several official and unofficial hymnbooks for The Church of Jesus Christ of Latter-day Saints have been published. They include *The Latter-day Saints' Psalmody* (1889),

DID YOU KNOW?

- The first hymn in Emma Smith's collection was "Know Then That Ev'ry Soul Is Free," and the last, "The Spirit of God."

- The current hymnbook used by the Church (in English) contains twenty-six hymns found in the original hymnal prepared by Emma Smith.

Deseret Sunday School Songs (1909), *Latter-day Saint Hymns* (1927), and *Hymns: The Church of Jesus Christ of Latter-day Saints* (1948).

The current hymnal, *Hymns of The Church of Jesus Christ of Latter-day Saints* (1985), contains twenty-six hymns that appeared in Emma's 1835 hymnal.[7] Her influence in the selection of hymns continues to inspire participants in worship services worldwide in the Church today.

Notes

1. Kirtland Council Minute Book 1, Sept. 16, 1835, 108, josephsmithpapers.org.
2. Crawley, *Descriptive Bibliography*, 1:59.
3. *A Collection of Sacred Hymns for the Church of the Latter Day Saints*, 1835, iii–iv, josephsmith papers.org.
4. Hicks, *Mormonism and Music*, 20.
5. *Collection of Sacred Hymns,* 1835, 1, 120–21, josephsmithpapers.org. For more information on "Know This That Every Soul Is Free," see Cornwall, *Stories of Our Mormon Hymns*, 105; for "The Spirit of God," see Davidson, *Our Latter-day Hymns*, 30.
6. History, 1838–1856, vol. C-1 [2 November 1838–31 July 1842], 972, josephsmithpapers.org.
7. *Hymns of The Church of Jesus Christ of Latter-day Saints*, preface; see *Collection of Sacred Hymns*, 1835, josephsmithpapers.org.

24
The Kirtland Temple Is Dedicated

1836

The Kirtland Temple, dedicated in 1836, a testament to the sacrifice and devotion of the early Saints.

The dedication of the Kirtland Temple marked the beginning of a great pentecostal season in the Church. Historian Milton V. Backman wrote of the dedicatory season:

"During a fifteen-week period extending from January 21 to May 1, 1836, probably more Latter-day Saints beheld visions and witnessed other unusual spiritual manifestations than during any other era in the history of the Church."[1] In the days preceding and following the dedicatory services, hundreds of people testified of visions of heavenly beings, manifestations of spiritual gifts, and even appearances of the Savior.[2]

In January 1831, the Lord commanded Joseph Smith to gather the Saints to Ohio, for there they would be endowed "with power from on high" (D&C 38:32). To facilitate the endowment of power, the Lord commanded the Saints in Ohio to build a temple. "A house of prayer, a house of fasting, a house of faith, a house of learning, a house of glory, a house of order, a house of God" was to be constructed (D&C 88:119). One Latter-day Saint suggested the temple be built of logs. "Shall we, brethren, build a house for our God, of logs?" Joseph asked. "No," he said, "I have a better plan than that. I have a plan of the house of the Lord, given by himself."[3]

The Lord's plan for the Kirtland Temple was intricate and multifaceted in design. The external design was similar to that of other houses of worship at the time, but plans for the interior were unique. It was to be fifty-five feet wide and sixty-five feet long, with a lower and a higher court. The lower court was to be dedicated "for your sacrament offering, and for your preaching, and your fasting, and your praying, and the offering up of your most holy desires unto me, saith your Lord." The higher court was to be dedicated for "the school of mine apostles" (D&C 95:16–17).[4]

"Notwithstanding the Church was poor," the followers of Joseph Smith moved forward with the temple the Prophet had envisioned.[5]

On June 5, 1833, George A. Smith hauled "the first load of stones for the Temple" from the quarry, and Hyrum Smith "commenced digging a trench for the wall, he ha[v]ing declared that he would strike the first blow upon the house."[6]

The cornerstone was laid on July 23, 1833. By the end of summer of 1833 nearly every able-bodied Latter-day Saint had contributed time and labor to construct the temple. Lucy Mack Smith wrote: "There was but one main spring to all our thoughts and actions; and that was, the building of the Lord's House."[7]

The joy of building the temple was countered by a mob who threatened to tear down the temple walls and kill the Prophet Joseph Smith. Heber C. Kimball wrote: "Our enemies were raging and threatening destruction upon us, and we had to guard ourselves . . . and were obliged to lie with our fire-locks in our arms."[8] For what seemed like months, men "gave no . . . sleep to their eyes, nor peaceful slumber to their eyelids," to protect the temple walls and Joseph Smith.[9] Nevertheless, construction of the temple moved ahead.

On March 27, 1836, an estimated one thousand people gathered inside the temple for the dedication. Dedicatory anthems were sung—"Now Let Us Rejoice" and "The Spirit of God."[10] The dedicatory prayer, which had been written under the direction of the Lord was read by the Prophet (D&C 109).

In the prayer, Joseph said, "Thou knowest that we have done this work through great tribulation; and out of our poverty we have given of our substance to build a house to thy name, that the Son of Man might have a place to manifest himself to his people" (D&C 109:5). Joseph asked God to "let the anointing" of worthy brethren "be fulfilled upon them, as upon those on the day of Pentecost" (D&C 109:35–36).

The "endowment" the Saints were promised was different from the sacred ceremonies performed in temples today. As the Saints prepared for the dedication of the temple, Joseph Smith taught "concerning the endowment, all who are prepared and are sufficiently pure to abide the presence of the Saviour will see him."[11]

Joseph's petition was granted, for "the Savior made His appearance to some, while angels ministered unto others, and it was a pentecost and an endowment indeed, long, long to be remembered."[12] Eliza R. Snow observed, "The ceremonies of that dedication may be rehearsed, but no mortal language can describe the heavenly manifestations of that memorable day."[13] After the dedicatory prayer, the congregation rose to their feet and with hands uplifted, shouted hosannas to God and the Lamb.

On April 3, 1836, one week later, other epochal manifestations were seen in the Kirtland Temple. Joseph wrote, "Attended meeting in the Lord's house and assisted the other presidents of the church [the First Presidency and quorum presidents] in seating the congregation. . . . In the afternoon, I assisted the other Presidents in distributing the Lord's supper to the Church, receiving them from the Twelve, whose privilege it was to officiate in the sacred desk this day. After having performed this service to my brethren, I retired to the pulpit, the veils being dropped, and bowed myself, with Oliver Cowdery, in solemn prayer, but silently, to the Most High."[14]

While Joseph Smith and Oliver were in the act of prayer, "the veil was taken from their minds, and the eyes of their understandings were opened. They saw the Lord standing upon the breast work of the pulpit before them. And under his feet was a paved work of pure gold, in color like amber: his eyes were as a flame of fire; the hair of his head was like the pure snow, his countenance shone above the brightness of the sun, and his voice was as the sound of the rushing of great waters, even the Voice of Jehovah." The Savior said, "I have accepted this house. . . . And the fame of this House shall spread to foreign lands, and this is the beginning of the blessing, which shall be poured out upon the heads of my people."[15]

When that vision closed, the heavens again were opened. Moses appeared and committed unto Joseph and Oliver "the keys of the gathering of Israel from the four parts of the earth, and the leading of the ten tribes from the land of the north. After that, Elias appeared, and committed the dispensation of the gospel of Abraham," which is the blessings and responsibilities of the Abrahamic covenant (D&C 110:11–12; see also Abraham 2:9–11). And then "another great and glorious vision" was opened—Elijah appeared and bestowed priesthood keys to turn "the hearts of the fathers to the children, and the children to the fathers" (D&C 110:13, 15).

Difficult days followed the temple dedication and the heavenly manifestations. The mob element combined with religious dissenters could not be kept at bay. Most Church members left Kirtland in 1838, and the Latter-day Saints were forced to abandon the Kirtland Temple in the years following. Some Saints remained in Kirtland until April 5, 1845, when most of them voted to gather with the main body of the Church in Nauvoo.

Other groups took control of the temple in the late 1840s, and the Latter-day Saints have never regained possession. Shortly after most of the Saints left Kirtland in 1838, the Reverend Nelson Slater obtained a five-year lease on the second and third storeys of the temple, using the structure as a school throughout the 1840s and 50s. After the school closed, the temple was abandoned until the Reorganized Church of Jesus Christ of Latter Day Saints (today called the Community of Christ) took possession of the building in 1880.[16]

Today the Kirtland Temple is maintained by the Community of Christ. Though no ordinances take place within its walls and it now functions primarily as a historic site, it remains a sacred place for all believers in the Restoration and one of the few places on earth where prophets ancient and modern—and Jesus Christ himself—visited and carried out their sacred work.[17]

DID YOU KNOW?

• Joseph Smith told the Saints that the plan for the Kirtland Temple came directly from the Lord.

• The hymns "The Spirit of God" and "Now Let Us Rejoice" were first sung at the dedication of the Kirtland Temple.

Notes

1. Backman, *Heavens Resound*, 285; Anderson, *Joseph Smith's Kirtland*, 174.
2. See Anderson, *Joseph Smith's Kirtland*, 174.
3. Lucy Mack Smith, History, 1844–1845, bk. 14, p. 1, josephsmithpapers.org.
4. Revelation, 1 June 1833 [D&C 95], 60, josephsmithpapers.org.
5. History, 1838–1856, vol. A-1 [23 December 1805–30 August 1834], 297, josephsmithpapers.org.
6. History, 1838–1856, vol. A-1 [23 December 1805–30 August 1834], 302, josephsmithpapers.org; Lucy Mack Smith, History, 1845, 226, josephsmithpapers.org.
7. Lucy Mack Smith, History, 1845, 227, josephsmithpapers.org.
8. Kimball, *Times and Seasons*, Jan. 15, 1845, 771.
9. Lucy Mack Smith, History, 1844–1845, bk. 14, p. 2, josephsmithpapers.org
10. History, 1838–1856, vol. B-1 [1 September 1834–2 November 1838], 716, 722, josephsmithpapers.org.
11. Jessee et al., *Journals,* 1:99, or josephsmithpapers.org.

12. History, 1838–1856, vol. B-1 [1 September 1834–2 November 1838], 726, josephsmithpapers.org.

13. *Joseph Smith* [manual], 307.

14. History, 1838–1856, vol. B-1 [1 September 1834–2 November 1838], 727, josephsmithpapers.org.

15. Revelation, Apr. 3, 1836 [D&C 110], 192, josephsmithpapers.org; see D&C 110:7– 10.

16. Backman, *Heavens Resound*, 371–72.

17. Howlett, *Kirtland Temple,* 112–13.

25
The First Mission to Great Britain

Map showing Great Britain, where the first Latter-day Saint missionaries, led by Heber C. Kimball, arrived in 1837.

On July 19, 1837, a small boat carrying Latter-day Saint missionaries moved from the passenger ship towards the seaport of Liverpool. The missionaries were so anxious to go ashore that they found space in the small boat instead of waiting for a steamer to come alongside the ship as was the custom. Elder Heber C. Kimball leapt out of the boat when it was still several feet from the shore. With this bold act, Elder Kimball became the first Latter-day Saint missionary to arrive in Great Britain. It was a beginning that would one day alter the course of Church history, for the numbers of converts from the British Isles and soon other countries of Europe would strengthen the Saints in America.

In 1837 increasing economic problems, coupled with the struggling Kirtland Safety Society, had induced tensions between Church members and Church leaders. With an apostasy looming, Joseph Smith launched the first mission of the Church outside North America. "God revealed to me that something new must be done for the salvation of his church," he recorded.[1]

Heber C. Kimball, one of two apostles leading the mission, seemed an unlikely choice for the task. Amid these trying times, the Prophet Joseph approached him in the Kirtland Temple and whispered, "Brother Heber, the Spirit of the Lord has whispered to me: 'Let my servant Heber go to England and proclaim my Gospel, and open the door of salvation to that nation.'" Elder Kimball was overwhelmed. "The idea of such a mission was almost more than I could bear up under. I was almost ready to sink under the burden which was placed upon me." Nevertheless, he determined to follow the prophetic direction. "All these considerations did not deter me from the path of duty; the moment I understood the will of my Heavenly Father, I felt a determination to go at all hazards."[2]

Less than a month later, Elder Kimball, along with Willard Richards, Joseph Fielding,

John Goodson, Isaac Russell, John Snider, and fellow apostle Orson Hyde, boarded a ship bound for England. Shortly after they arrived in Liverpool, the missionaries journeyed north to Preston. There they witnessed the unfurling of a large election banner reading "TRUTH WILL PREVAIL" in large, gilt letters. "It being so very seasonable and the sentiment being so appropriate to us in our situation, we were involuntarily led to exclaim, 'Amen! So let it be,'" wrote Elder Kimball.[3]

Early in their stay, the missionaries were warmly received by Reverend James Fielding, the brother of Elder Joseph Fielding. He invited them to speak to his congregation the following Sunday, perhaps not realizing the skill of these preachers from America or the power of their message. Within a few days, Elders Kimball and Hyde preached the first Latter-day Saint sermons heard in England. That Sunday, they baptized nine converts. As others of Reverend Fielding's congregation converted to the new faith, the reverend lamented, "Kimball bored the holes, Goodson drove the nails, and Hyde clinched them."[4]

Early success for the missionaries was plentiful, but opposition to the work also began to increase, including direct attacks by the servants of the adversary. The most vivid of these incidents began one night when Isaac Russell woke up Elders Kimball and Hyde and asked them for a priesthood blessing. As the two apostles placed their hands on Russell's head, Elder Kimball later recorded, "I was struck with great force by some invisible power and fell senseless to the floor as if I had been shot." Elders Hyde and Russell helped him back to his bed. In intense pain, Elder Kimball fell to his knees and began to pray. He and others then beheld a vision: "[I] sat up on the bed . . . and could distinctly see the evil spirits, who foamed and gnashed their teeth at us. We gazed upon them for about an hour and half. . . . I shall never forget the vindictive malignity depicted on their countenances . . . ; and any attempt to paint the scene which then presented itself, or portray their malice and enmity, would be vain."[5]

A year later, when Elder Kimball related the harrowing story to Joseph Smith, the Prophet rejoiced and declared, "I then knew that the work of God had taken root in that land. It was this that caused the devil to make a struggle to kill you."[6]

Opposition did little to halt the enthusiasm of new converts. Two of the first candidates for baptism were so eager to be baptized that they raced to the nearby River Ribble. George D. Watt won the contest. Among those baptized was Elizabeth Ann Walmsley, an invalid who was carried to the river by her husband. Elder Kimball promised Elizabeth that if she were baptized, the Lord would heal her affliction. At her confirmation, her disease was rebuked and less than a week later Elizabeth was attending to her household duties. She later journeyed to Zion and died in full fellowship at age eighty-two in Idaho.[7]

As the missionary labors continued in the Preston area, the simple manner and preaching style of Heber C. Kimball proved a perfect fit for the people they taught. Brigham Young recalled, "Brother Kimball would say, 'Come, my friend, sit down; do not be in a hurry;' and he would begin and preach the Gospel in a plain, familiar manner, and make his hearers believe everything he said, and make them testify to its truth, whether they believed or not, asking them, 'Now, ain't that so?'" Elder Kimball made his hearers feel so welcome, Brigham continued, that "the people would want to come to see him early in the morning, and stay with him until noon, and from that until night; and he would put his arm around the necks, and say, 'Come, let us go down to the water.'"[8]

Elder Kimball and his companions departed from England in April 1838 after nine months of missionary service. They left behind more than 1,500 converts, who were organized into branches in the greater Preston area. Presiding over the branches was the presidency of Joseph Fielding, Willard Richards, and William Clayton.[9]

Elders Kimball and Hyde returned to Great Britain in 1840 with other members of the Quorum of the Twelve. They succeeded in converting thousands more to the gospel of Jesus Christ. Over the course of the next century, more than fifty thousand Latter-day Saints voyaged from Great Britain to America. In so doing, they provided a foundation for future Church growth. As prophesied by Joseph Smith, the actions of Heber C. Kimball and his companions in 1837 not only opened the doors to a new corner of the earth but played a critical role in the salvation of the LDS Church by swelling its numbers.

NOTES

1. History, 1838–1856, vol. B-1 [1 September 1834–2 November 1838], 761, josephsmith papers.org.
2. Whitney, *Life of Heber C. Kimball*, 104.
3. Bloxham, Moss, and Porter, *Truth Will Prevail*, 73.
4. Allen et al., *Men with a Mission*, 40.
5. Whitney, *Life of Heber C. Kimball*, 130–31.
6. Whitney, *Life of Heber C. Kimball*, 132.
7. Whitney, *Life of Heber C. Kimball*, 135–36.
8. Van Wagoner, *Complete Discourses of Brigham Young*, 1253.
9. Allen et al., *Men with a Mission*, 53. Allen et al. estimated that baptisms in England during this period totaled between 1,500 and 2,000, although all did not remain in the Church. Other sources similarly place the figure at just over 1,500. See Evans, *Century of "Mormonism" in Great Britain*, 244.

26
The Failure of the Kirtland Safety Society

A banknote issued by the Kirtland Safety Society.

1837

During the construction of the Kirtland Temple, Latter-day Saints from the east and north of the United States sent funds to Kirtland, "which temporarily bolstered the town's economy." But outside funding ended once the temple was dedicated in March 1836. This shift placed Church leaders in a precarious situation. The debts of the Kirtland Saints were growing, and bills accrued in the temple construction went unpaid.[1]

Hoping to increase cash flow and lessen indebtedness, Church leaders gave serious consideration to establishing a bank in Kirtland. On November 2, 1836, Church leaders drafted an article of agreement to organize the Kirtland Safety Society. Elder Orson Hyde was dispatched to Columbus, Ohio, with the articles of agreement and the charge to petition the Ohio legislature for a bank charter.

As the 1836 Ohio state senate was examining applications for bank charters, Mr. Samuel Medary of Clermont County, Ohio, moved to amend the article of agreement or bill by adding a section which included the proviso: "The capital stock of which, shall be three hundred thousand dollars." When Mr. Medary called for a senate vote on the amended bill—"Yeas 11, Nays 24."[2]

Undeterred by this failure, Church leaders met in Kirtland on January 2, 1837, and organized the Kirtland Safety Society Anti-Banking Company, "for the promotion of our temporal interests, and for the better management of our different occupations, which consist in agriculture, mechanical arts, and merchandising."[3]

Joseph Smith posted a notice in the *Latter Day Saints' Messenger and Advocate:* "We invite the brethren from abroad, to call on us, and take stock in our Safety Society."[4] Stock certificates were issued, and "private land owned by the stock-holders along with what specie—gold and silver—that was received, became the capital basis upon which the firm operated."[5]

Most of the stock was backed by land in possession of the stockholders. The stock ledger book of the Kirtland Safety Society lists the names of 205 LDS members holding accounts with the society and includes most of the leaders among its 287 account pages.

The First Presidency of the Church took a decided stand about those who refused to support the new institution or recognize notes (currency) drawn on it. Wilford Woodruff was present at services held in the Kirtland Temple on Sunday, April 9, 1837, and recorded President Sidney Rigdon saying, "As many of the Church had refused Kirtlan[d] Currency which was their temporal salvation in consequence of this they put strength in the hands of their enemies & those that had done this thing must suffer by it." Elder Woodruff also recorded that Joseph Smith spoke on that occasion: "Yea, in the name of God, he proclaimed that severe judgment awaited those characters that professed to be his friends & friends to humanity & the Kirtland Safety Society but had turned traitors & opposed the currency & its friends. . . . Such have become covenant breakers, for which they will feel the wrath of God."[6]

The Kirtland Safety Society Anti-Banking Company was short-lived due to multiple problems stemming from the failure to obtain a corporate charter from the state of Ohio. The unchartered banking society had difficulty circulating its notes. Demand for the redemption of notes caused the early suspension of specie payment. This proved devastating to an institution already suffering from lack of capital.

Under an 1816 Ohio statute that prohibited the conducting of banking business unless by an authorized corporation, Joseph Smith and Sidney Rigdon were charged in February 1837 with operating the Kirtland Safety Bank as an illegal institution. Joseph Smith and Sidney Rigdon were found guilty of violating the 1816 statute and fined $1,000 each. On May 10, 1837, New York City banks, after a run had taken at least a million in specie (silver and gold) out of their own vaults, suspended

payments in specie. Banks across the country speedily followed suit, including banks in Ohio. This led to a nationwide banking panic followed by seven years of financial depression.

In June 1837 Joseph Smith, then serving as treasurer of the Kirtland Safety Society Anti-Banking Company, withdrew his support from the society. The society functioned for a short time under the direction of Warren Parrish and his associates. In August 1837 Joseph Smith denounced the business practices of Parrish and his associates and warned subscribers to beware. The Kirtland Safety Society Anti-Banking Company closed its doors in November 1837.[7] Some two hundred investors lost all or nearly all of their investment. It was difficult to reconcile their losses with the reasons for the bank's failure. After all, Joseph Smith had played a key role in the society.

Like the defaulting Kirtland Safety Society, many Saints wavered and ended their affiliation with the Church.[8] Convert Benjamin Johnson lamented, "Men in high places began to complain of and reproach each other, and brotherly love was found smothered. . . . All was now forgotten by many, who were like Judas, ready to sell or destroy the prophet Joseph and his followers."[9]

The turncoats denounced the presiding leaders as heretics and attempted to establish a new church organization and take control of the Kirtland Temple. It seemed to the faithful "as though all the powers of earth and hell were combining their influence in an especial manner to overthrow the church at once, and make a final end."[10]

The controversy in Kirtland was about more than just the failure of the bank. Historian Ronald Esplin wrote: "What was at issue was not simply prosperity or economic decline or the failure of the bank, although all of those were important. The central issue for many was their understanding of prophetic leadership: What was the role of a prophet? Was a prophet, like the Protestant minister in American tradition, expected to preach to us on Sunday out of the Book of Mormon or modern revelation, but not lead the community? Or was a prophet to lead a community of gathered Saints into a new way of organizing themselves, where all of their labors worked together to build the kingdom of God on earth?"[11]

The apostasy in Kirtland was one of the first serious tests of the role of the Prophet as a leader in both spiritual and temporal matters, and opinions over the role of prophetic leadership caused deep divisions among the Kirtland Saints.

During what Joseph called this "siege of darkness," Brigham Young declared, "I stood close by Joseph, and with all the wisdom and power God bestowed upon me, put forth my utmost energies to sustain the servant of God, and unite the Quorums of the Church."[12] Many in the quorums refused to unite as relentless accusations and persecutions raged.

As for Joseph, there were tender moments in these dark times. One was the night he overheard a little boy praying for his safety. After listening to the boy's humble prayer, Joseph told his friends "to go to bed and all sleep and rest themselves that night, for God had heard and would answer that boy's prayer."[13] They did as advised, and none was disturbed.

Choice moments, however, proved too few as tensions escalated. Lucy Mack Smith wrote of persecution becoming so violent that "Joseph regarded it as unsafe to remain any longer in Kirtland."[14]

The Prophet sought confirmation from the Lord and was told: "Thus saith the Lord, let the Presidency of my Church, take their families as soon as is practicable, and a door is open for them, and move to the west [Far West, Missouri], as fast as the way is made plain before their faces. . . . Verily I say unto you, the time has come, that your labors are finished in this place for a season."[15]

Joseph Smith and the remaining faithful members of the Church were forced to abandon Kirtland and relocate to Missouri, where a new conflict awaited them.

Notes

1. Backman, *Heavens Resound*, 314.
2. Journal of the Senate of the State of Ohio, 364–65.
3. *History of the Reorganized Church*, 2:90.
4. "Articles of Agreement," *Latter Day Saints' Messenger and Advocate*, Jan. 1837, 443.
5. Max H. Parkin, "Conflict at Kirtland: A Study of the Nature and Causes of External and Internal Conflict of the Mormons in Ohio between 1830 and 1838," master's thesis, Brigham Young University (1966), 167.
6. Kenney, *Wilford Woodruff's Journals*, 1:137–38.
7. See Scott H. Partridge, "The Failure of the Kirtland Safety Society," *BYU Studies* 12, no. 4 (Summer 1972): 437–54.
8. See Scott C. Esplin, "The Fall of Kirtland: The Doctrine and Covenants' Role in Reaffirming Joseph," in *Religious Educator* 8, no. 1 (2007): 13–24.
9. Johnson, *My Life's Review*, 20, 21.
10. History, 1838–1856, vol. B-1 [1 September 1834–2 November 1838], 761, josephsmith papers.org.
11. Ronald K. Esplin, "Joseph Smith and the Kirtland Crisis," in Holzapfel and Jackson, *Joseph Smith, the Prophet and Seer*, 265.
12. "History of Brigham Young," *Millennial Star*, Aug. 1, 1863, 487.
13. Oliver B. Huntington Autobiography, Special Collections and Archives, Merrill-Cazier Library, Utah State University, Logan, Utah.
14. Anderson, *Lucy's Book*, 615.
15. Journal, March–September 1838, 53, josephsmith papers.org.

27
The Mormon War in Missouri

Millstone believed to be an original from Hawn's Mill, Missouri.

In July 1838, Parley P. Pratt wrote, "It was a common boast that, as soon as we had completed our extensive improvements, and made a plentiful crop, they would drive us from the State [Missouri], and once more enrich themselves with the spoils."[1]

This sentiment of mob rule, combined with a provocative speech given by Sidney Rigdon the previous July and the accusations of disaffected Latter-day Saint leaders, created an evironment of conflict. The situation erupted when a brawl between Mormon and non-Mormon men broke out over block voting in the primary election at Gallatin, the county seat of Daviess County. Of the distortions and realities of this incident and others, Joseph Smith said, "There is great excitement at present among the Missourians seeking if possible an occasion against us. . . . We do not fear them for the Lord God the Eternal Father is our God and Jesus . . . is our strength and confidence."[2]

Church leaders appealed to governor Lilburn W. Boggs to quell mob mentality in his state. Instead, on October 9, 1838, the governor replied that "'the quarrel was between the Mormons and the Mob,' and that 'we might fight it out.'"[3] The governor's callous response led to more plundering and burning on both sides.

In several different meetings, the Saints in Missouri covenanted to defend themselves and their cause. When several Latter-day Saints were kidnapped by rogue elements of the Missouri militia, apostle David W. Patten—called "Captain Fearnot" by the Saints—led a group to rescue them. On October 25, 1838, sixty Latter-day Saints led by Elder Patten engaged in a pitched battle against the Missouri militia at Crooked River in Ray County. The fight lasted only a few minutes. There were casualties on both sides, including Elder Patten, who received a fatal wound.[4]

When an exaggerated account of the battle reached Governor Boggs, he "ordered out the First, Fourth, Fifth, Sixth and Twelfth divisions of the Missouri militia" on October 26.[5] The next day he issued his infamous "extermination order" against Latter-day Saints in Missouri: "The Mormons must be treated as enemies, and must be exterminated or driven from the State, if necessary, for the publick good. Their outrages are beyond all description."[6]

Boggs's executive order put in harm's way every Latter-day Saint who would not deny his or her faith. Hyrum Smith "endeavored to find out for what cause" the Latter-day Saints were subjected to such violence and even death. "All that we could learn was because we were Mormons," said Hyrum.[7]

On October 30 an armed mob of more than two hundred men attacked Hawn's Mill, where they shot and killed seventeen Latter-day Saints. Of the horrors of Hawn's Mill, Amanda Smith wrote, "Though we were women, with tender children, in flight for our lives, the demons poured volley after volley to kill us."[8]

Hiding in the woods until the firing ceased, Amanda returned to the blacksmith shop in the center of the settlement to find that her husband and one of her sons, Sardius, had been killed by the mob. Her oldest son carried to safety his brother Alma, who seemed to have received a mortal wound, with the bone of his hip shot away. Amanda later wrote, "I could not weep then. The fountain of my tears was dry; the heart overburdened with its calamity, and all the mother's sense absorbed in its anxiety for the precious boy which God alone could save."

Amanda worked through the night in the midst of the tears and cries from other settlers mourning the loss or wounding of their own families. "Yet was I there, all that long, dreadful night, with my dead and my wounded, and none but God as our physician and help," she later recorded. In her grief Amanda felt directed

by the Spirit to make a poultice for the deep wound her son had received.

She turned to her son and asked, "Alma, my child, . . . you believe that the Lord made your hip?"

"Yes, mother," he replied.

"Well, the Lord can make something there in the place of your hip, don't you believe He can, Alma?"

Over the next few weeks, Amanda continued to care for her son. She recorded, "A flexible gristle [grew] in place of the missing joint and socket, which remains to this day." More than forty years later she wrote, "Alma has never been the least crippled during his life, and he has traveled quite a long period of time as a missionary of the gospel and a living miracle of the power of God."[9]

On the same day Hawn's Mill was attacked, a short distance away a thousand militiamen surrounded Far West, the center of the Mormon communities in Missouri, in preparation for an armed attack. Hoping to forestall it, Joseph Smith and his closest associates left Far West to speak with military generals stationed on the periphery of the town. Instead of having a civilized conversation, Joseph and his associates were taken prisoner by the military.

As news of their capture passed from man to man in the encampment, militiamen yelled like a lawless mob or like "so many bloodhounds let loose upon their prey," wrote captive Parley P. Pratt. "If the vision of the infernal regions could suddenly open to the mind, with thousands of malicious fiends, all clamoring, exulting, deriding, blaspheming, mocking, railing, raging and foaming like a troubled sea, then could some idea be formed of the hell which we had entered."[10]

During the long evening hours that followed, military guards "kept up a constant tirade of mockery, and the most obscene blackguardism and abuse. They blasphemed God; mocked Jesus Christ; swore the most dreadful oaths; taunted brother Joseph and others; demanded miracles; wanted signs, such as: 'Come, Mr. Smith, show us an angel.' 'Give us one of your revelations.' 'Show us a miracle.' . . . 'Or, if you are Apostles or men of God, deliver yourselves, and then we will be Mormons.'"[11]

A military court martial convened to determine whether the prisoners should be permitted to live or die. Generals, local ministers, and judges demanded the execution of the prisoners. General Alexander Doniphan defended the prisoners, arguing that Joseph Smith and a significant number of the defendants "were not members of militia and were not subject to its disciplinary system."[12] He further argued that the assembled court martial was "illegal as hell."[13]

Despite his arguments, the prisoners were condemned to death, and General Doniphan was ordered to carry out their execution the next day. Doniphan refused, telling General Samuel Lucas, "You hurt one of these men if you dare and I will hold you personally responsible for it, and at some other time you and I will meet again when in mortal combat and we will see who is the better man."[14]

Instead of executing the prisoners, the next day General Lucas ordered the captives to climb into wagons for the journey to Independence. The wagons rolled through Far West at an early

hour on the morning of November 1, 1838. One stopped in front of Joseph's home, and a guard of six soldiers escorted him inside. "Father, is the mob going to kill you?" Joseph's young son asked. The guard retorted, "You damned little brat, go back, you will see your father no more."[15] The well-guarded wagons then rolled out of Far West.

As for the Saints who remained behind, on November 6, General John B. Clark addressed them and said: "I do not say that you shall go now, but you must not think of staying here another season, or of putting in crops. . . . As for your Leaders, do not once think, do not imagine for a moment, do not let it enter into your minds that they will be delivered and restored to you again, for their fate is fixed, the die is cast, their doom is sealed."[16]

Latter-day Saints appealed to the Missouri legislature for assistance as they prepared to leave the state of Missouri. The legislature appropriated two thousand dollars to relieve the suffering of the Saints throughout Caldwell County.

The suffering of the Latter-day Saints and their leaders is recounted in the Saints' Missouri redress petitions.[17] To date, these petitions remain unanswered. Yet the wrongs perpetrated against the Saints have not stopped the spread of the restored gospel, for "as well might man stretch forth his puny arm to stop the Missouri river in its decreed course, or to turn it up stream, as to hinder the Almighty from pouring down knowledge from heaven upon the heads of the Latter-day Saints" (D&C 121:33).

NOTES

1. *Autobiography of Parley P. Pratt*, 218.
2. History, 1838–1856, vol. B-1 [1 September 1834–2 November 1838], 818, josephsmith papers.org.
3. History, 1838–1856, vol. B-1 [1 September

1834–2 November 1838], 835, josephsmith papers.org.

4. Alexander L. Baugh, "David W. Patten," in Ludlow, ed., *Encyclopedia of Mormonism*, 3:1068.

5. R. J. Robertson, "The Mormon Experience in Missouri, 1830–1839," *Missouri Historical Review* 68, no. 3 (Apr. 1974): 289.

6. "Copy of a Military Order by the Governor of Missouri," Letterbook 2, Oct. 27, 1838, 34, josephsmithpapers.org.

7. Lucy Mack Smith, History, 1845, 273, josephsmith papers.org.

8. Andrew Jenson, *Historical Record* 5, no. 7 (July 1866): 84. Research by Brigham Young University professor Alexander L. Baugh led to the recent discovery of Jacob Hawn's grave in Yamhill, Oregon, and the correct spelling of his name; mormonhistoricsites.org.

9. *Historical Record* 5, no. 7 (July 1886): 83–88.

10. *Autobiography of Parley P. Pratt*, 235.

11. *Autobiography of Parley P. Pratt*, 235.

12. History, 1838–1856, vol. D-1 [1 August 1842–1 July 1843], 1636, josephsmithpapers.org.

13. Launius, *Alexander William Doniphan*, 63.

14. J. Wickliffe Rigdon, "I Never Knew a Time When I Did Not Know Joseph Smith," 36, in Launius, *Alexander William Doniphan*, 64.

15. History, 1838–1856, vol. D-1 [1 August 1842–1 July 1843], 1636, josephsmithpapers.org.

16. History, 1838–1856, vol. D-1 [1 August 1842–1 July 1843], 1627, josephsmithpapers.org.

17. Johnson, *Mormon Redress Petitions*, rsc.byu.edu.

28
Revelations in Liberty Jail

1839

Reconstruction of the jail in Liberty, Missouri.

The arrest of Joseph Smith and his associates at Far West was only the beginning of their troubles. The first day after their capture, the Prophet and his friends were taken to Crooked River, twelve miles from their homes. Joseph offered a word of assurance to his friends, telling them, "Be of good cheer, brethren, the word of the Lord came to me last night that our lives should be given us; and that whatever we might suffer during this captivity, not one of our lives should be taken."[1]

Joseph's prophecy was fulfilled but only after the men endured terrible hardships and deprivations.

In the following days, the prisoners were taken to jail, first in Independence and then in Richmond, Missouri, where they were subjected to jeers and taunting over their faith. At the Richmond Jail, the guards boasted about defiling Latter-day Saint women during atrocities committed in the weeks previous. Parley P. Pratt was "so disgusted, shocked, horrified, and so filled with the spirit of indignant justice that I could scrcely refrain from rising upon my feet and rebuking the guards; but had said nothing to Joseph, or any one else, although I lay next to him and knew he was awake. On a sudden he arose to his feet, and spoke in a voice of thunder, or as the roaring lion . . . :

"'*SILENCE, ye fiends of the infernal pit. In the name of Jesus Christ I rebuke you, and command you to be still; I will not live another minute and hear such language. Cease such talk, or you or I die THIS INSTANT!*'

"He ceased to speak. He stood erect in terrible majesty. Chained and without a weapon; calm, unruffled, and dignified as an angel, he looked upon the quailing guards, whose weapons were lowered or dropped to the ground; whose knees smote together, and who, shrinking into a corner, or crouching at his feet, begged his pardon, and remained quiet until a change of guards.

"I have seen the ministers of justice, clothed in magisterial robes, and criminals arraigned before them, while life was suspended on a breath, in the Courts of England; I have witnessed a Congress in solemn session to give laws to nations; I have tried to conceive of kings, of royal courts, of thrones and crowns; and of emperors assembled to decide the fate of kingdoms; but dignity and majesty I have seen but *once,* as it stood in chains, at midnight in a dungeon, in an obscure village in Missouri."[2]

Soon afterward, on December 1, 1838, Joseph Smith, Hyrum Smith, Sidney Rigdon, Lyman Wight, Caleb Baldwin, and Alexander McRae were taken to the jail in Liberty on charges of treason against the state of Missouri.[3] Elder Jeffrey R. Holland referred to the Liberty Jail confinement of the Prophet and his associates as "one of the most trying times in the history of the Church, both in terms of its impact on the Church generally and in the life of the Prophet Joseph Smith personally. . . . There was no more burdensome time in Joseph's life than this cruel, illegal, and unjustified incarceration." Yet, he added, "how empty our lives as Latter-day Saints would be if we did not have sections 121, 122, and 123 of the Doctrine and Covenants!"[4]

Fellow prisoners Baldwin and McRae acted as scribes for Joseph Smith in writing "to the scattered and destitute Latter-day Saints" in Missouri.[5] Portions of this letter were later canonized as Doctrine and Covenants 121–23.

Events leading up to the incarceration in Liberty Jail began in 1831 when the Prophet Joseph Smith identified Jackson County, Missouri, as Zion, and Independence as its "center place" (D&C 57:3). By 1833 nearly 1,200 Saints had gathered in Jackson County. Unfortunately, religious, political, and cultural differences between the Missouri settlers and the Saints led to misunderstandings, controversies, and ultimately conflict. When the Saints refused to leave Jackson County at the request of their neighbors, a Missouri mob raided

W. W. Phelps's home, where they destroyed the printing press of *The Evening and the Morning Star,* and they tarred and feathered Bishop Edward Partridge and Charles Allen.

In October 1838, General Samuel D. Lucas, a leader in the Missouri militia, took several Latter-day Saints prisoner, among them the Prophet Joseph Smith and his brother Hyrum. General Lucas transported the prisoners to a jail in Independence and from there to Richmond, Missouri. From November 12 to 29, 1838, Judge Austin A. King listened as alleged evidence was presented against the Mormon prisoners in a so-called court of inquiry held at Richmond.

At the end of what Hyrum Smith referred to as the "pretended court," Judge King found probable cause of treason against Joseph Smith, Hyrum Smith, Caleb Baldwin, Alexander McRae, and Lyman Wight for acts committed in Daviess County near Gallatin.[6] Judge King found probable cause for a charge of treason against Sidney Rigdon for acts committed in Caldwell County, based on two speeches given by Rigdon at Far West. The judge ordered the men so charged to be confined in Liberty Jail in Liberty, Missouri, and bound over to a grand jury.

Liberty Jail was a two-story limestone structure shaped like a box with a gabled roof. It measured "twenty-two and one-half feet long, twenty-two feet wide and twelve feet high to the square."[7] Conditions inside the jail were wretched. For example, the food was so contaminated and filthy that McRae said they "could not eat it until [they] were driven to it by hunger."[8] Joseph wrote, "Our souls have been bowed down" and "my nerve trembles from long confinement."[9]

While the Prophet languished in Liberty Jail, the Latter-day Saints fled Missouri, hoping for relief from the extermination order issued by Governor Lilburn W. Boggs. Elder Holland said, "The Saints, too, were without homes and without their prophet. They were leaving Missouri, heading for Illinois, but who knew what tragedies were awaiting them there? Surely . . . it was the bleakest and darkest of times."[10]

Emma Smith and her children were among those who made their way to safety in Quincy, Illinois, in the winter of 1838–39. On March 7, 1839, Emma wrote to Joseph: "No one but God, knows the reflections of my mind and the feelings of my heart when I left our house and home, and almost all of everything that we possessed excepting our little children, and took my journey out of the state of Missouri, leaving you shut up in that lonesome prison. But the recollection is more than human nature ought to bear. . . . The daily sufferings of our brethren in travelling and camping out nights, and those on the other side of the river would beggar the most lively description."[11]

Upon learning of the deprivations of the Latter-day Saints, Joseph cried out: "O God where art thou? And where is the pavilion that covereth thy hiding place? How long shall thy hand be stayed, and thine eye, yea thy pure eye, behold from the eternal heavens the wrongs of thy people and of thy servants, and thine ear be penetrated with their cries? Yea, O Lord, how long shall they suffer these wrongs and unlawful

DID YOU KNOW?

• Joseph Smith, Hyrum Smith, Sidney Rigdon, Lyman Wight, Caleb Baldwin, and Alexander McRae were incarcerated in Liberty Jail for nearly four months.

• Fellow prisoners Baldwin and McRae acted as scribes for Joseph Smith's letter "to the scattered and destitute Latter-day Saints," portions of which were canonized as Doctrine and Covenants 121, 122, and 123.

oppressions, before thine heart shall be softened toward them, and thy bowels be moved with compassion toward them?" (D&C 121:1–3).

Joseph then detailed the "suffering of the poor and much injured saints," as well as his own plight in Liberty Jail.[12] After writing seven pages recounting the deeds of the persecutors, Joseph received the Lord's reassurance of better days: "My son, peace be unto thy soul; thine adversity and thine afflictions shall be but a small moment; and then, if thou endure it well, God shall exalt thee on high; thou shalt triumph over all thy foes" (D&C 121:7–8).

The Lord reminded Joseph that "if the very jaws of hell shall gape open the mouth wide after thee, know thou, my son, that all these things shall give thee experience, and shall be for thy good. The Son of Man hath descended below them all. Art thou greater than he?" (D&C 122:7–8).

Historian Justin R. Bray explained: "These comforting words triggered a sense of confidence in Joseph. He said that God 'would have a tried people' and that the Latter-day Saints' experience in Missouri was 'a trial of our faith equal to that of Abraham.' Inasmuch as Abraham was saved from sacrificing his son Isaac, so would the Latter-day Saints be delivered from their trials if they remained faithful."[13]

The prisoners were taken from Liberty Jail to Gallatin, Missouri, on April 6. While being transported, the prisoners were allowed to escape from their captors.

Joseph Smith's lengthy letter has had a lasting effect on the lives of Latter-day Saints. It has proven wise counsel not only to the Prophet Joseph Smith and the suffering Saints scattered in the midwest but also to members of the Church in every era. The letter was reprinted in the *Times and Seasons, Millennial Star,* and *Deseret News,* and extracts were canonized as Doctrine and Covenants 121 to 123. As Elder

Holland taught, "The truths Joseph received while in Liberty Jail reveal that God was not only teaching Joseph Smith in that prison circumstance, but He was also teaching all of us, for generations yet to come."[14]

Elder Holland summarized the lessons of the Liberty Jail experience: "In one way or another, great or small, dramatic or incidental, every one of us is going to spend a little time in Liberty Jail—spiritually speaking. We will face things we do not want to face for reasons that may not be our fault. Indeed, we may face difficult circumstances for reasons that were absolutely right and proper, reasons that came *because* we were trying to keep the commandments of the Lord. We may face persecution, we may endure heartache and separation from loved ones, we may be hungry and cold and forlorn. Yes, before our lives are over we may all be given a little taste of what the prophets faced often in their lives.

"But the lessons of the winter of 1838–39 teach us that every experience can become a redemptive experience if we remain bonded to our Father in Heaven through it. These difficult lessons teach us that man's extremity is God's opportunity, and if we will be humble and faithful, if we will be believing and not curse God for our problems, He can turn the unfair and inhumane and debilitating prisons of our lives into temples—or at least into a circumstance that can bring comfort and revelation, divine companionship and peace."[15]

NOTES

1. *Autobiography of Parley P. Pratt,* 239.
2. *Autobiography of Parley P. Pratt,* 262–63.
3. Justin R. Bray, "Within the Walls of Liberty Jail, Doctrine and Covenants 121, 122, 123," history.lds.org.
4. Holland, "Lessons from Liberty Jail," *Ensign,* Sept. 2009, 29.
5. Letter to the Church and Edward Partridge, Mar. 20, 1839–A, josephsmithpapers.org; Bray, "Within the Walls of Liberty Jail."
6. "Hyrum Smith Sworn," *Times and Seasons,* July 1, 1843, 254.
7. See Jenson, *Historical Record,* 7:670–71.
8. Alexander McRae, "Incidents in the History of Joseph Smith," *Millennial Star,* Mar. 3, 1855, 135.
9. Holland, "Lessons from Liberty Jail," 28.
10. Holland, "Lessons from Liberty Jail," 33.
11. Letter from Emma Smith, Mar. 7, 1839, 37, josephsmithpapers.org.
12. Letter to the Church and Edward Partridge, March 20, 1839-A, 7, josephsmithpapers.org.
13. Bray, "Within the Walls of Liberty Jail."
14. Holland, "Lessons from Liberty Jail," 29.
15. Holland, "Lessons from Liberty Jail," 28.

29
The Nauvoo Charter

City of Nauvoo, whose charter gave the Saints some protection after the persecutions in Missouri.

1840

"The place was literally a wilderness," said Joseph Smith of Commerce, Illinois. "The land was mostly covered with trees and bushes, and much of it so wet that it was with the utmost difficulty a foot man could get through, and totally impassible for teams."[1]

He further observed, "Commerce was unhealthy, very few could live there; but believing that it might become a healthy place by the blessing of heaven to the saints, and no more eligible place presenting itself, I considered it wisdom to make an attempt to build up a city."[2]

On April 24, 1839, Joseph "advised the brethren, who could do so, to go to Commerce," which consisted of "one stone house, three frame houses, and two block houses."[3]

Joseph Smith and his family lived in one of the block houses, known as the Homestead, beginning in May 1839. By June, they had moved into a tent to make room for the sick who had fallen prey to illnesses rampant in the Mississippi Valley. To thwart the spread of what some called "swamp fever," a plan was proposed to dig ditches to drain the wetlands. By 1840 the Saints had drained the wetlands and built about "two hundred and fifty houses . . . mostly block houses, a few framed, and many more in lively operation."[4]

Chief architect of the wetlands transformation was Joseph Smith. Under his direction Latter-day Saint craftsmen, artisans, and skilled laborers tamed a swamp, reclaimed a wilderness, built a progressive community from the flats to the bluffs, renamed the settlement, and created a legendary city—a city set upon a hill of singular beauty. They built Nauvoo.[5]

As Nauvoo grew from a fledgling community on the Mississippi, Joseph believed it necessary to establish the town on a clear legal basis with a city charter approved by the Illinois legislature and signed into law by Thomas Carlin, governor of Illinois. Joseph shared his beliefs with convert John C. Bennett, who was well-versed in military and educational matters. Bennett had been the quartermaster general of the Illinois state militia and had petitioned the state legislatures of Virginia, Indiana, and Ohio to incorporate medical schools and universities. By 1838 he had established at least six schools in various midwest towns, although critics had dubbed him a "diploma peddler."[6]

At an October 1840 general conference, Bennett was appointed to a committee to draft a bill that would incorporate the city of Nauvoo. Bennett and his committee patched together a charter that in many respects mirrored the city charters of Galena, Quincy, and Springfield, Illinois. For example, the phraseology in the Nauvoo charter about the city council's legislative authority is the same as that in the Springfield charter, and the power granted justices of the peace and a municipal court is found in the charters that incorporated the cities of Chicago and Alton, Illinois.

Unique to the Nauvoo charter was the geographical area designated as the "City of Nauvoo" that allowed for expansion of city boundaries. Of the other unusual sections in the charter, perhaps the most unusual were sections on education and military. Joseph believed that by establishing a more complete educational opportunity for his followers, his "people whose minds [are] cultivated and manners refined by education" would have "great and precious enjoyments that [the] ignorant [do] not."[7]

Such a belief contrasted with established educational practices in Illinois. Educating one child in six was the desired goal of state-sponsored education at the time. The reason given was that surviving on the land "was too pressing to allow children the luxury of 'idle' hours at school."[8] This reasoning was unacceptable to Joseph Smith, who held that all youth and adults had the right to an education.

As for the military clause of the charter, after the experiences of Missouri, Joseph wanted to protect Nauvoo from untoward outside forces and said of Bennett, "He has been one of the instruments in effecting our safety and deliverance from the unjust persecutions and demands of the authorities of Missouri. . . . He is a man of enterprise, extensive acquirements, and of independent mind, and is calculated to be a great blessing to our community."[9]

After drafting the bill for the Nauvoo charter, Bennett became a "delegate, to urge the passage of said bill through the legislature," as per assignment received at the October 1840 general conference.[10] Bennett joined Almon W. Babbitt in Springfield for the December convening of the Illinois legislature. As a delegate, Bennett renewed his acquaintance with Whig and Democrat legislators, including Stephen A. Douglas and Abraham Lincoln. The bill to incorporate Nauvoo moved quickly through both houses of the legislature with little discussion or debate, with the exception of Senator Sidney H. Little's reservations over the "extraordinary militia clause."[11] On December 17, 1840, the bill was signed into law by Governor Thomas Carlin.

When the Nauvoo charter became law, Bennett said, "Every power we asked has been granted, every request gratified, every desire fulfilled. . . . Many members in the House . . . were warmly in our favor; and with only one or two dissenting voices, every representative appeared inclined to extend to us all such powers as they considered us justly entitled to, and voted for the law: and here I should not forget to mention that [Abraham] Lincoln . . . had the

DID YOU KNOW?

- The name of Commerce, Illinois, was changed to Nauvoo, from a Hebrew word meaning "beautiful."

- The Nauvoo charter established the University of Nauvoo at a time when educating one child in six was the goal of state-sponsored education in Illinois.

magnanimity to vote for our act . . . and cordially congratulated me on its passage."[12]

Under the authority of the charter, the First Presidency of the Church wrote: "The Nauvoo Legion will enable us to perform our military duty by ourselves, and thus afford us the power, and privilege, of avoiding one of the most fruitful sources of strife, oppression, and collision with the world. It will enable us to show our attachment to the state and nation as a people . . . thus proving ourselves obedient to the paramount laws of the land."[13]

With the charter established, on February 3, 1841, Bennett was elected the first mayor of Nauvoo, the Nauvoo Legion was officially founded, and the University of the City of Nauvoo had its origin. Yet from the outset, opponents of the Nauvoo charter sought for its repeal. Even the state legislature debated more than once whether to seek for repeal. In a letter published in the *Warsaw Signal* on February 14, 1844, Governor Thomas Ford of Illinois expressed irritation with the state senate for not moving ahead with the repeal. The following year, on January 29, 1845, the Illinois House of Representatives voted seventy-five to thirty-two to approve the senate bill to repeal the Nauvoo charter.

This action was followed by a delegation from Warsaw, Illinois, petitioning Governor Ford to expel all Mormons from the state. Recognizing the mob mentality that was increasing, Governor Thomas Ford advised Latter-day Saint leaders, "It would be good policy for your people to move to some far distant country. Your religion is new and it surprises the people as any great novelty in religion generally does. . . . I do not foresee the time when you will be permitted to enjoy quiet."[14]

Latter-day Saints prepared to leave their beloved city of Nauvoo for the uncharted Territory of Iowa on their way to a new home in the West.

Notes

1. History, 1838–1856, vol. C-1 [2 November 1838–31 July 1842], 954, josephsmithpapers.org.
2. Roberts, *Comprehensive History*, 2:9.
3. Roberts, *Comprehensive History*, 2:8–9.
4. History, 1838–1856, vol. C-1 [2 November 1838–31 July 1842], 1060, josephsmithpapers.org.
5. Nauvoo Journals, Dec. 1841–Apr. 1843, josephsmithpapers.org.
6. See Andrew C. Skinner, "John C. Bennett: For Prophet or Profit," in Garrett, *Illinois*, 251.
7. Joseph Smith, Jan. 12, 1841, in Ehat and Cook, *Words of Joseph Smith*, 62.
8. Givens, *In Old Nauvoo*, 237.
9. History, 1838–1856, vol. C-1 [2 November 1838–31 July 1842], 1146, josephsmithpapers.org.
10. History, 1838–1856, vol. C-1 [2 November 1838–31 July 1842], 1104, josephsmithpapers.org.
11. Flanders, *Nauvoo*, 96.
12. John C. Bennett, "Communications," *Times and Seasons*, Dec. 1840, 266–67.
13. "Statement of the First Presidency," *Times and Seasons*, Jan. 15, 1841, 274.
14. Thomas Ford to Brigham Young, 8 Apr. 1845, Brigham Young Papers, Utah Division of State History, Salt Lake City, Utah.

30
The Mission of the Twelve to Great Britain

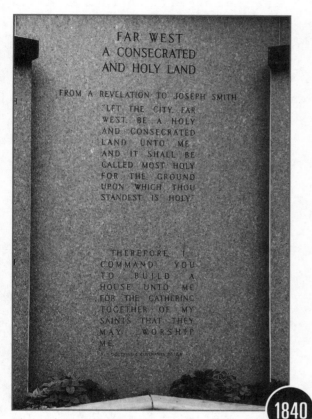

The temple site in Far West, Missouri, where the Twelve Apostles officially began their mission to Great Britain.

1840

On July 8, 1838, in Far West, Missouri, the Prophet Joseph Smith received a revelation in response to his supplication, "Show us thy will, O Lord, concerning the Twelve."[1] The revelation was a mission call that sent the Twelve "over the great waters [to] promulgate my gospel, the fulness thereof, and bear record of my name" (D&C 118:4).

This mission to the British Isles was not the first time that members of the Twelve had served in England. Heber C. Kimball and Orson Hyde opened the British mission in 1837. But the call in July 1838 was different, for it was issued to all members of the Twelve to commence their service in Britain "in the city of Far West, on the Twenty sixth day of April" the following year (D&C 118:5).[2]

Between the time the revelation was received and the appointed April departure date, however, the Latter-day Saints were expelled from Missouri under the Extermination Order issued by Missouri governor Lilburn W. Boggs on October 27, 1838. Most of the Saints, including the apostles, took refuge from the persecutions in the town of Quincy, Illinois, about two hundred miles from Far West. The question was whether the Twelve would risk their lives and return to Far West on April 26, 1839, to obey the revelation.

Not all of the Twelve were present at Far West on the appointed April date, but Brigham Young, Heber C. Kimball, Orson Pratt, John E. Page, Wilford Woodruff, George A. Smith, and John Taylor were there. In spite of the dangers in returning to Far West, early in the morning of April 26, 1839, these faithful brethren dedicated themselves to the Lord and their mission to the British Isles. Theodore Turley, a Latter-day Saint who had accompanied the Twelve to Missouri, could not resist telling Isaac Russell, an apostate still residing in town, that the revelation had been fulfilled. And so began the mission of the Twelve to England.[3]

Although the meeting at Far West marked the official beginning of their mission, the

95

distressed conditions of the Saints in the summer of 1839 delayed the departure of the Twelve. Most of the Twelve spent several months attempting to resettle their families and other destitute Saints in Commerce, Illinois. The malaria-infested swamp of Commerce, Illinois, and the land across the river at Fort Des Moines took its toll on the already weakened Saints.

The Twelve and their families suffered from illness indigenous to the swamplands, but they were fixed in their determination to fulfill the mission to England. As Wilford Woodruff lay on the ground to rest after journeying only a short distance from his home, the Prophet Joseph Smith happened upon him and cheerfully remarked, "'Well, Brother Woodruff,' . . . 'you have started upon your mission.'" Wilford replied, "'Yes,' . . . 'but I feel and look more like a subject for the dissecting room than a missionary.'"[4] Brigham Young and Heber C. Kimball, knowing the condition in which they were leaving their suffering families and their own precarious health, stopped their wagon and with great effort arose to shout three times to their wives, "Hurrah, hurrah for Israel!"[5] After traveling a modest distance, they were forced to rest for several days in Quincy.

The journey across the states and the voyage across the ocean proved slow and arduous for the Twelve. Not until April 14, 1840, did most of the Twelve reached English shores. At

DID YOU KNOW?
• The Quorum of the Twelve Apostles risked their lives to fulfill Joseph Smith's prophecy that the Twelve would commence their mission to England at Far West, Missouri.
• Wilford Woodruff baptized forty-five preachers and 160 new members in one place just thirty days after his arrival in England.

a council meeting on that date in the home of Willard Richards at Preston, England, Elder Richards was ordained an apostle as specified in the July 1838 revelation.

Now with eight apostles on English soil, the work of spreading the good news of the Restoration moved forward. The encouragement and enthusiasm for the work was much needed in 1840, because persecution and lack of strong local leadership had left the English Saints struggling to keep their faith. The Twelve strengthened the Latter-day Saints, reinvigorated the work in the British Isles, and spread the gospel at an unprecedented rate. Elder John Taylor explained why they enjoyed such success: "I feel the word of the Lord like fire in my bones. . . . You may rejoice with us in those great & glorious things which God has revealed for the salvation of the world."[6]

Elder George A. Smith was so busy sharing the gospel that he had little time to record his experiences. He wrote, "For the last twenty days I have been so busy with preaching, counselling, baptizing, confirming, and teaching the people that I had not time to journalize any; and have seldom gone to bed before 2 o'clock in the morning, as people were constantly in my room enquiring about the work of the Lord."[7]

The most dramatic stories of missionary work are the labors of Elder Wilford Woodruff in Herefordshire, England, when he learned that a religious group known as the United Brethren were seeking a restoration of the gospel. Wilford recorded, "I went in secret before the Lord, and asked Him what His will was concerning me. The answer I got was, that I should go to the south [Herefordshire], for the Lord had a great work for me to perform there, as many souls were waiting for the word of the Lord."[8]

Elder Woodruff soon arrived in Herefordshire at the farmhouse of John and Jane

Benbow. They immediately took him in and embraced his message of the Restoration. The Sunday following their conversion, Woodruff preached three sermons at three different locations to more than a thousand people. The Anglican vicar became so concerned with Woodruff's preaching that he sent a constable to arrest him. The constable listened to one of Woodruff's sermons and requested baptism. The vicar then sent two members of his congregation to stop Woodruff from preaching; they also asked for baptism. At this point, the clergyman decided not to send anyone else to stop the preacher.

Elder Woodruff recorded some of these events: "The first thirty days after my arrival in Herefordshire I had baptized forty-five preachers and one hundred and sixty members of the United Brethren, who put into my hands one chapel and forty-five houses, which were licensed according to law to preach in."[9]

The work of the Twelve in sharing the gospel was not without opposition. At one baptismal service, a mob disrupted the proceedings by tossing a dog into the water. At another baptismal service, Wilford Woodruff was pelted with stones as he entered the water, one hitting his head and nearly knocking him unconscious.

Although persecution intensified, the Twelve continued their work. Through their efforts and those of others, by 1841 more than four thousand people throughout the British Isles had joined the Church. Several hundred of these converts journeyed with the Twelve as they voyaged across the Atlantic and settled in the new Church center of Nauvoo. In the decades that followed, thousands of converts from the British Isles joined the Saints in the United States in the Intermountain West. Another success from the British mission was the unification of the Twelve under the able leadership of Brigham Young. Joseph Smith, noting the confidence and unity of the quorum, expanded their responsibilities and gave them the keys of the kingdom.

The mission to England commenced with the sacrifice to fulfill Joseph's prophecy that on April 26, 1839, at Far West, Missouri, the Twelve would journey "over the great waters [to] promulgate my gospel, the fulness thereof, and bear record of my name" (D&C 118:4). Few witnessed their dedication at Far West, but thousands reaped the benefit of their devotion to the Lord and his servant Joseph Smith. The blessings of the gospel of Jesus Christ became rooted in Great Britain through their sacrifice and willingness to serve the Lord.

NOTES

1. Jenson, *Historical Record,* 7, nos. 1–3 (Jan. 1888): 437.
2. Revelation, 8 July 1838–A [D&C 118], 55, josephsmithpapers.org.
3. Allen et al., *Men with a Mission,* 56–57.
4. Cowley, *Wilford Woodruff,* 109.
5. Whitney, *Life of Heber C. Kimball,* 266.
6. John Taylor to Leonora Taylor, Jan. 30, 1840, in Allen et al., *Men with a Mission,* 366.
7. Allen et al., *Men with a Mission,* 161.
8. Woodruff, *Leaves from My Journal,* 93.
9. Woodruff, *Leaves from My Journal,* 97; Allen et al., *Men with a Mission,* 126.

31
Introduction of Ordinances for the Dead

The resting place of some early Saints.

1840

In 1836 in an upper room of the Kirtland Temple, the Prophet exclaimed, "I [see] Fathers Adam and Abraham, and my father and mother, [and] my brother, Alvin, that has long since slept." In reference to Alvin, he "marveled how it was that he had obtained an inheritance in that kingdom, seeing that he had departed this life before the Lord had set His hand to gather Israel the second time, and had not been baptized for the remission of sins." When Joseph sought clarification, the voice of the Lord declared, "All who have died without a knowledge of this gospel, who would have received it if they had been permitted to tarry shall be heirs of the celestial Kingdom of God."[1]

In July 1838, in reply to the query, "What has become of all those who have died since the days of the apostles?" Joseph Smith answered, "All those who have not had an opportunity of hearing the gospel, and being administered

unto by an inspired man in the flesh, must have it hereafter, before they can be finally judged."[2]

Two years passed before Joseph again spoke of the deceased hearing the gospel of Jesus Christ. The occasion was the funeral of Seymour Brunson, held on August 15, 1840. The Prophet eulogized the life of Seymour Brunson, concluding that he "died in the triumph of faith."[3] According to the account of Simon Baker, Joseph Smith then read 1 Corinthians 15 and acknowledged that the apostle Paul was "talking to a people who understood baptism for the dead, for it was practiced among them." Upon seeing a widow whose son had died without baptism, the Prophet said, "Except a man be born of water and of the spirit he cannot enter the kingdom of heaven" and that "not one jot nor tittle of the Savior's words should pass away, but all should be fulfilled." Joseph Smith then announced that the time to fulfill the Savior's teaching had arrived—the Saints could now "act for their friends who had departed this life, and that the plan of salvation was calculated to save all who were willing to obey the requirements of the law of God."[4]

Latter-day Saints soon waded into the Mississippi River to be baptized for their deceased kindred and friends.[5] Joseph Smith continued to receive revelations that clarified this glorious doctrine: "If we can baptize a man in the Name of the Father of the Son & of the Holy Ghost for the remission of sins, it is just as much our privilege to act as an agent & be baptized for the remission of sins for & in behalf of our dead kindred who have not heard the gospel or fulness of it."[6]

Joseph said that those who neglect the great work for the dead "do it at the peril of their own salvation."[7] Most memorable were his words, "Brethren, shall we not go on in so great a cause? Go forward and not backward. Courage, brethren; and on, on to the victory! Let your hearts rejoice, and be exceedingly glad. Let the earth break forth into singing. Let the dead speak forth anthems of eternal praise to the King Immanuel, who hath ordained, before the world was, that which would enable us to redeem them out of their prison; for the prisoners shall go free" (D&C 128:22).

Wilford Woodruff recalled, "Joseph Smith himself . . . went into the Mississippi river one Sunday night after meeting, and baptized a hundred. I baptized another hundred. The next man, a few rods from me, baptized another hundred. We were strung up and down the Mississippi baptizing for our dead. . . . Why did we do it? Because of the feeling of joy that we had, to think that we in the flesh could stand and redeem our dead."[8]

In October 1841 Joseph Smith declared, "There shall be no more baptisms for the dead, until the ordinance can be attended to in the font of the Lord's House."[9] Joseph invited architect William Weeks to prepare drawings for a baptismal font. Those drawings depicted twelve oxen bearing a molten sea, symbolic of the twelve tribes' encampment that encircled the tabernacle in the days of Moses. When finished, the "baptismal Font [was] situated in the center of the basement room, under the main hall of the temple."[10]

On November 8, 1841, the font was dedicated by Joseph Smith. Baptisms were performed on Sunday, November 21, 1841, with officiators Brigham Young, Heber C. Kimball, and John Taylor baptizing about forty persons in behalf of the deceased. Before long, the font was in such great demand that some of the Saints returned to the Mississippi River to perform baptismal work. Harrison Burgess wrote, "Sabbath day in August [1843], I was called on to administer baptism in the Mississippi River. On this occasion I administered one hundred and sixty baptisms before I came out of the water."[11]

At the death of Joseph Smith on June 27, 1844, baptisms both in the font in the temple and in the Mississippi River were generally stopped, though some additional baptisms were performed. In August 1844, for example, Wilford Woodruff and his wife, Phoebe, went into the Mississippi River "to be baptized for some of our dead friends."[12] On the afternoon of August 24, 1844, "several of the Twelve Apostles were baptized for their dead" in the font.[13]

In January 1845, the wooden font was removed from the Nauvoo Temple site. On April 6, 1845, Brigham Young announced plans to create a stone font. Although a stone font was constructed, there is some question about whether baptisms for the dead were performed in it. If not, it might be asked why the Saints did not continue with that important work. The answer is not found in neglect but in a change of emphasis. The Saints turned their time and energy to preparing themselves to receive the endowment in the Nauvoo Temple and make preparations for the westward trek.

Except for three documented instances, the work of performing baptisms for the dead

DID YOU KNOW?

- The first baptisms for the dead took place in the Mississippi River near Nauvoo.

- The practice of baptism for the dead was halted in 1845 and not reinstituted until 1867.

ceased after the Saints' exodus from Nauvoo until it was reinstituted in 1867, in a font in the Endowment House in Salt Lake City. When the St. George Temple was completed in 1877, baptisms for the dead were performed exclusively within the walls of the temple, and has remained so ever since.[14]

Notes

1. History, 1838–1856, vol. B-1 [1 September 1834–2 November 1838], 696, josephsmith papers.org.
2. *Elders' Journal,* July 1838, 43.
3. *History of the Church,* 4:179.
4. Journal History of the Church, Aug. 15, 1840, Church History Library, The Church of Jesus Christ of Latter-day Saints, Salt Lake City, Utah; see John 3:5; Matthew 5:18.
5. Alexander L. Baugh, "'For This Ordinance Belongeth to My House': The Pracice of Baptism for the Dead Outside the Nauvoo Temple," *Mormon Historical Studies* 3, no. 1 (Spring 2002): 48; see D&C 127–28.
6. Discourse, Mar. 27, 1842, as reported by Wilford Woodruff, 139, josephsmithpapers.org; see D&C 128:16.
7. History, 1838–1856, vol. C-1 [2 November 1838–31 July 1842], 1230, josephsmith papers.org.
8. Wilford Woodruff, Journal, Apr. 6, 1891.
9. History, 1838–1856, vol. C-1 [2 November 1838–31 July 1842], 1230, josephsmith papers.org; see D&C 124:30, 35.
10. History, 1838–1856, vol. C-1 Addenda, 44, josephsmithpapers.org.
11. Burgess, in Susan Easton Black, "'A Voice of Gladness for the Living and the Dead' (D&C 128:12)," *Religious Educator* 3, no. 2 (2002): 137–49.
12. Kenney, *Wilford Woodruff's Journal,* 2:455.
13. In Black, "'A Voice of Gladness.'"
14. Baugh, "'This Ordinance Belongeth to My House,'" 54–55.

32
Doctrinal Developments and the Nauvoo Temple

The Nauvoo Temple, ca. 1845.

1841

"I am not capacitated to build according to the world," Joseph Smith told a *Pittsburg Gazette* editor. "I know nothing about architecture and all that."[1]

Yet he had definite plans about how the Nauvoo Temple should be constructed. Joseph invited architects to submit proposals and drawings of a temple for his consideration. The renderings of William Weeks captured his attention. "You are the man I want!" Joseph exclaimed after examining his drawings.[2] "I wish you to carry out *my* designs. I have seen in vision the splendid appearance of that building illuminated, and will have it built according to the pattern shown me."[3]

The pattern was intricate in design and meticulous in detail. It called for a three-storey gray limestone structure measuring 128 feet in length and 88 feet in width. Crescent moonstones, sunstones, and five-pointed star-stones were to be carved into the exterior to ornament thirty pilasters. A belfry and a clock tower with a gilded weathervane was planned to give height and beauty to the temple.

As the walls of the temple rose, Joseph Smith began to introduce some of the newly revealed ordinances of the temple to a small group of associates.[4] Joseph's understanding of the endowment had grown since the dedication of the Kirtland Temple. The first endowment ceremonies took place on Wednesday and Thursday, May 4 and 5, 1842.

The Prophet's history speaks of his giving the instruction to nine close associates: Hyrum Smith, Brigham Young, Heber C. Kimball, Willard Richards, William Law, William Marks, James Adams, George Miller, and Newell K. Whitney. The ceremony consisted of "instructing them in the principles and order of the Priesthood, attending to washings, anointings, endowments and the communication of Keys pertaining to the Aaronic Priesthood, and so on to the highest order of Melchizedek Priesthood." The Prophet explained the importance of these ordinances in "setting forth the order pertaining to the ancient of Days, and all those plans and principles, by which any one is enabled to secure the fulness of those blessings, which have been prepared for the Church of the first born, and come up and abide in the presence of the Eloheim in the Eternal worlds."[5]

As part of the revelation of the higher ordinances of the temple, Joseph Smith also introduced the ordinance of eternal marriage. On May 16, 1843, while staying in the home of Benjamin and Melissa Johnson, the Prophet introduced the new ordinance to them. Benjamin later wrote that Joseph "called me and my wife to come and sit down, for he wished to marry us according to the law of the Lord." In response Benjamin joked that he would not marry his wife again "unless she courted me." Benjamin continued, "He chided me for my levity, told me he was in earnest, and so it proved, for we stood up and were sealed by the Holy Spirit of Promise."[6]

Linked to the revelation of eternal marriage, came also the doctrine of the plurality of wives. Joseph Smith began to introduce the practice cautiously among a small group of followers in Nauvoo. The practice was difficult for many to accept. While some evidence suggests the Prophet may have known some of the principles as early as 1831, he recorded a revelation on July 12, 1843, explaining the practice in its fulness.[7] The Lord declared, "I reveal unto you a new and an everlasting covenant" (D&C 132:4).

Acceptance of the new doctrine was a test for even the most faithful Saints. Brigham Young later recalled his feelings upon learning of the teachings of plural marriage: "Some of [you] know what my feelings were at the time Joseph revealed the doctrine; I was not desireous of shrinking from any duty, nor of failing in the least to do as I was commanded, but it was the first time in my life that I had desired the grave. . . . When I saw a funeral, I felt to envy the corpse its situation, and to regret that I was not in the coffin."[8]

Nevertheless, the closest associates of the Prophet received all the temple ordinances faithfully. These ordinances, first introduced to this small group, were later introduced to the main body of the Saints in the completed temple.

While Joseph and his associates worked to set the doctrinal framework and develop the ordinances, construction of the temple continued at great sacrifice. Volunteers tithed their labor, giving one day in ten to cut and haul limestone blocks to the temple site. One day Byrum Bybee "hitched his team to his wagon and with his son had gone to the quarry to load a large stone into the wagon [when] their wagon became stuck in a mud hole." Joseph Smith waded "in mud halfway to his knees and [got] his shoulder covered with mud to help" get the wagon moving again.[9]

Luman Shurtliff wrote, "We labored ten hours a day and got something to take to our families for supper and breakfast. . . . I mention this not to find fault or to complain, but to let my children know how the temple of Nauvoo was built, and how their parents as well as hundreds of others suffered to lay a foundation on which they could build and be accepted of God."[10]

While men such as Bybee and Shurtliff blasted limestone and pushed and pulled the stone to the temple site, other men journeyed by riverboat to Wisconsin to cut timber for lumber needed for the temple. Women made

DID YOU KNOW?

• During the construction of the Nauvoo Temple, Joseph Smith began to reveal the higher ordinances of the temple to a small, select group of associates.

• After the Saints left Nauvoo, the temple was burned by an arsonist, and two walls were knocked down by a tornado.

clothing for the temple workers, gave pennies to purchase glass and nails, and bartered household goods to give of their means, for "every talent and exertion [was] peculiarly needed for the erection of the Temple."[11] Laborers from every state in the union and from nations across the sea came to help build the house of the Lord.

Wandle Mace recorded, "Men were as thick as blackbirds busily engaged upon the various portions" of the temple.[12] The architect with his sand shaker box and laborers with a chisel or wedge, gauging tools, turning pegs, wooden mallets, and block planes worked to build the House of God in Nauvoo. No one with a willing heart and a capacity for work was turned away, not even those who lacked tools. From the oval basin resting on twelve carved wooden oxen to the tower with the gold-leafed weather vane symbolic of "another angel flying in the midst of heaven," Joseph Smith and the Latter-day Saints built a temple to glorify God and, unintentionally, a memorial of their unwavering testimony (Revelation 14:6).

At six o'clock in the morning of May 24, 1845, Church leaders and laborers watched as under Brigham Young's supervision, the capstone on the temple was placed. On that occasion Brigham said, "The last stone is now laid upon the temple, and I pray the Almighty, in the name of Jesus, to defend us in this place, and sustain us until the temple is finished." Those assembled shouted, "Hosanna! Hosanna! Hosanna to God and the Lamb! Amen! Amen! Amen and Amen!"[13]

The spirit of God seemed to descend upon the people, gladness filled every heart, and tears of joy coursed down many cheeks. For Brigham Young, that day seemed "like a foretaste of celestial enjoyment and Millennial glory."[14]

But before that glory could be realized, the Latter-day Saints of Nauvoo would "suffer much affliction and would be driven to the Rocky Mountains."[15] Knowing the afflictions that awaited his people and that the time of their exodus was near, Brigham encouraged the Saints to prepare. By fall 1845 Nauvoo became "one vast mechanic shop, as nearly every family was engaged in making wagons."[16] Blacksmiths, carpenters and wheelwrights were on call day and night. From the shop to the parlor, every available space was used to assemble boxes, covers, wheels, and harnesses.

The stark dichotomy, an oddity of grand proportions, was not lost on observers. On the one hand was a scene of dogged determination to finish the temple, and on the other to build sturdy boxes with wheels to transport families to unknown and uncharted regions of the Rocky Mountains. One preparatory process, surely the most vital, was for the Latter-day Saints to receive their promised blessings in the temple—covenants between God and his people that would unite them to their families for all eternity. From December 1845 to February 1846, more than 5,600 Church members received their blessings in the Nauvoo Temple.

With the Saints' departure and the subsequent mob fury, Nauvoo's glory was gone. The once beautiful city of Nauvoo declined into crumbling ruin. On October 9, 1848, the temple was damaged by an arsonist. On May 27, 1850, a severe wind ripped through the temple and destroyed most of the north and west walls and so severely weakened the east and south walls that they had to be removed. In 1865 the Nauvoo city council ordered the removal of the remaining southwest corner as a safety measure. The once glorious temple was reduced to rubble.[17]

For generations the grandeur of Nauvoo lay shrouded in ruin. Nineteenth-century travelers scoffed at assertions that the town had once been a beautiful city that contained the jewel of the Mississippi Valley—the Nauvoo Temple. Scoffing has subsided since restoration efforts recreated the quaint, historic town of Nauvoo. A milestone in this restoration came in April 1999 when President Gordon B. Hinckley announced, "I feel impressed to announce that among all the temples we are constructing, we plan to rebuild the Nauvoo Temple."[18]

Translating past images into present-day reality proved difficult, yet the work of building a restored Nauvoo Temple went forward. The new builders created a masterpiece, from the foyer to the assembly room and from the mezzanine to the celestial room—a house of God. The reconstructed Nauvoo Illinois Temple was dedicated on June 27, 2002, by President Gordon B. Hinckley.

NOTES

1. Arrington, "William Weeks, Architect of the Nauvoo Temple," *BYU Studies* 19, no. 3 (Spring 1979): 341.
2. Arrington, "William Weeks," 340.
3. Arrington, "William Weeks," 346.
4. History, 1838–1856, vol. C-1 [2 November 1838–31 July 1842], 1328, josephsmithpapers.org.
5. History, 1838–1856, vol. C-1 [2 November 1838–31 July 1842], 1328, josephsmithpapers.org.
6. Johnson, *My Life's Review*, 85–86.
7. Some evidence suggests that Joseph Smith may have married a young woman named Fanny Alger as his first plural wife while living in Kirtland, Ohio. Little is known about this marriage, Emma Smith's involvement, or the terms on which it ended. After leaving Kirtland, Joseph Smith appears to have set aside the question of plural marriage until relocating to Nauvoo. See Hales, *Joseph Smith's Polygamy*, 1:93–99; lds.org/topics.
8. Young, in *Journal of Discourses*, 3:266
9. T. Edgar Lyon, "Recollections of 'Old Nauvooers' Memories from Oral History," *BYU Studies* 18, no. 2 (Winter 1978): 148.
10. Luman Shurtliff Autobiography, Church History Library, The Church of Jesus Christ of Latter-day Saints, Salt Lake City, Utah.
11. Maureen Ursenbach, "Eliza R. Snow's Journal," *BYU Studies,* Summer 1975, 405–6.
12. Wandle Mace Autobiography, L. Tom Perry Special Collections, Harold B. Lee Library, Brigham Young University, Provo, Utah.
13. *Millennial Star,* June 6, 1892, 365.
14. Brigham Young, in Arrington and Bitton, *Mormon Experience,* 65.
15. History, 1838–1856, vol. D-1 [1 August 1842–1 July 1843], 1362, josephsmithpapers.org.
16. Tullidge, *Women of Mormondom*, 321.
17. Allen and Leonard, *Story of the Latter-day Saints,* 231.
18. Gordon B. Hinckley, "Thanks to the Lord for His Blessings," *Ensign,* May 1999, 89.

33
The Female Relief Society of Nauvoo

1842

A statue in Salt Lake City commemorating Emma and Joseph Smith.

Between 1800 and 1840 female benevolent societies evolved into large organizations across the United States. Women united in bonds of sisterhood through missionary work, distribution of Bibles, and charitable acts of service. On the surface, the Female Relief Society of Nauvoo resembled the benevolent societies—it raised funds, relieved the poor, petitioned, and prayed. Yet, as poetess Eliza R. Snow admonished the Nauvoo sisterhood, "The popular Institutions of the day should not be our guide—. . . as daughters of Zion, we

should set an example for all the world, rather than confine ourselves to the course which had been heretofore pursued."[1]

Reynolds Cahoon, one of Joseph's close associates, observed, "There are many Benevolent Societies abroad designed to do good but not as this," meaning the Relief Society. He added, "Ours is according to the order of God, connected with the priesthood according to the same good principles. . . . The Relief Society was organized according to the mind of God."[2]

From the beginning, the central purpose of Relief Society was to assist Latter-day Saint women with temporal and spiritual aid, or, in the Prophet Joseph Smith's words: "The best measure or principle to bring the poor to repentance is to administer to their wants—the Society is not only to relieve the poor, but to save souls."[3]

The Relief Society was an integral part of the Church, for, Joseph said, "The organization of the Church of Christ was never perfect until the women were organized."[4]

On March 4, 1842, at Sarah Granger Kimball's home in Nauvoo a group of Latter-day Saint women met to discuss how they could best contribute to building the temple. Their initial plan was to make clothing to replace the tattered clothes worn by the brethren working in the temple quarries. Eventually, their discussion moved to forming a "Ladies' Society" or benevolent society like those in large cities in the United States. Sarah Kimball was assigned to ask Eliza R. Snow to draft a constitution and bylaws for the anticipated society. After reading the document Eliza had prepared and calling it "the best he had ever seen," Joseph said to Eliza, "Tell the sisters their offering is accepted of the Lord, and he has something better for them than a written constitution. . . . next Thursday afternoon, . . . I will organize the women under the priesthood after the pattern of the priesthood."[5]

On March 17, 1842, twenty women met in Joseph Smith's Red Brick Store on Water Street in Nauvoo for what was to be the first official meeting of the Female Relief Society of Nauvoo, or what Joseph would later call "a select Society separate from all the evils of the world, choice, virtuous, and holy."[6] At that founding meeting, Emma Smith was elected president of the society. She selected Elizabeth Ann Whitney and Sarah Cleveland as her counselors. Other officers were soon selected.

The officers of the new society were sustained without a challenge, but deciding on the name of the society was another story. The Prophet Joseph Smith and Elder John Taylor thought the society should include the word *benevolent*. "Pres. Emma Smith, said the *popularity* of the word benevolent is one great objection—no person can think of the word as associated with public institutions, without thinking of the Washingtonian Benevolent Society, which was one of the most corrupt Institutions of the day. [I] do not wish to have it called after other Societies in the world."[7]

When Eliza R. Snow pointed out that *relief*

suggested "some great calamity—that we intend appropriating on some extraordinary occasions instead of meeting the common occurrences," Emma replied, "We are going to do something *extraordinary!* When a boat is stuck in the rapids with a multitude of Mormons on board, we shall consider *that* a loud call for *relief.* We expect extraordinary occasions and pressing calls." With that, Joseph conceded, and it was decided that the name of the organization would be the Female Relief Society of Nauvoo.[8]

In that founding meeting, the Prophet clearly outlined the purposes of the society: to "provoke the brethren to good works in looking to the wants of the poor—searching after objects of charity, and in administering to their wants—to assist; by correcting the morals and strengthening the virtues of the female community, and save the Elders the trouble of rebuking; that they may give their time to other duties &c. in their public teaching." Emma Smith then spoke about "the object of the Society—its duties to others, also its relative duties to each other, viz., to seek out and relieve the distressed—that each member should be ambitious to do good—that the members should deal frankly with each other—to watch over the morals—and be very careful of the character and reputation—of members of the Institution &c."[9]

The Female Relief Society of Nauvoo grew quickly. Within two months, there were more than 600 members, and within two years, 1,300. Elizabeth Ann Whitney explained the reason for the rapid growth: "We rejoiced that we could enjoy the privilege of associating together to converse on things of the kingdom to comfort and edify each other."[10]

The society also provided the women of Nauvoo with an opportunity for spiritual communion. After the April 19, 1842, meeting, Eliza R. Snow recorded, "Nearly all present

DID YOU KNOW?

• The Prophet Joseph Smith declared, "The organization of the Church of Christ was never perfect until the women were organized."

• Emma Smith was one of the leaders responsible for choosing the name Relief Society.

arose and spoke, and the spirit of the Lord like a purifying stream, refreshed every heart." Lucy Mack Smith said at another meeting, "We must cherish one another, watch over one another, comfort one another and gain instruction that we may all sit down in heaven together."[11]

In addition to offering spiritual aid, the Female Relief Society of Nauvoo became known for its charitable acts. Society members prepared meals, cared for the sick, provided assistance to homeless converts, and comforted grieving mothers. The minutes from one meeting of the Relief Society details efforts of the sisters to visit the sick, assist an orphan, gather bedding for the Saints, make quilts, make clothing, and assist those in "extreme want."[12] These are just a sampling of the contributions of women of the sisterhood of Relief Society.

Beginning with seemingly small efforts of a few women in the spring of 1842 in Nauvoo, a great women's organization has emerged that continues to focus on small and simple acts of service. Through this service, the Relief Society has assisted millions of people across the world. Commenting on the extraordinary work of the early women of the Relief Society, Julie B. Beck, the General Relief Society President at the time, said, "As we learn how [God] helped them, we will gain a testimony that He will also help us today. We will learn that if, through the Holy Ghost, God could guide a woman more than a hundred years ago, He can do the same for women in our day."[13]

NOTES

1. Minutes of the Female Relief Society of Nauvoo, Mar. 17, 1842, in Derr et al., *First Fifty Years of Relief Society,* 35.
2. Minutes of the Female Relief Society of Nauvoo, Aug. 13, 1843, in Derr et al., *First Fifty Years,* 115–16.
3. Minutes of the Female Relief Society of Nauvoo, June 9, 1842, in Derr et al., *First Fifty Years,* 79.
4. Sarah M. Kimball, "Early Relief Society Reminiscence," Mar. 17, 1882, Relief Society Record, 1880–1892, in Derr et al., *First Fifty Years,* 6.
5. Sarah M. Kimball, "Auto-biography," *Woman's Exponent,* Sept. 1, 1883, 51, in *Daughters in My Kingdom,* 12.
6. Minutes of the Female Relief Society of Nauvoo, Mar. 31, 1842, in Derr et al., *First Fifty Years,* 43.
7. Minutes of the Female Relief Society of Nauvoo, Mar. 17, 1842, in Derr et al., *First Fifty Years,* 34–35.
8. Minutes of the Female Relief Society of Nauvoo, Mar. 17, 1842, in Derr et al., *First Fifty Years,* 35.
9. Minutes of the Female Relief Society of Nauvoo, Mar. 17, 1842, in Derr et al., *First Fifty Years,* 31, 36.
10. Minutes of the Female Relief Society of Nauvoo, July 15, 1843, in Derr et al., *First Fifty Years,* 106.
11. Minutes of the Female Relief Society of Nauvoo, Mar. 24, 1842, in Derr et al., *First Fifty Years,* 52, 40.
12. Minutes of the Female Relief Society of Nauvoo, Sept. 2, 1843, in Derr et al., *First Fifty Years,* 118–21.
13. Beck, "Relief Society History: A Look at the Lord's Vision for His Daughters," *Ensign,* Sept. 2011, 40.

34
The Church Expands into the Pacific

1843

Missionary work in the islands of the Pacific began in the days of the Prophet Joseph Smith.

In the spring of 1843, Joseph Smith called Addison Pratt, Benjamin F. Grouard, Noah Rogers, and Knowlton F. Hanks to take the restored gospel to the peoples of Oceania.[1] They traveled aboard the whaling ship *Timoleon* bound for the Society Islands (French Polynesia). Their voyage, which began on October 9, 1843, took them around the Cape of Good Hope. Elder Hanks died of consumption during the voyage and was buried at sea. On April 30, 1844, the remaining three missionaries landed on the island of Tubuai, 350 miles south of Tahiti. Their arrival marked the

beginning of Latter-day Saint missionary work in the Pacific Islands.

Missionary work in the Pacific was expanded in the fall of 1850. Brigham Young sent Elder Charles C. Rich, of the Quorum of the Twelve Apostles, to mining camps in California to find young Latter-day Saint men and set them apart as missionaries to the Sandwich Islands (Hawaii). When Elder Rich arrived at the mining camps near Sacramento, he announced himself as "Brigham Young's personal representative to all the Latter-day Saints in the Pacific Coast area."[2]

By October 1850 ten missionaries had been called by Elder Rich—including George Q. Cannon, a future member of the First Presidency. Elder Rich appointed Hiram Clark president of the group. In early November the missionaries journeyed from the Sacramento gold fields to the San Francisco Harbor, where they took passage to the islands aboard the *Imaum of Muscat*.

Aboard ship, missionary George Q. Cannon had a dream about their future labors in the Islands: "I dreamed one night that this party of brethren were heaving at the windlass, having a rope attached to it reaching forward to the anchor at the bow of the vessel. We were working with all our might endeavoring to raise the anchor, but seemingly we made but little progress. While thus engaged I thought the Prophet Joseph came from the after part of the vessel dressed in his temple clothes, and tapping me on the shoulder told me to go with him. I went, and he climbed on to the forecastle . . . and there he knelt down, also telling me to kneel down with him. He prayed according to the order of prayer which is revealed.

"After prayer, he arose upon his feet. 'Now,' said he, 'George, take hold of that rope'—the rope we had been pulling on with all our might. I took hold of it, and with the greatest ease and without the least effort, the anchor was raised. 'Now,' said he, 'let this be a lesson to you; remember that great things can be accomplished through the power of prayer and the exercise of faith in the right way.'"3

After nearly a month at sea, the missionaries landed at Honolulu on December 12, 1850. Historian R. Lanier Britsch observed, "The missionaries assumed that they had been sent to the islands to preach the gospel only to white people; but surveying the situation later in the day they realized that very few whites were available for proselyting. Since there was obviously not enough work to be done among the *haoles* (whites) in and around Honolulu, the missionaries decided to divide into pairs and go to other islands to preach."4

Many Latter-day Saint missionaries served in Hawaii after the introduction of the gospel in 1850. Most notable among the early missionaries was future Church President Joseph F. Smith, who at age fifteen began a three-year mission (1854–1857) in the Sandwich Islands.5

Some of the first conversions took place on the island of Maui, and the first Latter-day Saint branch was organized in the Kula District near Pulehu on August 6, 1851. Membership in Maui and the other islands grew quickly. By 1854 there were more than four thousand Hawaiian converts. These early believers worshiped in fifty-three branches. There were also several small schoolhouses and meetinghouses built by the Saints. The Book of Mormon was translated into the Hawaiian language

by Elder Cannon and early convert Jonatana (Jonathan) H. Napela, and it was published in 1855. The first generation of Hawaiian Saints saw the founding of a remarkable community that would influence the Church in the region into the twenty-first century.6

In 1864, the village of Laie, on the north shore of Oahu, was a small community seemingly without much promise. Yet several remarkable visions and experiences given to Church leaders pointed towards Laie becoming a special place of gathering for the Saints.7 The first such vision took place in 1864, when Elder William R. Cluff prayed in a small grove of trees in Laie. "Suddenly and to my astonishment, President Brigham Young came walking up the path and met me face to face. . . . [he] said: 'Brother William, this is the place we want to secure as headquarters for this mission.'"8

Elder Cluff's missionary companion Francis Hammond also had a dream-visitation in which Brigham Young and Heber C. Kimball appeared to him and told him that Laie was "the chosen spot."9

After Elder Cluff told Brigham Young of his vision, President Young called Francis A. Hammond and George Nebeker as co-presidents of the Hawaiian Mission and asked them to gather the Saints and live the principles of the gospel. Elders Hammond and Nebeker arrived in Honolulu on December 23, 1864, and immediately began to search for a place for the Hawaiian Saints to gather to. They learned that Thomas T. Dougherty, United States vice consul, owned a six-thousand-acre plantation called Laie in northeast Oahu.

On January 26, 1865, Elder Hammond purchased the plantation from Dougherty. Church leaders opened a sugar mill on the plantation. Missionaries under the direction of Jonathan H. Napela organized the Hawaiian

Saints into teams to work on the plantation and at its mule-powered mill.[10]

The next prophecy about Laie came twenty years later, at a time when the Hawaiian Saints were discouraged with work on the plantation due to drought, debt, and declining sugar prices. Many expressed a desire to leave Laie and voiced their complaints to Joseph F. Smith, who was serving his third mission in the islands (1885 to 1887).[11] After listening to their concerns, Joseph F. Smith instructed the Saints to "not leave this land, for this place has been chosen by the Lord as a gathering place for the Saints of The Church of Jesus Christ of Latter-day Saints in Hawaii."[12]

On December 22, 1900, President George Q. Cannon spoke of Hawaiians needing the blessings of the temple. After that, temple work was discussed frequently in mission conferences, and in April 1915, mission president Samuel Woolley prophesied of a future temple in Laie: "I tell you that there are people here today who if they continue in the work of the Lord, shall enter into the temple or other temples; and the time will come, in my judgment, that a temple will be built here."[13]

President Woolley's words were prophetic, for two months later President Joseph F. Smith selected a site for a temple at Laie and dedicated the site to the Lord. The Hawaiian Temple, described by newspaper editors as the "Taj Mahal of Hawaii," was dedicated on November 27, 1919—Thanksgiving Day.

President Heber J. Grant offered the dedicatory prayer, asking the Lord to provide a way for Hawaiians and other Pacific Islanders to attend "this holy house and become saviors unto their ancestors."[14]

The next prophecy occurred on February 7, 1921, when Elder David O. McKay attended a flag-raising ceremony held at an elementary school in Laie. He was impressed with the children of various nationalities pledging allegiance to the United States of America. Elder McKay envisioned the same scene on a larger scale, in which the community of Laie would become the intellectual center of the Pacific.

This vision stayed with him for the next thirty-four years. In 1951, one of his first acts as President of the Church was to establish a college in Laie. In 1955, President McKay dedicated the Church College of Hawaii and blessed the community to become "a missionary factor, influencing not thousands, not tens of thousands, but millions of people who will come."[15] The Church College of Hawaii, now Brigham Young University–Hawaii, continues to fulfill President McKay's prophecy. It is known as "the most culturally diverse campus in the United States."[16]

To provide the students at the school with employment opportunities, in 1959 Church leaders established the Polynesian Cultural Center (PCC). The center covers forty-two acres, with huts and a lagoon representing six different types of villages: Hawaiian, Samoan, Tongan, Fijian, Maori, and Tahitian. Since opening, the PCC has become Hawaii's most successful paid-admission attraction. In September 2013 the PCC celebrated its fiftieth anniversary and welcomed its 37-millionth visitor.[17] Home to both the PCC and BYU–Hawaii, Laie has become showcase for the unique fusion of Latter-day Saint culture and the diverse cultures of the peoples of the Pacific.

President Gordon B. Hinckley once remarked, "I never come to Laie that I don't have a feeling that this place occupies some peculiar position in the plan of the Lord."[18]

With Laie an important hub of activity, The Church of Jesus Christ of Latter-day Saints has grown and flourished in the Pacific. Hawaii served as the introduction for missions in Samoa, Tonga, French Polynesia, New Zealand, Australia, and a host of other places. The Saints in the region enjoy a heritage that stretches as far back as the days of the Prophet Joseph Smith. By the beginning of the twenty-first century, the Pacific had become a great center of growth for the Church. The nations of Samoa, American Samoa, and Tonga have had the largest proportion of Church members in countries anywhere in the world.[19]

Notes

1. Britsch, *Unto the Islands of the Sea*, 3.
2. Britsch, *Moramona*, 3.
3. Cannon, in *Journal of Discourses*, 22:289; or "Discourse," *Logan Leader*, Dec. 16, 1881, udn.lib.utah.edu.
4. Britsch, *Moramona*, 5.
5. Smith, *Life of Joseph F. Smith*, 164.
6. Britsch, *Moramona*, 18–19, 24–25.
7. William Cluff, Journal, cited in Beebe, *Cluff Missionaries in the Sandwich Islands*, 61–62.
8. "William W. Cluff's Second Mission," cited in Beebe, *Cluff Missionaries*, 56.
9. "William W. Cluff's Second Mission," cited in Beebe, *Cluff Missionaries*, 57.
10. Brigham Young to King Kamehameha V, March 24, 1865, Outgoing Correspondence of Brigham Young, in Moffat et al., *Gathering to Laʻie*, 196.
11. Smith, *Life of Joseph F. Smith*, 164.
12. Russell T. Clement, "Apostle in Exile: Joseph F. Smith's Third Mission to Hawaii, 1885–1887," *Mormon Pacific Historical Society* 7, no. 1 (1986): 53.
13. General Minutes, Hawaiian mission conference, April 3, 1915, in Britsch, *Unto the Islands of the Sea*, 153.
14. Heber J. Grant, "Dedicatory Prayer of the Hawaiian Temple," *Honolulu Star-Bulletin*, Dec. 6, 1919, in Richard J. Dowse, "The Laie Hawaii Temple: A History from Its Conception to Completion," master's thesis, Brigham Young University (2012), 153.
15. Alton L. Wade, "Laie—A Destiny Prophesied," *Ensign*, July 1994, 70.
16. Moffat et al., *Gathering to Laʻie*, 185.
17. polynesia.com.
18. Moffat et al., *Gathering to Laʻie*, 1.
19. Plewe, *Mapping Mormonism*, 239.

35
Joseph Smith's Campaign for President of the United States

Joseph Smith, candidate for president of the United States.

1844

In 1843, newspaper editors across the nation were asking, "Who shall be the next President?" To editor John Taylor, the answer was the "man who will be the most likely to render us [the Latter-day Saints] assistance in obtaining redress for our grievances" against the state of Missouri.[1]

Joseph Smith agreed with Taylor's assessment and acting "in behalf of the Church of Jesus Christ of Latter-day Saints," sent letters to five leading presidential candidates—Martin Van Buren, Lewis Case, Henry Clay, John C. Calhoun, and Richard Johnson—asking, *"What will be your rule of action relative to us as a people,* should fortune favor your ascension to the chief magistracy?"

Henry Clay, leading candidate of the Whig Party, wrote in response, "Should I be a candidate, I can enter into no engagements, make no promises, give no pledges, to any particular portion of the people of the United States."[2]

On January 29, 1844, Joseph Smith invited leading men in Nauvoo to counsel with him on the proper course to pursue in relation to the coming presidential election. At that informal caucus, the motion by Willard Richards was unanimously accepted "that Joseph Smith be a candidate for the next Presidency; and that we use all honorable means in our power to secure his election."[3]

Joseph accepted the nomination. According to Wilford Woodruff, the Prophet explained that the only reason he was "permitting his name to go forth as a Candidate for the Presidency of the United States" was that the Latter-day Saints had been deprived of their constitutional rights.[4]

Soon afterward, on February 7, 1844, *General Smith's Views of the Powers and Policy of the Government of the United States* was published. Joseph Smith definitely sounded presidential. Although William W. Phelps is credited with writing *Views,* Joseph guided the wording of the document.

Views included a list of solutions for the nation's ills, such as "pay every man a reasonable price for his slaves out of the surplus revenue arising from the sale of public lands, and from the deduction of pay from the members of Congress" and "[grant] the president full power to send an army to suppress mobs."[5]

Views concluded: "We have had Democratic Presidents, Whig Presidents, a pseudo-Democratic-Whig President, and now it is time to have a *President of the United States.*"[6]

Copies of *Views* were mailed to United States president John Tyler, his cabinet, justices of the Supreme Court, members of Congress, and other prominent men in the nation. Other copies of *Views* were carried by electioneering volunteers called from Nauvoo to push forward Joseph's campaign. At first 244 men volunteered, and within weeks, their numbers swelled to 337.

As they campaigned from New York to Washington and from Michigan to Alabama, John Taylor actively reported their activities. He notified Latter-day Saints living outside Illinois where elders would be speaking on national politics. He printed in the *Times and Seasons* a schedule of forty-seven political conferences to be held in fifteen states, beginning with Illinois on May 4, 1844, and ending with Washington, D.C., on September 15, 1844.

He even reported a mock vote on a steamboat: "We learn from the polls of the steamboat *Osprey,* on her last trip to [Nauvoo], that the vote stood for General Joseph Smith, 20 gents and 5 ladies; Henry Clay, 16 gents and 4 ladies; Van Buren, 7 gents and 0 ladies."[7]

On June 26, 1844, the day before the martyrdom of Joseph Smith, John Taylor called for greater support of Joseph's bid for the United States presidency: "Let us now have a righteous man at the head of the government. Citizens of the United States awake! . . . let all citizens of this vast republic answer, *at the polls* next fall, GEN. JOSEPH SMITH."[8]

But there would be no vote for Joseph Smith. Shots were fired on June 27, 1844, and Joseph Smith, a candidate for president of the United States, lay dead. Electioneering volunteers were called back from the twenty-six states and the Territory of Wisconsin. Copies of *Views* remained in circulation, but the demand was gone. In the fall of 1844, most Latter-day Saints voted for James K. Polk of Tennessee as president and Silas Wright of New York as vice-president. The Latter-day Saint vote helped give Polk and Wright a 54 percent to 42 percent victory over Whig candidate Henry Clay in Illinois.

DID YOU KNOW?

• Joseph Smith ran for president of the United States as an independent candidate, unaffiliated with any of the principal political parties of the time.

• One of Joseph Smith's campaign proposals was a plan for the peaceful elimination of slavery in the United States.

Notes

1. *Times and Seasons,* Oct. 1, 1843, 343–44.
2. "Correspondence between Gen. Joseph Smith and the Hon. Henry Clay," *Times and Seasons,* June 1, 1844, 544.
3. Joseph Smith Journal, 29 Jan. 1844, in Hedges et al., *Journals,* 3:169, or josephsmithpapers.org; see Arnold K. Garr, "Joseph Smith: Candidate for President of the United States," in Garrett, *Illinois,* 151–68.
4. Woodruff, in Hedges et al., *Journals,* 3:176n175; Garr, "Joseph Smith," 149–68.
5. "General Smith's Views of the Powers and Policy of the Government of the United States," 3–8, contentdm.lib.byu.edu.
6. "For President, Gen. Joseph Smith, Nauvoo, Illinois," *Nauvoo Neighbor,* May 8, 1844, 2.
7. *Nauvoo Neighbor,* May 3, 1844.
8. Libertas, "The Mormons," *Nauvoo Neighbor,* June 26, 1844, 3.

36
The Martyrdom of Joseph and Hyrum Smith

The jail in Carthage, Illinois, site of the martyrdom of Joseph and Hyrum Smith.

1844

The tentative peace of Nauvoo ended in the winter of 1843–44, some six months before Joseph Smith was killed. Ridicule, arrest warrants, and evil speaking accelerated as apostates searched for ways to thwart the plans of God and malign the character of the Prophet. Sacred doctrines declared by Joseph were distorted to disprove his claims to divine revelation and heighten angry public sentiment. Unfounded rumors of a secret plan for a military invasion of Nauvoo to capture the Mormon prophet were declared as truths.

To Mormons and anti-Mormons alike, open conflict between residents of the city of Nauvoo and neighbors in outlying communities seemed the only resolution. Leaders of neighboring communities, jealous of the emerging city, its temple, and its growing prosperity, threatened violence against all Latter-day Saints in Nauvoo if they did not abandon their holdings and leave the state.

Editor Thomas Sharp of the *Warsaw Signal* predicted, "War and extermination is inevitable! CITIZENS ARISE, ONE AND ALL!!! Can you stand by, and suffer such INFERNAL DEVILS! to rob men of their property and RIGHTS, without avenging them. We have no time for comment; every man will make his own. LET IT BE MADE WITH POWDER AND BALL!!!"[1]

Of Joseph Smith, Sharp penned, "Joe Smith is not safe out of Nauvoo. We would not be surprised to hear of his death by violent means in a short time."[2] Mormon dissidents shared Sharp's sentiments and pledged to murder Joseph Smith.

Although Joseph believed these men "would not scare off an old setting hen," their evil plans ignited public sentiment to fever pitch when they printed the *Nauvoo Expositor*.[3] Joseph, acting as mayor of Nauvoo, met with the Nauvoo city council to discuss the libelous accusations printed in the *Expositor*. The official decision resulting from the discussions was to denounce the anti-Mormon newspaper as a public nuisance and to authorize the Nauvoo sheriff to stop future publication of it.

The swift actions of the sheriff and his posse led publishers of the *Expositor*—Charles A. Foster, Robert D. Foster, Chauncy L. Higbee, Francis M. Higbee, Charles Ivins, William Law, and Wilson Law—to charge the mayor and the Nauvoo city council with starting a riot that resulted in the destruction of their newspaper. Joseph was arrested and discharged twice for charges related to the destruction of the newspaper.[4]

The legal process, however, did not pacify his enemies, who clamored for blood. Despite their boisterous threats, Joseph Smith confidently said, "God Almighty is my shield; and what can man do if God is my friend? I shall not be sacrificed until my time comes; then shall I be offered freely."[5]

According to John Taylor, Joseph decided to depart from Nauvoo to alleviate tensions. Elder Taylor later wrote, "It was Brother Joseph's opinion that, should we leave for a time, public excitement, which was so intense, would be allayed."[6]

Joseph crossed the river to Iowa but remained for only a few hours before word came from some of the frightened citizens of Nauvoo. Vilate Kimball later wrote to her husband, Heber, that "some were tried almost to death to think Joseph should leave them in the hour of danger." With his brother Hyrum and wife Emma both urging him to return, Joseph and his party returned to Nauvoo.[7]

On Monday morning, June 24, 1844, Joseph and Hyrum journeyed to Carthage. In Carthage accusations of riot, stemming from the *Nauvoo Expositor* incident, were turned to charges of treason. Rumors once whispered in secret now were shouted. John Taylor recalled that when the party arrived in Carthage, "a great deal of excitement prevailed on and after our arrival. . . . The governor had received into his company all of the companies that had been in the mob; these fellows were riotous and disorderly, hallooing, yelling, and whooping about the streets like Indians, many of them intoxicated; the whole presented a scene of rowdyism and low-bred ruffianism only found among mobocrats and desperadoes, and entirely revolting to the best feelings of humanity."[8]

While in the jail at Carthage, Joseph sent a letter to Emma, striking a hopeful note that "when the truth comes out we have nothing to fear" and telling her, "I hope the people of Nauvoo will continue placid, pacific, and prayerful."[9]

On June 27, 1844, Joseph dictated another letter to Emma and then wrote this postscript: "Dear Emma, I am very much resigned to my lot knowing I am justified and have done the best that could be done. Give my love to the children and all my friends."[10] Joseph and Hyrum and two members of the Quorum of the Twelve Apostles, John Taylor and Willard Richards, remained in the east bedroom of the jail.

Around five o'clock in the afternoon, Richards saw a hundred or more men running around the corner of the jail. Taylor described them as "an armed mob—painted black—of from 150 to 200 persons" (D&C 135:1). The mob easily overpowered the guards, rushed the stairs, and began shooting into the east bedroom. Despite attempts to protect themselves from lawless

DID YOU KNOW?

• Joseph Smith was arrested and discharged twice on the charge of destroying the *Expositor*, a newspaper published by apostates in Nauvoo.

• Joseph Smith prophesied to Willard Richards that "the time would come that the balls would fly around him like hail, and he should see his friends fall on the right and on the left, but that there should not be a hole in his garment."

violence, the four men were no match for the disguised mobbers.

Hyrum Smith was the first to fall from an assassin's bullet. As he backed away from the door to the center of the room, one bullet pierced the upper panel of the door and struck him on the left side of the nose. Falling to the floor, he exclaimed, "*I am a dead man!*" (D&C 135:1). Bending over the body of his lifeless brother, Joseph sobbed, "Oh! My poor, dear, brother Hyrum!"[11] Hyrum was hit by three other bullets—one in his left side, another near his throat, and a third in his left leg.

According to eyewitness John Taylor, Joseph then calmly and deliberately picked up a six-chambered pepperbox pistol that had been smuggled into the jail and fired back into the mob from around the corner of the door. Only three of the chambers fired, but Joseph's action provided a brief respite from the men shooting from behind the door.[12]

From the murderous mob outside, however, a steady stream of fire continued to pour into the room. John Taylor was the second to be shot. A bullet fired from the doorway struck his thigh and another his watch. After crawling under a bed for protection, Elder Taylor was hit by three more bullets. Willard Richards was relatively unscathed, in fulfillment of Joseph's earlier prophecy that "the time would come that the balls would fly around him like hail, and he should see his friends fall on the right and on the left, but that there should not be a hole in his garment."[13]

As Joseph moved toward the bedroom window, two bullets hit him from the doorway, and two struck him from the outside. As he fell from the second-storey window to the ground below, he was heard to exclaim, "*O Lord, My God!*" (D&C 135:1). The mob had finished its murderous work. Joseph lay dead outside the jail. But the workers of destruction left more than the corpses of two men. They left "a broad seal affixed to 'Mormonism' that cannot be rejected by any court on earth . . . [and] truth of the everlasting gospel that all the world cannot impeach" (D&C 135:7). Their senseless brutality forged two martyrs' crowns.

The testators are dead, yet their testament lives on. Josiah Quincy, once the mayor of Boston, said, "It is by no means improbable that some future textbook . . . will contain a question something like this: What historical American of the nineteenth century has exerted the most powerful influence upon the destinies of his countrymen? And it is by no means impossible that the answer to the interrogatory may be thus written: Joseph Smith, the Mormon Prophet."[14]

NOTES

1. *Warsaw Signal,* June 12, 1844.
2. *Warsaw Signal,* May 29, 1844.
3. Ehat and Cook, *Words of Joseph Smith,* 337.
4. Taylor, *Witness to the Martyrdom,* 36–43.
5. Ehat and Cook, *Words of Joseph Smith,* 158.
6. Taylor, *Witness to the Martyrdom,* 54.
7. Bushman, *Rough Stone Rolling,* 546; Taylor, *Witness to the Martyrdom,* 57–58.
8. Taylor, *Witness to the Martyrdom,* 60.
9. Joseph Smith letter to Emma Smith, June 25, 1844, in History, 1838–1856, vol. F–1 [1 May 1844–8 August 1844], josephsmithpapers.org.
10. Joseph Smith to Emma Smith, June 27, 1844, in History, 1838–1856, vol. F–1 [1 May 1844–8 August 1844], 175, josephsmithpapers.org.
11. Taylor, *Witness to the Martyrdom,* 89.
12. Taylor, *Witness to the Martyrdom,* 89.
13. Vogel, *History of Joseph Smith,* 6:695.
14. Roberts, *Comprehensive History of the Church,* 2:349–50.

37
Brigham Young and the Mantle of Joseph

1844

Statue of Joseph Smith and Brigham Young at This Is the Place State Park, near Salt Lake City, Utah.

In the summer of 1844, The Church of Jesus Christ of Latter-day Saints was in crisis. The martyrdom of Joseph and Hyrum Smith in Carthage Jail had created an atmosphere of fear and uncertainty regarding the future of the Church and the fate of its members. Could the Church endure without the Prophet Joseph Smith? Who would take his place? Opportunists circled like wolves even as the Prophet and his brother were laid to rest. Rumors of the disintegration of the Church circulated throughout the country. One

Connecticut newspaper editor asked, "Is it possible that a sect so singular and fanatical can exist and maintain itself in this age of the world?" Almost gleefully he wrote, "It has been said, that now their prophet and leader was dead, the sect would be dispersed and come to an end." Then he warily added, "But this does not seem to be the case."[1]

When Brigham Young, then on a mission in New Hampshire, received word of the murder of Joseph and Hyrum Smith, "the first thing I thought of was whether Joseph had taken the keys of the kingdom with him from the earth."[2]

He contemplated that thought with "Brother Orson Pratt [who] sat on my left. We were both leaning back on our chairs. Bringing my hand down on my knee, I said, the keys of the kingdom are right here with the Church."[3] Secure in this knowledge, Brigham set off at once for Nauvoo.

When Brigham arrived in the city on August 6, he found the Latter-day Saints still reeling over the deaths of the martyrs and confused about the issue of succession in the Presidency of the Church. William Marks, president of the Nauvoo Stake, urged local priesthood quorums to appoint a trustee to manage Church financial affairs. Others pressed for the Council of Fifty to take over leadership. Sidney Rigdon, who had served as counselor in the First Presidency, proclaimed himself "a guardian through whom Joseph will speak to the people . . . as a god to this dispensation."[4]

Brigham declared, "I do not care who leads the Church. But one thing I must know, and that is what God says about it." He added, "I have the keys and means of obtaining the mind of God on the subject."[5]

On Thursday morning, August 8, 1844, Sidney Rigdon spoke to a large Latter-day Saint congregation and presented his claim to Church leadership. Standing in a wagon in front of the preaching, Rigdon spent nearly an hour and a half explaining his proposal.[6]

At the end of Rigdon's speech, Brigham Young announced a meeting to convene at 2 o'clock that afternoon. While the Saints gathered for that meeting, Brigham seated himself on the stand next to other members of the Quorum of the Twelve. Elder John Taylor, who was still recovering from the injuries he sustained in Carthage Jail, was not present. Wilford Woodruff later recorded that Brigham Young told the people "that the quorum of the Twelve have the keys of the kingdom of God in all the world. They stand next to Joseph and are the presidency of the Church and hold the keys."[7]

In recording this event, Brigham simply wrote, "I arose and spoke to the people. My heart was swollen with compassion towards them, and by the power of the Holy Ghost, even the spirit of the prophets, I was enabled to comfort the hearts of the Saints in the afternoon."[8]

Many present recorded a likewise simple but profound and life-altering experience. According to multiple accounts, as Brigham Young began speaking, many heard or saw Joseph Smith. Some even jumped to their feet to see for themselves if the Prophet Joseph had returned.

Historians have collected more than 120 accounts of Brigham Young's transfiguration. Accounts cut across lines of age, experience, and gender. The accounts do not agree as to the exact time the "Mantle of Joseph" took place. Some record it occurring as Brigham stood up after Sidney Rigdon concluded speaking in the morning meeting. Other accounts report it occurring in the afternoon meeting. Some have recorded the date incorrectly. One of the earliest accounts was written by Caroline Barnes Crosby:

"Sidney Rigdon came to the stand and tried to show to the people that he was the rightful successor of Joseph. And his arguments were so powerful that many were almost persuaded to believe him such. But as soon as the twelve apostles with bro Brigham Young at their head took the stand it was shown conclusively where the power rested. It was the first time that I ever thought he [Brigham] resembled bro Joseph. But almost every one exclaimed that the mantle of Joseph had fallen on Brigham. For one I never had any doubts afterward."[9]

George Romney recorded: "I testify to you in all fervor, before God, that the mantle of Joseph Smith fell upon Brigham Young. It was Joseph's voice and manner, as Brigham Young addressed the people and told them who should be their leader. Now this is no fiction; this is true as I stand here after so many years, passing from the year 1844 up to the present time."[10]

Aurelia Spencer Rogers recorded the testimony of her sister Ellen: "Brigham Young, who was President of the Quorum of Apostles, arose to speak, when 'The Mantle of Joseph' fell upon him, and he was like one transformed; his countenance, voice and form were like those of the late Prophet. Many in the congregation, even children saw this miracle; it satisfied the people and decided the question who was to be the leader."[11]

George Q. Cannon wrote, "If Joseph had risen from the dead and again spoken in their hearing, the effect could not have been more startling than it was to many present at that meeting; it was the voice of Joseph himself; and not only was it the voice of Joseph which was heard, but it seemed in the eyes of the people as if it were the very person of Joseph which stood before them."[12]

Another eyewitness reported, "The voice of the people was in favor of sustaining the [Quorum of the] Twelve."[13]

As for Sidney Rigdon, he continued to speak against the Twelve and was excommunicated from the Church. Other challengers presented themselves in the months that followed, including William Marks, James Strang, and Joseph Smith's younger brother William. But none of these opportunists held as strong a claim as Sidney Rigdon appeared to. He eventually founded his own church and gained a number of followers but was "seldom content after 1844." His biographer recorded, "Racked by poverty, poor health, and mental instability, he spent much of his dotage studying on his own cloud-encircled peak the ineffable secrets of God."[14]

Brigham Young, as president of the Quorum of the Twelve Apostles, became the leader of the Church, later reestablishing the First Presidency. But none of these subsequent events was set in stone on the August day in 1844 when Brigham Young stood before a crowd of Latter-day Saints and claimed leadership of the Church for the Twelve. Without a doubt, Brigham Young possessed a forceful and charismatic presence, and it is entirely possible that he could have persuaded the Saints on his own to follow the Twelve, but the spiritual manifestation of the mantle of Joseph cemented in the minds of Latter-day Saints that Brigham Young was the true successor of the Prophet Joseph Smith.

Notes

1. *Hartford [Connecticut] Daily Courant,* July 25, 1844, in Baker, *Murder of the Mormon Prophet,* 639.
2. Arrington, *American Moses,* 111.
3. Manuscript History of Brigham Young, 171, Church History Library, The Church of Jesus Christ of Latter-day Saints, Salt Lake City, Utah.
4. William Huntington Diary, Aug. 4, 1844, L. Tom Perry Special Collections, Harold B. Lee Library, Brigham Young University, Provo, Utah.
5. Brigham Young, in "History of the Church," *Millennial Star,* Apr. 4, 1863, 216.
6. Leonard, *Nauvoo,* 435.
7. Kenney, *Wilford Woodruff's Journal,* 2:436.
8. Brigham Young, Diary, Aug. 8, 1844, Church History Library; Dean C. Jessee, "The Writings of Brigham Young," *Western Historical Quarterly,* July 4, 1973, 284.
9. Caroline Barnes Crosby, "Memoirs Begun at Tubuai, Society Islands, 1851," in Lynne Watkins Jorgensen, "The Mantle of the Prophet Joseph Passes to Brother Brigham: One Hundred Twenty-One Testimonies of a Collective Spiritual Witness," in Welch and Carlson, *Opening the Heavens,* 158.
10. George Romney, typescript account of testimony, in Jorgensen, "Mantle of the Prophet," 132.
11. Rogers, *Life Sketches of Orson Spencer and Others,* 332.
12. George Q. Cannon, in Roberts, *Comprehensive History,* 2:418.
13. *Times and Seasons,* Sept. 2, 1844, 650.
14. Van Wagoner, *Sidney Rigdon,* 359.

38
The Camp of Israel at Winter Quarters

1846

The Visitors' Center at Winter Quarters, Nebraska.

After the long and arduous trek across Iowa, Latter-day Saints sought refuge along the banks of the Missouri river. Their primary settlement, dubbed simply Winter Quarters, became a temporary base of operations until permanent headquarters could be designated. More than four thousand Saints gathered at Winter Quarters during the winter of 1846–47.[1]

They arrived in the Nebraska wilderness without a firm idea of their next destination. In the squalid conditions of the camps along the Missouri, death and disease tested the limits of their faith and endurance. Yet for all its privations, this period in Church history witnessed the genesis of a new organization, new direction, and new leadership for the Saints.

From the outset, Brigham Young and the other leaders of the trek across Iowa knew the banks of the Missouri were not the ideal location to spend the winter. They had hoped to press on to Grand Island (Nebraska) that winter and send a party to the Rocky Mountains to identify the new refuge for the Saints. Brigham's hopes evaporated during the hardships and delays of the months-long journey across Iowa. Concerns for refugees still fleeing Nauvoo led Brigham to conclude it was time to regroup and reorganize before pushing farther west.

The location Brigham Young selected at present-day Florence, Nebraska, was not ideal. Fragile relations with the surrounding Indian nations, the swampy environment, and the approach of winter contributed to anxiety in the camps. Nevertheless, a settlement was carefully platted to include twenty-two wards organized with bishops appointed to look after the poor and the needy. Available manpower for the settlement had been diminished when Brigham Young encouraged the recruitment of five hundred men to form the Mormon Battalion.

In Winter Quarters, as well as in the string of temporary Latter-day Saint encampments along the Iowa trail, sickness prevailed. Louisa Barnes Pratt recalled, "The shaking ague fastened deathless fangs upon me [and] I shook till it appeared my very bones were pulverized. I wept, I prayed, I besought the Lord to have mercy on me."[2] Thomas L. Kane, a non-Mormon who observed the plight of the Saints, broke down and openly "sobbed like a child" when he saw the terrible conditions in the camps.[3] Wilford Woodruff recorded in his journal, "I have never seen the Latter Day Saints in any situation where they seemed to be passing through greater tribulations or wearing out faster than at the present time."[4] It is estimated that 723 deaths occurred in a population of 8,750 Saints, or a mortality rate of one in twelve.[5]

The extreme adversity led many to question the judgment and leadership of Brigham Young and the Quorum of the Twelve Apostles. Prominent Church leaders within the camps, most notably George Miller, opposed the route, the destination in the West, and the management of the camps. James J. Strang, an apostate claiming to be the rightful successor to Joseph Smith, offered an alternative to disaffected Saints. His followers pointed to the suffering at Winter Quarters as evidence of Brigham Young's folly.

To the faithful, there was no folly. On January 14, 1847, Brigham Young received a revelation, or what was titled "The Word and Will of the Lord concerning the camp of Israel" (D&C 136). The revelation provided answers to some of the difficult questions raised at Winter Quarters, including the martyrdom of Joseph Smith: "It was needful that he should seal his testimony with his blood, that he might be honored and the wicked might be condemned" (D&C 136:39). The revelation specified that the westward trek was to take place "under the direction of mine apostles," which left no doubt about who was the Lord's anointed (D&C 136:3). The revelation declared, "My people must be tried in all things," and they must "covenant and promise to keep all the commandments of the Lord" (D&C 136:2). The revelation directed the Saints to "praise the Lord with singing, with music, with dancing, and with a prayer of praise and thanksgiving" (D&C 136:28).

Hosea Stout recorded in his journal that the revelation was "to me a source of much joy and gratification" and added, "This will put to silence the wild bickering and suggestions of those who are ever in the way and opposing the proper council. They will now have to come to this standard or come out in open rebellion to the will of the Lord."[6]

George Miller and other opponents of Brigham Young disparaged the revelation. Most of the Saints, however, heeded its counsel and looked forward to spring when they could organize themselves into companies for the westward trek.

Besides the revelation to Brigham Young, which later was canonized, other spiritual experiences sustained the Saints huddled at Winter Quarters. Brigham told of several dreams or visions in which he conversed with the Prophet Joseph Smith. According to Brigham, in one dream Joseph told him to "be sure and tell the brethren that it is all important for them to keep the spirit of the Lord, to keep the quiet spirit of Jesus." Joseph "explained how the spirit of the Lord reflected on the spirit of man and set him to pondering on any subject, and he also explained how to know the spirit of the Lord from the spirit of the enemy."[7]

In addition to revelations and visions, temple ordinances were practiced among the Saints at Winter Quarters, including a peculiar iteration of eternal families called the law

DID YOU KNOW?

- More than one of every twelve Saints encamped at Winter Quarters died due to disease and harsh conditions.

- After receiving the "Word and Will of the Lord" in January 1847, Brigham Young announced that "he had no more doubts nor fears of going to the mountains."

of adoption. Brigham Young, for instance, adopted several individuals into his family and held meetings to provide family instruction. In one such meeting, he declared, "Those that are adopted into my family . . . I will preside over them throughout all eternity and will stand at their head."[8]

Other apostles, including John Taylor, Willard Richards, and Heber C. Kimball, adopted large numbers of men and women into their families. The desire to gather as families in Winter Quarters provides a valuable insight into the mindset of the Saints in the winter of 1846–47.

John R. Young referred to Winter Quarters as "the Valley Forge of Mormondom."[9] Like George Washington's army decades earlier, the Saints at the Missouri endured a crucible of testing and refinement in harsh conditions. They emerged from the grim winter more confident, united, and secure. After receiving the "Word and Will of the Lord" in January 1847, Brigham Young announced that "he had no more doubts nor fears of going to the mountains, and felt as much security as if he possessed the treasures of the east."[10]

Groups of Saints began leaving Winter Quarters early in April, with Brigham Young leaving on April 7, 1847, the day after general conference. Winter Quarters was soon abandoned when the Saints moved across the Missouri River to create the new hub for their migration—Kanesville (later Council Bluffs), Iowa. Winter Quarters had been a stopping place on their journey to the West. But the sacrifice, suffering, and sanctification of Winter Quarters lingered in their collective memory.

Notes

1. Bennett, *Mormons at the Missouri,* 68–69.
2. Bennett, *Mormons at the Missouri,* 132.
3. Grow, *Liberty to the Downtrodden,* 61.
4. Kenney, *Wilford Woodruff's Journal,* 3:95–96.
5. Bennett, *Mormons at the Missouri,* 141.
6. Hosea Stout, Diary, Jan. 14, 1847, in Brooks, *On the Mormon Frontier,* 1:227–29.
7. Hosea Stout, Diary, in Brooks, *On the Mormon Frontier,* 1:238.
8. Bennett, *Mormons at the Missouri,* 191–93.
9. John R. Young, in Rich, *Ensign to the Nations,* 92.
10. Brigham Young, in Bennett, *Mormons at the Missouri,* 159.

39
The March of the Mormon Battalion

Monument on the Mormon Battalion Trail near Albuquerque, New Mexico.

1846

New Mexico to the United States, and pay an additional $25 million for California. His attempts to negotiate land acquisitions were rebuffed by Mexican officials.

Angered by a breakdown in the negotiations, on January 13, 1846, President Polk ordered General Zachary Taylor to move troops across the Nueces River and take a defensive posture on the eastern bank of the Rio Grande. Polk then recommended to Congress that forts be built along the overland route to Oregon to provide protection for westering migrants.

Brigham Young sent Elder Jesse C. Little to Washington, D.C., with an offer to President Polk to build the proposed fortifications. President Young told Elder Little, "If our government shall offer any facilities for emigration to the western coast, embrace those facilities, if possible."[1]

Elder Little met with President Polk shortly after the United States' war with Mexico commenced. On June 3, 1846, President Polk wrote, "I told Mr. Little that we were at war with Mexico, and asked him if 500 or more of the Mormons now on the way to California would be willing on their arrival in that country to volunteer and enter the United States army in that war, under the command of a United States officer. He said he had no doubt they would willingly do so."[2]

The Army of the West, commanded by Stephen W. Kearny, had direct responsibility for the enlistment of the Mormon Battalion. Colonel Kearny ordered Captain James Allen of the First Dragoons to recruit four or five

United States president James K. Polk, an expansionist with a disposition to acquire New Mexico and California, took the oath of office in March 1845. With "Manifest Destiny" the theme of his presidential campaign, President Polk viewed his election as a mandate to acquire New Mexico and California for the United States. Polk was willing to assume $4.5 million in property damages due to American citizens for losses suffered in recent Mexican civil wars, pay $5 million if Mexico would cede companies from among the Mormons in Iowa. After receiving the instructions, Captain Allen and three soldiers made their first contact with the Latter-day Saints at their encampment at Mount Pisgah, Iowa.

On July 16, Captain Allen explained his orders from Colonel Stephen W. Kearny to a large assembly of Latter-day Saint men at Council Bluffs. His remarks were followed by those of Brigham Young, who said, "Let the Mormons be the first men to set their feet on the soil of California. . . . I proposed [to Captain Allen] that the five hundred volunteers be mustered, and I would do my best to see all their families brought forward, as far as my influence extended, and feed them when I had anything to eat myself."[3]

Due largely to the words of Brigham Young, on July 16, an estimated 543 men were mustered into the Mormon Battalion at Council Bluffs. They were accompanied by 33 women, 20 of whom served as laundresses, and 51 children.[4] After being formed into companies (A through E), the Mormon Battalion began its march.

On August 1, 1846, the newly enlisted soldiers arrived at Fort Leavenworth (Kansas) where they were issued military equipment. On August 13, Companies A, B, and E began the march from Fort Leavenworth to Santa Fe (New Mexico). Companies C and D followed on August 15.

On September 12, 1846, the battalion reached the Arkansas River, where they met William Crosby and seven other Latter-day Saints from Fort Pueblo (Colorado), a western post for mountaineers, traders, and trappers. The chance meeting of Crosby and his description of Pueblo presented an unexpected option to Lieutenant Colonel A. J. Smith, acting commander of the battalion. He was becoming alarmed at having to transport disabled soldiers, women, and children with the battalion. On September 16, Smith ordered Captain Nelson Higgins and a small contingent of soldiers to escort some of the women, children, and sick men to Fort Pueblo.

The main body of the battalion proceeded to march across what is now the state of Kansas, the southeast corner of Colorado, and the northwest tip of the Oklahoma panhandle. They reached Santa Fe on October 9, 1846. A gun salute ordered by Colonel Alexander W. Doniphan, commander of the garrison, welcomed Colonel Smith and his advance unit of 250 soldiers to Santa Fe. The rear unit marched into Santa Fe on October 12 with little fanfare.

Joining the soldiers at Santa Fe was Captain Philip St. George Cooke, appointed by General Kearny as acting lieutenant colonel of the Mormon Battalion. Colonel Cooke ordered Captain James Brown to form a detachment of women, children, and "men reported by the assistant Surgeon."[5] Brown's detachment, consisting of ninety-one men, eighteen women, and seven children, left Santa Fe on October 18, 1846, to join Higgins's detachment at Pueblo.

Under the command of Colonel Cooke, the main body of the battalion left Santa Fe. Upon reaching the Rio Grande River, Colonel Cooke sent a detachment of sixty-two ailing men, one woman, and one child under the command of Lieutenant William W. Willis back to Santa Fe, where they were reassigned to Fort Pueblo for the winter. Colonel Cooke's reduced battalion,

DID YOU KNOW?

• The Mormon Battalion carried out one of the longest infantry marches in American military history, roughly 1,900 miles.

• An estimated 543 men were mustered into the Mormon Battalion at Council Bluffs, Iowa. They were accompanied by 33 women, 20 of whom served as laundresses, and 51 children.

now numbering 343 men and four women, left the Rio Grande River and crossed the southeast corner of present-day Arizona before reaching the ruins of Rancho San Bernardino, in present-day California, on December 2, 1846.

Reentering what is now Arizona, they marched along the San Pedro River. But rather than follow the San Pedro River all the way to its junction with the Gila River, Colonel Cooke marched the battalion overland to Tucson. On December 18, the battalion left the garrison at Tucson to the Mexican inhabitants and continued their epic march. After trekking through the Imperial Deseret, the battalion veered northeast before, in mid-January, entering Box Canyon, in present-day San Diego County. After carving a wagon road through the canyon using only hand tools, the soldiers reached Warner's Ranch and, on January 27, the deserted San Luis Rey Mission. About a mile south of the mission, battalion soldiers had their first glimpse of the Pacific Ocean.

On February 4, 1847, Colonel Cooke said to the battalion soldiers, "History may be searched in vain for an equal march of infantry. Nine-tenths of it has been through a wilderness where nothing but savages and wild beasts are found; or deserts where, for want of water, there is no living creature."[6]

At an approximate distance of 1,900 miles, the march of the Mormon Battalion is one of the longest in American military history.[7]

On March 15, after six weeks at the San Luis Rey Mission, Company B was sent to San Diego, the only naval port south of San Francisco. They served out their military term at the peacetime garrison in San Diego. The other four companies headed to Ciudad Los Angeles to serve out their military term at the peacetime garrison of Los Angeles.

On Friday, July 16, 1846, 317 soldiers assembled in companies at Fort Moore in Los Angeles. Lieutenant Andrew J. Smith of the First Dragoons marched down one line and back up another. When he finished, he returned to the front and said, "You are discharged."[8]

One military historian, Sherman L. Fleek, noted, "The Mormon Battalion was the only religious unit in American military history in federal service, having been recruited solely from one religious body and having a religious title as the unit designation." In addition, the morale and integrity of the Mormon Battalion make it unique in the history of the Mexican War. During that war, the desertion rate among American troops was 8 percent, nearly double that of any other war fought by the United States. The Mormon Battalion experienced only one desertion during its one year service.[9]

Placed in the context of the Saints fleeing the United States in search of freedom from persecution, the sacrifices of the men and women in the Mormon Battalion are extraordinary. The service of the battalion provided a vital injection of funds necessary to complete the westward trek of the main body of the Saints and was a bright spot in the tense relationship between the Church and the United States federal government.

NOTES

1. Little, Report, in Roberts, *Comprehensive History*, 3:67.
2. Nevins, *Polk*, 110.
3. Watson, *Manuscript History of Brigham Young*, July 1, 1846, 205.
4. Tyler, *Concise History of the Mormon Battalion*, 125–26.
5. "Orders No. 8," in Tyler, *Concise History*, 166–67.
6. Cooke, "Cooke's Journal of the Mormon Battalion, 1846–1847," in Bieber, *Exploring Southwestern Trails*, 239–40.
7. Fleek, *History May Be Searched in Vain*, 324–25.
8. Tyler, *Concise History*, 298.
9. Fleek, *History May Be Searched in Vain*, 27.

40
The Vanguard Company

1847

Ensign Peak, where Brigham Young and the vanguard pioneer company raised an "ensign to the nations," similar to the flag on right.

On April 7, 1847, a select company of 143 men, 3 women, 2 children, 72 wagons, 93 horses, 66 oxen, 52 mules, 19 cows, 17 dogs, and several chickens left Winter Quarters, Nebraska, en route to the Rockies.[1] Led by Brigham Young, their objective was nothing less than to find a permanent home for the Latter-day Saints. Approximately a thousand miles of rolling plains, arid steppes, and the intimidating slopes of the Rocky Mountains separated them from their destination. The vanguard company would follow the best guides and maps available at the time but ultimately journey into an unknown and forbidding region of the continent. Nevertheless, the need to find a new home for the Saints was critical.

The vanguard company was not the only pioneer group venturing across the plains the summer of 1847, but they were unusual in their makeup and discipline. Brigham Young gathered company captains together and presented to them a strict schedule and set of rules to govern the camp. According to Wilford Woodruff, "The bugle was to be blown at half past 8 o'clock at night when all was to go to prayers in their several wagons and retire to bed by 9 o'clock. The bugle will blow at 5 o'clock in the morning to arise and pray and two hours will be allotted the camp to dress, pray, cook, eat, feed horses, harness and start at the blow of the bugle at 7 o'clock."[2]

Despite the strict regimen, the journey across the plains was an exhilarating adventure after the confinement of Winter Quarters. Some of the pioneers recorded the wonders of the unfamiliar landscape, and others wrote of the herds of buffalo encountered on the trek. Wilford Woodruff recorded, "Thousands upon thousands [of buffalo] would crowd together as they came from the bluffs to the bottom land . . . It looked as though the face of the earth was alive and moving like the waves of the sea."[3]

William Clayton remarked, "No pen nor tongue can give an idea of the multitude now in sight continually. . . . Truly, the Lord's cattle upon the thousand hills are numerous."[4] Men hunted the buffalo, though President Young forbade them to kill any more than were needed for meat. The bison gave sustenance to the pioneers, and their "buffalo chips" provided needed fuel on the nearly treeless plains.

For the most part, the journey passed peacefully. Near Scott's Bluff, Nebraska, however, Brigham became irritated over excessive levity in camp. He delivered a stern rebuke to the pioneers, telling the company, "If you do not open your hearts so that the Spirit of God can enter your hearts and teach you the right way, I know that you are a ruined people and will be destroyed." He added, "Unless there is a change and a different course of conduct, a different spirit to what is now in the camp, I go no farther."[5]

Brigham's words were perhaps a manifestation of anxiety, for he commented privately, "We are the pioneers for the whole Church of God on the Earth seeking for a place to establish the Kingdom, but we have not found it yet."[6]

Several incidents occurred when the company arrived at Fort Laramie, in present-day eastern Wyoming. First, the vanguard company found that they were not the first Mormons to arrive at the fort. Latter-day Saints who had left Mississippi several months earlier anxiously awaited the arrival of the vanguard company. Robert Crow, the leader of the small Mississippi group, reported that a Mormon Battalion detachment was making its way north from Fort Pueblo, Colorado, to meet the main body of the Saints at Fort Laramie.

The newly arrived Saints were also surprised to learn that former governor Lilburn W. Boggs of Missouri had stopped at the fort en route to California. Boggs had spoken disparagingly of Mormons while at the fort. One man was reported to have said, "Let the Mormons be as bad as they would, they could not be any worse than [Boggs] and his men were."[7]

Departing from Fort Laramie, the vanguard company trekked across the high plains of Wyoming, passing such landmarks as Independence Rock, Devil's Gate, and South Pass. During this phase of the journey, the pioneers encountered Jim Bridger, the legendary mountain man who offered advice and encouragement about the unfamiliar territory stretching before them. Bridger spoke optimistically, though cautiously, about the Salt Lake Valley.[8] Wilford Woodruff recorded, "He spoke . . . highly of the great Salt Lake for a settlement," but warned "there was but one thing that could operate against it . . . that would be frost."[9]

With Bridger's warning still ringing in their ears, less than two days later the party met Sam Brannan, the colorful leader of the Saints who had sailed around the horn of South America and settled in northern California. Brannan brought tales of the ill-fated Donner-Reed party and gave a full-fledged sales pitch to Brigham Young and others of the beautiful, temperate country on the Pacific Coast. Brigham listened with cautious skepticism but remained undeterred in his search for a new home in the Rocky Mountains.

As the vanguard company neared their chosen destination, danger stalked the camp. Rocky Mountain fever, an illness spread by ticks and characterized by chills, a hacking cough, severe headaches, acute pains throughout the body, fevers, and delirium, proved debilitating and sometimes deadly.[10]

Elder Heber C. Kimball, second in command of the camp, asked that the pioneers "humble ourselves before the Lord that we may obtain power with him to turn away sickness and disease from our midst." Elder Wilford

DID YOU KNOW?

- The vanguard company sought advice from the legendary mountain man, Jim Bridger, about the best location to settle.

- Brigham Young almost died from mountain fever only a few days before his arrival in the Salt Lake Valley.

Woodruff said, "The devil was constantly striving to hinder our progress and thwart the purposes of God, and now, by causing the President to be sick, hinder our getting through in time to return to our families."[11]

With Brigham Young languishing, Heber C. Kimball sent Orson Pratt, John Brown, and a few others in an advance party to locate the Salt Lake Valley. Elder Pratt and his small group entered the valley on July 20. After counseling with them on their return, Brigham declared, "I know it is the spot and we have come here according to the suggestion and direction of Joseph Smith who was martyred. The word of the Lord was to go to that valley and the best place you can find in it is the spot. I prayed that he would lead us directly to the best spot, which he has done, for after searching we can find no better."[12]

The still weak but recovering Brigham Young saw the Salt Lake Valley for the first time on July 28. According to the familiar story, Brigham Young gazed at the view and remarked, "This is the right place; drive on."[13]

There is little evidence from the vanguard company that Brigham made this proclamation, however. If he did, it went unrecorded in the contemporary accounts of the event. Though President Young's exact words on the occasion might not be known, Wilford Woodruff summed up Brigham's reaction to seeing the valley: "President Young expressed his full satisfaction in the appearance of the valley as a resting place for the Saints and was amply repaid for his journey."[14]

Wilford recorded his personal reaction: "This is an important day in the history of my life and the history of the Church of JESUS CHRIST of Latter Day Saints. . . . After traveling from our encampment six miles . . . we came into full view of the great valley or basin [of] the Salt Lake and land of promise held in reserve by the hand of GOD for a resting place

for the Saints upon which a portion of the Zion of GOD will be built."[15]

Today a grand stone monument near the mouth of Emigration Canyon honors the entrance of the Latter-day Saints into the Salt Lake Valley. Brigham Young, Heber C. Kimball, and Wilford Woodruff are depicted in heroic fashion standing atop an impressive granite pillar. The permanence of the monument, along with the perpetuity of festivities associated with July 24, gives the impression that the success of the vanguard party was a foregone conclusion to an epic journey. But contemporary accounts of the company show that anxiety and hope existed in equal portions. Faced with an unfamiliar country and an uncertain destiny, the fate of the vanguard company was not known when they departed from Winter Quarters. Their courage not only provided a new home for the Saints but a story of faith that has inspired generations.

Notes

1. See Whitney, *History of Utah*, 1:298–305; Evans, *One Hundred Years of Mormonism*, 440; Roberts, *Comprehensive History of the Church*, 3:163; McGavin, *Mormon Pioneers*, 176.
2. Wilford Woodruff, Journal, Apr. 18, 1847, in Staker, *Waiting for the World's End*, 111.
3. Wilford Woodruff, Journal, May 8, 1847, in Staker, *Waiting for the World's End*, 113–14.
4. *William Clayton's Journal*, May 8, 1847, 137.
5. *William Clayton's Journal*, May 29, 1847, 191.
6. Norton Jacob, Journal, May 28, 1847, in Barney, *Mormon Vanguard Brigade*, 150.
7. Bennett, *We'll Find the Place*, 172–76.
8. Norton Jacob, in Barney, *Mormon Vanguard Brigade*, 188–89.
9. Kenney, *Wilford Woodruff's Journal*, 3:219.
10. Norton Jacob, in Barney, *Mormon Vanguard Brigade*, 211.
11. Norton Jacob, Journal, July 17, 1847, in Barney, *Mormon Vanguard Brigade*, 211.
12. Norton Jacob, Journal, July 28, 1847, in Barney, *Mormon Vanguard Brigade*, 227.
13. See Bennett, *We'll Find the Place*, 218–19.
14. Kenney, *Wilford Woodruff's Journal*, 3:234.
15. Kenney, *Wilford Woodruff's Journal*, 3:233.

41
The Mormon Tabernacle Choir Is Begun

The Tabernacle on Temple Square, Salt Lake City, Utah.

1847

The Mormon Tabernacle Choir has been called "an extraordinary chorus," "the lyrical voice of Mormonism since pioneer days," "a company of angels," and "America's Choir."[1] From its humble beginnings in 1847 to its global renown today, the Choir has entertained countless audiences with powerful music ranging from hymns and classical numbers to patriotic songs and tunes from Broadway shows.

Although the Choir's role as an emissary for the Church has grown throughout the years,

its purpose has always been the same: "To give voice to the gospel of peace and human brotherhood."[2] The Mormon Tabernacle Choir has played an important role in helping the Church move out of obscurity and become well known and respected around the world.

Less than a month after the vanguard company arrived in the Salt Lake Valley in July 1847, Brigham Young organized a small choir to perform at a Church conference. Two years later, talented converts from Wales joined the fledgling choir. Over the next twenty-four years, the choir grew from the original core of pioneers to more than three hundred voices. On July 4, 1873, the first Mormon Tabernacle Choir concert was presented in the Tabernacle on Temple Square.[3]

In 1893 the Mormon Tabernacle Choir performed its first out-of-state concert at the Chicago World's Fair. The choir won second place and a prize of one thousand dollars, but more important than the prize was the national recognition. One listener at the event commented, "Your choir looked and sang like a chorus of angels." The Chicago journal *Music* noted the youthfulness of choir members, with "many of them under twenty years of age, good, hearty boys and girls, full of spirit and determination." Apostle Abraham Cannon noted in his diary, "It is said by those who are thought to be competent to judge that [our Choir] should really have been awarded the first prize."[4]

President Wilford Woodruff, who accompanied the choir on its tour, was impressed at the goodwill the choir inspired in such places as Denver and Kansas City. After a meeting with the mayor of Independence, Missouri, President Woodruff reflected, "I went through Jackson County . . . in 1834 on a mission to the Southern States. At that time we traveled secretly lest our lives should be taken by mobocrats; now in 1893, the mayor of Independence and hosts of others bid us welcome to the city."[5]

The Choir visited Denver in 1896, the San Francisco World's Fair in 1902, and the Alaska Yukon Exposition in Seattle in 1909. Newspapers across the country described the choir as "an extraordinary chorus," a "group of 350 singers [that] had heart . . . conviction . . . [and a] firm belief in what it was singing."[6]

In addition to national tours, the choir began making sound recordings. In September 1910, the choir made its first recording with the Columbia Phonograph Company. Since then, the Choir has released more than 175 albums, including two that have each sold over a million copies.[7] The choir received a Grammy Award for their recording of the "Battle Hymn of the Republic" in 1959 and were nominated for Grammy awards in 1967, 2007, and 2009.[8]

Other firsts for the choir include performing for United States president William Howard Taft in 1911 and later at the inaugurations of Lyndon B. Johnson (1965), Richard M. Nixon (1969), Ronald Reagan (1981), George H. W. Bush (1989), and George W. Bush (2001).[9]

In 1955 the choir went on its first international tour, performing for six weeks in large cities in Great Britain, Holland, Denmark,

Germany, Switzerland, and France. Other tours followed, with the choir performing in Japan, Korea, Australia, New Zealand, Mexico, Brazil, Scandinavia, eastern Europe, and Israel. Choir concerts gave opportunities for peoples of the world "to be touched by the Spirit and, in spite of language barriers, to communicate through music the expressions of love for each other and for God."[10]

Sound recordings and tours gave the Mormon Tabernacle Choir national and international recognition. They also brought acceptance throughout the world. While traveling in Europe in 1998, the choir had as its goal to "make friends with the people and raise the level of acceptance of the Church and its members in countries visited." Reflecting on their goal, Elder Dieter F. Uchtdorf, then serving as president of the Europe West Area, said, "The Church's growth here in the next century will be built on the results of these concerts."[11]

At the end of that European tour, Elder Gene R. Cook of the First Quorum of the Seventy said, "I don't know when we have had more news coverage for The Church of Jesus Christ of Latter-day Saints than we've had in the past three weeks. . . . The impact in the press was great. . . . I don't know of anything that has brought the Church out of obscurity in the time that I've been here any more than what has happened these last few weeks. It has been phenomenal."[12]

Part of the Mormon Tabernacle Choir's success comes from its individual members, who are set apart as music missionaries. They have many opportunities to interact with people on their tours. The conversations they have often clarify misconceptions about the Church. A government official in Brussels said, "We've never really understood your people. . . . But you've given us a whole new appreciation for what 'Mormon' means. In terms of your concert

DID YOU KNOW?

- *Music and the Spoken Word* is the longest continuous nationwide network broadcast in America.

- The Mormon Tabernacle Choir has released more than 175 albums, including two that have sold over a million copies.

and its themes tonight, it was absolutely magnificent. And if the songs you sang are the things you believe, then we know who you are."[13]

Besides their touring, one tradition of the Mormon Tabernacle Choir is *Music and the Spoken Word,* a weekly Sunday morning program broadcast continually since 1929, when it began as a radio program. The "oldest continuous nationwide network broadcast in America," it has produced more than four thousand episodes and airs on over two thousand radio and television stations.[14]

Today, the Mormon Tabernacle Choir continues to fulfill its objective of missionary work through music. *Music and the Spoken Word* and national and international tours continue. In 2012 the Choir launched its own YouTube channel and other online access points so that the Tabernacle Choir's music is accessible anywhere in the world. The Choir's music, mission, and members have come together to "strengthen the Saints, open doors for the Church, build bridges of goodwill and understanding, and share the message of the restored gospel."[15]

President Gordon B. Hinckley said of the Mormon Tabernacle Choir: "In seasons of conflict its voice has been one of peace. In times of doubt and cynicism it has brought reassurance and faith. To those in distress, in sorrow and in despair, it has given hope and strength and resolution. To a world at times unsure of God, it has spoken without equivocation and with certainty, singing His praises with majestic and moving power. In a culture of shifting values and changing tastes, it has won and held the love and the loyalty of a vast audience spanning the generations and reaching across the continent and to foreign lands."[16]

NOTES

1. Petersen, *Mormon Tabernacle Choir,* 76; Kirk Johnson, "Mormons on a Mission," *New York Times,* Aug. 20, 2010; Jay M. Todd, "A Company of Angels," *Ensign,* Oct. 1998, 30; Katie Harmer, "The Mormon Tabernacle Choir's Path to Prominence," *Deseret News,* Sept. 5, 2013.
2. R. Scott Lloyd, "Choir Looks Back on 60 Years of Broadcasting 'Voice of Peace,'" *LDS Church News,* 22 July 1989, 5; K. Newell Dayley, "Mormon Tabernacle Choir," in Ludlow, *Encyclopedia of Mormonism,* 2:950.
3. Swinton, *America's Choir,* 17; Harmer, "Mormon Tabernacle Choir's Path to Prominence."
4. Hicks, *Mormon Tabernacle Choir,* 42–43.
5. Cowley, *Wilford Woodruff,* 583.
6. Petersen, *Mormon Tabernacle Choir,* 74.
7. Richard E. Turley Jr., "The First Mormon Tabernacle Choir Recordings," *Ensign,* Sept. 2010, 59.
8. Turley, "First Mormon Tabernacle Choir Recordings," 59; "The Mormon Tabernacle Choir's GRAMMY Awards History," mormontabernaclechoir.org.
9. Swinton, *America's Choir,* 73; "The Significance of January 20th in Mormon Tabernacle Choir History," mormontabernaclechoir.org.
10. Cynthia Doxey, "International Tours of the Tabernacle Choir," in Black et al., *Out of Obscurity,* 81.
11. Todd, "Company of Angels," 30.
12. Cook, to Tabernacle Choir, July 1, 1998, in Doxey, "International Tours of the Tabernacle Choir," 76.
13. Todd, "Company of Angels," 33–34.
14. Harmer, "Mormon Tabernacle Choir's Path to Prominence."
15. Cynthia Doxey and Lloyd D. Newell, "The Mormon Tabernacle Choir's Pacific Tour, 1988," in Neilson et al., *Pacific Isles,* 144.
16. Lloyd, "Choir Looks Back on 60 Years of Broadcasting 'Voice of Peace.'"

42
The First Sunday School

1849

Richard Ballantyne, founder of the first Latter-day Saint Sunday School.

"Even before I joined the Church I was moved upon to work for the young," Richard Ballantyne wrote. "I saw that the children, from the very nature and circumstances of the people, were being neglected; and I wanted to gather them into the school where they could learn to read and write, by the goodness of God, and the true gospel of salvation given by Jesus Christ."[1]

In the spring of 1849, less than a year after his arrival in the Salt Lake Valley and while still living in two wagons, Brother Ballantyne envisioned building a home with a large room—twenty feet long and eighteen feet wide—for a Sunday school. It would have a large glass window to provide light and an fireplace for warmth. In the months that followed, he secured the needed timber, rock, and adobe for the home. He constructed wooden benches and dedicated that one large room for the teaching of the gospel.[2]

This Sunday school was not the first to be launched among the Latter-day Saints. Helen Mar Whitney recalled lining up in front of the schoolhouse in Kirtland, Ohio, each Sunday morning at 10 o'clock to walk with her teacher up to the Kirtland Temple for instruction.[3] Other reminiscences tell of Sunday school classes held in England as early as 1841. But Ballantyne's Sunday school was the first that took root in the Church.[4]

Instruction began on December 9, 1849, when Ballantyne welcomed neighborhood children to his home. The children of John Taylor, Wilford Woodruff, Parley P. Pratt, Franklin D. Richards, and other Church leaders were among the fifty or so children, ages eight to fourteen, who enrolled in his Sunday School. "The children took delight in attending the school, and there was no trouble in getting them there, although it opened at eight o'clock in the morning. In those days general Sabbath services were held at ten o'clock, a.m., and the school dismissed in time to give its members an opportunity to attend them."[5]

Sunday school continued weekly in the Ballantyne home for about a year. Each class began with a song and prayer, followed by lessons from the Bible, Book of Mormon, or Doctrine and Covenants. When a meetinghouse was built in the ward where Ballantyne resided, Sunday instruction was relocated to the meetinghouse. Ballantyne continued to teach and serve as the Sunday School superintendent until a mission call to India in 1852 necessitated his resignation. Responsibility for the Sunday School was passed to Joseph Horne.

Recollecting his work with young children Ballantyne wrote, "I felt . . . that the Gospel was too precious to myself to be withheld from the children. They ought to have the privilege of Gospel teaching, and that was the main purpose—to teach them the Gospel—because I felt it was very precious to me, and I thought it would be precious to them; and it was my duty to do that."[6]

Throughout the early 1850s, Sunday schools were started in wards throughout the Utah Territory. They functioned independently basis, with their own curriculum and administrative guidelines. As the movement spread across the Intermountain West, the need for training and curriculum grew. In 1866, Elder George Q. Cannon began publishing the *Juvenile Instructor,* a journal intended to provide lesson materials, instructions, and encouragement to Sunday school teachers. He later founded George Q. Cannon and Sons (precursor of Deseret Book Company) to publish manuals and materials for use in the Sunday schools.[7]

In 1867 the Deseret Sunday School Union was organized with Cannon as president from 1867, which position he retained until his death in 1901. Under his leadership, the Sunday School program became an established part of Sabbath day worship for Latter-day Saints.

In 1876 the Deseret Sunday School Union published a circular "with a view to secure uniformity" in the Sunday Schools. The circular contained guidelines for Sunday School, such as "no loud talking, or playing, or running." Brethren were told to remove their hats upon entering any Sunday School meeting, and teachers were counseled to make their lessons "varied and interesting, with singing, instrumental music, brief addresses, asking questions, recitations, etc."[8]

That same year, the First Presidency issued instructions to administer the sacrament to children in Sunday School meetings, in order to "give the children a better understanding of the divine mission of the Savior."[9] The practice of administering the sacrament ended in 1980, when Sunday School was incorporated into the consolidated three-hour block.

Over the years, Sunday School has remained an integral part of study and learning in the Church. In the early 1900s, new classes for older children and youth were added. In 1904 the first Sunday School class for adults was taught in the Weber Utah Stake. Thereafter, adult Sunday School classes became a regular part of the Church program. In the 1970s the curriculum for Sunday School was standardized. In 1971, under the direction of General Superintendent Russell M. Nelson, an eight-year curriculum cycle was introduced. It was later simplified to four years—one year for teaching each of the standard works. At that time, the name of the organization was changed from the Deseret Sunday School Union to simply Sunday School.

DID YOU KNOW?

- While still living in a wagon in the Salt Lake Valley, Richard Ballantyne planned to build a room in his new home for housing a Sunday school.

- George Q. Cannon founded a publishing company for the express purpose of providing materials for the Sunday schools of the Church.

The teaching and methodology of Sunday School have changed over the years, but the aims of the organization—the oldest formal teaching organization of the Church—remain remarkably close to those set forth by Richard Ballantyne in 1849. At the fiftieth anniversary of the Sunday School, in 1899, Church leaders placed a letter in a box of memorabilia underlining the object of Sunday School instruction: "We beseech you that whatever . . . may be the changes wrought in the fifty years to come, that you never forget for an instant the object of the great Sunday School work, viz: To teach the children the principles of the Gospel of Jesus Christ; to make Latter-day Saints of them."[10]

NOTES

1. Sonne, *Knight of the Kingdom,* 46.
2. *Jubilee History,* 9–10.
3. Whitney, "Life Incidents," *Women's Exponent* 9, no. 5 (August 15, 1880): 42.
4. David O. McKay, "Sunday Schools of the Church," *Improvement Era,* May 1930, 480–81.
5. *Jubilee History,* 11–12.
6. *Jubilee History,* 12.
7. Bitton, *George Q. Cannon,* 151.
8. *Jubilee History,* 26.
9. *Jubilee History,* 26–27.
10. "In Celebration of Sunday School," *Ensign,* Oct. 1998, 67.

43
The Perpetual Emigration Fund

1849

Pioneers make their way through Echo Canyon on their way to Salt Lake City.

In 1849 Elder Lorenzo Snow was called by Brigham Young "to assist in gathering funds for bringing the poor Saints to Zion."[1] Elder Snow's call led directly to the founding of the Perpetual Emigration Fund Company, announced at the October 1849 general conference. Brigham Young served as the first president of the Perpetual Emigration Fund. He was succeeded by Horace S. Eldredge in 1870, who was succeeded by Albert Carrington in 1873.

The purpose of the Perpetual Emigration Fund was to assist Latter-day Saints from the eastern United States and Europe to heed the Lord's command to gather to the Salt Lake Valley:

Israel, Israel, God is calling,
Calling thee from lands of woe.
Babylon the great is falling;
God shall all her tow'rs o'er-throw.[2]

Funding for the Perpetual Emigration Fund came from Church assets and private contributions. Its financial foundation never grew as large as Brigham Young and other Church leaders hoped it would. In fact, resources for the Perpetual Emigration Fund strained and even exhausted Church tithing contributions. "The Fund," as it was called by Church leaders, was promoted as the best answer to emigration woes. As contributions were received, accurate accounting of expended funds was essential to the process. Tempers flared over the slightest discrepancy.

Each year European Church leaders were asked to determine how many Latter-day Saints were ready to journey to the Salt Lake Valley. If local Fund donations were below the needed amount, leaders transferred tithing funds to assist Saints on their westward journey. Elder Widerborn, president of the Scandinavian Mission, wrote, "The spirit of gathering is great among the Saints, and those who can are preparing to emigrate next season. Would to God we had means enough to emigrate the poor . . . souls who are struggling here in poverty . . . work being scarce and wages low."[3]

The distribution of Perpetual Emigration Fund funds was commensurate with the individual or family's inability to pay for the journey. Unfortunately, more Latter-day Saints were seeking assistance than there was money to give. Determining who received funding took into consideration length of membership in the Church, whether a person's skills were needed to build settlements in the West, and whether relatives or friends had donated to the Fund.

To stretch limited funding, cost-cutting measures became a high priority. Church agents served as brokers and purchased group tickets for Latter-day Saints aboard sea-going vessels. At every step of the way, whether purchasing tickets, choosing routes, selecting commodities, and so forth, converts were guided by experienced leaders. Every detail of outfitting, lodging, feeding, and transporting was arranged beforehand. Even railroad fares and what were called "Church trains" (ox teams, wagons, and teamsters sent from Utah to a designated frontier post in the Midwest to transport Perpetual Emigration Fund travelers to the Salt Lake Valley) were prearranged, using this credit-based transportation system. Families were asked to double up in wagons. The handcart experiment used from 1856 to 1860 was a means of lowering costs for immigrants.

These detailed preparations took time and means and were not without difficulties. For example, Church agents in the Copenhagen mission office were accused of profiting from ship and railroad passenger rebates and of fleecing unsuspecting emigrants. Denials of such actions were dismissed as false. A few converts never understood that the 5 percent brokerage discounts given to Latter-day Saint leaders were not kept by the leaders at the mission office. The financial discounts were turned back into the Fund, "making welcome cash available to emigrants with marginal resources."[4] The unresolved misunderstanding marred the Scandinavian emigration process for years.

Money from the Fund was not a gift to the traveler. It was a loan, a debt to be repaid whether by cash, commodities, or labor. Cash was always preferred. Before the journey commenced, notes were signed that obligated the traveler to repay the specified amount. In theory, the repayment provided for a "perpetual source of assistance for others. In practice, however, only about one-third of the [Fund's] beneficiaries repaid their loans in full, sometimes with interest; about one-third made partial repayment; the rest repaid nothing."[5]

A Danish-language monthly periodical printed in Salt Lake City reminded fund recipients of their obligation: "Have you forgotten how eagerly you seized every means which would make your emigration possible?"[6]

In 1880, at the fiftieth anniversary of the organization of The Church of Jesus Christ of Latter-day Saints, President John Taylor said, "It occurred to me . . . that we ought to do something, as they did in former times, to relieve those that are oppressed with debt, to assist those that are needy, to break off the yoke of those that may feel themselves crowded upon, and to make it a time of general rejoicing."[7]

With the tradition of the Israelite jubilee year on his mind, President Taylor announced that he "forgave half of the outstanding debt

DID YOU KNOW?

- The first of the Latter-day Saints aided by the Perpetual Emigration Fund were pioneers stranded in Iowa and the last were Icelandic immigrants to Utah.

- Only about a third of the Saints assisted by the Perpetual Emigration Fund were able to pay back the debt that they owed.

owed by the poor to the fund."[8] The amount owed the Perpetual Emigration Fund at that time was "$1,604,000; thus $802,000 of the debt was to be cancelled." Those who had the means to repay their loan were not relieved of their indebtedness in 1880, for as President Taylor said, "For in former times, . . . they did not release the rich [from debt], it was the poor."[9]

In 1887 the United States government, under provisions in the Edmunds-Tucker Act, dissolved the Fund and took its assets, consisting of "mainly promissory notes totaling more than $400,000."[10] These funds were "disposed of by the secretary of the interior for the use and benefit of the public schools."[11]

The Perpetual Emigration Fund was a useful, credit-based transportation system for Latter-day Saint emigrants from 1849 to 1887. The first of the Latter-day Saints aided by the Fund were pioneers stranded in Iowa and the last were Icelandic immigrants. It is estimated that more than thirty thousand Latter-day Saints were assisted by the Perpetual Emigration Fund on their journey to the American West.

Notes

1. Rich, *Ensign to the Nations*, 443; Richard L. Jensen, "Perpetual Emigrating Fund Company," historytogo.utah.gov.
2. "Israel, Israel, God Is Calling," *Hymns*, no. 7.
3. Bjork, *West of the Great Divide*, 107.
4. Mulder, *Homeward to Zion*, 143.
5. Powell, *Utah History Encyclopedia*, 419; Jensen, "Perpetual Emigrating Fund Company."
6. "Betal Eders Emigrationsgjaeld," *Morgenstjernen* 1 (1882): 186, in Mulder, *Homeward to Zion*, 151.
7. Nibley, *Presidents of the Church*, 87.
8. David F. Boone, "Perpetual Emigrating Fund," in Ludlow, *Encyclopedia of Mormonism*, 3:1075.
9. Rich, *Ensign to the Nations*, 409.
10. Powell, *Utah History Encyclopedia*, 420.
11. Arrington and Bitton, *Mormon Experience*, 253.

44
The Public Announcement of Plural Marriage

1852

Elder Orson Pratt.

At a Church conference held in the Salt Lake Tabernacle in late August 1852, Elder Orson Pratt boldly announced, "It is quite unexpected to me, brethren and sisters, to be called upon to address you this forenoon; and still more so, to address you upon the principle which has been named, namely, a plurality of wives." Elder Pratt acknowledged that although the congregation was aware that "the Latter-day Saints have embraced the doctrine of plurality of wives," but noted, "it is new ground to the inhabitants of the United States."[1]

Several factors led to Elder Pratt's 1852 announcement. Although the practice was not announced publicly during the Nauvoo era (1839–1846), Church leaders became increasingly open about it on the westward trek to the Rockies and during the years that followed. United States government officials in the Territory of Utah decried the practice in the early 1850s. Judge Perry E. Brocchus in a September 1851 speech in Salt Lake City called upon Mormon women to be "virtuous," undoubtedly a veiled reference to plural marriage. His speech elicited an angry response from Brigham Young, who defended the honor of Latter-day Saint women. Undeterred, Brocchus and other federal officials reported to eastern newspaper editors that Mormons were "openly sanctioning and defending the practice of polygamy or plurality of wives."[2]

In response to the outcry that followed, Church leaders selected Orson Pratt to publicly announce the practice of plural marriage at the August 1852 conference. The choice was curious, for Elder Pratt had not always been a proponent of the practice. When first taught the doctrine of plural marriage, Pratt rejected it. After a period of estrangement, he reconciled himself to the Church and to the doctrine and returned to his place in the Quorum of the Twelve. About a decade later, he publicly explained and defended the doctrine in the Salt Lake Tabernacle.[3]

Elder Pratt began his address by speaking about the most pressing concern of the doctrine: "It is not, as many have supposed, a doctrine embraced by them [the Latter-day Saints] to gratify the carnal lusts and feelings of man; that is not the object of the doctrine." Pratt then presented the reasons why Latter-day Saints were commanded by God to practice plural marriage. The foremost reason was that marriage is a central institution in the plan of God. "What is the object of this union?" Pratt asked. "It is clearly expressed; for, says the Lord unto the male and female, I command you to multiply and replenish the earth." He spoke of plural marriage being a fulfillment of the promise made to Abraham and other ancient patriarchs: "Lift up your eyes, and behold the stars; so thy seed shall be, as numberless as the stars" (Genesis 13:14–16).[4]

Elder Pratt continued his address by railing against the immoral practices that prevailed in the world, declaring, "Whoredom, adultery, and fornication, have cursed the nations of the earth for many generations." He taught that immorality is to "be prevented in the way the Lord devised in ancient times; that is, by giving to His faithful servants a plurality of wives, by which a numerous and faithful posterity can be raised up, and taught in the principles of righteousness and truth." He added, "After they fully understand those principles that were given to the ancient Patriarchs, if they keep not the law of God, but commit adultery, and transgressions of this kind, let their names be blotted out from under heaven, that they have no place among the people of God."[5]

Elder Pratt then spoke of many "great and mighty ones" reserved to come forth in the dispensation of the fulness of times "through a noble parentage." He concluded, "Among the Saints is the most likely place for these spirits to take their tabernacles through a just and righteous parentage."[6]

Elder Pratt explained that plural marriages were performed not in a random or haphazard way but under the direction of the priesthood as in ancient times. He cited specifically the example of David being rebuked by the prophet Nathan for taking a wife without the Lord's sanction (2 Samuel 12:1–12). Pratt declared, "One man has power to turn the key to inquire of the Lord, and to say whether I, or these my brethren, or any of the rest of this congregation, or the Saints upon the face of the whole earth, may have this blessing of Abraham conferred upon them; he holds the keys of these matters now, the same as Nathan, in his day."[7]

In the conference session that followed Pratt's speech, Brigham Young bore a fervent testimony of the prophetic role of Joseph Smith. The revelation Joseph received concerning celestial marriage was read aloud to the congregation (D&C 132.) The proceedings of the conference sessions were later published in the *Deseret News* and other Church periodicals.

In the decades following the 1852 announcement, Orson Pratt was a fierce defender of the revelations on plural marriage. Brigham Young once declared, "If Brother Orson were chopped up in inch pieces, each piece would cry out Mormonism was true."[8]

Perhaps the highest point in Elder Pratt's public defense of plural marriage came in 1870 when he debated J. P. Newman, chaplain of the United States Senate. The subject of the debate was, "Does the Bible Sanction Polygamy?" The debaters were given one hour each day for three days to present their arguments in the Salt

DID YOU KNOW?

• The practice of plural marriage was announced publicly at a general conference in 1852.

• Elder Orson Pratt publicly debated Dr. J. P. Newman, the chaplain of the United States Senate, over whether the Bible sanctioned plural marriage.

Lake Tabernacle. The two men fired out biblical passages in support of their stance, at times delving into the Hebraic roots of the biblical text to make their point. Elder Pratt matched Chaplain Newman at every turn. The clear and incisive arguments of Pratt showed that Latter-day Saints did not violate scriptural injunctions in their adherence to Joseph Smith's teaching on plural marriage.

At the end of the debate, both sides declared victory, although later evaluations favored Pratt's arguments and skills as a debater. For example, a Catholic writer reasoned, "Newman, whatever his qualifications as chaplain of the Senate or his merits as an orator, proved neither a scripture scholar nor an apt debater." A newspaper reporter lamented, "Someone carrying more guns than Dr. Newman will have to be sent out missionarying among the Mormons."[9]

More than a century after the practice of plural marriage was ended, many Latter-day Saints are uncomfortable with the legacy of plural marriage. Taken in their historical context, the clear and incisive arguments of Orson Pratt first delivered in 1852 put the opponents

of the Church on notice that plural marriage was a biblically sanctioned practice and the Latter-day Saints violated no scriptural injunctions in their adherence to Joseph Smith's revelation. Elder Orson Pratt demonstrated how sincere the Saints were in following the revelations of God and in staying true to the covenants they had made.

NOTES

1. Pratt, in *Journal of Discourses,* 1:53–54; Hardy, *Solemn Covenant,* 14.
2. David J. Whittaker, "The Bone in the Throat: Orson Pratt and the Public Announcement of Plural Marriage," *Western Historical Quarterly,* July 1987, 295.
3. England, *Life and Thought of Orson Pratt,* 77–80.
4. Pratt, in *Journal of Discourses,* 1:54, 59–60.
5. Pratt, in *Journal of Discourses,* 1:61–62.
6. Pratt, in *Journal of Discourses,* 1:62–63.
7. Pratt, in *Journal of Discourses,* 1:64.
8. Brigham Young, Office Journal, Oct. 1, 1860, in England, *Life and Thought of Orson Pratt,* 217.
9. Brigham Young Office Journal, Oct. 1, 1860, in England, *Life and Thought of Orson Pratt,* 245–46.

45
The Mormon Reformation

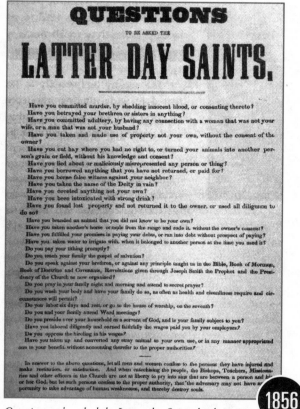

Questions to be asked the Latter-day Saints by their leaders as part of the Mormon Reformation of 1856.

In 1848, a year after the arrival of the first pioneers in the Salt Lake Valley, Jedediah M. Grant approached a house where Brigham Young was nailing shingles and called out, "Brother Brigham, we have some urgent public business that we need to discuss with you." When Brigham replied that he was busy with his own work, Grant responded, "President, we want you to quit working with tools. We need you to work with men. We have got plenty of

carpenters in Zion, but there is only Brigham Young."[1]

That was just the beginning for the zealous Jedediah M. Grant, the most recognized figure of the 1856–57 Mormon reformation. He was known among the Saints as "Mormon Thunder." The reformative efforts of Grant and other leaders produced a renewed commitment to living the tenets of the gospel during a time when the Saints were still striving to survive in their new home in the Intermountain West.

The Mormon reformation began as an effort to increase righteousness among the Saints. Brigham Young was concerned that a spiritual complacency was developing. This led Church leaders to express concern for the spiritual welfare of those living in the Utah Territory. Crop failures and famines suggested the Lord was displeased with the behavior of his people, too. In 1851 Heber C. Kimball, a counselor in the First Presidency, declared, "There is a reformation about to commence and my heart and soul is in it."[2]

In the fall of 1856, Jedediah M. Grant, who had been been called to the First Presidency in 1854, was sent to Kaysville, Utah, to deliver a sermon. Grant noted a "dark and dull spirit" among the people in Kaysville. His companion, Joseph Young, suggested that they preach in nearby Farmington instead. Grant replied: "Do you know how I feel about it? In the name of the Lord Jesus Christ, I will never leave this land, until the people surrender. . . . Shall we give up and let the wicked and ungodly overcome us? No, in the name and by the power of

God we will overcome them. We will cleanse the inside of the platter and have Israel saved."[3]

That Sunday, Grant preached a series of fiery sermons calling upon the Saints in Kaysville to repent and seek forgiveness for their sins. That same day, Brigham Young gave a similar address in Salt Lake City, rebuking the congregation for lying, stealing, swearing, committing adultery, and quarrelling in their families. Wilford Woodruff noted, "It was one of the strongest addresses . . . ever delivered to this church." He added that Brigham's "voice and words were like the thundering of Mt. Sinai."[4]

With that, the reformation had begun. Over the next few months a series of conferences were held throughout the Utah Territory so that Church leaders could call the Saints to repentance. The conferences often led to rebaptisms, as many members signified through this means a repentance of sins and recommitment to the Church.

Church leaders set apart "home missionaries" to visit the homes of members and ask a series of twenty-seven questions. The questions—printed and sent out to bishops, home missionaries, and teachers—gave evidence of the deep concern Church leaders had for the Saints. Questions ranged from "Have you committed murder, by shedding of innocent blood, or consenting thereto?" to "Do you wash your body and have your family do so as often as health and cleanliness require and circumstances permit?" Other questions related to issues of honesty, such as "Have you lied about or maliciously misrepresented any person or thing?" or the more specific, "Have you branded an animal that you did not know to be your own?"[5]

The zeal manifested by Church leaders for the reformation did not always produce positive results. Drawing on wording from Old Testament passages, several Church leaders taught that some sins were so serious that the sinner's own blood must be shed for the sinner to receive forgiveness. In the years that followed, critics took this counsel to imply that it was appropriate to use violence as a means of suppressing dissent within the community.[6]

Years after the reformation ended, the First Presidency and Quorum of the Twelve declared: "This Church views the shedding of human blood with the utmost abhorrence. . . . We denounce as entirely untrue the allegation which has been made that our church favors or believes in the killing of persons who leave the church or apostatize from its doctrines."[7]

Historian Paul H. Peterson noted that "many of Brigham Young's utterances were rhetorical and designed to encourage (or sometimes even frighten) Saints into gospel conformity."[8] Peterson also noted that "Brigham's later speeches featured less overstatement and hyperbole, less bombast and militancy. Once the overwhelming fervor of the Reformation had cooled, Brigham observed that 'people are not to be driven into heaven by preaching hell-fire.' Instead, he observed the virtues of 'instructing people until the increase in knowledge and understanding, until their traditions pass away, and they will become of one heart and one mind in the principles of godliness.'"[9]

The heightened rhetoric of the period often overshadowed the results of the reformation.

DID YOU KNOW?

- During the Mormon reformation of 1856–57, all Church members were asked a series of twenty-seven questions to test their commitment to the faith.

- The preaching of the reformation was so effective that Orson Hyde, Wilford Woodruff, and Lorenzo Snow offered to give up their apostolic callings to more persuasive speakers.

Elders Orson Hyde, Wilford Woodruff, and Lorenzo Snow were so affected by the preaching of Brigham Young, Jedediah Grant, and others that they offered to give up their Church positions.[10] Church attendance surged, at times resulting in people being turned away from services because of lack of space. The payment of tithes and offerings increased dramatically. The number of letters addressed to Brigham Young from those seeking to repent grew significantly. The number of covenant marriages, including plural marriages, skyrocketed. Scholar Stanley Ivins concluded that there were 65 percent more plural marriages in the two years of the reformation than during any other comparable time.[11]

The reformation came at a great cost, however. Jedediah M. Grant worked himself to death with a strenuous schedule of preaching and travel. In one of his final sermons, President Grant declared, "When you are right we will cease to chastise, we will cease to rebuke; we will cease telling you to surrender, to repent of all your sins. But until you do this, we will continue to throw the arrows of God through you."[12]

Worn down by the toil of his efforts, Grant contracted typhoid fever and collapsed in November 1856. While he lay on his deathbed, he saw a vision of the spirit world. According to one account, "he saw many of the Saints and found them pure and clean. They were clothed in pure white. There was not dirt or filth in the Spirit World, or darkness. Everything was in perfect order."[13] Just days before President Grant's passing, his last child, Heber, was born. A future Church President, Heber J. Grant was in many ways as vigorous a reformer as his father.

The waves of the Reformation reached as far as the shores of Great Britain before they receded. Similar attempts at reformation took place in 1877, again at the urging of Brigham Young, and in 1884 under the leadership of John Taylor, though neither effort reached the same level of intensity as the reformation of 1856–57. Stoked by the fervor of the teaching of Jedediah Grant and others, the fires of recommitment prompted by the 1856 reformation burned in the hearts of the Saints as they moved into a most difficult period of their history.

NOTES

1. Sessions, *Mormon Thunder*, 3.
2. Paul H. Peterson, "The Mormon Reformation," PhD diss., Brigham Young University (1981), 13.
3. Sessions, *Mormon Thunder*, 259.
4. Peterson, "Mormon Reformation," 24.
5. "Questions to Be Asked the Latter-day Saints," Church History Library, The Church of Jesus Christ of Latter-day Saints, Salt Lake City, Utah. See Gustive O. Larson, "The Mormon Reformation," *Utah Historical Quarterly* 26 (1958): 45–63.
6. See "Peace and Violence among 19th Century Latter-day Saints," lds.org.
7. Roberts, *Comprehensive History of the Church*, 4:136.
8. Paul H. Peterson, "Reformation (LDS) of 1856–1857," in Ludlow, *Encyclopedia of Mormonism*, 2:1197.
9. Paul H. Peterson, "Brigham Young and the Mormon Reformation," in Black and Porter, *Lion of the Lord*, 258.
10. Staker, *Waiting for the World's End*, 185; Peterson, "Mormon Reformation," 45.
11. Stanley Ivins, "Notes on Mormon Polygamy," *Western Humanities Review*, Summer 1956, 231, in Peterson, "Mormon Reformation," 45.
12. Sessions, *Mormon Thunder*, 311.
13. Sessions, *Mormon Thunder*, 315.

46
The Rescue of Handcart Pioneers

1856

Handcart pioneers, pressing forward through harsh winter storms.

From 1856 to 1860, nearly three thousand Latter-day Saints pulled their possessions and supplies in two-wheeled carts from Iowa City to the Salt Lake Valley.[1] Two companies made the journey successfully in 1856, but disaster struck the Saints in the third and fourth handcart companies and the two wagon companies that traveled with them. Late starts, unexpected delays, insufficient provisions, and unseasonably cold weather led to much suffering and death among the Saints in those four companies.

The sailing ship *Thornton,* with 764 Latter-day Saints aboard it under the leadership of James Willie, departed on May 3, 1856, from Liverpool. The vessel *Horizon,* carrying 856 Saints under the direction of Edward Martin, sailed May 25. The late departure dates put them behind schedule. The Willie company arrived in Iowa City on June 26 and the Martin company on July 8. On July 15, nine days after the Willie company reached Iowa City, they proceded west. The Martin company didn't start west until July 28, twenty days after arriving in Iowa City. The handcart companies were accompanied by two companies of oxen-drawn wagon trains carrying provisions for the emigrants.[2]

For both companies, the journey across Iowa to Florence, Nebraska, was completed in four weeks without incident. In Florence, each company paused to repair carts, procure supplies, and, more importantly, decide whether to proceed to the Salt Lake Valley or wait until the next season. Levi Savage, a leader in the Willie handcart company, feared the groups "could not cross the mountains with a mixed company of aged people, women, and little children, so late in the season." When company leaders disagreed, Savage replied, "Brethren and sisters, what I have said I know to be true; but, seeing you are to go forward, I will go with you, will help you all I can, will work with you, will rest with you, will suffer with you, and, if necessary,

I will die with you. May God in his mercy bless and preserve us."[3]

The Martin company, the last handcart pioneer group for the year, left Florence on August 27, 1856. Because of delays along the trail, it was not until late September 1856, when the Willie company reached Fort Laramie, that provisions became an issue. Captain Willie reduced rations and set a faster pace for the pioneers in their journey toward the Salt Lake Valley. A few days later, Willie reduced rations again, this time to only ten ounces of flour per day. Lacking proper nourishment, few pioneers could sustain the pace needed to reach their destination. Yet they pushed on as snow-capped mountains in the distance signaled that winter was imminent.

Snow began to fall on the trail on October 19. Provisions continued to run lower, and tragedy followed. Lack of proper clothing and bedding combined with scanty shelter took a deathly toll. Pioneer John Chislett wrote, "Many a father pulled his cart, with his little children on it, until the day preceding his death. . . . The snow fell several inches deep as we travelled along, but we dared not stop."[4]

The Martin company reached Fort Laramie October 8. Not finding provisions there for his company, Captain Martin shortened daily rations: "First, the pound of flour was reduced to three-fourths, then to one-half of a pound, and afterwards to still less per day. However we pushed ahead." He lamented, "I almost wish God would close my eyes to the enormity of the sickness, hunger and death among the Saints."[5]

Meanwhile, on October 4, 1856, Brigham Young was informed that two handcart companies and two wagon companies were still en route to the Salt Lake Valley. The next day, October 5, at the semiannual conference of the Church, President Young said, "Many of our brethren and sisters are on the plains with hand-carts, and probably many are now 700 miles from this place, and they must be brought here. . . . Go and bring in those people now on the plains."[6]

On October 7, the first of 250 rescuers and teams moved out of the Salt Lake Valley toward the windswept plains of north-central Wyoming. Their journey of some three hundred miles was challenging, but their determination was sure. On October 21, rescuers reached the snowbound Willie company, and "shouts of joy rent the air; strong men wept till tears ran freely down their furrowed and sun-burnt cheeks."[7]

Some in the first rescue party stayed with the Willie company while others pushed on in search of the Martin company. Among them was George Grant, who recounted, "We found the Martin Company in a deplorable condition, they having lost fifty-six of their number since crossing the North Platte, nine days before. . . . There were old men pulling and tugging their carts, sometimes loaded with a sick wife or children—women pulling along sick husbands. . . . The sight is almost too much for the stoutest of us." Anxious to relieve the suffering pioneers, Grant said, "We will move every day toward the valley if we have to shovel snow to do it, the Lord helping us."[8] Such determination bound

DID YOU KNOW?

• From 1856 to 1860 nearly three thousand Latter-day Saints successfully pulled their earthly possessions in two-wheeled carts from Iowa City to the Salt Lake Valley.

• Though the Martin and Willie handcart companies became the most famous because of the extreme hardships they suffered, there were ten handcart companies in total, most of which suffered relatively few deaths.

the rescuers to the handcart immigrants on the frozen plains of Wyoming as perhaps nothing else could.

On November 9 rescuers delivered the first of the Willie company to the Salt Lake Valley. Twenty-one days later, on November 30, those bringing survivors of the Martin company began their descent into the valley. President Young, in speaking to a congregation assembled in the bowery on Temple Square, said:

"When those persons arrive I do not want to see them put into houses by themselves; I want to have them distributed in the city among the families that have good and comfortable houses; . . . I wish the sisters to go home and prepare to give those who have just arrived a mouthful of something to eat, and to wash them and nurse them up. . . . Prayer is good, but when baked potatoes, and pudding, and milk are needed, prayer will not supply their place on this occasion."[9]

The last of the pioneers in the Hodgetts and Hunt wagon trains reached Salt Lake City in mid December.

In the years following the tragedy of the Martin and Willie companies, the story of the courage and rescue of the handcart pioneers became a symbolic narrative of the westward movement of the Church. Every year, thousands of Church youth participate in reenactments of the handcart treks as a reminder of the sacrifices of the Saints of the early Church, and their story continues to inspire the Saints of our time to continue forward.

NOTES

1. Hafen and Hafen, *Handcarts to Zion,* 194; Olsen, *Price We Paid,* 477–78.
2. Olsen, *Price We Paid,* 26.
3. Hafen and Hafen, *Handcarts to Zion,* 96–97.
4. Olsen, *Price We Paid,* 126–27.
5. "Leaves from the Life of Elizabeth Kingford Jackson," in Hafen and Hafen, *Handcarts to Zion,* 108.
6. "Brigham Young Speech at the Bowery, Oct. 5, 1856," *Deseret News,* Oct. 15, 1856.
7. "Mr. Chislett's Narrative," in Stenhouse, *Rocky Mountain Saints,* 325.
8. "Captain George Grant's Report from Devil's Gate to President Brigham Young, November 2, 1856," *Deseret News,* Nov. 19, 1856.
9. "Brigham Young Remarks on November 30, 1856," *Deseret News,* Dec. 10, 1856.

47
The Utah War

1857

Albert S. Johnston, commander of the United States forces in the Utah War.

The Utah War was an expensive conflict for the United States. Referred to by some historians as the nation's first civil war, the conflict set Brigham Young, president of The Church of Jesus Christ of Latter-day Saints, against James Buchanan, president of the United States. It also aligned the Nauvoo Legion, Utah's territorial militia, against nearly one-third of the United States Army.[1]

Although the Utah War saw no military battles and ended peacefully, it was a catalyst for dramatic changes within the Church and the western region of the United States.

For the most part, the conflict was a result of poor communication and false charges against Church leadership in Utah. Federal officials, out of step with the people in Utah, fled from the territory in the early 1850s and spread rumors of rebellion in the valleys of the West. Believing the rumors and with almost no investigation, United States president James Buchanan sent an armed expedition to subdue the territory.

President Buchanan delivered a blistering message to the Congress in December 1857, informing the legislative body of Brigham Young's "absolute [power] over both church and State." Agitated by reports of the "fanatical spirit" of citizens in Utah Territory, Buchanan speculated that if Brigham's "government shall come into collision with the government of the United States, the members of the Mormon Church will yield implicit obedience to his will."[2]

With sentiment running strong against Mormon leadership in Utah, Illinois senator Stephen A. Douglas declared in 1857, "When the authentic evidence shall arrive, if it shall establish the facts [about Utah] which are believed to exist, it will become the duty of Congress to apply the knife and cut out this loathsome, disgusting ulcer."[3]

Buchanan's moves met with mixed support from the Congress, and he ordered the Utah Expedition to depart during a congressional recess.[4] In April 1857 President Buchanan ordered a force of 2,500 military personnel to escort Alfred Cumming, the newly appointed territorial governor, to Utah.

The Utah Expedition was sent west without so much as a committee investigating whether a rebellion was really taking place. When Captain Stewart Van Vliet arrived in Salt Lake City, Brigham Young confronted him: "Congress has promptly sent investigating committees to Kansas and other places, as occasion has required; but upon the merest rumor it has sent 2,000 armed soldiers to destroy the people of Utah, without investigating the subject at all."[5]

Captain Van Vliet believed the Mormons had the upper hand when it came to the anticipated conflict. The narrow mountain passes that led to the Salt Lake Valley formed a natural fortress, and Brigham Young announced in a Speptember 1857 sermon the Mormon strategy in the impending conflict. Captain Van Vliet, attending the sermon, wrote to his superiors, "Their plan of operations will be, burn up the grass, cut up the roads, and stampede the animals, so as to delay the troops until snow commences to fall, which will render the road impassable."[6] Van Vliet's assessment was a fair summary of the Nauvoo Legion's proposed plan of defense.

Throughout the summer and fall of 1857, a contingent of the Legion, commanded by Lot Smith, harassed Johnston's Army and delayed its approach to the Salt Lake Valley. The most dramatic encounter took place on October 4, 1857. The captain of a wagon train contracted to carry supplies to the army was confronted by Smith and his raiders. Upon learning that Smith planned to burn the supply wagons, he exclaimed, "For God's sake don't burn the trains!" To which Smith replied, "It was for His sake I was going to burn them."[7]

Raids and bad weather hampered the progress of the army across the high plains. The army expected to winter on the edge of Utah Territory at Fort Bridger but found the fort a smoldering pile of ashes due to the work of Smith's raiders. Johnston, his soldiers, and Governor Cumming settled in for a miserable winter. In the meantime, Lot Smith and his raiders ranged about, pillaging government supplies. Other Mormon soldiers dug in on the rim of Echo Canyon to guard the entry to the Salt Lake Valley.

The first sign of hope for a peaceful resolution came that winter. Thomas L. Kane, a long-standing non-Mormon friend of the Latter-day Saints, and John M. Bernhisel, the congressional delegate of the Utah Territory, negotiated in the nation's capital for a settlement before blood was shed. At a meeting with President Buchanan on Christmas Day 1857, Kane was allowed to seek a peaceful resolution between the opposing military forces.[8]

Wanting to avoid snowy mountain passes, Kane traveled by sea to Panama, crossed the isthmus overland, and then sailed to San Francisco. From there, he journeyed to Utah. Brigham Young was so moved at seeing the "very pale and worn down" Kane that he pronounced a blessing upon him: "Brother Thomas, the Lord sent you here and he will not let you die. No, you cannot until your work is done. I want you to have your name live with the Saints to all eternity. You have done a great work and you will do a greater work still."[9]

After conferring with Church leaders, Kane journeyed to the army's camp, arriving on

DID YOU KNOW?

• The Utah conflict pitted a small territorial militia against nearly one-third of the United States Army.

• Thomas L. Kane, a nonmember friend to the Church, nearly wore himself out negotiating a truce between the two parties.

March 12, 1858. He was greeted with skepticism by the army commander and the soldiers who had spent the winter languishing in the cold. A series of misunderstandings led Kane to challenge Johnston to a duel. Fortunately, the duel was called off, and Kane convinced Governor Cumming to accompany him to Salt Lake City without a large military escort. As Kane and Cumming passed through Echo Canyon, bonfires were lit on both sides of the canyon by Nauvoo Legion forces. By the time Kane and Cummings arrived in the valley, they were convinced the defenders in Echo Canyon numbered far beyond their previous estimates.[10]

A settlement was reached when Brigham Young agreed to step down as governor and allow the army to enter Utah Territory as long as the troops did not occupy Salt Lake City. But before the army arrived, Brigham took precautions to ensure the safety of his people by ordering thousands of Latter-day Saints residing in Salt Lake City to relocate to Utah Valley and other points south.

When the army arrived in Salt Lake City, they found the settlement abandoned except for a small force ready to burn the settlement if given the command. Johnston and his soldiers marched through the city and on to Cedar Valley, about forty miles southwest. There the army built Camp Floyd and remained there until the outbreak of the Civil War.

The Utah War effectively ended the period of theodemocracy—civil and ecclesiastical government united under Brigham Young's leadership.[11] Alfred Cumming proved to be a fair and just governor of the Utah Territory. He returned to his home in Georgia at the outbreak of the Civil War, and the army was ordered back to the eastern states.

The heroic efforts of Thomas L. Kane averted a potentially bloody conflict. Though the army and the Saints found a peaceful way to resolve the conflict in the winter of 1857–58, the struggle between the United States federal government and the Church lasted for decades afterward.

Notes

1. Richard D. Poll and William P. MacKinnon, "Causes of the Utah War Reconsidered," *Journal of Mormon History* 20, no. 2 (Fall 1994): 17.
2. James Buchanan, in Thomas G. Alexander, "Carpetbaggers, Reprobates, and Liars: Federal Judges and the Utah War (1857–58)," *Historian*, Summer 2008, 210.
3. MacKinnon, *At Sword's Point*, 136.
4. MacKinnon, *At Sword's Point*, 137.
5. Poll and MacKinnon, "Causes of the Utah War Reconsidered," 21–22.
6. Hafen and Hafen, *Mormon Resistance*, 53.
7. "Narrative of Lot Smith," in Hafen and Hafen, *Mormon Resistance*, 222.
8. See Grow, *Liberty to the Downtrodden*, 149–206.
9. Kenney, *Wilford Woodruff's Journal*, 5:168–70.
10. Whitney, *History of Utah*, 1:672. See Grow, *"Liberty to the Downtrodden,"* 176–87.
11. Patrick Q. Mason, "God and the People: Theodemocracy in Nineteenth-Century Mormonism," *Journal of Church and State*, Winter 2015, 2.

48
The Mountain Meadows Massacre

Monument to the victims of the Mountain Meadows Massacre, Washington County, Utah.

1857

The Mountain Meadows Massacre took place against the backdrop of hysteria that surrounded the approach of the Johnston's army during the so-called Utah War. The basic facts of the massacre are these: A contingent of the Utah Territorial Militia, all Latter-day Saints, were assisted by a group of Native Americans in slaughtering members of an emigrant wagon train. Of approximately 120 men, women, and children, only seventeen children under age six were spared.[1]

Different versions of the atrocity have circulated for decades, with blame being laid on various groups and individuals. The massacre still haunts the public image of Latter-day Saints and raises a number of troubling questions for Latter-day Saints. How did such a horrific act take place? What factors led to the senseless slaughter? How were the perpetrators, most of whom lived exemplary lives before and after the massacre, convinced to take part in it?

The name of the wagon train was the Fancher party. This company consisted primarily of families from Arkansas who had banded together to journey to California. The Fancher wagon train arrived in the Salt Lake Valley in the summer of 1857, just as tensions over the approaching army reached a peak. As the train took a southward route through Utah Territory, a number of unfortunate incidents contributed to the animosity between the Fancher party and Mormon settlers. An allegation that the Fancher party deliberately poisoned a dead cow, which led to the death of an Indian near Corn Creek (present-day Kanosh) heightened Mormon fears. While the exact cause of the Indian's death is still unknown, scholars reinvestigating the circumstances of the massacre, have pointed to an outbreak of anthrax, a deadly virus found in westward wagon trains in the summer of 1857.[2]

Tensions continued to escalate as the emigrants traveled southward, boiling over at a stop in Cedar City. Tempers flared when local mill operators demanded a cow in return for grinding the emigrants' grain—an exorbitant price. Men in the Fancher party railed against the Mormon businessmen and threatened to join the approaching army and return to Cedar City to exact their revenge. According to one account, emigrants boasted that "they had helped to Kill Joseph Smith . . . and other Mormons at Nauvoo & Missouri, and that . . . they would kill some more yet."[3] Captain Fancher reprimanded these men and tried to mend relationships with the Mormons.

From Cedar City, the Fancher party moved on to Mountain Meadows, a well-known stop on the California trail. Isaac Haight, stake president and mayor of Cedar City, ordered local militia to find the emigrants and chasten them for their words. Some accounts suggest that Haight encouraged the militia to take the cattle of the Fancher party as compensation for their threats. Haight's request was soundly rejected by William Dame, commander of the local militia and stake president in nearby Parowan.

Undeterred, Haight and other leaders in Cedar City hatched a new plan, more sinister in its calculations. Their plan was to persuade the local Paiute Indians to ambush the Fancher party encamped at Mountain Meadows, kill some or all of the men, and take the cattle by force. To carry out the new plan, leaders enlisted the help of John D. Lee, a militia major with jurisdiction over the area where the attack was to take place.

At first the Paiutes showed reluctance to take part in the attack, but Lee persuaded them to agree. When all was in place, Haight presented the plan to a council of local leaders. The cold-blooded nature of the planned attack set off a sharp debate. The council asked if Haight had consulted Brigham Young on the matter, to which Haight replied he had not. Haight agreed to send a messenger to Salt Lake City to seek counsel.

The next day, however, just before the messenger departed to consult with Brigham Young, John D. Lee and a group of Paiutes attacked the wagon train at Mountain Meadows.[4] Several emigrants were killed in the first ambush. The survivors fought off the attackers, some of whom were white men disguised as Paiutes. The emigrants circled their wagons and took up defensive positions. Attacks continued, and both sides settled in for what was to be a five-day siege.

Events worsened when two Cedar City militiamen fired on two riders in the Fancher party who were outside the defensive corral of the encampment. One rider escaped and informed the emigrants of seeing white men in the attacks, not just Indians. With the militia's collaboration in the attacks known, the scheme began to collapse. Haight, Lee, and the other leaders realized the possible consequences if the army learned of Mormon involvement in attacks on the California-bound emigrant train.

A council was held in Parowan to explain the situation to President William Dame and other local leaders. Dame called for men to volunteer to help the emigrants move along to California. After the council meeting, Haight and one of his counselors met with Dame privately and told him that the emigrants most likely knew militiamen were involved in the attacks. They told Dame most of the emigrants were already dead and asked for his permission to silence the survivors. Dame reluctantly consented. Haight then gathered as many militiamen as possible and left for Cedar City.

On Friday, September 11, 1856, John D. Lee approached the emigrant train under a flag of truce. He convinced the emigrants that the Utah militia was interceding to end the attacks and that the militia would provide an escort to safety, providing the emigrants laid down their weapons. Soon afterward, the emigrants filed out of the wagon corral—women, children, and the wounded first, the men following with militia escorts. After they had walked roughly a mile, a signal was given and militiamen turned and killed the emigrant nearest them. At the same time, Indians arose from their hiding places and attacked, murdering women and children. When the slaughter ended a few minutes later, all of the Fancher party had been killed except for seventeen children deemed too young to be witnesses against the militia for the atrocity.[5]

James Haslam, the messenger sent to Brigham Young, returned to Cedar City two days after the Mountain Meadows massacre. He carried a letter from the Church President, which read in part, "In regard to emigration trains passing through our settlements, we must not interfere with them until they are first notified to keep away. You must not meddle with them . . . let them go in peace." When Haight received the message he broke into sobs, repeating the words, "Too late, too late."[6]

In the months and years that followed, attempts were made to assign responsibility for the massacre to the Native Americans involved in the incident. Some historians blamed the deaths on Brigham Young, though much evidence contradicts this theory. The chief architects of the massacre swore a vow of silence and argued over how to report the crime to the Church President. Eventually, John D. Lee reported the massacre to Brigham Young but in so

doing lied about the collaboration of the Utah militia. When militiaman Nephi Johnson was brought before Brigham, he recalled, "While I was relating it to him he walked the floor, and was deeply impressed by the statement, and several times said why did Lee lie to me?"[7]

Lee was later indicted for the crimes, convicted, and executed. Before his death, however, Lee wrote a salacious memoir accusing Brigham Young of involvement in the massacre. When historians Ronald W. Walker, Richard E. Turley, and Glen M. Leonard published a detailed study on the massacre in 2008, they set aside Lee's memoir because of inconsistencies and "the cumulative effect of other sources [that] contradicted it."[8]

The massacre has cast a dark shadow over southern Utah for decades. Juanita Brooks, one of the first Latter-day Saint historians to approach this difficult story, was driven to research by whispered stories of the killings she had heard in her childhood. One of Brooks' earliest memories was being at the deathbed of a former militiaman, who screamed, "Blood! BLOOD! BLOOD!" shortly before his passing.[9]

Brooks and others who brought the story of the massacre to light deserve credit for their efforts to lay to rest the disturbing events of September 11, 1857. At an event commemorating the sesquicentennial of the massacre, President Henry B. Eyring offered these words of reconciliation:

"The gospel of Jesus Christ that we espouse abhors the cold-blooded killing of men, women, and children. Indeed, it advocates peace and forgiveness. What was done [at Mountain Meadows] long ago by members of our Church represents a terrible and inexcusable departure from Christian teaching and conduct. We cannot change what happened, but we can remember and honor those who were killed here."[10]

DID YOU KNOW?

- A combined force of Mormon militiamen and Native Americans massacred members of the Fancher party, a wagon train traveling across Utah Territory.

- The seventeen survivors of the massacre were all under the age of six years.

Notes

1. Walker et al., *Massacre at Mountain Meadows*, 208–9.
2. Walker et al., *Massacre*, 121–23.
3. Walker et al., *Massacre* 132–33.
4. See "Peace and Violence among 19th Century Latter-day Saints," lds.org.
5. Walker et al., *Massacre at Mountain Meadows*, 208–9. The children lived with nearby settlers for a time, before being returned to their next of kin during the investigations of the massacre. See Moorman, *Camp Floyd and the Mormons*, 123–40.
6. Walker et al., *Massacre*, 226.
7. Nephi Johnson's 1908 statement, in "Selections from the David H. Morris Collection," *BYU Studies* 47, no. 3 (2008): 141.
8. Walker et al., *Massacre*, xxii.
9. Peterson, *Juanita Brooks*, 41.
10. Henry B. Eyring, in "150th Anniversary of Mountain Meadows Massacre," Sept. 11, 2007, mormonnewsroom.org.

49
The Retrenchment Movement

Ten of Brigham Young's daughters.

1867

Linking the railroads across North America in 1869 led some of the Church's enemies to project the end of the Latter-day Saints. Elder George Q. Cannon noted in 1868: "We are told—openly and without disguise, that when the railroad is completed there will be such a flood of so-called 'civilization' brought in here that every vestige of us, our church and our institutions, shall be completely obliterated."[1]

When the question of the approaching railroad was raised to Brigham Young, he replied, "[Mormonism] must indeed be a ——— poor religion, if it cannot stand one railroad."[2]

Before the gold and silver spikes were driven in the railroad tracks at Promontory Summit, Utah, steps were taken to strengthen Latter-day Saints against outside influences, a movement generally labeled "retrenchment." In 1867 Eliza R. Snow, acting under Brigham Young's direction, reestablished the Relief Society as the women's organization in the Church.[3] Relief Society had ceased to function after the death of Joseph Smith, the evacuation of Nauvoo, and the trek to the American West. Although small Relief Societies had been formed in Salt Lake City during the 1850s, most were quickly abandoned with the threat of invasion by Johnston's army and the Utah war. The reestablishment of Relief Society signaled a new permanent and prominent role for the organization.

The revitalized Relief Society in 1867 led directly to the Retrenchment Association being organized two years later.[4] At a family meeting held in his home in Salt Lake City on November 28, 1869, Brigham Young spoke to his family about his concern over worldly trends. "All Israel are looking to my family and watching the example set by my wives and children," Brigham said. "For this reason I desire to organize my own family first into a society for the promotion of habits of order, thrift, industry, and charity; and above all I desire to retrench them from their extravagance in dress in eating and even in speech." He then spoke of his larger vision:

"I have long had it in my mind to organize the young ladies of Zion into an association so that they might assist the older members of the Church, their fathers and mothers, in propagating, teaching, and practicing the principles I have been so long teaching. There is need for the young daughters of Israel to get a living testimony of the truth. . . . We are about to organize a Retrenchment Association, which I want you all to join."[5]

A few weeks after the family meeting, the first Retrenchment Association was organized. The aims of the new organization were, first, to "not condescend to imitate the pride, folly and fashions of the world" and second, to "set examples for others, instead of seeking to pattern after them."[6] Twenty-three-year-old Ella Young Empey was selected as the first president of the Retrenchment Association.

Within the first year of her leadership, chapters of the Retrenchment Association were organized in nearly every ward in Salt Lake City, with additional chapters in nearby Ogden, Logan, Provo, Bountiful, and Brigham City. The overarching parent association was called the Senior and Junior Cooperative Retrenchment Association. Adult women participated in the "Senior Retrenchment Association," and young women participated in "Junior Retrenchment."[7] This organization influenced thousands of young Latter-day Saint women in the Intermountain West.

An important convert to the value of this organization was Junius F. Wells, a son of Daniel H. Wells of the First Presidency. At the time, Junius Wells was a returned missionary with a burning desire to provide better preparation for young men planning to serve missions. One of the most painful moments on his own mission to England came when he first spoke at an LDS branch in Liverpool. "It took the president of the branch several minutes to introduce me," Wells recalled, "but it took me just one and one-quarter minutes to say all that I knew."[8]

Upon returning to Salt Lake City, Elder Wells was called upon to speak on missionary preparation at several ward meetings. In this process, he noted the effect of the Retrenchment Association on young women, and he met with Eliza R. Snow to learn more about it. Soon after his meeting with Sister Snow, his father Daniel H. Wells presented him with a directive from Brigham Young: "The President wants you to organize the young men."[9]

Junius Wells met with Brigham Young, who advised, "We want them to hold meetings where they will stand up and speak—get into the habit of speaking—and of bearing testimony. These meetings are to be for our young men, to be composed of young men for their improvement—for their mutual improvement—a society of young men for mutual improvement." President Young then bestowed a name on the new association: "The Young Men's Mutual Improvement . . . Association" (YMMIA).[10]

At the founding meeting of the YMMIA in the Salt Lake Thirteenth Ward, Brother Wells emphasized the success of the Retrenchment Association, saying, "Sister Snow and those associated with her have organized the young ladies, and their labors have been crowned with success." He asked the young men, "How many of you, my young brethren, realize the responsibility of seeking unto God, to know for yourselves that what your parents have taught you is of God?" In short, he declared, "We need the cultivation of the heart as well as of the mind."[11]

In the months that followed, Wells journeyed throughout the settlements in Utah Territory, organizing branches of the YMMIA. In 1877, when Brigham Young and other Church leaders carried out a reorganization of all stakes and wards, a directive was

DID YOU KNOW?

• The retrenchment movement led to the reconstitution of Relief Society, with Eliza R. Snow as general president.

• The creation of the young women's and young men's organizations likewise grew out of the retrenchment movement.

sent to all wards to establish a branch of the YMMIA and the Retrenchment Association. Brigham Young asked that the Retrenchment Association be known as the Young Ladies' Mutual Improvement Association.[12]

In the decades that followed, "Mutual" became the standard program for young Latter-day Saint men and women. Author Wallace Stegner, a non-Mormon who attended Mutual as a young man growing up in Salt Lake City, wrote of the importance of the organization in the lives of young Latter-day Saints:

"The social life of Mormondom is centered in the Ward House as surely as the religious life is, and every Mormon child from the age of twelve upward is a member of . . . the M.I.A., or Mutual. . . . Designed as a faith-promoting scheme among the young people, the M.I.A. is in practice a highly developed youth movement. . . . All the way from hikes, outings, picnics, swimming parties, and hayrides to movies, dances, community singing, amateur theatricals, and athletic contests, the M.I.A. is the orbit within which the young Saint's life moves."[13]

The reinstitution of Relief Society, along with the fruits of the retrenchment movement and the creation of the Young Men's Mutual Improvement Association, resulted in three enduring and important auxiliaries in the Church.

As Latter-day Saints seek to fortify themselves against the growing influence of a worldly society, the strategies employed by Church leaders to meet the challenges of a world brought closer by the coming of the railroad to Utah are still relevant today.

NOTES

1. George Q. Cannon, in *Journal of Discourses,* 12:290.
2. Bowles, *Our New West,* 260.
3. Carol Cornwall Madsen, "Retrenchment Association," in Ludlow, *Encyclopedia of Mormonism,* 3:1223–24.
4. Derr et al., *First Fifty Years of Relief Society,* 236–37.
5. Gates, *History of the Young Ladies' Mutual Improvement Association,* 9.
6. Gates, *History,* 11.
7. Gates, *History,* 36–37.
8. Gates, *History,* 81.
9. Gates, *History,* 81.
10. Junius F. Wells, "Historic Sketch of the Y.M.M.I.A.," *Improvement Era,* June 1925, 715.
11. Wells, "Historic Sketch of the Y.M.M.I.A.," 717.
12. Gates, *History,* 83–84. The name was changed to the Young Women's Mutual Improvement Association in 1934 and simplified to Young Women in 1974 (Peterson and Gaunt, *Keepers of the Flame,* xiii).
13. Stegner, *Mormon Country,* 16, 18, in Janet Peterson, "Young Women of Zion: An Organizational History," in Whittaker and Garr, *Firm Foundation,* 284.

50
The Trial of George Reynolds

1874

George Reynolds, secretary to the First Presidency and defendant in legal case testing the legality of plural marriage.

After the public announcement of plural marriage in 1852, opposition to the practice was heightened in the United States. During elections of the late 1850s, both Republican and Democratic parties had anti-polygamy platforms that proposed new laws to outlaw the practice. The 1856 Republican platform categorized polygamy and slavery as the "twin relics of barbarism."[1]

Although the outbreak of the American

Civil War focused the attention of the nation at large on slavery, ending polygamy was also a top priority for American lawmakers. On July 8, 1862, President Abraham Lincoln signed the Morrill Anti-Bigamy Act, a law passed by the Congress specifically designed to punish and prevent plural marriages in the Utah Territory.

The issue was that Latter-day Saints viewed the practice of plural marriage as exercising their religious belief, and they believed the Morrill Anti-Bigamy Act violated the First Amendment to the United States Constitution, which guarantees that no laws will "[impede] the free exercise of religion."[2] Latter-day Saints viewed marriage as a religious and not a civil ordinance. The faithful felt a higher obligation to obey the commandments of God than an unjust federal law. The most immediate effect of the Anti-Bigamy Act was a marked increase in plural marriages in Utah, which suggests that Latter-day Saints wanted to preserve their right to practice plural marriage before the government intervened.[3]

The stage was set for a legal battle to determine the constitutionality of the Morrill Anti-Bigamy Act. Yet for several years, no action was taken. The federal government was embroiled in a civil war, and after the war, the reconstruction of the southern states. When enthusiasm for reconstruction ebbed, lawmakers turned to halting polygamy among the Mormons. Knowing the increasing federal pressure to end the practice of plural marriage, Church leaders decided to put forward a test case to establish the illegality of the Morrill Anti-Bigamy Act.[4]

In October 1874, after several weeks of discussion, thirty-year-old George Reynolds was asked to serve as the defendant in the test case.

Reynolds was a devout and faithful Latter-day Saint who worked as a bookkeeper and private secretary to several prominent Church leaders. Reynolds had married Amelia Jane Schofield as his second, plural wife only a few months earlier, in August 1874. In contrast to the popular images in the national press of wicked patriarchs ruling over scores of women, Reynolds was modest and unassuming, the opposite of the lecherous stereotypes of polygamists.

Latter-day Saint leaders hoped for a gentlemanly test case, but acrimony over the issue of polygamy ran high, and federal judges were anxious to mete out punishment. In February 1875 Brigham Young was sentenced to spend a night in prison on a charge of unlawful cohabitation. Accompanied by a hundred armed followers who were determined to protect him at all costs, President Young submitted to the authorities. His imprisonment sparked outrage among both Mormon and non-Mormon residents of Salt Lake City. The judge who had sentenced the elderly prophet was soon removed from his position.[5]

Conditions continued to deteriorate between Church leaders and government officials as the date for the trial of George Reynolds approached. The trial itself degenerated into a lurid and exploitive display, even though the defense argued that plural marriage was a religious rite and Reynolds, in entering his second marriage, was performing what he saw as a religious duty. The low point came when Reynolds' second wife, Amelia, obviously pregnant, was summoned before the court and compelled to admit her status as a plural wife of George Reynolds.

J. G. Sutherland, a defense attorney for Reynolds, argued, "They [the Mormons] believe it [polygamy] to be a divine institution, and they will be indebted for their highest happiness in another life to their fidelity and obedience to it in this."[6] Sutherland's argument failed to persuade the jury, and promises made to Reynolds by the prosecution were not kept. Reynolds was convicted and sentenced to one year of hard labor in the territorial penitentiary.

Reynolds and his legal team appealed to the Utah Territorial Supreme Court, who dismissed the case due to irregularities in the composition of the grand jury. In the fall of 1875 Reynolds was again indicted, convicted, and sentenced to two years of hard labor and imprisonment. Through the appeals process, the case against George Reynolds moved through the court system until it reached the Supreme Court of the United States.

In July 1879 the Supreme Court upheld Reynolds' conviction. That was a devastating blow to Church leaders. Chief Justice Morrison R. Waite delivered the opinion of the court: "Suppose one believed that human sacrifices were a necessary part of religious worship, would it be seriously contended that the civil government under which he lived could not interfere to prevent a sacrifice? Or if a wife religiously believed it was her duty to burn herself upon the funeral [pyre] of her dead husband, would it be beyond the power of the civil government to prevent her carrying her belief into practice?"[7]

The outcome of the Reynolds case has raised serious legal questions about the protections afforded by the First Amendment. Legal scholars Firmage and Mangrum wrote that Chief Justice Waite "concluded that the First Amendment protected only religious belief, not conduct. . . . Religion exists as much through the conduct of an individual as through belief, and conflict over freedom of religion will arise when the majority of any community is offended by the specific practices of a minority. . . . Thus, unless at least some practices for the majority are protected by the First Amendment, the free exercise clause is redundant, and devoid of practical content."[8]

When asked about the decision, George Reynolds said, "I regard [the decision] a nullification of the Constitution, so far as religious liberty is concerned. To say the Constitution simply grants freedom of religious opinion but not the exercise of that opinion is twaddle."[9]

Reynolds submitted himself to the authorities and spent eighteen months in deplorable conditions in penitentiaries in Nebraska and Utah. He passed his time in prison preparing the first concordance of the Book of Mormon. He was spoken of among the Saints as "a living martyr to the cause of Zion" and a "representative prisoner suffering for the conscientious faith of the whole people."[10]

For the Latter-day Saints, the outcome of the Reynolds case set the stage for a serious conflict escalation between the Church and the federal government.[11] In the wake of the Reynolds decision, President John Taylor said, "Our revelation given in August, 1831, specifically states that if we keep the laws of God we

need not break the laws of the land. Congress has since, by the act placed us in an antagonism to what we term an unconstitutional law, and now it becomes a question of whether we should obey God or man."[12]

The conflicts eventually ended when the practice of plural marriage ceased in the Church, but not before thousands among the Saints suffered and many were imprisoned on account of their faith.

Notes

1. Gordon, *Mormon Question,* 57.
2. "First Amendment," Cornell University Law School Legal Information Institute.
3. Daynes, *More Wives Than One,* 102–3.
4. See Van Orden, *Prisoner for Conscience' Sake,* 58–65.
5. Van Orden, *Prisoner for Conscience' Sake,* 67; Arrington, *American Moses,* 372; Roberts, *Comprehensive History,* 5:445–46.
6. Van Orden, *Prisoner for Conscience' Sake,* 70.
7. Reynolds v. United States, Supreme Court of the United States, 98 U.S. 145, Oct. 1878, 166, in Firmage and Mangrum, *Zion in the Courts,* 155.
8. Firmage and Mangrum, *Zion in the Courts,* 155.
9. "Interview of W. Cox with George Reynolds," manuscript in George Reynolds Papers, L. Tom Perry Special Collections, Harold B. Lee Library, Brigham Young University, Provo, Utah, in Van Orden, *Prisoner for Conscience' Sake,* 88.
10. Junius F. Wells, "A Living Martyr," *Contributor,* Feb. 1881, 154; "Biography of George Reynolds," Perry Special Collections, Lee Library, 18–19; Van Orden, *Prisoner for Conscience' Sake,* 93, 106–7.
11. Firmage and Mangrum, *Zion in the Courts,* 156–59.
12. Taylor, in Van Orden, *Prisoner for Conscience' Sake,* 87. The revelation referred to by President Taylor is D&C 58:21; see Godfrey et al., *Documents,* 2:15–16, or josephsmithpapers.org.

51
The St. George Temple Is Dedicated

The St. George Utah Temple.

1877

In a place that George A. Smith, counselor to Brigham Young, described as "the most wretched, barren, god-forsaken country in the world" stands the oldest and longest operating temple in the Church.[1] Wilford Woodruff was called as its first president, the first temple president in this dispensation. In that temple the first endowments for the dead and other ordinances were performed for the founding fathers of the United States and other noble and great men and women of ages past.[2]

On January 31, 1871, at a meeting of the St. George School of the Prophets, Brigham Young asked, "What [are your thoughts] of building a temple in St. George?" Erastus Snow instantly responded, "Glory! Hallelujah!!"[3]

Elder Bruce C. Hafen noted what would be required of the people of the region to built a temple: "Brigham Young knew that the 1,100 Saints that lived there were in extreme poverty. . . . But he also knew of their willingness to sacrifice."[4] On November 5, 1871, Latter-day Saints in the St. George area voted to sustain President Young's decision to build a temple.

Four days later, on November 9, after Brigham Young had lifted the first shovelful of dirt at the temple site, the dedicatory prayer was offered by President George A. Smith: "May Thy peace be upon the pioneers of this desert and upon all those who have labored to reclaim the same: may eternal blessings rest upon them and their posterity forever."[5]

Brigham Young assigned architect Truman O. Angell to design the St. George Temple with an outside measurement of 142 feet by 96 feet. President Young asked Angell to pattern the temple after the Kirtland and Nauvoo temples with two large assembly halls with pulpits representing the Aaronic and the Melchizedek Priesthood. Angell worked to create architectural drawings, and Elder Erastus Snow of the Quorum of the Twelve and construction superintendent Miles Romney worked to find laborers and building materials for the temple. Many men gave one day in ten to work on the temple as tithing labor, and some four hundred men from northern settlements labored as temple missionaries. Others "worked on the temple for wages, receiving pay half in cash and half in Tithing Office checks." To meet the expense of the laborers, President Young allotted all tithes from the Saints living south of Beaver, Utah, for the building of the temple.[6]

Progress on the temple was slow. The turnover of workers was an issue, but nothing compared to the issue of underground water that needed to be channeled away from the temple site. To solve the problem of wet soil, laborers quarried and hauled volcanic rock to the temple site. The rock was pounded into the ground with an old cannon barrel filled with lead that was hoisted thirty feet in the air and then dropped. It took two years of quarrying, hauling, and pounding volcanic rock into the soil to complete the foundation and the basement. Yet, laborers were not discouraged.

Supervisor Milo Andrus wrote, "There are over one hundred men engaged directly on the ground: over one hundred men working in the quarry, and over forty men at Mount Trumbull getting out the lumber. In addition some men are on the road for the purpose of getting, wood, coal, etc." Wanting to provide for these laborers, President George A. Smith exhorted the Saints to "remember the brethren who are laboring on the Temple at St. George. . . . some of them are destitute of clothing, and other necessaries."[7]

By April 1874 most of the laborers were erecting the red sandstone walls. Others worked on the baptismal room in the basement and the oxen to support the baptismal font. Although progress was evident at every turn, George A. Smith said of Brigham Young, "You cannot realize . . . how anxious he is to get this temple completed. He feels he is getting old, and is liable to drop off anytime, and he has keys he wants to give in the temple."[8]

President Young watched as plasterers and painters put a coat of white over the sandstone as a symbol of purity and light. He knew that immigrant artists from Norway and Denmark—Dan Weggeland, C. C. A. Christensen, and Samuel Jepperson—were painting murals to adorn the temple and thousands of wagonloads of rich soil were being hauled to the temple site so that the barren ground could support vegetation.[9]

When everything was in readiness for the dedicatory services, President George Q. Cannon and other Church leaders traveled to St. George for the occasion. Upon seeing the temple, President Cannon wrote, "When we saw it, it stood out in bold relief and in marked contrast with the black and red hills which surround the little valley in which St. George stands. . . . It excited peculiar emotions in all the parties to witness once more a temple erected to the Most High God."[10]

A private dedication was held on January 1, 1877, for parts of the temple. On that day temple president and apostle Wilford Woodruff wrote, "This is a very important day to the Church and Kingdom of God upon the Earth."[11]

As Brigham Young walked to the stand to speak to the assembled, "the house seemed filled with a heavenly host and the President's face fairly shone with the light of the Holy Ghost."[12]

Brigham said, "All the angels in heaven are looking at this little handful of people. Can the fathers be saved without us? No. Can we be saved without them? No."[13]

DID YOU KNOW?

- The St. George Utah Temple is the oldest temple in operation in the Church.

- The first endowments for the dead were performed in the St. George Temple.

He asked if those in attendance thought he was satisfied with the temple. He responded, "I am not half satisfied, until I have whipped . . . the devils from off this earth."[14] He then crashed his hickory cane down on the pine pulpit.

After the ceremony, the Saints began to leave the temple but stopped when President Young advised, "Sit down and calm yourselves and let the devil roar."[15] When they did leave the temple, they found their buggies had been upset and trees blown down in a terrible windstorm.

On April 6, 1877, a processional to the St. George Temple marked the day of dedication. Two men carried Brigham on a chair through the temple doors to the waiting crowd. President Daniel H. Wells offered the dedicatory prayer and said, "We now dedicate and consecrate it to Thee that it may be holy unto Thee the Lord our God, for sacred and holy purposes."[16]

The temple in St. George stands today as a house of the Lord and as a monument to the courageous pioneers of nearly a century and a half ago who labored to build it.[17] They heeded Brigham Young's advice: "This is a desert country, but it is a splendid place to rear Saints."[18] With the dedication of the temple, the great work to redeem the dead began anew.

Notes

1. Jace Whatcott, "Brigham Young, Wilford Woodruff, and the St. George Temple," *LDS Church News*, July 3, 2015.
2. Cowan, *Temples to Dot the Earth*, 78–80.
3. James G. Bleak, "Annals of the Southern Utah Mission, Book B, 81–82," in Yorgason et al., *All That Was Promised*, 80.
4. Whatcott, "Brigham Young, Wilford Woodruff, and the St. George Temple."
5. George A. Smith, in Yorgason et al., *All That Was Promised*, 91–92.
6. "The St. George Temple: One Hundred Years of Service," *Ensign,* Mar. 1977, 92–93.
7. Smith, in *Journal of Discourses*, 17:163–64.
8. George A. Smith, in Robert Gardner Journal, in Carter, *Heartthrobs of the West*, 10:321.
9. "St. George Temple," 94.
10. Bitton, *George Q. Cannon*, 201.
11. Woodruff Journal, Jan. 1, 1877, in Yorgason et al., *All That Was Promised*, 268.
12. "St. George Temple," 94.
13. Young, in *Journal of Discourses*, 18:303–5.
14. "St. George Temple," 94.
15. Maggie Cragun Interview, "Dedication of the St. George Temple," WPA Federal Writers' Project Collection, Library of Congress, Manuscript Division, Washington, D.C.
16. See Daniel H. Wells dedicatory remarks, in Kirk M. Curtis, "History of the St. George Temple," master's thesis, Brigham Young University (1964), 992–96.
17. Cowan, *Temples to Dot the Earth*, 77–80.
18. Bleak, "Annals of the Southern Utah Mission, Book B, 182," in Yorgason et al., *All That Was Promised*, 88.

52
Brigham Young Restructures Church Organization

1877

Brigham Young's winter home in St. George, Utah.

The last great work of Brigham Young's life was a reorganization of the Quorum of the Twelve Apostles and a realignment of thirteen stakes (to make twenty), 101 wards (to make 241), hundreds of priesthood quorums, and more than a thousand leadership positions.[1] It was a work that affected all the quorums in the Church, from the general authorities to the ward priesthood quorums.[2] George Q. Cannon, a counselor in the First Presidency, recalled that Brigham Young "seemed to be anxious and restless until he had thoroughly organized the Church."[3] In large measure, the priesthood reorganization of 1875 to 1877 led to the current operational structure of the Church.

Most of the reorganization took place in the last five months of Brigham Young's life, but his first step was taken in 1875 to clarify seniority in the Twelve. In June 1875 two apostles, Orson Hyde and Orson Pratt, were serving as the senior members of the Twelve. Both had been excommunicated during Joseph Smith's presidency, but both had also been returned to their earlier positions in the quorum, even though others had been called to the Twelve during their absence from it. After discussing the matter with the Quorum of the Twelve Apostles, President Young determined to reorganize seniority according to the length of uninterrupted service within the Twelve. His decision placed John Taylor, Wilford Woodruff, and George A. Smith ahead of Elders Hyde and Pratt, with John Taylor as president of the Twelve. In so doing, President Young clarified the process for succession in the presidency of the Church.

In 1876 Brigham clarified the relationship of stakes to one another. He stated that the Salt Lake Stake did not hold a special "center stake" status over the other stakes but that all stakes were equal. Stakes that had grown too large were split. Brigham felt strongly that more concentrated and localized priesthood units would better serve the steadily increasing Church population. He presided at nine of the reorganizing conferences, beginning with that of the St. George Stake.

When the stake reorganizations were complete, the number of stakes had been increased from thirteen to twenty. President Young released members of the Twelve who were also serving as stake presidents, reminding them of their service as general Church officers and giving instruction that they were not to be encumbered with local assignments.[4]

To assure the clarity of this change and others in the restructuring, the First Presidency sent an epistle explaining the purpose of the reorganization, teaching principles governing priesthood quorums, and giving an array of instructions. The instructions were so extensive that some consider this First Presidency epistle a forerunner to the handbook used by Church leaders today. Historian William G. Hartley characterized the epistle as "the most comprehensive policy statement about priesthood practices since the Doctrine and Covenants was first published."[5]

Many practices outlined in the epistle are taken for granted today as standard practices in the Church. For instance, the epistle called for bishoprics to be composed of three high priests—the bishop and two counselors. Before that time, the makeup of bishoprics was somewhat haphazard, with a number of creative configurations. Some locations had acting bishops who had not been properly ordained as high priests or had only one counselor, and in some cases counselors were serving in bishoprics without having been ordained high priests.[6]

The epistle instructed priesthood quorums to follow the numerical size for quorums stated in the Doctrine and Covenants—ninety-six elders, forty-eight priests, twenty-four teachers, and twelve deacons. The epistle directed that young men be ordained to Aaronic Priesthood offices. Furthermore, parents were instructed to send their children to Sunday School. Each ward bishopric was to organize a Mutual Improvement Association for young men and women. Better record keeping was emphasized: minutes were to be taken of Church meetings and reports made by wards and stakes. Many wards did not have records before 1877, though some wards had existed since the 1850s.

The First Presidency epistle also directed that "all members are to be enrolled in a ward or a branch, visited regularly, and brought to repentance when necessary."[7] This meant that every Latter-day Saint was to be assigned to a geographical congregation with a priesthood leader assigned to watch over them. The action made wards the primary units of the Church.

Although wards had existed as organizational units beginning in Nauvoo, outside of temporal needs the ward structure had been underused. Now ward meetings became the primary gathering place for Latter-day Saints. When the reorganization began, there were 101 wards in the Church. By the end of the summer of 1877, 140 new wards had been organized, a hundred new bishops ordained, and another eighty-five acting bishops, or presiding elders, called. Of the 241 bishops serving, 185 (or three of every four), were called during the brief period of reorganization.[8]

Brigham Young presided over his last reorganization meeting on August 19, 1877—just ten days before his death. By the end of the restructuring, he had put in place a change un-paralleled in importance since the restoration of the priesthood nearly fifty years earlier. It was unmatched in its scope and significance until the beginnings of Church Correlation in the 1960s.

After Brigham's death, George Q. Cannon summarized what the venerable "Lion of the Lord" had accomplished in his final months:

"He set the priesthood in order as it has never before been since the first organization of the church upon the earth. He defined the duties of the apostles, he defined the duties of the seventies, he defined the duties of the high priests, the duties of the elders and those of the lesser priesthood, with plainness and dis-tinction and power—the power of God—in a way that is left on record in such unmistakable language that no one need err who has the Spirit of God resting down upon him."[9]

NOTES

1. Arrington, *Brigham Young,* 398; Orton and Slaughter, *40 Ways to Look at Brigham Young,* 258.
2. Allen and Leonard, *Story of the Latter-day Saints,* 380.
3. William G. Hartley, "The Priesthood Reorgani-zation of 1877: Brigham Young's Last Achieve-ment," in Hartley, *My Fellow Servants,* 237.
4. Hartley, "Priesthood Reorganization," 229.
5. Hartley, "Priesthood Reorganization," 244.
6. Hartley, "Priesthood Reorganization," 230.
7. Hartley, "Priesthood Reorganization," 244.
8. Hartley, "Priesthood Reorganization," 257.
9. Roberts, *Comprehensive History of the Church,* 5:507.

53
The Beginning of the Primary Association

1878

Aurelia Spencer Rogers, founder of the Primary Association, which became the Church's organization for children.

The worldwide Primary Association traces its beginnings to Farmington, Utah. In 1878 Aurelia Spencer Rogers, a forty-four-year-old mother of twelve, was concerned about the delinquency of young boys in Farmington.[1] "Many of them were allowed to be out late at night," she remembered, "and certainly some of the larger ones well deserved the undesirable name of 'hoodlum.'"[2]

Bishop John W. Hess of the Farmington Ward shared her view and invited mothers to discuss with him ways to curb delinquent tendencies in their children. "A fire seemed to burn within me," Sister Rogers wrote. "Could there not be an organization for little boys wherein they could be taught everything good and how to behave"? She later added that little girls could also benefit, for an organization focused on the young wouldn't "be complete without them."[3]

Within weeks Sister Rogers found a receptive listener for her idea in Eliza R. Snow, general president of the Relief Society. Knowing that Sister Snow was "truly a woman of God" and that "the Lord had not given her children of her own, but her loving care was extended to all the dear children everywhere," Rogers explained to her the delinquency problem in Farmington.[4] Snow quickly grasped the situation and promised to discuss a possible children's organization with President John Taylor.

President Taylor was enthusiastic about forming such an organization. Following his counsel, Snow wrote to Rogers and invited her to begin an association "for the cultivation of the children in Zion" and suggested the name be "Primary." Snow added, "The angels and all holy beings especially the leaders of Israel on the other side of the veil will be deeply interested."[5]

After receiving Sister Snow's letter, Bishop Hess set Aurelia Spencer Rogers apart as the first president of Primary. As she began to function in her calling, she wrote, "I seemed to be carried away in the Spirit. . . . Nothing could worry or irritate me; if my little ones were fretful, or the work went wrong, I had patience, could control in kindness, and manage my household affairs easily. This was a testimony to me that what was being done was from God."[6]

Before the first children's meeting was held, Sister Rogers and her two counselors, Louisa L. Haight and Helen H. Miller, visited homes in Farmington in hopes of enrolling every child in Primary. Within weeks, they succeeded in enrolling 215 out of 224 children in town.[7]

On Sunday, August 25, 1878, the first Primary children's meeting was held in the Farmington Ward. The boys and girls sat in rows with the youngest children seated in the front. At the end of each row, an older child was strategically placed to monitor the younger children. On that occasion Rogers spoke of the purpose of Primary—to help children grow up to become good men and women. Brother Mads Christensen, a carpenter assigned to help the Primary presidency, then spoke briefly. When the meeting ended, the children were instructed to come again on Saturday, September 7, and on every Saturday thereafter.

As the organizational procedures of Primary unfolded over the next few weeks, a simple pattern for conducting the meetings emerged. At the beginning of each meeting, a member of the presidency asked the children if they knew anyone who was sick or needed special help so they could be remembered in their prayers. The presidency then encouraged the children to be helpful at home: "Sometimes we would ask them how many would like to try for one week, and see how much they could do for father and mother without grumbling, and not quarrel with their brothers and sisters. A good many would try." As for singing, in the beginning the "children were very timid," Rogers wrote. But as time passed "their voices rang out sweet and clear, and in some cases much talent was displayed."[8]

Eliza R. Snow was a frequent visitor to the Primary meetings in Farmington. She soon recognized the benefits and blessings that came to the children from attending such an association. Wanting boys and girls throughout the Church to experience what she saw happening in Farmington, Sister Snow "went from place to place, in company with Sister Zina D. H. Young and others, organizing with the assistance of the Bishops until nearly every settlement [in Utah] had a Primary Association."[9]

Sister Snow then approached Sister Rogers, seeking suggestions for the name of a woman who could best serve as general president of the Primary Association. Snow felt strongly that the president should live in Salt Lake City near the headquarters of the Church. Rogers suggested Louie B. Felt. When Sister Felt was called as president, some Latter-day Saints were upset, believing the position should have been Rogers'. "I never had a moment's jealousy over anyone holding office," Rogers said, "for no person will ever take my honors from me; I shall have all that I deserve."[10] Sister Felt served as the general president of the Primary Association for forty-five years. Sister Rogers served on the Primary general board until her death in 1923.

The Primary Association continued to grow. Beginning in 1900, the first lesson materials were published in *The Children's Friend*. Shortly thereafter, the children were separated into age categories for instruction. Four rotating one-hour meetings were held each month—Lesson Hour, Story Hour, Busy Hour and Social Hour.[11] The purpose of Lesson Hour was to teach children stories from the scriptures and Church history. Story Hour was devoted to sharing edifying and instructive moral stories. Busy Hour was a time for developing handicraft talents, and Social Hour was a time for games, dances, and parties designed to teach children good manners and deportment.

DID YOU KNOW?

- The Primary was founded because of the rowdy behavior of several young children in the settlement of Farmington, Utah.
- Some of the earliest Primary curriculum included Lesson Hour, Story Hour, Busy Hour, and Social Hour.

In 1928, on the fiftieth anniversary of the founding of the children's association, Primary was second only to Sunday School in the number of participants worldwide.[12] In 1980, when the Church consolidated most of its meetings into a three-hour block, Primary became part of Sabbath-day worship.[13]

Historian Leonard J. Arrington observed that in Latter-day Saint history there is a "centrifugal bias," or a "tendency to believe the notion that the important influences and forces in Mormon history originated in the center and moved outward from there."[14] But the work of Aurelia Spencer Rogers suggests that the course of Church history can be affected by the sincere efforts of one Latter-day Saint working outside the center to influence the greater whole.

Though the work of Eliza R. Snow and other Church leaders shaped Primary, it is fitting that the children's organization of the Church started with a concerned and engaged mother.

NOTES

1. Rogers, *Life Sketches*, 205–8.
2. Rogers, *Life Sketches*, 207, 209.
3. Rogers, *Life Sketches*, 221–22.
4. Rogers, *Life Sketches*, 210–12.
5. Rogers, *Life Sketches*, 212.
6. Conrad Harward, "A History of the Growth and Development of the Primary Association of the LDS Church from 1878 to 1928," master's thesis, Brigham Young University (1976), 19. Sister Louisa Haight's given name was pronounced "LoIZA," according to her grandson Elder David B. Haight.
7. Rogers, *Life Sketches*, 215–17.
8. Rogers, *Life Sketches*, 221–22.
9. Rogers, *Life Sketches*, 222–23.
10. Harward, "History of the Growth and Development of the Primary," 91–95.
11. Harward, "History of the Growth and Development of the Primary," 91; Rogers, *Life Sketches*, 205–6.
12. "Church Consolidates Meeting Schedules," *Ensign*, Mar. 1980, 73.
13. Arrington, "The Search for Truth and Meaning in Mormon History," *Dialogue*, Summer 1968, 63.

54
The Pearl of Great Price Is Added to the Scriptures

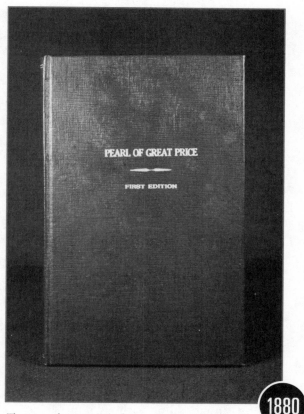

The original 1851 Pearl of Great Price *published in England by Elder Franklin D. Richards.*

1880

The title of the missionary pamphlet *Pearl of Great Price* came from the Savior's parable of "a merchant man, seeking goodly pearls . . . when he had found one pearl of great price, went and sold all that he had and bought it" (Matthew 13:45–46).[1] In this parable, a pearl of great price is a precious gem, signifying sacred information "worth more than any earthly fortune."[2]

The origin of the now-canonized Pearl of Great Price dates to 1851 when Elder Franklin D. Richards of the Quorum of the Twelve Apostles was presiding over the European Mission. He had responsibility for more than 32,000 Latter-day Saints in Britain and the publishing center for the Church in Liverpool. Through the *Latter-Day Saints' Millennial Star,* Elder Richards announced on June 15, 1851, that the "Pearl of Great Price, is the title of a new work which will soon be ready for sale. . . . [It is] a source of much instruction and education to many thousands of the Saints, who will by an acquaintance with its precious contents, be more abundantly qualified to set forth and defend the principles of our Holy Faith before all men."[3]

When the book became available for purchase, the full title was *The Pearl of Great Price, Being a Choice Selection from the Revelations, Translations, and Narrations of Joseph Smith, First Prophet, Seer, and Revelator to the Church of Jesus Christ of Latter-day Saints.*

The contents of the first edition included a preface by Elder Richards explaining that the reason for the publication was "the repeated solicitations of several friends of the publisher, who are desirous to be put in possession of the very important articles contained therein. . . . It is presumed that true believers in the Divine mission of the Prophet Joseph Smith, will appreciate this little collection of precious truths as a *Pearl of Great Price* that will increase their ability to maintain and to defend the holy faith by becoming possessors of it."[4]

The first edition included the following:

1. Extracts from the prophecy of Enoch,

2. The word of God to Moses,

3. The book of Abraham,

4. An extract from Joseph Smith's translation of the Bible,

5. A key to the revelations of John (now D&C 77 and Matthew 24),

6. A revelation and prophecy by the Prophet received on December 25, 1832 (D&C 87),

7. Extracts from the 1838 history of Joseph Smith (an account of the First Vision, visitations of the angel Moroni, and the restoration of the Aaronic Priesthood,

8. The Articles of Faith,

9. The poem "Truth" by John Jaques ("Oh, Say, What Is Truth?" *Hymns*, no. 143), and

10. Selections from revelations in the Doctrine and Covenants (20; 27; 107).[5]

The second edition of the *Pearl of Great Price* was published in Salt Lake City in 1878. Editing and additions in the second edition were largely the work of apostle Orson Pratt. Elder Pratt omitted Elder Richards's preface and included a more "complete text of the Adam, Enoch, Noah, and Moses material" and a "Revelation on the Eternity of the Marriage Covenant, Including Plurality of Wives," today's Doctrine and Covenants 132.[6]

Two years later, on October 10, 1880, the Pearl of Great Price was canonized. During general conference, President George Q. Cannon declared, "I hold in my hand the book of Doctrine and Covenants and also the book The Pearl of Great Price, which books contain revelations of God. . . . As there have been additions made to it . . . it has been deemed wise to submit these books with their contents to the Conference, to see whether the Conference will vote to accept the books and their contents as from God, and binding upon us as a people and as a Church." President Joseph F. Smith added: "I move that we receive and accept the revelations contained in these books, as revelations from God to The Church of Jesus Christ of Latter-day Saints, and to all the world. The motion was seconded and sustained by unanimous vote of the whole conference."[7]

Of the ratifying vote, President Wilford Woodruff wrote, "This is a great day for Israel."[8]

The 1902 edition of the Pearl of Great Price was the work of a committee headed by James E. Talmage under the supervision of the First Presidency. Elder Talmage recorded in his journal, "Had interview with the First Presidency in a matter which has been under informal consideration for some time, viz: that of preparing a revised edition of the 'Pearl of Great Price,' one of the standard works of the church. I was appointed today to prepare the same. . . . I undertake this as I have attempted other labors in connection with Church work in a missionary spirit without hope or expectation of reward. Indeed I doubt that I will be known as the reviser even if the work be completed, and a revised edition published."[9]

During the April 1902 general conference President Joseph F. Smith announced: "The Latter-day Saints generally are familiar with the book called the Pearl of Great Price. The old edition of it has been accepted by the Church as an authentic doctrinal work. It has now been re-published, with some improvements. It has been divided into chapters and verses, with references on the bottom of the pages. . . . We

DID YOU KNOW?

- The present Pearl of Great Price was originally published as pamphlet to provide the British Saints access to several of revelations of Joseph Smith.

- The first *Pearl of Great Price*, a missionary pamphlet, contained a poem and several revelations now found in the Doctrine and Covenants.

have eliminated from the Pearl of Great Price those revelations it formerly contained which are to be found, and always were, in the Book of Doctrine and Covenants."[10]

In the October 1902 general conference the revised Pearl of Great Price was presented to an assembly of Saints: "It was moved and seconded that the book be accepted as a standard work of the Church, and the motion was carried unanimously."[11] Elder Talmage recorded on October 6, 1902: "The Pearl of Great Price in the revised form prepared by the Committee and myself, was accepted by vote as one of the standard works of the Church."[12] This was the last vote on the Pearl of Great Price as a standard work of the Church.

During the April 1976 general conference, President N. Eldon Tanner announced: "At a meeting of the Council of the First Presidency and Quorum of the Twelve held in the Salt Lake Temple on March 25, 1976, approval was given to add to the Pearl of Great Price."[13] The additions were Joseph Smith's vision of the celestial kingdom, received in the Kirtland Temple on January 21, 1836, and Joseph F. Smith's vision of the redemption of the dead, received in the Beehive House in Salt Lake City on October 3, 1918.

Three years later, in June 1979, the First Presidency announced that Joseph Smith's vision would become section 137 of the Doctrine and Covenants and Joseph F. Smith's vision of the redemption of the dead would become section 138.[14] In 1982, these two revelations were moved from the Pearl of Great Price to the Doctrine and Covenants.[15]

Since 1981, the Pearl of Great Price has remained unchanged: selections from the book of Moses, the book of Abraham (including three facsimiles), Joseph Smith–Matthew 24, Joseph Smith–History, and the Articles of Faith. This diverse, inspired, collection of sacred works has taken its rightful place with the Bible, Book of Mormon, and Doctrine and Covenants as a standard work of The Church of Jesus Christ of Latter-day Saints.

Notes

1. *Millennial Star*, July 15, 1851, 217.
2. James R. Clark, "Our Pearl of Great Price: From Mission Pamphlet to Standard Work," *Ensign*, Aug. 1976, 12–17.
3. *Millennial Star*, July 15, 1851, 217.
4. *Pearl of Great Price* (1851), v.
5. Draper et al., *Pearl of Great Price*, 5–7.
6. Draper et al., *Pearl of Great Price*, 7–8.
7. Journal History of the Church, Oct. 10, 1880, Church History Library, The Church of Jesus Christ of Latter-day Saints, Salt Lake City, Utah.
8. Wilford Woodruff Journal, Oct. 10, 1880, Church History Library.
9. Talmage, personal journal no. 10, Feb. 2, 1900, in Clark, "Our Pearl of Great Price," 15.
10. Smith, in Conference Report, Apr. 1902, 91.
11. Joseph F. Smith, in Conference Report, Oct. 6, 1902, 83.
12. Talmage, personal journal no. 10, 471, in Clark, "Our Pearl of Great Price," 16.
13. Tanner, "The Sustaining of Church Officers," *Ensign*, May 1976, 19.
14. *LDS Church News*, June 2, 1979, 3.
15. Cowan, *Answers to Your Questions about the Doctrine and Covenants*, 152.

55
Mormon Colonies in Mexico and Canada

1885

The Cardston Alberta Canada Temple, the second (after Hawaii) to be built outside the continental United States, was dedicated in 1923.

With the passage of the Edmunds Act in 1882 and the Edmunds-Tucker Act in 1887, pressure to end the practice of plural marriage reached a fever pitch. The decade of the 1880s marked a period of prolonged conflict between Latter-day Saints, who saw defending the principle of plural marriage as a charge from God, and federal officials who sought to destroy the practice at any cost. As persecution increased, Church leaders looked for places of sanctuary outside the United States.[1]

In December 1884, the First Presidency sent a letter to Christopher Layton at St. Joseph, Arizona, asking him to "obtain a place of refuge under a foreign government to which our people can flee." The letter continued, "Better for parts of families to remove and go where they can live in peace than to be hauled to jail and . . . incarcerated with thieves and murderers and other vile characters."[2]

Almost immediately Latter-day Saints in Arizona made preparations to move to Mexico.

The prospect of Mormon colonization in Mexico was considered for at least a decade before the first colonists arrived there in 1885. Under the direction of Brigham Young, a missionary expedition into Mexico had searched for new lands to settle. Favorable reports from the expedition were considered but not implemented until the crisis with the federal government in the 1880s.

Some of the early Mormon colonists saw their situation in biblical terms. Amy Theresa Richardson, a bride of only a few weeks, wrote, "Very soon we set out for Snowflake to prepare for our flight, not into Egypt, but to Old Mexico. I tell you the road was not strewn with roses, neither was it all thorns. Going into a strange land among a different people and a new government was not a sweet dream. But there was a jolly crew of us and we had many good evenings of entertainment on the way."[3]

Within six weeks of the First Presidency's request, more than 350 Mormon colonists were encamped on the banks of the Casas Grandes River in Mexico.[4] Their first few months in Mexico were filled with tense negotiations with government officials to secure suitable land. At one point, the governor of Chihuahua signed an expulsion order, giving the Saints sixteen days to leave the state. Through the efforts of Church leaders, government officials in Chihuahua reversed their position and welcomed the settlers.

More and more Latter-day Saint refugees poured into northern Mexico, where they established eight settlements and a thriving commonwealth. The largest of the settlements was Colonia Juárez, named after Benito Juárez, a hero and former president of the Mexican Republic. The settlers saw a number of miracles in their early years in Mexico—one being an earthquake that providentially increased the water supply in Chihuahua.[5]

With early signs of success in the Mexican colonies, in 1887 Church leaders asked Charles Ora Card to lead Mormon settlers to southern Alberta, Canada. On May 1, 1887, the first furrow was ceremoniously plowed where the town of Cardston was later established. By 1901 more than 3,200 Saints lived in a constellation of settlements stretching across southern Alberta.

The colonists in Mexico continued to prosper and established schools, homes, and dozens of thriving fruit orchards. The colonies remained of high interest to the entire Church partly because six apostles lived in Colonia Juárez between 1885 and 1895.[6] In addition, Latter-day Saints in the Mexican colonies continued to perform plural marriages after the 1890 Manifesto issued by President Wilford Woodruff. Most Latter-day Saints believed the Manifesto applied only to Church members in the United States. Plural marriages continued to be performed in the colonies until the First Presidency ended the practice throughout the Church in the early twentieth century.[7]

In 1911 a revolution erupted in Mexico that threatened the Mormon colonies. When fighting between the Mexican government and insurgents reached nearby settlements, Latter-day Saint colonists tried to maintain their neutrality but were caught in the crossfire of conflict. Rebels raided the Mormon colonies for food and supplies, threatening Saints at every turn. When stake president Junius Romney met with rebel leader I. Salazar to discuss Mormon grievances, Salazar hinted that the raids were only the beginning of the colonists' troubles.

President Romney later recorded, "Up to this moment of time it had never crossed my mind that the colonists would have to leave Mexico, but from this moment I was perfectly convinced that unless Salazar changed his attitude toward the colonists there would be nothing for us to do but evacuate the country, or in the alternative, actually fight the revolutionists. His manner and expression were such to convince me that he had already formed a definite plan for the oppression, if not extermination, of the colonists."[8]

As threats and depredations continued, the situation grew more tenuous. In July 1912 President Romney evacuated all the women and children. Several thousand colonists—now refugees—were transported on trains to El Paso, Texas, where they lived in horrendous conditions awaiting news of loved ones in Mexico.

Orrin P. Miller, a counselor in the Presiding Bishopric, visited the refugees and wrote, "The sight presented to my view is one of the most heart-rending I have ever witnessed—to see over 2,000 people, mostly women and children, driven from their homes without time to gather

DID YOU KNOW?

• Seeking safety from American antipolygamy laws, Church leaders sought out places of refuge in Canada and Mexico.

• Mormon settlers in Mexico faced famines, floods, earthquakes, and even threats from armed revolutionaries.

even their personal effects and most of them without a dollar to assist themselves with."[9]

The brethren who had remained in the colonies were evacuated a month later.

President Joseph F. Smith lamented the suffering of the colonists in a general conference address but praised their choice to avoid violence: "[The Lord] has given us a chance to get up like gentlemen and come away from the scene of strife and hypocrisy to where we can find peace and freedom. That is far better than to have the stain of blood upon our hands."[10]

Most of the 4,500 exiles never returned to Mexico. Only a small group, roughly 1,000, returned. They rebuilt two of their stricken towns, Colonia Juárez and Colonia Dublán.[11]

In contrast to their counterparts in Mexico, the colonists in southern Canada prospered in relative peace. In 1912, the same year as the exodus from Mexico, the First Presidency announced plans for a temple in Cardston, the first temple to be built outside the United States.

In 1999, more than a century after the first Mormon colonists arrived and eighty-seven years after most of them fled, a temple was constructed in northern Mexico in Colonia Juárez. It was among the first of the smaller temples announced by President Gordon B. Hinckley, who envisioned the concept of small temples on a visit to the colonies.

Mormon colonization outside the United States during the late nineteenth century met with varying degrees of success. The colonists in Canada experienced little persecution, whereas colonists in Mexico experienced severe adversity. Regardless, these colonization efforts represented the first permanent Church presence outside the United States and the first stepping-stone for the Church in becoming a global faith.

NOTES

1. Richard L. Jensen, "Colonization," in Ludlow, *Encyclopedia of Mormonism,* 1:291, 294.
2. Whetten, *Colonia Juarez,* 7.
3. Johnson, *Heartbeats of Colonia Diaz,* 19.
4. Whetten, *Colonia Juarez,* 10–27.
5. Whetten, *Colonia Juarez,* 10–27.
6. Whetten, *Colonia Juarez,* 34. The six apostles who lived in Colonia Juarez during this time were Brigham Young Jr., Erastus Snow, Moses Thatcher, Francis M. Lyman, George Teasdale, and John W. Taylor.
7. See "The Manifesto and the End of Plural Marriage," lds.org.
8. Romney, *Mormon Colonies in Mexico,* 173.
9. Romney, *Mormon Colonies in Mexico,* 190.
10. Joseph Fielding Smith, in Romney, *Mormon Colonies in Mexico,* 218.
11. Whetten, *Colonia Juarez,* 55.

56
The Mormon Underground

1886

Several Latter-day Saint men convicted and imprisoned for practicing plural marriage, including President George Q. Cannon (center, holding flowers), ca. 1889.

On a late summer afternoon in 1886, President John Taylor was sitting in George Stringfellow's parlor when a glass bulb in a nearby lamp burst, sending broken glass throughout the room. At the time, little was thought of the incident. A week later, however, President Taylor dreamed that there was symbolism in the broken light bulb. Bodyguard Samuel Bateman recorded in his journal that the "breaking of the globe was interpreted to him [President Taylor] in a dream that the deputies surprised us and we were scattered and nary two of us were together."[1]

Latter-day Saints today might be surprised to learn that John Taylor lived a clandestine existence in constant danger of being arrested by federal marshals and imprisoned. Precipitating this situation was legislation that made it easy

for government officials to prosecute polygamists. In March 1882, "upon learning of the passage of the [Edmunds] law," President George Q. Cannon wrote to Church attorney Franklin S. Richards that "he [President Taylor] would be selected as a target for attack."[2] President Taylor ultimately was forced into hiding.

The first federal legislation against plural marriage was the Morrill Anti-Bigamy Act, signed into law on July 1, 1862, by United States president Abraham Lincoln.[3] Little was done at the time to enforce the Morrill Act because the federal government was occupied with the Civil War.

In 1882, twenty years later, Senator George Edmunds stirred up interest in legal action against polygamy. He proposed an amendment to the Morrill Act that required marriage licenses and restricted polygamists' right to serve in public office, vote, or be called to jury duty. The amendment also proposed to grant amnesty to anyone who denounced polygamy. The Edmunds Act was signed into law on March 14, 1882, by United States president Chester Arthur.

The next legislation to target polygamy was the Edmunds-Tucker Act, signed in 1887. It disincorporated the Church and the Perpetual Emigration Fund "on the ground that they fostered polygamy."[4] The act authorized the seizure of Church real estate not directly used for religious purposes and the takeover of Church funds in excess of $50,000, a limit imposed by the Morrill Act.

Anticipating arrest and imprisonment as the result of these noxious laws, on February 1, 1885, President Taylor delivered his last public address in the Tabernacle in Salt Lake City. Federal marshals and deputies stood at the exits of the Tabernacle to arrest President Taylor when the meeting ended. Uncertainty filled the air as President Taylor spoke:

"It may suit others to violate the law, to trample upon human rights and desecrate the sacred [temple] of liberty . . . in the name of justice; but we profess to be governed by higher, by nobler, and more exalted principles . . . and if Jesus could afford to endure the attacks of sinners . . . we ought to be able to endure a little of the same thing. . . . When men begin to tear down the barriers and tamper with the fundamental principles and institutions of our country, they are playing a very dangerous game, and are severing the bonds which hold society together."[5]

After addressing the congregation for almost two hours, as was customary at the time, President Taylor closed his remarks with a final warning:

"You will see trouble, TROUBLE, TROUBLE enough in these United States. . . . I tell you in the name of God, woe! to them that fight against Zion, for God will fight against them."[6]

He then went down the stairs to the basement of the Tabernacle, where his bodyguards, Charles Barrell and Samuel Bateman, escorted him to safety.

The writings of President Taylor reveal that he attached meaning to his hardships. He was not simply hiding from officers of the law but was suffering a necessary persecution that would refine him for future glory. He wrote to his wife Margaret:

"When men shall revile you and persecute you and say all manner of evil against you for my name's sake, rejoice and be exceedingly glad, for great is your reward in heaven, for so persecuted they the prophets which were before you. . . . It was true in the prophets' days, it was true in the days of Jesus, it is true in our day. . . . You may ask, 'Do you do this?' Yes. I feel to thank God that I am a Latter-Day Saint and considered worthy to share . . . what the former-day saints had to pass through. And it is only a very little that I and my brethren endure when compared to that what the Saints endured in former times."[7]

In spite of his positive outlook, President Taylor's ability to lead the Church was greatly diminished. Meetings with other Church leaders were rare. Most Church business was conducted through correspondence. His addresses were written and sent to others to read at gatherings held in outlying areas rather than in the Salt Lake Tabernacle. Though the administrative duties of his counselor Joseph F. Smith were not as great as President Taylor's, President Smith recorded that while he too was in hiding, he received eight pounds of mail in one day.

These were difficult days not only for Church leaders but for Latter-day Saints in general. In the late 1880s, more than 1,300 Mormon men were jailed as "cohabs" for failure to abide by the federal laws that outlawed polygamy. Although federal officials had their hands full with the number of men imprisoned for conscience' sake, the search for John Taylor and his counselors continued unabated. As late as February 9, 1887, just five months before President Taylor's death, deputies searched the

DID YOU KNOW?

• President Abraham Lincoln signed the Morrill Act (1862), the first antipolygamy legislation passed by the Congress of the United States.

• President John Taylor died while in hiding from persecution brought on by federal antipolygamy laws.

temple, tithing offices, the Gardo House, and the Lion House for clues to the whereabouts of the First Presidency. They offered $800 for information leading to the capture of President Taylor and his counselor George Q. Cannon. In May 1887, President Cannon wrote to John W. Young, "President Taylor's health is not good and I heartily wish that something would be done in his case. It seems a most cruel and barbarous proceeding for him to be kept as he is."[8]

On July 29, 1887, George Q. Cannon and Joseph F. Smith announced in the *Deseret News* the death of President John Taylor. They informed readers that "his constant desire was to do everything in his power to relieve the Latter-day Saints from the oppression under which they suffer."[9] A newspaper editorial by Charles W. Penrose insisted that exile was the leading factor in President Taylor's declining health and subsequent death.[10]

The prophetic interpretation of the broken lamp in John Taylor's dream of September 1886 was fulfilled. With his death, his bodyguards returned to their families. President Taylor's counselors continued to live in exile until President Cannon was arrested and imprisoned. As the dream suggested, those in hiding faced loneliness when they were separated from their loved ones. For those forced to remain in

hiding, that loneliness lasted until President Wilford Woodruff issued the Manifesto in 1890, which marked the beginning of the end of the practice of plural marriage.

NOTES

1. Diary of Samuel Bateman, 1886–1909, Sept. 14, 1886, 3, L. Tom Perry Special Collections, Harold B. Lee Library, Brigham Young University, Provo, Utah.
2. George Q. Cannon to Franklin S. Richards, Apr. 1887, 6, Perry Special Collections, Lee Library.
3. Ray Jay Davis, "Antipolygamy Legislation," in Ludlow, *Encyclopedia of Mormonism*, 1:52.
4. Davis, "Antipolygamy Legislation," 1:52.
5. Taylor, in *Journal of Discourses*, 26:149-54.
6. Taylor, *Last Pioneer*, 335.
7. Taylor to Margaret Taylor, Feb. 2, 1887, in Margaret M. Taylor Papers, Church History Library, The Church of Jesus Christ of Latter-day Saints, Salt Lake City, Utah.
8. George Q. Cannon to John W. Young, May 20, 1887, in John Taylor Family Papers, Special Collections, Willard J. Marriott Library, University of Utah, Salt Lake City, Utah.
9. Cannon and Smith, "Announcement of the Death of President John Taylor," *Deseret News: Semi-weekly*, July 29, 1887, in John Taylor Family Papers, Special Collections, Marriott Library.
10. Eric Perkins and Mary Jane Woodger, "Administration from the Underground," in Woodger, *Champion of Liberty*, 362.

57
The Manifesto

President Wilford Woodruff.

1890

From the 1830s to the 1880s, many Latter-day Saints participated in the practice of plural marriage. It took a revelation to the Prophet Joseph Smith to begin the practice of plural marriage, and it took a revelation to end the practice. The latter revelation was given to President Wilford Woodruff and is found in the Doctrine and Covenants as Official Declaration 1. This revelation constitutes a dramatic turning point in the history of the Church.

During the nineteenth century, most citizens of the United States viewed the practice of plural marriage as immoral. This attitude led to an increasingly stringent series of antipolygamy laws leveraged against the Saints. Beginning in 1862, the United States Congress passed a series of laws intended to end the practice. These laws, particularly the Edmunds-Tucker Act of 1887, exerted great pressure on Church leaders. By 1890 the United States federal government had disincorporated the Church, seized its assets, and imprisoned many prominent leaders. Wives and children of these leaders were at risk of being subpoenaed to testify in court against their husbands and fathers.

With Latter-day Saints being forced to live under such difficult circumstances, President Wilford Woodruff sought guidance from the Lord about continuing the practice of plural marriage. In May 1890, when the United States Supreme Court upheld the constitutionality of the Edmunds-Tucker Act, the Lord showed President Woodruff in vision "exactly what would take place if we did not stop this practice. . . . All the temples [would] go out of our hands." He explained, "[God] has told me exactly what to do, and what the result would be if we did not do it."[1]

In his journal President Woodruff recorded, "The Lord has commanded me to put the following question to the Saints . . . Which is the wisest course for the Latter-day Saints to pursue—to continue to attempt to practice plural marriage with the laws of the nation against it and the opposition of 60,000,000 of people and at the cost and confiscation and loss of all the temple and the stopping of all the ordinances?"

Shown the ramifications of continuing, President Woodruff instead chose to "cease the practice and submit to the law," that in so doing he might "leave the temples in the hands of the Saints so they can attend to the ordinances of the Gospel both for the living and the dead." In making such a significant change, President Woodruff declared that "the Latter-day Saints throughout Israel should understand that the First Presidency of the Church and the Twelve Apostles are led and guided by the inspiration of the Lord, and the Lord will not permit me nor any other man to lead the people astray."[2]

On September 25, 1890, the First Presidency issued the Manifesto, which declared, "Inasmuch as laws have been enacted by Congress forbidding plural marriages, which laws have been pronounced constitutional by the court of last resort, I hereby declare my intention to submit to those laws, and to use my influence with the members of the Church over which I preside to have them do likewise." The Manifesto addressed the United States government when it specified, "We are not teaching polygamy, or plural marriage, nor permitting any person to enter into its practice."[3]

Within a week of President Woodruff's issuance of the Manifesto, the Quorum of the Twelve Apostles voted to sustain his actions. At the October 1890 general conference, the Manifesto was sustained by common consent and became "authoritative and binding" upon all Church members living in United States territories.[4]

Nevertheless, it proved difficult to stop the practice of plural marriage within the Church.[5] Part of the problem was a difference of opinion on how to implement the Manifesto. For example, the Manifesto had no bearing on plural marriages that already existed. President Woodruff explained, "This Manifesto only refers to future marriages, and does not affect past

conditions. I did not, I could not, and would not promise that you would desert your wives and children. This you cannot do in honor."[6]

Even with this strong affirmation, some Latter-day Saints who had entered polygamous relationships began to live monogamously. The Manifesto began the process of ending the practice of plural marriage within the Church; "the ending of the practice after the Manifesto was . . . gradual."[7] Plural marriages continued to be performed in Canada and Mexico, where polygamy was believed to be legal.

Some among the Church hierarchy continued to perform new plural marriages in defiance of the law. A second manifesto was issued by President Joseph F. Smith in 1904 that made the solemnization of new plural marriages punishable by excommunication. Two apostles, Matthias Cowley and John W. Taylor, refused to submit to the new directive and were dropped from the Quorum of the Twelve.[8]

By 1908 the Manifesto of 1890 had been canonized and was being published in the Doctrine and Covenants. It has been included in every edition of the Doctrine and Covenants since. Today plural marriage is not allowed among living Church members.[9]

Speaking of the practice ninety years after the Manifesto, President Gordon B. Hinckley taught, "If any of our members are found to be practicing plural marriage, they are

DID YOU KNOW?

- Although the Manifesto marked the beginning of the end of plural marriage among Church members in the United States, the practical end of polygamy took place over a generation.

- Speaking of the Manifesto, President Wilford Woodruff said, "[God] has told me exactly what to do, and what the result would be if we did not do it."

excommunicated, the most serious penalty the Church can impose. . . . It is against the law of God. Even in countries where civil or religious law allows polygamy, the Church teaches that marriage must be monogamous and does not accept into its membership those practicing plural marriage."[10]

Notes

1. "Remarks Made by President Wilford Woodruff," *Deseret Evening News*, Nov. 7, 1891; Official Declaration 1.
2. Kenney, *Wilford Woodruff's Journal*, 9:171.
3. "Official Declaration," *Deseret Evening News*, Sept. 25, 1890, 2.
4. *Deseret Evening News*, Oct. 6, 1890, in "The Manifesto and the End of Plural Marriage," lds.org.
5. "The Manifesto and the End of Plural Marriage."
6. Wilford Woodruff, in Marriner W. Merrill, in Hardy, *Solemn Covenant*, 141.
7. Antone, *Becoming True Saviors of Men*, 75.
8. "The Manifesto and the End of Plural Marriage."
9. Consistent with the teachings of Joseph Smith, deceased persons may be sealed to more than one spouse, though the exact nature of these relationships in the eternities is not known. See "Plural Marriage in Kirtland and Nauvoo," lds.org.
10. Hinckley, "What Are People Asking about Us?" *Ensign*, Nov. 1998, 71–72.

58
The Salt Lake Temple Is Dedicated

1893

The Salt Lake Temple, ca. 1896.

The invitation "Come, Come, Ye Saints" each year beckons millions to Temple Square in the valley of the Great Salt Lake. There a house of the Lord—a temple to God—rises majestically heavenward as a symbol of pioneer industry, fortitude, and devotion.

Four days after the first Mormon pioneer company entered the Salt Lake Valley in 1847, Brigham Young struck his cane to the ground where the temple now stands and declared, "Here we will build the Temple of our God."[1]

Young selected architect Truman O. Angell to draw the plans for the temple. "I labored as hard as any man could," Angell wrote. "All this is a labour of the mind and hence is a labour that no one perhaps will see."[2] As Angell refined his architectural drawings, on February 14, 1853, Brigham Young began the groundbreaking for the temple by turning the first shovelful of desert soil.

The original foundation of the Salt Lake Temple was made of red sandstone quarried in Red Butte Canyon northeast of Salt Lake City. Workers hacked against stone that broke their crude tools and exhausted the unskilled masons. Despite the hardships, by 1855 the massive foundation, laid sixteen feet below ground level, was finished.

Work on the temple halted when news reached Brigham Young of the United States Army heading to Utah with a presidential order to quell rumored sedition.[3] President Young ordered the foundation to be buried under mounds of dirt that were smoothed over to resemble a freshly plowed field. Young offered a prayer of protection for the temple foundation on August 13, 1857, petitioning the Lord for strength to finish the temple.[4]

Work on the temple did not start again for several years. When the foundation was unearthed, it was found that the stones had deteriorated. Upon close inspection, Brigham Young observed that sandstone could not support the temple. He instructed the Saints to begin anew: "I want to see the Temple built in a manner that it will endure through the Millennium."[5]

The crumbling sandstone was discarded for a more enduring foundation of granite found in Little Cottonwood Canyon, about twenty-three miles southeast of Salt Lake City.[6]

Mining granite was an energetic undertaking. Men drilled a series of holes about four inches deep every seven inches along the grain of the stone. When the holes formed a dotted line across the length of the mountain, wedges were driven and a rhythmic pounding from one wedge to another began. Large slabs of granite were taken from the mountain using these methods. One such slab provided 2,960 stones that weighed about 2,500 pounds each.

One witness recalled seeing the first stones brought to Temple Square in 1860: "The sight of the great stones one at a time being hauled along the streets by two yoke of oxen and we would all stand for them to pass with a feeling of awe and reverence."[7]

Large derricks were used to place the stones on the temple walls. The process was slow and the task arduous, yet the pioneers labored patiently. They built the temple walls eight feet thick at ground level and six feet thick at the top. After hoisting the last stones to their appointed places, masons chiseled celestial symbols into the granite. Fifty moonstones depicting the 1878 lunar cycle, stars including the Big and Little Dippers, and sunstones were carved into the stones.

Latter-day Saint artisans studying in Paris, France, returned to the Salt Lake Valley to decorate the interior of the temple. Under inspired direction, they created symbolic illustrations depicting aspects of holy temple ordinances.[8] Other talented artists created fine woodcarvings, delicate lace draperies, and exquisite silk curtains. The grandeur of the interior, from the marble inlaid floors to the frescoed ceilings, blends to perfection a monument of pioneer ingenuity, creativity and, most of all, devotion to God.

The final creation for the temple was a statue of the angel Moroni by non-Mormon sculptor Cyrus E. Dallin. The gold-leafed copper statue represents the fulfillment of the prophecy, "And I saw another angel fly in the midst of heaven, having the everlasting gospel to preach unto them that dwell on the earth" (Revelation 14:6).

By April 6, 1893, the Salt Lake Temple was finished. Saints from settlements throughout the Rocky Mountains gathered to Temple Square to attend the dedication of the great temple. They were greeted with snow and a "wind velocity of sixty miles per hour."[9] Despite the inclement weather, many waited for the temple doors to open and to be ushered into the beautiful, gold-trimmed assembly room. Their reverential awe for the temple began a season of rejoicing and a united new beginning.

President Wilford Woodruff offered the dedicatory prayer on April 6: "We come before Thee with joy and thanksgiving, with spirits jubilant and hearts filled with praise, that Thou hast permitted us to see this day for which, during these forty years, we have hoped, and toiled, and prayed, when we can dedicate unto Thee this house which we have built to Thy most glorious name . . . We pray Thee, Heavenly Father, to accept this building in all its parts from foundation to capstone, with the statue that is on the latter placed, and all the finals and other ornaments that adorn its exterior . . . We thank Thee with all the fervor of

DID YOU KNOW?

- Construction of the Salt Lake Temple was halted for nearly ten years by the approach of an army meant to subdue the Saints.

- Brigham Young declared that he wanted the Salt Lake Temple to "endure through the Millennium."

overflowing gratitude that Thou hast revealed the powers by which the hearts of the children are being turned to their fathers and the hearts of the fathers to the children, that the sons of men, in all their generations can be made partakers of the glories and joys of the kingdom of heaven."[10]

The Salt Lake Temple continues to be a symbol of purity, peace, and oneness with God to millions of Latter-day Saints worldwide. This temple is unique among all the temples that dot the earth, for within its walls the First Presidency and the Twelve Apostles meet weekly, as do other leading quorums of the priesthood. But as in all other temples, inside this holy place the beautiful relationships between husband and wife and parent and child are made eternal by restored priesthood authority.

Notes

1. Journal History of the Church, July 28, 1847, Church History Library, The Church of Jesus Christ of Latter-day Saints, Salt Lake City, Utah; Brigham Young, in Gates, *Life Story of Brigham Young,* 104.
2. Truman O. Angell, Journal, 1851–1856, Dec. 15, 1857, in Paul L. Anderson, "Truman O. Angell: Architect and Saint," in Cannon and Whitaker, *Supporting Saints,* 133, 161.
3. Cowan, *Temples to Dot the Earth,* 100.
4. Cowan, *Temples to Dot the Earth,* 64–67.
5. Young, in *Journal of Discourses,* 10:254.
6. Cowan, *Temples to Dot the Earth,* 100.
7. Annie Wells Cannon, "Passing Thoughts," *Woman's Exponent,* May 1, 1893, 157.
8. Rachel Cope, "John B. Fairbanks: The Man Behind the Canvas," master's thesis, Brigham Young University (2003).
9. *Deseret Evening News,* Apr. 6, 1893.
10. *Deseret Evening News,* Apr. 6, 1893.

59
The Genealogical Society of Utah Is Founded

Genealogical records collected to facilitate the performance of temple ordinances for the dead.

1894

On April 14, 1894, President Woodruff announced during general conference a new policy that had great bearing on genealogical work and subsequent temple activity. The announcement came as a result of President Woodruff's pleadings before the Lord regarding the temple sealing ordinance. At that time most sealing ordinances were limited to the first generation of Latter-day Saints who had remained true to the faith. Beyond that generation,

Latter-day Saints often adopted themselves into the family of a Church leader, believing that such an adoption would bring a greater chance of salvation.[1] This practice "raised doctrinal questions about the organization of eternal families" in the mind of President Woodruff.[2] After much prayer, he received a revelation from the Lord telling him that the time had come to prohibit such "sealing adoptions." His landmark announcement at the 1894 conference was as follows:

"When a man receives the endowments, adopt him to his father; not . . . to any other man outside the lineage of his fathers. That is the will of God to this people. . . .

"We want the Latter-day Saints from this time to trace their genealogies as far as they can and to be sealed to their fathers and mothers. Have children sealed to their parents and run this chain through as far as you can get it."[3]

President Woodruff's announcement made the collecting and organizing of family records for the purpose of temple work binding upon all Latter-day Saints. Yet it seemed impossible to fulfill such a command, for a major impediment to genealogical research was inaccessibility of ancestral records. Most source materials for genealogical research were stored in homes, institutions, archives, or churches beyond the reach of the Latter-day Saints in the Intermountain West. Something needed to be done to further genealogical research and relieve the burden on the Saints to be "baptized for those of their relatives who are dead, who they believe would have embraced the gospel, if they had been privileged with hearing it, and who have received the gospel in the Spirit, through the instrumentality of those who have been commissioned to preach to them while in prison."[4]

On November 13, 1894, the First Presidency authorized the organization of the Genealogical Society of Utah and appointed Elder Franklin D. Richards as president. The society has been known as The Genealogical Society of The Church of Jesus Christ of Latter-day Saints (1944), the Genealogical Department (1976), and the Family History Department (1987). It was "established primarily as an aid to temple work, its chief function being the gathering, classification, and tabulation of genealogical information to be used by those engaged in the performance of vicarious ordinances for their dead kindred."[5]

To provide research materials to Latter-day Saints, the society began a library with charter members contributing 11 volumes. By 1995 the library had grown to more than 258,000 volumes. Today the Family History Library not only has thousands of additional volumes but more than 4,600 local family history centers throughout the world.

The society created a Temple Index Bureau to check the reliability of the ancestral names sent in for temple ordinances and to prevent duplication.[6] Not many years later, the society began microfilming records throughout the world. The introduction of microfilm as a way of preserving irreplaceable genealogical records greatly enhanced their availability. Microfilm has an estimated life of 500 years if it is stored properly. To store the rolls and rolls of microfilm created by the society, in 1963 the Granite Mountain Records Vault in Salt Lake City was constructed. This climate-controlled vault contains roughly 35 billion

images of genealogical images on 2.4 million rolls of film.[7]

In 1984 the society helped create the first desktop genealogy management software. In 1999 FamilySearch, a digital program for genealogy, was launched, and in 2013, FamilySearch introduced a free online service. FamilySearch International has "grown . . . into the premier global leader in online genealogy research, touting billions of records and millions of subscribers. . . . [Said Paul Nauta, spokesman for Family Search:] 'What started out on index cards went to microfilm, to discs, and is now at our fingertips.'"[8]

George Durrant, a former director of the Family History Department, commented, "These and other resources have aided millions of researchers in finding their 'roots,' and have made possible the performance of temple ordinances for millions who lived and died without that opportunity."[9]

The commandment to the Latter-day Saints to seek out their ancestors and their commitment in providing temple ordinances for them has been greatly advanced by the Genealogical Society of Utah. This organization, known by various names throughout its history, has "enabled millions of genealogists throughout the world to develop a strong association between

DID YOU KNOW?

• The Genealogical Society of Utah, which grew into the family history program of the Church, started because of an effort by Church leaders to discourage members from having themselves sealed to people to whom they were not related.

• The Granite Mountain Records Vault constructed by the Church contains some 35 billion images of genealogical images on 2.4 million rolls of microfilm from over 120 different countries.

family history and The Church of Jesus Christ of Latter-day Saints."[10]

Notes

1. Gordon Irving, "The Law of Adoption: One Phase of the Development of the Mormon Concept of Salvation, 1830–1900," *BYU Studies* 14, no. 3 (1974): 291–314.
2. James B. Allen, Jessie L. Embry, and Kahlile B. Mehr, "Small Beginnings," *BYU Studies* 34, no. 2 (1994–95): 42.
3. Durham, *Discourses of Wilford Woodruff,* 156–57; Irving, "Law of Adoption," 291, 311–14.
4. History, 1838–1856, vol. C-1 [2 November 1838–31 July 1842], 1118, josephsmithpapers.org.
5. R. B. Summerhays, "The Genealogical Society of Utah," *Improvement Era,* Oct. 1927, 1104.
6. George D. Durrant, "Genealogical Society of Utah," in Ludlow, *Encyclopedia of Mormonism,* 2:537; Merrill S. Lofthouse, "A History of the Genealogical Society of The Church of Jesus Christ of Latter-day Saints to 1970," master's thesis, Brigham Young University (1971), 45.
7. Scott Taylor, "Mormon Church's Storied Granite Mountain Vault Opened for Virtual Tour," *Deseret News,* Apr. 29, 2010.
8. Genelle Pugmire, "LDS Church Celebrates 120th Anniversary of Genealogical Society, Now FamilySearch," *Provo [Utah] Daily Herald*, Nov. 12, 2014.
9. Durrant, "Genealogical Society of Utah," 2:538.
10. Durrant, "Genealogical Society of Utah," 2:538.

60
The Political Manifesto

1896

Portrait of Moses Thatcher.

Latter-day Saints have always been engaged in civic affairs of the cities and nations where they reside. For instance, Joseph Smith served as a mayor of Nauvoo, Brigham Young served as the first governor of the Utah Territory, and apostles Reed Smoot and Ezra Taft Benson served in the Senate and the Cabinet of the United States, respectively. For the first sixty years after the Church was organized, leaders were engaged in political processes at every level. In the 1890s, after the Manifesto ending the practice of plural marriage, Church leaders faced questions about the appropriate separation of church and state. At the center of the controversy was Moses Thatcher, a member of the Quorum of the Twelve.

Called to the Quorum of the Twelve in 1879, Thatcher had long been active in Utah politics. He served in the territorial legislature, as an advocate for the Church in Washington, D.C., and as a member of the convention that drafted the Utah state constitution. For most of his political career, Thatcher was an energetic member of the People's Party, the political arm of the Church that dominated Utah politics for years. Before Utah could be granted statehood, however, citizens were advised to dissolve their territorial parties and affiliate with the national political parties. The People's Party was disbanded in 1891. Those who had been active in the People's Party, like Moses Thatcher, joined either the Republican or the Democratic party.

Thatcher affiliated with the Democratic Party, where he became known for his fiery rhetoric. In an 1892 speech printed in the *Ogden Standard,* Thatcher boldly declared that Jesus Christ would have been a Democrat and Lucifer a Republican. When his remarks appeared in print, Thatcher responded that he had been misquoted. The First Presidency was alarmed at such partisan talk. Within a few days, a letter protesting the use of the name of Jesus Christ in pursuit of political gain was printed in the *Ogden Standard* under the signatures of Joseph F. Smith, a counselor in the First Presidency, and John Henry Smith, a member of the Twelve.

This was not the first time Thatcher's rhetoric had led to conflict with the other Church leaders. Over the years he publicly criticized a number of Church leaders, including George Q. Cannon, Joseph F. Smith, John Henry Smith, Heber J. Grant, Brigham Young Jr., Franklin D. Richards, and Marriner W. Merrill. In most cases Thatcher worked to heal the wounds he had inflicted, but his relationship with the First Presidency and the Twelve was marked by distrust.

The situation was not helped by Thatcher's poor health, which often led to his absence from meetings of the Twelve. George Q. Cannon, a counselor in the First Presidency, privately wrote in 1895 that Thatcher "has not been for a long time in full harmony with his quorum or the presidency" and worried that Thatcher "would lose the faith unless he repents."[1]

The situation continued to deteriorate until September 1895, when the Utah Democratic Party nominated B. H. Roberts, of the presidency of the Seventy, as their candidate for the Congress of the United States and Moses Thatcher as their candidate for the Senate. Thatcher's selection was based on the assumption that Democrats would gain control of the state legislature and the legislators would select him as their candidate. At that time, state legislatures chose Senators.

Heber J. Grant, who had declined a nomination from the Democratic Party to be a gubernatorial candidate, felt strongly that Thatcher should not have accepted the Democratic nomination "without having had a full and free chat with his brethren of the apostles and also with the First Presidency." When Thatcher was asked to meet with the First Presidency about his political nomination, he reproved President Wilford Woodruff for trying to dictate in political matters and accused the First Presidency of trying to deprive him of his agency. Elder Brigham Young Jr., who attended the meeting, conceded some of Thatcher's points but was alarmed that his fellow apostle would "throw down the responsibilities of his priesthood and pick up politics without consulting the authorities under which he has covenanted to labor."[2]

A few days later, at the priesthood session of the October 1895 general conference, President Joseph F. Smith delivered a stern warning to Church leaders who entered the political arena without first consulting their presiding authority. Leaders of the Utah Democratic Party interpreted the remarks of President Smith, a Republican, as a rebuke of Elders B. H. Roberts and Moses Thatcher. When the Democrats failed to achieve most of their goals in the November elections, charges began to swirl about Church involvement in politics. With evidence of a growing partisan divide among Church leaders, President Woodruff looked for a remedy.

In the meantime, accusations against B. H. Roberts and Moses Thatcher were on the rise. In the days leading up to the April 1896 general conference, President Woodruff and his counselors drafted a document that became known as the political manifesto. This document stated, "Before accepting a nomination or entering into engagements to perform new duties," Church leaders should counsel with their presiding authorities and "learn from

DID YOU KNOW?

- Until the early 1890s the Church sponsored its own political party.

- The political manifesto, which advised Church members to counsel with their presiding authority before entering the political arena, was signed by all of the general authorities except apostle Moses Thatcher, who refused.

them whether he can, consistently with the obligations already entered into with the church, upon assuming his office take upon himself the added duties and labors and responsibilities of the new position." The document also declared that Church leaders did not "in the least desire to dictate to them concerning their duties as American citizens or to interfere with the affairs of the state," adding, "neither do we consider that in the remotest degree we are seeking the union of church and state."[3]

The document was signed by all the general authorities except Elder Moses Thatcher, who refused. He could not accept certain provision in the document "without stultification."[4]

When the political manifesto was read in general conference in April 1896, Thatcher's name was not included. In the months that followed, President Woodruff and other Church leaders sought to reconcile with Thatcher but could not. Thatcher insisted on a public trial if he was to be removed from his ecclesiastical position. When he refused to meet with the First Presidency and Twelve privately, the Twelve voted to remove him from their quorum. Thatcher lost his position as an apostle but was not excommunicated. He remained a member of the Church, even testifying on behalf of the Church at the Reed Smoot hearings in Washington, D.C.

The political manifesto was an important benchmark in the integration of the Church into American society. The document was read to all congregations of the Church for a sustaining vote. During this process, suggestions were offered to clarify that only general authorities must consult with Church leaders before seeking political office, not rank and file members of the priesthood.

Over the years the Political Manifesto was applied at various times. For instance, in 1934 when J. Reuben Clark Jr., second counselor in the First Presidency, was suggested as a candidate for the United States Senate, Clark consulted with President Heber J. Grant and decided not to run. A few years later when Ezra Taft Benson was asked to serve as Secretary of Agriculture in the Cabinet of Dwight D. Eisenhower, Elder Benson consulted with President David O. McKay, received clearance, and served for the duration of the Eisenhower administration.

NOTES

1. Edward Leo Lyman, "The Alienation of an Apostle from His Quorum: The Moses Thatcher Case," *Dialogue*, Summer 1985, 77, 79.
2. Lyman, "Alienation of an Apostle," 80.
3. *Autobiography of B. H. Roberts,* 203.
4. Alexander, *Things in Heaven and in Earth,* 315.

61
The First Sister Missionaries

1898

Amanda Inez Knight (left) and Lucy Jane (Jennie) Brimhall (right), the first full-time proselyting sister missionaries in the Church.

The early history of the Church is filled with missionary accounts of the brethren. Only occasionally is found a brief account of a wife accompanying her husband to the mission field. During the presidency of Brigham Young and later nineteenth-century leaders women traveled as genealogical missionaries or were sent to study at universities outside the Intermountain West. None of these women, who numbered fewer than two hundred, served as proselyting missionaries.

In 1898 Amanda Inez Knight and Lucy Jane (Jennie) Brimhall were called as the first full-time proselyting female missionaries. One reason for this dramatic break from the past was that these women could provide an opposite view of the stereotype of Latter-day Saint women in the postpolygamy era. Susa Young Gates, a daughter of Brigham Young and a public figure in her own right, recognized the

advantages of missionary service for women: "It was felt that much prejudice could be allayed, that many false charges against the women of the Church could thus be refuted, while the girls themselves would receive quite as much in the way of development and inspiration as they could impart through their intelligence and devotion."[1]

Jennie Brimhall and Inez Knight were schoolmates at Brigham Young Academy (later Brigham Young University). Jennie was the daughter of George H. Brimhall and Alsina E. Wilkins. When her father became a professor at Brigham Young Academy, Jennie attended the academy and graduated in 1895. She taught school in Bluff City, Utah, until the next year, when she returned to Brigham Young Academy to teach third and fourth graders. She accepted the marriage proposal of Jesse Will Knight, also a classmate and the brother of Inez Knight. During his engagement to Jennie, Jesse accepted a mission call to the British Isles.

Inez Knight was the daughter of Utah mining magnate Jesse Knight and his wife Amanda McEwan. After studying at Brigham Young Academy, Inez pursued genealogical research in St. George, Utah.

In 1898, twenty-two-year-old Jennie Brimhall and twenty-three-year-old Inez Knight made plans to travel abroad. When Jennie's bishop, J. B. Keeler, learned of their plans, he suggested the two friends go to Europe as missionaries instead. That single women had never been called to serve proselyting missions did not deter Jennie, who followed the counsel of Church leaders on matters ranging from proper dress to waltzing. Jennie replied without hesitation that she would be willing to be a missionary if she were formally called.

Bishop Keeler wrote to President Wilford Woodruff about the matter. In a subsequent letter from the First Presidency of the Church, President Edward Partridge of the Utah Stake was authorized to set apart Jennie and Inez as missionaries to Great Britain. He did so on April 1, 1898, and the two women thus became the first sister missionaries in the Church.

The next day, they departed for Liverpool, England. Upon arriving at the seaport, they were assigned by mission president Platt D. Lyman to "do all things required of male missionaries along the same lines: visiting, tracting, preaching, and exerting themselves to the utmost to spread . . . the truth."[2]

Next day, Jennie spoke to a crowded hall full of curious Britons. Her audience listened "with rapt attention" as she delivered her message with "intelligence and sincerity."[3]

Inez and Jennie also participated in street meetings. After five street-corner meetings in one night, Inez wrote in her journal: "Most of the elders . . . stood like brave soldiers on the street that night and different young men in all humility and yet with intelligence told the people gospel truths. I was never prouder to know that I was numbered with the L.D. Saints."[4]

The first permanent assignment for Inez and Jennie was in the town of Bristol, England. After tracting all day, Inez wrote in her journal: "At three houses they took my tract and spoke civilly to me, but at the fourth, a woman asked me who I was, and learning that I was a Latter-day Saint, she said, 'You don't know as much about them as I do, or you would not carry their trash around.' I told her I had lived among them all my life and ought to know. She then asked me if I knew Mary ————. I answered no. 'Well then you're a liar; you either did not come from Utah, or else you know her, because Mormon Elders took her out six years ago.' She followed me to each gate through the street, to inform them at each house who I was. Girl-like, I went home and cried."[5]

Tracting statistics in Inez's journal reveal that in the first month of their mission, she and Jennie distributed 523 tracts, visited 295 houses in tracting, visited 14 homes by invitation, had 22 gospel conversations, and distributed two books. Inez also noted that they often drew an "eager crowd" when speaking.[6]

Due in part to the successful service of these first female missionaries and others, the First Presidency began to consider extending a missionary invitation to all the young women of the Church. Their considerations were greatly enhanced by the request of European Mission president Joseph W. McMurrin for a number of bright and intelligent women to be called as missionaries to England.

On March 11, 1898, President George Q. Cannon of the First Presidency announced, "'It has been decided to call some of our wise and prudent women into the missionary field.' He spoke of the labors performed by Sister Elizabeth Claridge McCune in England and

DID YOU KNOW?

- Although many married women served missions with their husbands, the first single female missionaries were not called until 1898.

- The first assignment given to the sister missionaries was to "do all things required of male missionaries along the same lines: visiting, tracting, preaching, and exerting themselves to the utmost to spread . . . the truth."

other sisters who had spoken in public places; and added that great good could be accomplished by the sisters in this direction."[7]

After three months in the mission field, Jennie Brimhall was honorably released in November 1898 for health reasons. She journeyed to the States with other recently released missionaries, including her fiancé, Jesse Will Knight, whom she married the next year.

Sister Liza Chipman took the place of Jennie as the missionary companion of Inez. These sisters enjoyed much success, except in January 1899 when the Anti-Mormon League threw stones and trash at them. Inez recorded:

"We escaped being hurt, save in our feelings, though our clothing was badly soiled and our hats somewhat crumpled. The noise made by our pursuers drew people out of shops and buildings for some distance ahead of us, and as we at home stand to view a circus parade, so they watched us pass along, all save one man who accompanied us most of the way, endeavoring to protect us. About five minutes before we reached the police station we met Brothers James and Haddock, with three policemen, who at once stepped between us and the crowd, which, however, had so increased by this time that it was impossible to turn them back. Arriving at the station, we were at once hurried into a back room, and after waiting there about an hour (in which time some tears were shed and a Gospel conversation held) the chief of police took us out of the rear entrance and saw us safe home."[8]

Despite such occasional difficulties, the sister missionaries grew to love the people they served, and the British Saints, in turn, made sacrifices to serve them. For instance, one evening the sisters stayed with a woman who insisted that the two missionaries have her bed while she slept on the floor. In the morning, this woman gave them her children's breakfast while the hungry children looked on.

In March 1899, the mission president approached the sisters about being released. Inez Knight wrote of their response, "Sister C. and I are both willing to remain until the Lord calls us home."[9] Inez served for fourteen additional months in London, Ashford, and Kent, England, before boarding a vessel bound for America on May 19, 1900.

The work of the first sister missionaries opened the door for a new era in missionary work, and a new era for Latter-day Saint women. Today women make up a substantial and important portion of the missionary force, serving in nearly every country where the Church is organized. The brave pioneering efforts of these first sister missionaries laid the foundation for the work of the sister missionaries of our time.

NOTES

1. Susa Young Gates, in Jessie L. Embry, "Oral History and Mormon Women Missionaries: The Stories Sound the Same," *Frontiers* 19, no. 3 (1998): 172.
2. Whitney, *History of Utah*, 4:614; Evans, *Century of "Mormonism,"* 242.
3. Whitney, *History of Utah*, 4:614.
4. "Inez Knight Allen Missionary Journal," Mormon Missionary Diaries, L. Tom Perry Special Collections, Harold B. Lee Library, Brigham Young University, Provo, Utah, 17–18.
5. Whitney, *History of Utah*, 4:611.
6. Diane L. Mangum, "The First Sister Missionaries," *Ensign*, July 1980, 64.
7. "Biographical Sketches: Jennie Brimhall and Inez Knight," *Young Woman's Journal*, June 1898, 245.
8. Whitney, *History of Utah*, 4:612–13.
9. "Inez Knight Allen Missionary Journal," 141–42.

62
President Lorenzo Snow Receives Revelation on Tithing

1899

President Lorenzo Snow.

In 1898, the Church was facing a financial disaster. Several factors contributed to it, but chief among them were the draconian measures employed by the United States federal government in its drive to end the practice of plural marriage. The 1887 the Edmunds-Tucker Act dissolved the corporation of the Church and placed all its assets over the value of $50,000 in the hands of federal authorities. Church leaders attempted to counter the effects of the Edmunds-Tucker Law by placing deeds of Church-owned properties in the names of trusted members.

Ending plural marriages in 1890 significantly lessened tensions between Church leaders and the federal government, but the residue of their conflict and its devastating effects on the finances of the Church lingered for years. Combined with the fallout from a severe economic crisis in the the 1890s, the Church was nearly insolvent by the end of the decade.

In 1898 when Lorenzo Snow became President of the Church, he expressed his determination to solve the financial problem created, in large part, by the federal government. President Snow deplored debt, saying to one audience that he had borrowed money only once—$60 to help defray the costs of his first mission. As an apostle, Elder Snow had helped design and operate the united order in Brigham City, Utah, one of the most successful cooperative ventures in the Church. Soon after becoming Church President, Lorenzo Snow asked his counselors, George Q. Cannon and Joseph F. Smith, to create a report that detailed the financial condition of the Church. Their report revealed deeply disturbing news: the Church was on the verge of bankruptcy.

The first step taken by President Snow to reform Church finances was to issue a million dollars in short-term bonds with an interest rate of 6 percent per year. The bonds sold within a year, but the measure was only a stopgap. Something more permanent was needed for the long-range financial well-being of the

Church. The question weighed heavily upon President Snow.

In early May 1899, President Snow's son LeRoi entered his father's room and saw him "sitting upright in his bed. His face was almost white and his eyes shone as I had never seen them before. All he said was: 'I am going to St. George.'"[1] Not long afterward, President Snow publicly announced his intention to journey to St. George and tour other Utah settlements. Yet he frankly admitted that he did not know why he was planning to travel to southern Utah.

Even with the availability of travel by railroads, the journey to southern Utah was long and arduous for the eighty-five-year-old President Snow. He was accompanied by his son LeRoi and several general authorities, including Joseph F. Smith and William B. Preston, the Presiding Bishop. The rail line south from Salt Lake City ended at Modena, Utah, which meant the traveling party were conveyed the next sixty-five miles to their destination in horse-drawn carriages. According to LeRoi, President Snow appeared very weak when the party finally arrived at St. George and slept restlessly that night, still unsure of the reason for the journey.

The next day President Snow was the first speaker at a meeting held in the St. George Tabernacle. According to contemporary accounts, President Snow praised the Saints in southern Utah for their faithfulness in paying tithes and offerings and emphasized the importance of "establishing Zion within our hearts." He declared that earlier attempts to establish Zion had met with failure, because the Saints valued "more of the dollar than serving the Lord."[2] Throughout his discourse, the faithful payment of tithes was a prominent theme.

According to contemporary accounts, there occurred in his address a dramatic moment when President Snow paused, looked at the back wall of the tabernacle as if he were seeing something, and then began speaking in depth about tithing. Several gathered in the tabernacle recalled that President Snow "appeared to [be] surrounded by a beautiful, bright white light."[3] He later said that on that occasion he received a revelation from the Lord.

At another meeting President Snow declared, "The word of the Lord to you is not anything new; it is simply this: THE TIME HAS NOW COME FOR EVERY LATTER-DAY SAINT WHO CALCULATES TO BE PREPARED FOR THE FUTURE AND TO HOLD HIS FEET STRONG UPON A PROPER FOUNDATION, TO GO AND DO THE WILL OF THE LORD AND TO PAY HIS TITHING IN FULL." He further declared this to "be the word of the Lord to every settlement throughout the land of Zion."[4]

After leaving St. George, President Snow's party preached the importance of tithing in settlements on their route to Salt Lake City. Records from meetings held in the settlements of Washington, Leeds, Toquerville, Kanarraville, Cedar City, Parowan, Beaver, Kanosh, Meadow, Fillmore, Holden, Scipio, and Nephi tell of President Snow speaking on tithing. In Holden, President Snow told the congregation of Latter-day Saints that when he had left Salt Lake City, he didn't know why he was to travel south, but "in the first meeting

DID YOU KNOW?

- Severe persecution by the United States government, combined with a worldwide financial panic, led the Church to a severe fiscal crisis.

- At one point, eighty-four-year-old President Lorenzo Snow traveled for seventeen days, holding twenty-four meetings in sixteen different settlements and speaking twenty-six times, all to urge the Saints to live the law of tithing.

in St. George" he came to know that "there is one important command that was given to the Latter-day Saints that has not been observed; it is the law of tithing."[5]

After seventeen days of travel, twenty-four meetings in sixteen different communities, and speaking twenty-six times, President Snow reached his home in Salt Lake City. Although he was weary, his zeal for the topic of tithing was not abated. Historian E. Jay Bell observed that during his sixty years of Church service before his speech in St. George, Lorenzo Snow had given only two or three recorded addresses on the subject of tithing. Afterward, he spoke on tithing on forty-four documented occasions. The effect of this emphasis is shown in statistics from the period, which show a marked increase in full-tithe payers. In addition to speaking on tithing, President Snow worked to end deficit spending and put in place mechanisms to increase the accountability for expenditures of Church funds. Gradually, the Church began to emerge from the dark cloud of debt and insolvency.

Unfortunately, President Snow did not live to see the full financial independence of the Church. Such independence was not reached until 1907. At the April 1907 general conference, President Joseph F. Smith announced,

"The Church of Jesus Christ of Latter-day Saints owes not a dollar that it cannot repay at once. At last we are in a position that we can pay as we go. We do not have to borrow any more, and will not have to if the Latter-day Saints continue to live their religion and observe this law of tithing. It is the law of revenue to the Church."[6]

Though the presidency of Lorenzo Snow from 1898 to 1901 was brief, it was crucial to freeing the Church from the dire straits of insolvency. Elder John A. Widtsoe referred to President Snow as "the financial liberator" of the Church.[7]

NOTES

1. LeRoi C. Snow, "From Despair to Freedom through the Law of Tithing," Church Section, *Deseret News*, Mar. 29, 1941, 5; E. Jay Bell, "The Windows of Heaven Revisited: The 1899 Tithing Reformation," *Journal of Mormon History* 20, no. 1 (1994): 57–58.
2. Bell, "Windows of Heaven Revisited," 63.
3. Bell, "Windows of Heaven Revisited," 64.
4. Bell, "Windows of Heaven Revisited," 72.
5. Bell, "Windows of Heaven Revisited," 73–74.
6. Smith, in Conference Report, Apr. 1907, 7.
7. Widtsoe, "Lorenzo Snow: The Financial Liberator," *Instructor*, Nov. 1938, 574.

63
Elder Heber J. Grant's Mission to Japan

1901

Missionaries to Japan: left to right, Horace S. Ensign, Alma O. Taylor, and mission president Heber J. Grant.

Perhaps no other mission faced as many challenges as the Japan Mission when it was opened at the turn of the twentieth century. From the moment mission president Heber J. Grant and his fellow missionaries arrived at Yokohama, they were confronted with language barriers, unfamiliar cultural mores, and difficulties in finding converts. After twenty-three years of failing to meet these challenges, the mission was closed.

Despite this bleak beginning, the opening of the Japan Mission was an important event for the Church. The mere fact that Westerners were allowed to enter Japan, after its years of isolation, was a giant step forward. Latter-day Saints believed the Lord was "at work in

His own way, breaking down the barriers . . . between the nations . . . [and] preparing the way for His servants to go forth to declare the glad tidings of salvation."[1] This work, though stopped for a time, ultimately led to growth and progress with the reopening of the Japan Mission in 1948.

Before the mid-nineteenth century, Japan had been closed to "commercial, diplomatic, and religious overtures of the West" for more than two hundred years, beginning in the 1600s.[2] The closure had led to the isolation of the people and their way of life. Not until 1854 did Japan reestablish trade and regular interaction with the Western world.

On February 14, 1901, George Q. Cannon, a counselor in the First Presidency, announced the opening of a mission in Japan. Elder Heber J. Grant, a member of the Quorum of the Twelve Apostles, recalled, "The moment he made this remark, I felt impressed that I would be called to open up this mission."[3]

Elder Grant was right. Not having served a proselytizing mission before, he faced the call with trepidation: "I do not know when anything has struck me much harder than being called to Japan. I really dreaded being called to the British mission . . . but I look upon the European mission in comparison to opening up the work in Japan, as a picnic on the one hand and a great labor on the other. However, I shall go and do the best I possibly can."[4]

On July 24, 1901, Elder Grant and his companions—Horace S. Ensign, Louis A. Kelsch, and Alma O. Taylor—left Salt Lake

City to begin their journey to Japan. After traveling over five thousand miles, the missionaries arrived in Yokohama on August 12. Their initial excitement over the new sights and sounds of Japan did not last long, for they found themselves in the middle of what Elder Taylor called "a heavy war"—Church doctrines and practices had been mistranslated and misunderstood by the Japanese long before their arrival.[5]

Japanese scholar Sara Cox Smith observed that Mormonism "was portrayed as ridiculous and indeed laughable in its doctrine but with an uncanny, almost eerie, power to attract believers. Many perceived it to be a threat to Japanese culture."[6]

Misunderstanding of the Church, combined with the missionaries' arrival in Yokohama, led to a strong reaction by the Japanese press. More than 160 editorials or essays were published in magazines or newspapers, some in opposition to the Latter-day Saints and some in support of them during the missionaries' first month in the country. Scholar Shinji Takagi wrote, "The amount of press coverage given the Mormon missionaries during the [first] month or so was unprecedented and has not been surpassed in the subsequent history of the Church in Japan." There was, however, a silver lining to the published opposition—the overall impact was more positive than negative and helped in "making sure that the news of the arrival of Mormonism in Japan penetrated every region and sounded in virtually every ear."[7]

On September 1, 1901, a month after their arrival, President Heber J. Grant and his companions walked to a beautiful grove of trees on a hillside that overlooked the Yokohama harbor. There Elder Grant dedicated the nation of Japan for the preaching of the gospel, the gathering of Israel, and the "establishment of righteousness upon the earth." He also prayed that the Lord might "touch the hearts of the people

. . . to recognize the truth when it was declared unto them."[8]

Nevertheless, the hearts of the people were slow to hearken. As historian Reid L. Neilson explained, "From the day they arrived in Japan until the day they returned to America, these men and women were unsure how to evangelize in a non-Christian, non-Western nation."[9] Popular phrases in Japan at the time included "Down with frivolous Europeanization! Keep to our national heritage! Japan for the Japanese!"[10] The missionaries struggled with these sentiments as well as "countering the assumption that the Church was based on the practice of polygamy."[11]

Another significant difficulty was translating the Book of Mormon into Japanese. The missionaries simply translated their message but did not adapt it to an Asian audience. The missionary model that had worked so well in Europe and America did not work well in Japan. Yet their efforts did yield results. On March 8, 1902, Nakazawa Hajime, the first Latter-day Saint convert in Japan, was baptized.[12]

Unfortunately, Nakazawa Hajime was later excommunicated. The hope and then disappointment over the first convert became emblematic of the missionaries' efforts as a whole in the country.[13] Over the next few years, other Mormon missionaries went to Japan, including members of Heber J. Grant's family. Nevertheless, the work was slow and conversions were few. After ten years, there had

DID YOU KNOW?

• During the first month of Elder Heber J. Grant's mission to Japan, 160 editorials or essays appeared in Japanese publications, some in opposition to the Church and some in support of it.

• The Japan Mission was opened in 1901 and closed in 1924; it was reopened in 1948.

been only 51 baptisms. In September 1903, Elder Grant was released and returned to Salt Lake City. When the Japan Mission was closed twenty-one years later, a total of 174 converts had been baptized.

Elder Grant's sadness over the mission was evident in his October 1903 general conference address: "I regret I am not able to tell you that we have done something wonderful over in Japan. To be perfectly frank with you, I acknowledge I have accomplished very little indeed, as the president of that mission; and very little has been accomplished—so far as conversions are concerned." Yet he expressed optimism for the Japanese mission: "I feel the assurance in my heart there will yet be a great and important labor accomplished in that land. The inhabitants are a wonderful people. What they have accomplished during the past fifty years, since the country was opened to foreigners, is little less than marvelous."[14]

Early Japanese missionary Alma O. Taylor believed that the beginnings of missionary labors in Japan were a success. He declared: "Is the Japan mission a failure? Is it premature? The shortest answer to both these questions is an emphatic 'No.' It is the mission of 'Mormonism' to preach the gospel to all the world for a witness before the end shall come. Therefore, counting its success or failure by the number of converts made, is a gross mistake. The aim of the Japanese mission is to preach the everlasting gospel and bear witness of Jesus Christ, that the people of this land, like those of all other lands, may be left without excuse. Our success or failure, then, must be determined by the answer to the question, 'What

has the Japan mission done, and what is it doing, for the spread of truth?'"[15]

The early efforts to preach the gospel to the people of Japan helped lay the groundwork for the reopening of the mission in 1948 and the remarkable growth of the Church in Japan today.

Notes

1. "Opening of Japan," *Millennial Star,* Sept. 2, 1854, 552.
2. Reid L. Neilson, "The Japan Mission: First Efforts," in Neilson and Gessel, *Taking the Gospel to the Japanese,* 31.
3. Ronald W. Walker, "Strangers in a Strange Land: Heber J. Grant and the Opening of the Japan Mission," in Neilson and Gessel, *Taking the Gospel to the Japanese,* 148.
4. Grant to Anthony W. Ivins, Feb. 15, 1901, in Walker, "Strangers in a Strange Land," 148.
5. Alma O. Taylor, Journal, Aug. 20, 1901, 123, byu.edu.
6. Sarah Cox Smith, "Translator or Translated? The Portrayal of The Church of Jesus Christ of Latter-day Saints in Print in Meiji Japan," in Neilson and Gessel, *Taking the Gospel to the Japanese,* 129.
7. Shinji Takagi, "Mormons in the Press: Reactions to the 1901 Opening of the Japan Mission," in Neilson and Gessel, *Taking the Gospel to the Japanese,* 179, 205–6.
8. Nielson, *Japanese Missionary Journals of Elder Alma O. Taylor,* 48–49.
9. Neilson, *Early Mormon Missionary Activities in Japan,* 79, 83.
10. Anesaki, *History of Japanese Religion,* 360.
11. Smith, "Translator or Translated?" 137.
12. Britsch, *From the East,* 53–55.
13. Britsch, *From the East,* 55.
14. Grant, in Conference Report, Oct. 1903, 7.
15. Taylor, "About Japan and the Japan Mission," *Improvement Era,* Nov. 1906, 6.

64
The Reed Smoot Hearings

Reed Smoot, ca. 1898.

1903

Reed Smoot was elected to the United States Senate by the Utah State legislature in January of 1903. Elder Smoot's ecclesiastical position as a member of the Quorum of the Twelve Apostles (since 1900) immediately ignited a firestorm of controversy.[1]

From 1904 to 1907 a series of congressional hearings led to an intense examination of Latter-day Saint history and practices. Remnants of the hearings linger even today, and for decades they have "conjured up claims

of religious persecution, duplicitous testimony and shocking admissions."[2]

Most historians agree that the highly publicized hearings had a great bearing on the public image of the Church. The Reed Smoot hearings, or the Smoot case, led to a profound shift in America's perception of the Latter-day Saints. The case consisted of a series of hearings on whether the United States Senate should seat the duly-elected Senator Smoot.

Smoot's election in 1903 stirred up a new wave of anti-Mormon sentiment. Protests began almost immediately. Eighteen prominent men in Salt Lake City, many of them ministers from other faiths, published a document protesting Smoot's election for the reason "that he is one of a self-perpetuating body of fifteen men who . . . claim, supreme authority, divinely sanctioned, to shape the belief and control the conduct of those under them in all matters whatsoever."[3]

Within a year, more than 3,100 petitions had arrived in Washington, D.C., requesting that Reed Smoot not be admitted to the Senate. The petitions led Senate leaders to form a committee to investigate the charges against Smoot. As historian Harvard Heath explained, "The prosecution focused on two issues: Smoot's alleged polygamy and his expected allegiance to the Church and its ruling hierarchy, which, it was claimed, would make it impossible for him to execute his oath as a United States senator. Though the proceedings focused on senator-elect Smoot, it soon became apparent that it was the Church that was on trial."[4]

In late February 1903 when Senator Smoot arrived in Washington, D.C., he was met by protestors who charged him with being a polygamist, and they wanted answers about the old issues of Danites and the Mountain Meadows Massacre. Senator Smoot prepared a rebuttal to these charges with the help of several non-Mormon lawyers.

The hearings began in March 1903 with subpoenas issued to every general authority and other Church leaders, asking them to testify about the power of the Church over its members. President Joseph F. Smith was questioned for three days.[5] Elders James E. Talmage and Francis M. Lyman of the Quorum of the Twelve were also questioned. Moses Thatcher, who had been dropped from the Quorum of the Twelve in 1896, was also asked to testify.[6] Their testimonies were published in the anti-Mormon press while federal agents in Utah searched for Smoot's other wife, only to find that there wasn't one. He was not and had never been a polygamist.

During the three-year trial, the Senators took sides for or against Smoot. Senator Fred Dubois of Idaho was vicious in his opposition. Senator Boies Penrose of Pennsylvania, while addressing the subject of polygamy, glared at colleagues who had a reputation for philandering: "As for me, I would rather have seated beside me in this chamber a polygamist who doesn't polyg than a monogamist who doesn't monog."[7]

Historian Kathleen Flake observed, "The four-year Senate proceeding created a 3,500-page record of testimony by 100 witnesses on every peculiarity of Mormonism, especially its polygamous family structure, ritual worship practices, 'secret oaths,' open canon, economic communalism, and theocratic politics."[8]

The trials themselves became a spectacle, with the public actively participating in the proceedings. Around the nation, the trials played out as a fascinating drama, depicted in the newspapers of the day. Flake noted, "At the height of the hearing, some senators were receiving a thousand letters a day from angry constituents. What remains of these public petitions fills 11 feet of shelf space, the largest such collection in the National Archives."[9]

On February 20, 1907, a vote was taken on whether to expel Reed Smoot from the United States Senate. The vote fell short of the necessary two-thirds majority. Senator Smoot retained his seat and was reelected four times, serving for twenty-six more years.

Historian Heath observed that the vote had more sweeping results than just seating the Senator from Utah. The victory for Smoot was a victory for the Church, providing greater political legitimacy in a time when the Church was moving closer to the mainstream of American society. The vote marked the beginning of three decades in the Senate in which Senator Smoot become one of the most powerful leaders in the American government. Heath argued, "Perhaps more than any other individual, Reed Smoot molded and shaped the positive national image the Church was to enjoy throughout the twentieth century."[10]

President Joseph F. Smith saw the seating of Senator Smoot as an important turning point in the way Latter-day Saints were viewed by the rest of the nation. Only a few months before his death, President Smith told Senator Smoot, "I cannot understand how anyone, not even

DID YOU KNOW?

- Reed Smoot was elected to the office of United States Senator while serving as a member of the Quorum on the Twelve Apostles.

- President Joseph F. Smith testified before a congressional committee during the Reed Smoot hearings.

your bitterest opponents, can fail to see the handwriting of an overruling providence in the success and honor you have won and achieved at the seat of government. Surely the Lord has magnified his servant."[11]

Notes

1. Roberts, *Comprehensive History of the Church,* 6:390–91.
2. Nick Literski, "Reed Smoot Hearings: A Review and What It Says about Today," mormonmatters.org.
3. Roberts, *Comprehensive History of the Church,* 6:391.
4. Harvard S. Heath, "Smoot Hearings," in Ludlow, *Encyclopedia of Mormonism,* 3:1363.
5. See Michael H. Paulos, "Under the Gun at the Smoot Hearings: Joseph F. Smith's Testimony," *Journal of Mormon History* 34, no 4 (Fall 2008): 181–225; Flake, *Politics of American Religious Identity,* 55.
6. Flake, *Politics of American Religious Identity,* 55.
7. Beers, *Pennsylvania Politics,* 51.
8. Flake, *Politics of American Religious Identity,* 5.
9. Flake, *Politics of American Religious Identity,* 5.
10. Heath, "Smoot Hearings," 3:1364.
11. Joseph F. Smith to Reed Smoot, Jan. 5, 1918, in Harvard S. Heath, "The Reed Smoot Hearings: A Quest for Legitimacy," *Journal of Mormon History* 33, no. 2 (2007): 77.

65
The End of the Physical Gathering

Missionaries in England with Church President Joseph F. Smith (middle row, second from right), mission president Heber J. Grant (middle row, far right), and members of the Grant family, 1906.

1906

The doctrine of gathering was consistently practiced in the Church throughout the nineteenth century. From the beginning of the Restoration, the Saints were encouraged to gather to a specific location to enjoy the fellowship of believers, to strengthen one another, and later to receive the ordinances of the temple.

At the beginning of the twentieth century, a change to the doctrine of gathering began to take place. With more and more converts residing outside the traditional Latter-day Saint strongholds in the Intermountain West, Church leaders began to encourage Latter-day Saints to stay in their own lands and build up the Church there.[1]

Several small events led to the change. The new policy marked the practical beginning of The Church of Jesus Christ of Latter-day Saints as a global faith.

In September 1830 the Lord commanded through his Prophet Joseph Smith that the Saints "gather in unto one place upon the face of this land, to prepare their hearts and be prepared in all things against the day when tribulation and desolation are sent forth upon the wicked" (D&C 29:8).[2]

It became clear a few months later that the gathering was not just spiritual but also temporal when the Lord commanded the Saints to "go to the Ohio" (D&C 37:1, 3). In obedience to that command, the newly baptized gathered to Kirtland, Ohio. Later, when the location for the city of Zion was revealed as Independence, Missouri, many of the Saints gathered to Missouri (D&C 57:1–2).[3]

Throughout the early history of the Church, Latter-day Saints moved to such specific places as Far West, Missouri, and Nauvoo, Illinois, in obedience to the doctrine of gathering. Joseph Smith asked, "What was the object of gathering the . . . people of God in any age of the world?" He answered, "The main object was to build unto the Lord a house whereby He could reveal unto His people the ordinances of His house and the glories of His kingdom, and teach the people the way of salvation."[4]

After the martyrdom of Joseph Smith, Brigham Young continued to emphasize a physical gathering. In 1845 Church leaders issued a proclamation declaring that the Lord "has commanded us to gather together his

Saints on the Continent, and build up holy cities and sanctuaries."[5] The commandment to gather stayed consistent throughout the remainder of the nineteenth century, with most converts immigrating to Church centers in the western United States. Unfortunately, the practice kept international units from gaining a strong foothold in foreign lands. The first indication of a new phase of gathering appeared in the 1890s, when difficult economic conditions led to a temporary suspension of the gathering movement.

In January 1899 President Lorenzo Snow led a discussion with the First Presidency and the Twelve about the inherent problems of gathering. The discussion was particularly poignant, because a hallmark of President Snow's brief tenure was the opening of new countries for missionary work and his focus on the international membership of the Church. President Snow's counselor George Q. Cannon expressed concern over those who "come here . . . who fail to secure employment and . . . return to their former homes." He added, "They either apostatize or to a great extent neutralize the efforts of our missionaries laboring in those regions." Elder Matthias Cowley noted that when converts had not gathered to the Intermountain West, their remaining in their homelands had been "beneficial, since they had in many cases built meetinghouses and helped raise up branches of the Church, as well as becoming seasoned in the faith."[6]

Another important moment came in 1906 when President Joseph F. Smith traveled to Europe, the first time a president of the Church had done so. During a conference held in Bern, Switzerland, President Smith prophesied, "The time will come when this land [Europe] will be dotted with temples, where you can go and redeem your dead." He further declared that "temples would be built in diverse countries of the world."[7]

This prophecy signaled President Smith's intention to remove one of the barriers that kept Latter-day Saints from remaining in their own lands. Instead of the Saints traveling to live near a temple in the western United States, the prophetic promise was that temples would go to them. Fifty years later, in 1955, the Bern Switzerland Temple was dedicated near the site of President Smith's 1906 prophecy, and just over a century after that prophecy, more than a dozen temples have been built in European countries.

In 1907 an editorial in the *Millennial Star,* a Church periodical published in England, offered advice to emigrating Saints and added, "The Church to which we belong is not using any influence to persuade its members or others to emigrate, but desires many of them shall stay and build up the work abroad."[8]

An epistle addressed to Latter-day Saints in the Netherlands gave even stronger indications of a growing shift in the implementation of the doctrine of gathering: "The policy of the Church is not to entice or encourage people to leave their native lands; but to remain faithful and true in their allegiance to their governments, and to be good citizens."[9]

Throughout his presidency, Joseph F. Smith looked for ways to make the blessings of the temple available to Latter-day Saints residing outside the United States. In 1912 he announced plans to build a temple in Cardston,

> **DID YOU KNOW?**
>
> • Near the beginning of the twentieth century, Church leaders began urging members to stay in their own nations.
>
> • In February 1996, the Church announced that more members were living outside the United States than inside it.

Alberta, Canada. Three years later, he announced a temple to be built in Laie, Hawaii, the first temple to be built outside North America.

By the 1920s Latter-day Saints were advised by Church leaders to remain in their native lands. A 1921 editorial in the *Millennial Star* declared, "Stay Where You Are!" The article did not fault Latter-day Saints who migrated to the United States, but it made it clear there was no longer a directive for Church members to physically gather to the Intermountain West. The editorial noted:

"The counsel of the General Authorities to the yet ungathered saints, is not to flock Zionward under existing conditions; but to remain in the countries where they now dwell, and honour the laws of those countries. Such as have homes and employment, especially, should stay and help build up the Lord's work . . . strengthening the hands of the elders and other missionaries labouring among them."[10]

The policy change did not signal an end to the doctrine of gathering, merely a different implementation. Church leaders now emphasized the doctrine of gathering as a spiritual ideal for Latter-day Saints. They cited an 1838 prophecy of the Prophet Joseph Smith, in which the Lord declared, "The gathering together upon the land of Zion, and upon her stakes, may be for a defense, and for a refuge from the storm" (D&C 115:6).

At an area conference held in Seoul, South Korea, in 1975, President Spencer W. Kimball taught, "In the early days of the Church we used to preach for the people to come to Utah as the gathering process, largely because it was the only place in the whole world where there was a temple. . . . It is no longer necessary that we bring all the people to Salt Lake City. . . . And so the gathering is taking place. Korea is the gathering place for Koreans, Australia is the gathering place for Australians, Brazil for the Brazilians, England for the English."[11]

On another occasion President Kimball taught, "The First Presidency and the Twelve see great wisdom in the multiple Zions, many gathering places where the Saints within their own culture and nation can act as a leaven in the building of the kingdom."[12]

In February 1996 the Church announced that more members were living outside the United States than in it.[13] Less than a century after the physical gathering to the Intermountain West ended, the gradual policy change initiated by Presidents Lorenzo Snow and Joseph F. Smith had led to the emergence of a truly global faith.

Notes

1. Journal History of the Church, Jan. 19, 1899, Church History Library, The Church of Jesus Christ of Latter-day Saints, Salt Lake City, Utah.
2. MacKay et al., *Documents,* 1:177, or josephsmith papers.org.
3. MacKay et al., *Documents,* 1:226–27; Godfrey et al., *Documents,* 2:5–12; or josephsmithpapers.org.
4. *Joseph Smith* [manual], 416.
5. "Proclamation of the Twelve Apostles of the Church of Jesus Christ of Latter-day Saints," in Clark, *Messages of the First Presidency,* 1:263.
6. Journal History of the Church, Jan. 19, 1899.
7. *Der Stern,* Aug. 1, 1906, 332; Serge F. Ballif, in Conference Report, Oct. 1920, 90; see Cowan, *Temples to Dot the Earth,* 120.
8. *Millennial Star,* May 23, 1907, 329.
9. Clark, *Messages of the First Presidency,* 4:165.
10. *Millennial Star,* Sept. 15, 1921, 585.
11. *Teachings of Spencer W. Kimball,* 440.
12. *Teachings of Spencer W. Kimball,* 440.
13. Samuel M. Otterstrom, "Membership Distribution, 1850–present," in Plewe, *Mapping Mormonism,* 174.

66
The Beginning of the Seminary Program

Thomas J. Yates, the first seminary teacher.

1912

One important development in Latter-day Saint history took place in the family home of Laura Merrill, a young mother residing in Salt Lake City. Her determination to teach her children from the scriptures gave rise to seminary, the most far-reaching educational program in the Church.

In 1912, Joseph F. Merrill, a professor of physics at the University of Utah, was appointed second counselor to President Frank Y. Taylor of the Granite Utah Stake. This stake,

a seedbed of innovation, had already implemented teacher training, systematized temple work under the direction of the priesthood, and a family night program announced in 1909. When President Merrill joined the stake presidency 1912, he was charged with creating additional innovations in the stake's educational programs.

At the time, youth in the Granite Utah Stake and elsewhere received their basic education at Church academies in the Intermountain West. The introduction of government-sponsored public schools in 1890 had led to a steady decrease in the number of Latter-day Saint students attending Church academies. As a result, fewer and fewer youth received the benefit of religious instruction offered at Church academies. With public school enrollment in Utah surpassing that of Church schools, President Merrill had a difficult problem to solve—how to provide daily religious instruction for members of his stake without intruding on the separation of Church and state.

During a stake-sponsored family night, President Merrill became intrigued by the stories his wife, Laura, shared with their children from the Bible and the Book of Mormon. He recalled, "Her list of these stories was so long that her husband often marveled at their number, and frequently sat as spellbound as were the children as she skillfully related them."[1]

When President Merrill asked his wife where she had learned to teach these stories, she spoke of attending Elder James E. Talmage's religion class at the Salt Lake Stake Academy.

Inspired by his wife's teaching and the seminars he had attended during his graduate studies at the University of Chicago, President Merrill formulated a plan to offer religious training to students in public high schools while honoring established barriers between church and state.

Merrill's plan was simple in its execution. A facility could be built near Granite High School, where students, temporarily released from school custody, could receive religious training. He presented his plan to the presidency and high council of the Granite Stake, the superintendent of Church schools, and the state superintendent of public instruction. With their approval, Merrill moved ahead with what he called seminary. He was given general supervision over selecting a teacher, subject to the approval of the stake presidency.

President Merrill sent a letter to the Church Board of Education, outlining expectations for the first seminary teacher:

"May I suggest it is the desire of the presidency of the stake to have a strong young man who is properly qualified to do the work in a most satisfactory manner. By young we do not necessarily mean a teacher who is young in years, but a man who is young in his feelings, who loves young people, who delights in their company, who can command their respect and admiration and exercise a great influence over them. . . . We want a man who is a thorough student, one who will not teach in a perfunctory way, but who will enliven his instructions by a strong, winning personality and give evidence of a thorough understanding of and scholarship in the things he teaches. . . . A teacher is wanted who is a leader and who will be universally regarded as the inferior of no teacher in the high school."[2]

The teacher selected for the first seminary class was Thomas J. Yates, a member of the Granite Stake high council. There were several factors against selecting the forty-year-old Yates, the most important being that he was not a professional educator. He had a full-time position as a construction engineer at the nearby Murray power plant.

But President Taylor saw Brother Yates as a man of utmost integrity who could teach the youth. At a stake conference, President Taylor said, "Brother Yates always reminds me of Joseph who was sold into Egypt, he is a tower of purity and strength."[3] Yates said, "This was a new venture. It had never been tried before. We could see wonderful possibilities if it were successful which would mean a complete change in the Church."[4]

Once the choice of Yates was confirmed, he and Merrill launched headlong into preparations to have a religious education program ready by the fall of 1912. The first problem they tackled was curriculum. After some discussion, they decided to center their program on the standard works—one class in the Old Testament, another in the New Testament, and a class combining the study of the Book of Mormon with a course in Church history.

Then there was the issue of keeping the seminary program separate from the high school, which meant constructing a building. Yates took part in purchasing the land, designing the building, and even overseeing its construction. "It took considerable thought to plan this building," Yates wrote. "We did not know the number of students to provide for,

DID YOU KNOW?

- The idea for seminary was inspired by a young mother teaching her children from the scriptures.

- The first seminary building had no electric lights, no textbooks, and only a single volume in its library.

and therefore the size of the classrooms, or the number of rooms. There was no precedent to guide us."[5]

The construction of the first seminary building, built at a cost of $2,500, was begun a few weeks before the beginning of the school year in 1912. The building had four rooms—a classroom, an office, a small library, and a cloakroom. The classroom was furnished with blackboards, seats with armrests, and a stove for heat. There were no lights and no textbooks other than the scriptures. The library consisted of a Bible dictionary owned by Yates. Seminary students were expected to make their own maps of the Holy Land, North America, South America, Mesopotamia, and Arabia.[6]

Seventy students enrolled when the seminary opened in the fall of 1912. Yates spent his mornings working at the Murray power plant and his afternoons at the seminary building. His salary was $100 a month. At the end of that first year, President Taylor urged Yates to continue teaching. The time-consuming task of traveling by horseback every day from Murray to the Granite seminary building and back home again had proven too much for Yates, however, and he declined the offer.

Asked to suggest his replacement, Yates recommended Guy C. Wilson, a professional educator who had recently moved to Salt Lake from the Mormon colonies in Mexico. Wilson later wrote of Yates, "Brother Thomas Yates had the previous year conducted classes in the Seminary, but it was felt that a lack of funds and other facilities had prevented him from giving the work a fair trial."[7]

The second seminary was established at Brigham City, Utah, in 1915, and from there the program grew quickly. By 1920 the Church board of education had examined the declining enrollments in Church schools and closed nearly all the academies. The board encouraged Latter-day Saint youth to attend public high schools and seminaries. The seminary program provided a way to build and staff a theology department for local high schools, without having to build and staff an entire school.[8]

The seminary program was adapted as the Church expanded from the Intermountain West to other areas throughout the world. The first early-morning seminary classes were begun in southern California in 1950. Home-study seminaries paved the way for international Latter-day Saint education in the 1960s and 1970s.

Five years after the first seminary was established, Laura Merrill passed away from cancer in 1917, unaware of the far-reaching effect of the example she had set for her husband. Joseph F. Merrill became the Church commissioner of education in 1928 and helped pioneer the application of seminary principles on the collegiate level in institutes of religion.

Although Thomas J. Yates continued to labor in relative obscurity in the Granite Utah Stake for the remainder of his life and his name is relatively unknown in the Church today, President Henry B. Eyring, at a gathering of religious educators in 2010, spoke of Yates as a master teacher:

"In that [seminary] roll book was the name of Mildred Bennion. She was 16 years old that year [the one year Thomas Yates taught at the Granite seminary]. Thirty-one years later she would become my mother. She was the daughter of a man we would today call 'less active.' Her mother was left a widow the fall of the year after that first seminary class began. She raised and supported my mother and five other children alone on a small farm. Somehow that one seminary teacher cared enough about her and prayed fervently enough over that young girl that the Spirit put the gospel down into her heart. That one teacher blessed tens of thousands because he taught just one girl in a crowd of 70."[9]

NOTES

1. Merrill, "A New Institution in Religious Education," *Improvement Era*, Jan. 1938, 12–15, 55–56.
2. Merrill, "New Institution," 55.
3. "Autobiography of Thomas J. Yates," 42, Church History Library, The Church of Jesus Christ of Latter-day Saints, Salt Lake City, Utah.
4. "Autobiography of Thomas J. Yates," 79.
5. "Autobiography of Thomas J. Yates," 80.
6. Charles Coleman and Dwight Jones, "History of Granite Seminary," unpublished manuscript, 1933, Church History Library, 7.
7. Coleman and Jones, "History of Granite Seminary," 32.
8. See Casey Paul Griffiths, "A Century of Seminary," *Religious Educator* 13, no. 3 (2012): 18–24.
9. Eyring, "To Know and Love God," address to religious educators, Feb. 26, 2010, 5.

67
The Boy Scout Program in the Church

A group of Boy Scouts, 1926.

1913

In the early 1900s, many young men, even though they had participated in the Primary Association, fell away from Church activity. President Joseph F. Smith was concerned about the issue and spearheaded Church programs to help young men stay more involved. For example, in 1909 he encouraged the Young Men's Mutual Improvement Association (YMMIA) to introduce athletic activities into their curriculum.[1] Another example was his decision to affiliate the Church with the Boy Scouts of America.

Boy Scouts began with Lord Baden-Powell, a lieutenant general in the British Army. After traveling throughout Great Britain, Powell expressed concern for the welfare of teenage boys and wanted to do something for them. In 1907 he took twenty-one young men on a campout for several days. On the campout, these boys learned camping skills, hiking, and woodworking, and discovered the wonders of nature. Honesty, service, and cheerfulness were also emphasized.

When the encampment turned out to be a happy experience for all concerned, Lord Baden-Powell wrote *Scouting for Boys* in 1908. His plan for Scouting called for young men to advance through the ranks of Tenderfoot, Second Class, and First Class. Over the years, the Scouting program has added the ranks of Star, Life, and Eagle as well as other distinctions.

The organizational outline of Scouting in Powell's book led to Scout troops being formed all over Great Britain. In 1910, newspaper entrepreneur and explorer William D. Boyce brought the Scouting movement to the United States and founded Boy Scouts of America (BSA).[2]

Enthusiasm for the BSA movement spread quickly across the United States. Thomas George Wood, a Latter-day Saint emigrant from England, started the first Latter-day Saint Scout troop in Utah on October 12, 1910, but Wood's troop was not affiliated with the BSA.[3] It was not long before similar Scout troops sprang up in wards of the Church throughout the Intermountain West.

Initially, Church leaders were hesitant to affiliate with the BSA on account of concerns about turning over leadership and religious training to a public organization. Though the concerns were still unresolved, the YMMIA was encouraged to organize MIA Scouts. During the early years of the MIA Scout program, YMMIA Athletic Director John H. Taylor visited many stakes to promote MIA Scouts and was often asked why MIA Scouts were not affiliated with the BSA.

In response, Taylor investigated the possibility of affiliating with the BSA. On January 8, 1913, he met with National Field Scout Commissioner Samuel A. Moffat to discuss a partnership between the Church and the BSA. On March 15, 1913, the YMMIA general board resolved to affiliate with the BSA. On May 2, 1913, the BSA national executive board voted to accept the MIA Scouts as a chartered organization, and a charter was issued on May 21, 1913.[4]

The LDS Church Scouting program has evolved through the years to meet the changing needs of youth. For example, when it was found that boys often dropped out of Scouting when they turned sixteen, the Church introduced the Vanguard Scout program for boys ages fifteen through eighteen. After five years of successful retention of older Latter-day Saint young men in Scouting through the Vanguard program, the National BSA Council adopted the Vanguard curriculum in their advanced Scouting program.

A Scout's entrance into BSA dropped in 1949 from age twelve to age eleven, which led to the introduction of Scouting in the Church's Primary Association. President David O. McKay asked general Primary president LaVern Parmley to adopt Cub Scouting for boys ages eight through eleven. By 1953 there were 114 Cub Scout packs functioning in wards throughout the Church. Women called to serve in Cub Scouts were asked to register as den mothers, but at first they could not serve on Cub Scout committees. This restriction was lifted when the BSA national executive board recognized that the needs of Cub Scouts could better be served with women directly involved with BSA committees. Sister Parmley served on the national Cub Scout committee with Elizabeth Reneker, wife of Robert W. Reneker, president of BSA. They were the first women to serve in a BSA national capacity.

Since Sister Parmley's service, other LDS leaders have also served on the BSA national executive board. Elder George Albert Smith served from 1931 to 1949. Elder Ezra Taft Benson was then appointed to take his place. Elder Benson served for twenty years, until Elder Thomas S. Monson took his place in 1969. President Monson continues to hold his position on the BSA national executive board (2017). In 2012, Wayne Perry, a Latter-day Saint and life-long Scouter from Seattle, Washington, became president of BSA—the first Latter-day Saint to hold the position.

Today the Church is the largest chartered organization affiliated with BSA, with about 17 percent of the BSA's membership in the United States. That proportion is even higher in the western United States.[5]

DID YOU KNOW?

- The Church of Jesus Christ of Latter-day Saints was the first chartered organization to affiliate with the Boy Scouts of America.

- The Church is ranked in the United States as the largest in total units and membership in the Boy Scouts of America, constituting about 17 percent of overall membership.

NOTES

1. "History Highlights #2: Zion's Youth 1870–1910," ldsbsa.org; "Athletic Work in the Ensign Stake," *Improvement Era*, Aug. 1909, 840–41.
2. See Hillcourt and Baden-Powell, *Baden-Powell*.
3. Francis, *Century of Honor*, 14.
4. Jason Swensen, "Century of Honor Book Celebrates 100 Years of LDS Scouting," *LDS Church News*, lds.org; Francis, *Century of Honor*, 31–32.
5. "Scouting and the Church of Jesus Christ of Latter-day Saints," 4, scouting.org.

68
The Family Home Evening Program

A depiction of family home evening, a program introduced by President Joseph F. Smith and his counselors in 1915.

1915

The concept of family home evening is rooted in the pioneer era. President Harold B. Lee observed: "In the last epistle written to the Church by President Brigham Young and his Counselors, it was urged that parents bring their children together and teach them the gospel in the home frequently. So family home evening has been urged ever since the Church was established in this dispensation."[1]

Family home evening is viewed as an application of the Church's doctrine of the eternal nature of the family unit and the scriptural mandate that parents bring up their children in light and truth (D&C 93:40; 68:25–28). The

institution of a formal family home evening began with a letter sent on April 27, 1915, to local Church leaders by President Joseph F. Smith and his counselors in the First Presidency of the Church. The letter stated:

"We advise and urge the inauguration of a 'Home Evening' throughout the Church, at which time fathers and mothers may gather their boys and girls about them in the home and teach them the word of the Lord. . . . This 'Home Evening' should be devoted to prayer, singing hymns, songs, instrumental music, scripture-reading, family topics and specific instruction on the principles of the Gospel, and on the ethical problems of life, as well as the duties and obligations of children to parents, the home, the Church, society and the Nation. For the smaller children appropriate recitations, songs, stories and games may be introduced. Light refreshments of such a nature as may be largely prepared in the home might be served. . . .

"If the Saints obey this counsel, we promise that great blessings will result. Love at home and obedience to parents will increase. Faith will be developed in the hearts of the youth of Israel, and they will gain power to combat the evil influence and temptations which beset them."[2]

In the forty-five years between 1915 and 1960, many Latter-day Saints moved from farms to cities. With these shifting demographics, President David O. McKay began emphasizing the importance of the family as never before. In the April 1964 general conference, President

McKay introduced the motto "No other success can compensate for failure in the home."[3]

A year later, under the direction of the First Presidency, a lesson manual for family home evening was given to each family to aid parents in teaching their children.[4] The manual emphasized practical everyday application of gospel principles taught in priesthood and auxiliary classes. From 1965 to 1984, "revised home evening manuals, with suggested weekly lessons and activities" were provided to parents.[5]

Beginning in 1966, stakes in the Church were urged to set aside a regular weeknight for family home evening and to avoid scheduling any other activities on that night—the night designated varied from stake to stake. This renewed emphasis on family home evening attracted the attention of the media and government leaders. In his October 1975 general conference address, Elder James A. Cullimore, Assistant to the Council of the Twelve, spoke of the national attention the practice was receiving. He quoted proclamations made by the mayor of Houston, Texas, and the governor of Arizona declaring Family Unity Month and Family Week within their jurisdictions and citing the Church's emphasis on families and the practice of family home evening. He also quoted an article by UPI journalist Louis Cassels giving a glowing report of family home evening as practiced in the Church.[6]

In 1970 President Joseph Fielding Smith, son of President Joseph F. Smith, who had issued the 1915 letter, designated Monday night as the preferred time to hold family home evening worldwide. He indicated that no competing ecclesiastical functions were to be held on Monday evenings.

In 1985, the Church produced and distributed the *Family Home Evening Resource Book*. Intended to be used for a decade, this volume provided resource materials for lessons and family activity ideas. "In 1987, a Family Home Evening video supplement was also made available. Nineteen video vignettes were included, treating important educational and moral topics."[7]

Over the years, Church leaders have counseled Latter-day Saints to hold family home evenings and have promised blessings to those who followed their counsel. The First Presidency promised in 1970:

"Well-planned family home evenings can be a source of long-lasting joy and influence. These evenings are times for group activity, for organizing, for the expressions of love, for the bearing of testimony, for learning gospel principles, for family fun and recreation, and of all things, for family unity and solidarity."[8]

In 1992 President Ezra Taft Benson promised, "Family home evenings should be scheduled once a week as a time for discussions of gospel principles, recreation, work projects, skits, songs around the piano, games, special refreshments, and family prayers. Like iron links in a chain, this practice will bind a family together, in love, pride, tradition, strength, and loyalty."[9]

In 2002 President Gordon B. Hinckley encouraged businesses and organizations to keep Monday night free of activities in order for Latter-day Saints to more easily hold family home evening.

For more than a century, faithful Latter-day Saint families have followed counsel and held family home evenings. As a result, family home evening has become a vital and integral part of the lives and beliefs of Latter-day Saints and a prominent institution of the teachings and culture of the Church.

NOTES

1. *Harold B. Lee* [manual], 125.
2. Joseph F. Smith, Anthon H. Lund, and Charles W. Penrose, "Home Evening," *Improvement Era*, June 1915, 733–34.
3. McKay, in Conference Report, Apr. 1964, 5; see McCulloch, *Home, the Savior of Civilization*, 42.
4. R. Scott Lloyd, "Family Home Evening: 2 Landmark Anniversaries," *LDS Church News*, Jan. 30, 2015.
5. James F. Mitchell and Terri Tanner Mitchell, "Family Home Evening," in Ludlow, *Encyclopedia of Mormonism*, 2:496.
6. Cullimore, in Conference Report, Oct. 1975, 39; Lloyd, "Family Home Evening."
7. Mitchell and Mitchell, "Family Home Evening," 2:496.
8. Joseph Fielding Smith, Harold B. Lee, and N. Eldon Tanner, "Letter to the Parents of the Church," *Family Home Evenings 1970–71*, v.
9. Benson, "Salvation: A Family Affair," *Ensign*, July 1992, 4.

69
The Father and the Son, a Doctrinal Exposition

1916

The First Presidency, 1901. Left to right, John R. Winder, Joseph F. Smith, Anthon H. Lund.

Since the beginning of Christianity, believers have debated the nature of God. This debate also existed among members of The Church of Jesus Christ of Latter-day Saints. Although most contemporary Latter-day Saints assume the theology of the Godhead has always been the position of the Church, perceptions about God and the Godhead have passed through several phases of development.

Historian Brian Ricks explained, "The clarification between the Father and the Son was one of the doctrinal pieces that took the longest to fall into place for the Latter-day Saints." According to Ricks, the reasons for the delay may have been "because it is through those roles that God interacts with men" and "the intimate nature of those interactions" may have made it difficult for early Latter-day Saints to "let go of previous traditions and beliefs."[1]

Most nineteenth-century converts had either been members of the Church of England or another Protestant faith and had not previously distinguished between individuals in the Godhead. One historian noted, "Early Mormon leaders, assuming a rather eclectic approach to the acquisition of knowledge, encouraged the saints to 'gather' truth from such disparate sources as infidels and Methodists, Universalists and Baptists, Catholics and Shakers."[2] With the revelations of the Restoration still unfolding, little distinction was made in most early Church literature between members of the Godhead and there was little concern with the identity of each divine Being.

In the early twentieth century, however, discussions arose among Church members about the roles of God the Father and his Son Jesus Christ. There was still some confusion among Latter-day Saints over the nature of the Godhead, particularly about the unity of the Father and the Son and the relationship between them.[3] President Joseph F. Smith was concerned about those misunderstandings and, more specifically, misunderstandings about the Only Begotten Son.

Both President Smith and his counselor Charles W. Penrose spoke to the question of the Godhead in their April 1916 general conference addresses. President Penrose stated, "I am sorry that [this issue] has not been rectified long ago, because plain answers have been given to brethren and sisters who write and desire to know about it, and yet it still lingers, and contentions arise in regard to it."[4] President Penrose then spoke about the distinct roles and personages of the Godhead.

Elder James E. Talmage, a member of the Quorum of the Twelve, was asked by the First Presidency to explain and clarify the Church's doctrine on the subject. Talmage had already produced a series of books explaining the belief and teachings of the Church, including *Articles of Faith* (1899), *The Great Apostasy* (1909), *The House of the Lord* (1912), and *Jesus the Christ* (1915).

Now he was asked to produce a document to clarify the roles of the members of the Godhead. Summarizing the accomplishments of Talmage's work, historian Brian Ricks noted, "[His] document answered questions regarding the Book of Mormon's use of 'Father' when referring to Jesus Christ. . . . Elder Talmage's efforts, as directed and overseen by the First Presidency, assisted in clarifying his predecessors' teachings on the Godhead."[5]

After it was written by Elder Talmage, the manuscript was reviewed, approved, and published in pamphlet form on June 30, 1916, by the First Presidency and the Quorum of the Twelve. It was entitled *The Father and the Son, a Doctrinal Exposition by The First Presidency and The Twelve.* This exposition clarified the meaning of certain scriptures in which Jesus Christ, or Jehovah, is designated as the Father.[6] The exposition was reprinted in the August 1916 *Improvement Era* and included in the 1924 edition of *The Articles of Faith,* by James E. Talmage.

The twofold purpose of the exposition was, first, to distinguish between the personages of Elohim and Jehovah and establish the correct use of these names in the Church, and second, to clarify why Jesus Christ is called the Father and the Son in the Book of Mormon, while maintaining separation between Elohim and Jehovah. Robert L. Millet, former dean of Religious Education at Brigham Young University, gave additional insights into the exposition:

"Jesus is the Son of God in at least three ways. First, he is the firstborn spirit child of God the Father and thereby the elder brother of the spirits of all men and women. . . . Second, he is the literal physical son of God, the Only Begotten in the Flesh. . . . Third, spiritually he is also a son by virtue of his submission unto the will of the Father. . . .

"Jesus Christ is also known by the title of Father. . . .

"Christ is sometimes called Father because of his role as Creator from the beginning. . . . Before his mortal birth, and acting under the direction of the Father, Jesus was Jehovah, . . . 'the Father of heaven and earth, the Creator of all things from the beginning.' . . .

"Jesus Christ is also known as Father through the spiritual rebirth of mankind. . . . Those who accept the gospel of Jesus Christ and receive its saving covenantal ordinances, living worthy of its sanctifying and enlightening powers, are 'born again' unto Christ and become known as the children of Christ, 'his sons and his daughters,' his 'seed.' . . . Christ thus becomes the Father of their salvation, the Father of life in the Spirit, the Father of the new birth."[7]

The exposition by the First Presidency established beyond question the doctrine of the Godhead. Since 1916 there has been no

DID YOU KNOW?

• On June 30, 1916, the First Presidency and the Quorum of the Twelve published in pamphlet form *The Father and the Son, a Doctrinal Exposition*, which clarified the meaning of certain scriptures in which Jesus Christ, or Jehovah, is designated as the Father.

• The exposition established beyond question the doctrine of the Godhead.

disagreement among Church leaders about the identification of Jesus Christ as Jehovah. The official declaration of 1916 is still referred to by Church leaders when commenting on the relationship between Jehovah and Elohim.[8]

In addition, the exposition's definition is taught in lesson manuals, periodicals, and other literature of the Church. Historian Ricks explained the significance of the exposition as follows:

"The influence of the doctrinal exposition on Latter-day Saints, past and present, cannot be underestimated. As an official document from the First Presidency, the orthodoxy of the Church regarding the Godhead was established. What Nicaea and Alexandria accomplished for the Catholic Church, this document accomplished for the Latter-day Saints. Regardless of what had been said before, this was the new standard for doctrinal accuracy."[9]

NOTES

1. Bryan W. Ricks, "James E. Talmage and the Nature of the Godhead: The Gradual Unfolding of Latter-day Saint Theology," master's thesis, Brigham Young University (2007), 192.
2. O. Kendall White Jr., "The Transformation of Mormon Theology," *Dialogue* 5, no. 2 (1970): 9–10.
3. Alexander, *Mormonism in Transition*, 280.
4. Penrose, in Conference Report, Apr. 1916, 17.
5. Ricks, "James E. Talmage and the Nature of the Godhead," ii.
6. Robert L. Millet, "Jesus Christ, Fatherhood and Sonship of," in Ludlow, *Encyclopedia of Mormonism*, 2:739–40.
7. Millet, "Jesus Christ, Fatherhood and Sonship of," 2:739.
8. Brian W. Ricks, "James E. Talmage and the Doctrine of the Godhead," *Religious Educator* 13, no. 2 (2012): 201–2.
9. Ricks, "James E. Talmage and the Nature of the Godhead," 132.

70

The Vision of the Redemption of the Dead

President Joseph F. Smith, 1901.

1918

Elder Boyd K. Packer called the canonization of President Joseph F. Smith's vision of the redemption of the dead one of the "great events relating to the scriptures."[1]

Yet, he said, "I was surprised, and I think all of the Brethren were surprised, at how casually that announcement of two additions to the standard works was received by the Church. But we will live to sense the significance of it; we will tell our grandchildren and our great-grandchildren, and we will record in our diaries, that we were on the earth and remember when that took place."[2]

Perhaps more is known about the events leading up President Smith's vision than about events leading up to most of the other revelations contained in the Doctrine and Covenants. In October 1918, President Joseph F. Smith was stricken by age and grief over the death of his son Hyrum. President Smith began an intensive study of the scriptures concerning the afterlife and the world of the spirits.

The text of President Joseph F. Smith's vision sets forth with clarity the Savior declaring liberty to the captives in the spirit prison. The vision clarifies that Jesus Christ did not go personally to the spirits in prison. Instead, he organized others to teach them the gospel message. The vision disclosed the pattern by which the doctrines of the gospel are to be shared with those who died without a knowledge of the gospel. It answers many questions that had perplexed not only Latter-day Saints but the entire Christian world and answers such difficult theological questions as what becomes of those who die without having had the opportunity to accept Jesus Christ while they lived.

President Joseph F. Smith was not expected at general conference in October 1918 because he had "been undergoing a siege of very serious illness for the last five months."[3] Nonetheless, he was determined to attend. He spoke to those who had assembled in the Salt Lake Tabernacle and alluded to the vision: "I shall postpone until some future time, the Lord being willing, my attempt to tell you some of the things that are in my mind, and that dwell in my heart. I have not lived alone these five months. I have dwelt in the spirit of prayer, of supplication, of faith and of determination; and I have had my communication with the Spirit of the Lord continuously."[4]

After the conference, President Smith dictated the vision of the redemption of the dead to his son Elder Joseph Fielding Smith. On October 31, 1918, the manuscript was presented by Elder Smith at a council meeting of the First Presidency, the Quorum of the Twelve Apostles, and the Church Patriarch. President Smith was too ill to attend.

Less than three weeks later, on November 19, 1918, President Joseph F. Smith died of pneumonia. Shortly thereafter, the text of the vision was published in the November 30 edition of the *Deseret Evening News*. It was also printed in the December *Improvement Era* and in the January 1919 editions of the *Relief Society Magazine,* the *Utah Genealogical and Historical Magazine,* the *Young Women's Journal,* and the *Millennial Star*. It appears from these publications that the general authorities were eager for the Latter-day Saints to have access to the text of the vision in a timely manner.

Over the next six decades, however, little was said in general conference about the vision. Then, in October 1975, six months before the vision was canonized, Elder Boyd K. Packer introduced his general conference address by saying, "I have reason . . . to feel very deeply about

DID YOU KNOW?

• President Joseph F. Smith received a vision of the redemption of the dead during the final weeks of his life, after struggling with illness for nearly five months.

• In 1976 the vision of the redemption of the dead was canonized as scripture.

the subject that I have chosen for today, and to feel more than the usual need for your sustaining prayers, because of its very sacred nature."[5]

The subject Elder Packer referred to was the vision of the redemption of the dead. For the first time in a general conference, a general authority, Elder Packer, quoted directly from the vision. It was fifty-seven years since the vision had been acknowledged as the word of God.

This was also the first time that the vision of the redemption of the dead was presented as the pivotal link to genealogical research. After quoting two verses from the future scripture, Elder Packer stated, "Here and now, then, we move to accomplish the work to which we are assigned. . . . We gather the records of our kindred dead, indeed, the records of the entire human family; and in sacred temples in baptismal fonts designed as those were anciently, we perform these sacred ordinances."[6]

At the April 1976 general conference, N. Eldon Tanner, a counselor in the First Presidency, stated: "At a meeting of the Council of the First Presidency and Quorum of the Twelve held in the Salt Lake Temple on March 25, 1976, approval was given to add to the Pearl of Great Price the following two revelations:

"First, a vision of the celestial kingdom given to Joseph Smith, the Prophet, in the Kirtland Temple, on January 21, 1836, which deals with the salvation of those who die without a knowledge of the gospel.

"And second, a vision given to President Joseph F. Smith in Salt Lake City, Utah, on October 3, 1918, showing the visit of the Lord Jesus Christ in the spirit world and setting forth the doctrine of the redemption of the dead.

"It is proposed that we sustain and approve this action and adopt these revelations as part of the standard works of The Church of Jesus Christ of Latter-day Saints."[7]

Those gathered in the Salt Lake Tabernacle

voted to sustain the action to accept the two revelations as scripture, and they were placed in the Pearl of Great Price.[8] After the visions were canonized, the doctrines in them became binding upon the Latter-day Saints. Five years later, the revelations were transferred to the 1981 edition of the Doctrine and Covenants as sections 137 and 138. The inclusion of these visions in the scriptural canon marked the dawning of an era of unprecedented temple building and technology, with the computer becoming an indispensable tool in genealogical research.

The canonization of the vision of the redemption of the dead played a large role in moving forward temple work for the deceased. The vision confirmed and expanded earlier prophetic insights concerning work for the dead and introduced doctrinal truths that were unknown before October 1918 and not fully instituted until 1976. The remarkable process of bringing this vision to scripture will provide the way, as Elder Boyd K. Packer counseled, that "we can redeem our dead by the thousands and tens of thousands and millions and billions and tens of billions. We have not yet moved to the edge of the light."[9]

Notes

1. Boyd K. Packer, "Teach the Scriptures," address to religious educators, Oct. 14, 1977, 4.
2. Packer, "Teach the Scriptures," 4.
3. Smith, in Conference Report, Oct. 1918, 2; George S. Tate, "'The Great World of the Spirits of the Dead': Death, the Great War, and the 1918 Influenza Pandemic as Context for Doctrine and Covenants 138," *BYU Studies* 46, no. 1 (2007): 5–40.
4. Smith, in Conference Report, Oct. 1918, 2.
5. Packer, "The Redemption of the Dead," *Ensign*, Nov. 1975, 97.
6. Packer, "Redemption of the Dead," 97.
7. Tanner, in James R. Clark, "Our Pearl of Great Price: From Mission Pamphlet to Standard Work," *Ensign*, Aug. 1976, 17.
8. Clark, "Our Pearl of Great Price," 17.
9. Packer, "The Edge of Light," BYU devotional address, Mar. 4, 1990, in Tate, *Boyd K. Packer*, 198.

71
Elder David O. McKay's Worldwide Tour

David O. McKay and Hugh J. Cannon visiting Egypt during their world tour.

1921

One important if understated twentieth-century event in the history of the Church is the yearlong, worldwide tour of Elder David O. McKay and Hugh J. Cannon, editor of Church publications.[1] In 1920 President Heber J. Grant asked these two brethren to conduct an international tour of missions and schools to gather firsthand information about Latter-day Saints throughout the world. They were specifically asked "to study their spiritual and, as far as possible, temporal needs, and to ascertain the effect of 'Mormonism' upon their lives."[2]

As it turned out, the worldwide tour of Elder McKay and Brother Cannon was "a major first step toward comprehending that a world-wide church would consist of more than a series of copies of the Great Basin church."[3] Assistant Church Historian Reid Neilson explained, "The globalization of the church, not merely its international diaspora, traces its roots to [this] around-the-world journey in the early 1920s."[4]

Joseph H. Stimpson, president of the mission in Japan, "acted as an important catalyst [for] McKay and Cannon's circumnavigation of the globe."[5] President Stimpson wrote that he "felt isolated and forgotten as the only Mormon mission president in Asia. . . . [He] had not spoken with a general authority in almost five years," so in 1920, "out of desperation, Stimpson finally sent a pleading missive to one of his former teachers at the Weber Academy in Ogden, Utah, Elder David O. McKay."[6]

President Stimpson asked Elder McKay if he would represent the Church and tour his mission. Stimpson suggested that the visit would give Elder McKay the ability to report "the true condition of the mission to the people in Zion in general and the Authorities in particular and re-sult in a closer co-operation." Stimpson also felt that a visiting general authority could "give an added testimony" and important instruction to the Japanese Saints, which would act as a "great incentive for more diligent effort on their part."[7]

For several months President Grant con-sidered Stimpson's proposal before granting his request and sending Elder McKay on a worldwide tour. As for Elder McKay, "the ju-nior apostle was caught by surprise; he was in the process of moving from Ogden to Salt Lake City. Still, [he] agreed to go."[8]

On October 15, 1920, a *Deseret News* head-line read, "Two Church Workers Will Tour

Missions of Pacific Islands." The article that followed stated, "[David O. McKay] will make a general survey of the missions, study conditions there, gather data concerning them, and in short, obtain general information in order that there may be someone in the deliberations of the First Presidency and the Council of the Twelve thoroughly familiar with actual conditions."[9]

A few days later, the *Deseret News* announced: "The two Church officials will study not only conditions in the L. D. S. colonies in each of the island groups, with regard to physical needs, missionaries, meeting places and spiritual affairs, but will also make a study of the customs and needs of the people in general at each place visited."[10]

During the 366-day tour, Elder McKay and Brother Cannon traveled 61,646 miles, visiting all the Church missions and schools except one in South Africa. Elder McKay also dedicated China for the preaching of the gospel. "As they crossed national and cultural boundaries," they met countless people from Asia, Africa, Europe, and the Polynesian Islands.[11] Elder McKay found that each culture possessed unique characteristics. For instance, in Japan he found courtesy and consideration; in Korea interest and beauty; in China wonder and inspiration; and in Polynesian a depth of love he had not experienced before.

On February 7, 1921, at a flag-raising ceremony held at a Church-owned elementary school in the town of Laie on the island of Oahu, he was impressed by the many nationalities of children pledging allegiance to their new country. Elder McKay envisioned the same scene being duplicated on a large scale and pictured the community of Laie as the intellectual center of the Pacific. He recorded his feelings on that day:

"As I looked at that motley group of youngsters, and realized how far apart their parents are in hopes, aspirations, and ideals, and then thought of these boys and girls, the first generation of their children, all thrown into what [Israel Zangwill] had aptly called the 'Melting Pot' and coming out Americans, my bosom swelled with emotion and tears came to my eyes, and I felt like bowing in prayer and thanksgiving for the glorious country which is doing so much for all these nationalities.

"But more than that, when I realize that these same boys and girls have the opportunity of participating in all the blessings of the Gospel which will transform the American into a real citizen of the Kingdom of God, I feel to praise His name for the glorious privileges vouchsafed to this generation. We held short services in the school room in which all—American, Hawaiian, Japanese, Chinese, Filipino—participated as though they had belonged to one nation, one country, one tongue."[12]

The inspired idea stayed with Elder McKay for the next thirty-four years. In that time, he supervised the establishment of small colleges in Samoa and Tahiti. One of his first official acts after he became president of the Church in 1951 was to establish a college in Laie, Hawaii. When the Church College of Hawaii was dedicated, President McKay expressed his view that the college would not only educate young Latter-day Saints but would have a significant impact on the world at large. He prophesied: "From this school, I'll tell you, will go men and women whose influence will be felt for good

DID YOU KNOW?

- During their 366-day world tour, Elder David O. McKay and Hugh J. Cannon traveled 61,646 miles, visiting nearly every Church mission and school.

- Elder McKay's travels led to the institution of Church programs that blessed the lives of members around the world.

towards the establishment of peace internationally. Four hundred and fifty million people waiting to hear the message over in China, a noble race . . . [and] I don't know how many million over in Japan. You prepare to go and carry that message. Three hundred and fifty million down in India. We have scarcely touched these great nations, and they're calling today."[13]

After visiting New Zealand, Elder McKay and Brother Cannon visited the Far East, Australia, Singapore, India, Israel, Egypt, Palestine, Italy, and Scotland. And in so doing, Elder McKay became the first general authority to have firsthand knowledge of every congregation in the Church.[14]

The lasting legacy of the journey of Elder McKay and Hugh Cannon was their conviction that the Church should provide a "comparable religious experience for its members around the world." To assure that that happened, President David O. McKay "instituted a building program unparalleled in Mormon history," including temples in New Zealand, England, and Switzerland.[15] President McKay regarded his efforts in transforming The Church of Jesus Christ of Latter-day Saints into a global religious organization as one of his greatest achievements.

NOTES

1. Neilson, *To the Peripheries*, ix–x.
2. Hugh J. Cannon, "Around-the-World Travels of David O. McKay and Hugh J. Cannon," ca. 1925, typescript, 1, microfilm, Church History Library, The Church of Jesus Christ of Latter-day Saints, Salt Lake City, Utah, in Neilson, *To the Peripheries*, ix.
3. Prince and Wright, *David O. McKay*, 358–59.
4. Neilson, *To the Peripheries*, ix.
5. First Presidency to Stimpson, Oct. 15, 1920, in Neilson, *To the Peripheries*, xx.
6. Stimpson to McKay, Mar. 18, 1920, in Neilson, *To the Peripheries*, xxi.
7. Stimpson to McKay, Mar. 18, 1920, in Neilson, *To the Peripheries*, xxi.
8. Neilson, *To the Peripheries*, xxiii.
9. "Two Church Workers Will Tour Missions of Pacific Islands," *Deseret News,* Oct. 15, 1920, 5, in Prince and Wright, *David O. McKay*, 358.
10. "Plan Visit to Island Missions," *Deseret News*, Oct. 23, 1920, 20, in Prince and Wright, *David O. McKay*, 359.
11. Neilson, *To the Peripheries*, xiv–xv.
12. Law, *Founding and Early Development*, 28.
13. "Groundbreaking Services: Excerpts from President David O. McKay's Church College of Hawaii/BYU–Hawaii dedication," newsroom .byuh.edu; Faldmo, *Church College of Hawaii*, 17.
14. Neilson, *To the Peripheries*, xxi–xxii.
15. Neilson, *To the Peripheries*, xxiii.

72
The Founding of the Institutes of Religion

1926

J. Wyley Sessions, director of the first institute of religion, on the steps of the Moscow, Idaho, institute building.

In October 1926 J. Wyley Sessions walked into the office of the First Presidency of the Church expecting to receive an employment offer with the Utah-Idaho Sugar Company. During the interview that ensued, Charles W. Nibley, second counselor in the First Presidency, turned to President Heber J. Grant and exclaimed, "Heber! We're making a mistake! I've never felt good about Brother Sessions in the sugar business. . . . There's

something else for this man." After a moment of silence, President Nibley looked directly at Sessions and said, "Brother Sessions, you're the man for us to send to the University of Idaho to take care of our boys and girls who are attending the University there, and to study the situation and tell us what the Church should do for Latter-day Saint students attending state universities."[1]

Stunned, Brother Sessions, who had recently returned from a seven-year mission in South Africa and was physically depleted and nearly destitute, exclaimed, "Oh no! We've been home just twelve days today, since we arrived from more than seven years in the mission system, are you calling me on another mission?" President Grant said, "No, no, Brother Sessions, we're just offering you a wonderful professional opportunity." Years later Sessions recalled his conflicted feelings over the new assignment: "I went, crying all the way. I didn't want to do it. But just a few days later our baggage was checked to Moscow, Idaho, and there [we] started the LDS Institute of Religion."[2]

The idea of offering religious education to college-age students was not new. Church leaders had long held the belief that some of the brightest young Latter-day Saints were losing their faith while attending college. In addition, the 1912 annual report of Church schools showed that there was a growing need for weekday religious instruction at the University of Utah and other state-run colleges in Utah.[3] Then there were the requests from the branch president in Moscow, Idaho, and George L.

Luke, a professor of physics at the University of Idaho, for a Latter-day Saint student center near the university campus.[4]

In 1926 Wyley Sessions undertook the assignment to start an institute program near the University of Idaho in the newly built, combined seminary and social center. Sessions's efforts were distinguished by his intention to launch a program designed to meet the spiritual, intellectual, and social needs of college students. Assisting Sessions in this endeavor was his wife, Magdalene, who created a varied program of social and cultural activities.

Seeking advice for this new undertaking, Sessions wrote to Elder Joseph F. Merrill, Church commissioner of education and pioneer of the seminary program. Merrill himself was a physicist who had spent most of his career at the University of Utah. Merrill informed Sessions that the objective of the Institute program should be to "enable our young people attending these colleges to make the necessary adjustments between the things they have been taught in the Church and the things they are learning in the university, to enable them to become firmly settled in their faith as members of the Church." Merrill further told Sessions, "You know that when our young people go to college and study science and philosophy in all their branches, that they are inclined to become materialistic, to forget God, and to believe that the knowledge of men is all sufficient." He then

asked, "Can the truths of science and philosophy be reconciled with religious truths?"[5]

Merrill concluded: "Personally, I am convinced that religion is as reasonable as science; that religious truths and scientific truths nowhere are in conflict; that there is one great unifying purpose extending throughout all creation; that we are living in a wonderful, though at the present-time deeply mysterious, world; and that there is an all-wise, all-powerful Creator at the back of it all. Can this same faith be developed in the minds of all our collegiate and university students? Our collegiate institutes are established as means to this end."[6]

Not everyone in the Moscow, Idaho, community welcomed Sessions or his plan for the institute of religion. The local ministerial association, some faculty members of the university, and several local businessmen appointed a committee to keep an eye on Sessions to make sure he didn't "Mormonize" the university.[7]

Recognizing the need for community support of his efforts, Sessions joined the Chamber of Commerce, spoke to and later joined the Kiwanis Club, and enrolled in the university to earn a master's degree. At a series of biweekly dinners held by the Chamber of Commerce, Sessions made every effort to sit by Fred Fulton, chair of the committee appointed to oppose his work. At one dinner Fulton said to Sessions, "You son-of-a-gun, you're the darndest fellow. I was appointed on a committee to keep you out of Moscow and every time I see you, you come in here so darn friendly that I like you better all the time." Sessions replied, "I'm the same way. We may just as well be friends."[8]

J. Wyley Sessions founded institute programs in Pocatello, Idaho, and Laramie, Wyoming. He later became head of Religious Instruction at Brigham Young University.

Growing out of Brother Sessions's pioneering efforts are hundreds of institutes in the

United States and throughout the world. In the 1990s the institute program was expanded to include all Latter-day Saints between the ages of eighteen and thirty years old, not just students attending colleges and universities. By 2014 there were 359,828 students enrolled in the institute program, making it the largest educational program for college-age students in the Church. By contrast, the largest Church-owned school, Brigham Young University, reported an enrollment of 29,672 in 2014, less than one-tenth the number of students enrolled in the institute program.[9]

Teachers in the worldwide institutes range from seasoned professionals to new converts. In the institutes of religion, young adults enjoy a safe haven in which to learn spiritual truths.

Notes

1. James Wyley Sessions and Magdalene Sessions, interview by Richard O. Cowan, June 29, 1965, private possession, 9; Arrington, "The Founding of LDS Institutes of Religion," *Dialogue*, Summer 1967, 137–47; Magleby, "1926—Another Beginning, Moscow, Idaho," *Impact*, Winter 1968.
2. Sessions and Sessions, 1965 interview, 9; Magleby, "1926—Another Beginning," 31–32; Merrill, "The Lord Overrules," *Improvement Era*, July 1934, 413, 447.
3. Berrett, *Miracle in Weekday Religious Education*, 47.
4. Berrett, *Miracle in Weekday Religious Education*, 48–49.
5. Magleby, "1926—Another Beginning," 31–32; see Merrill, "The Lord Overrules," 413, 447.
6. Magleby, "1926—Another Beginning," 32; see Merrill, "The Lord Overrules," 413, 447.
7. James Wyley Sessions, interview by Marc Sessions, Aug. 12, 1972, 5, MS 15866, Church History Library, The Church of Jesus Christ of Latter-day Saints, Salt Lake City, Utah.
8. Sessions, 1972 interview, 5; Sessions and Sessions, 1965 interview, 13.
9. Seminaries and Institutes of Religion, *Annual Report for 2014*, 2.

73
The Chicago Experiment

1930

Russel B. Swensen (left) and Sidney B. Sperry (right), both graduates from the University of Chicago and influential religious educators in the Church.

During the first century of the Restoration, Latter-day Saints took pride in the fact that there were no professional religious scholars in the Church. A few general authorities—most notably Parley and Orson Pratt, John Taylor, B. H. Roberts, and George Reynolds—had produced scholarly works on a par with those of other religionists of their day, but research and writing in the field of religion, for the most part, was confined to the general authorities. Even though the Church developed

its own school system in the late nineteenth century, teachers at these schools were to gain expertise in secular subjects—such as English and mathematics—and then teach one or two religion classes on the side. There were to be no full-time religion teachers.[1]

That practice began to change with the beginning of the seminary program in 1912. Two decades later, however, teachers were still hired for their ability to relate to young people rather than their training in the field of religion. As late as 1930 the Religion Department of Brigham Young University, consisted of one professor—George H. Brimhall, who had previously served as president of BYU.[2]

Yet there was a question to be addressed: In a Church whose leaders came from many different walks of life, was there a place for professional religionists? Three main factors led to the rise of religious scholars in the Church. First, the institutes of religion, designed to serve Latter-day Saint college-aged students, needed qualified instructors. Second, Church leaders recognized the need for increased scholarship to defend the Restoration. B. H. Roberts, in particular, emphasized the need for more scholarly work on the Book of Mormon. Finally, teachers in the seminary program needed training to teach the scriptures to the youth.

When Joseph F. Merrill was appointed Church commissioner of education in 1928, he determined to remedy the situation. As a former professor at the University of Utah, Commissioner Merrill thought Latter-day Saint religion teachers should attend divinity schools.

He reasoned: "We felt it very necessary . . . our [institute] Director[s] should have a scholarship in the Biblical and religious field comparable to the scholarship that the University would demand of any one appointed to head one of the departments. For example, if the University is looking for someone to head the department of Physics, it will limit its search to a trained physicist."[3]

The first step by Commissioner Merrill was to invite outside scholars who were experts in biblical studies to train seminary and institute teachers at Brigham Young University. Edgar Goodspeed, a world-renowned New Testament scholar from the University of Chicago, taught a series of classes at BYU. Commissioner Merrill and other Church leaders were so impressed with Goodspeed's knowledge of the New Testament that they arranged for him to speak in the Salt Lake Tabernacle.

Merrill's next step was to send promising young teachers—Sidney B. Sperry, T. Edgar Lyon, Daryl Chase, Russel B. Swensen, and Heber Snell—to the University of Chicago to receive graduate training at the School of Divinity. Merrill knew the risks of this experiment, for the Chicago Divinity School was among the most liberal in the nation. Its scholars regularly published radical interpretations of the Bible. Edgar Goodspeed, for instance, in his translation of the New Testament, questioned the authenticity of a significant portion of the biblical text. Nevertheless, the liberal attitude of the school made it likely one of the few schools of theology in the United States who would accept Latter-day Saint scholars.[4]

Some of the Latter-day Saint teachers were dazzled by the academic rigor of the Chicago scholars. Russel Swensen wrote home praising the "stimulus in study when sitting at the feet of brilliant professors" and expected that "the past year will be a bright spot in my life."[5]

Others grew uncomfortable with the liberal leanings of the theological scholars. T. Edgar Lyon wrote to his parents, "I fail to see how a young man can come here to school, then go out after graduation and still preach what we call Christianity. . . . They make no attempt to harmonize science and the Bible—they merely throw the Bible away, and teach scientific 'truths' as the only thing to follow."[6]

When these first students completed their graduate studies, Merrill sent each a letter urging a remembrance that "religion is based upon faith. And religious faith, of course, does not rest wholly on demonstrable facts."[7]

Was the experiment a success? Elder Boyd K. Packer, himself a veteran religious educator, wrote, "There was encouragement, both for the men in the institute program and for the teachers of religion at Brigham Young University to go away and get advanced degrees. 'Go study under the great religious scholars of the world,' was the encouragement, 'for we will set an academic standard in theology.'" Elder Packer offered this assessment, "Some who went never returned. And some of them who returned never came back. They had followed, they supposed, the scriptural injunction: 'Seek learning, even by study and also by faith' (D&C 88:118). But somehow the mix had been wrong. For they had sought learning out of the best books, even by study, but with too little faith."[8]

A few teachers returned to Utah and spread

DID YOU KNOW?

- In 1930 the Religion Department of Brigham Young University consisted of just one professor.

- Some of the earliest religion scholars in the Church had to attend the most liberal theological school in the United States because they wouldn't have been accepted anywhere else.

radical views of the scriptures through the seminary and institute program. In 1938 President J. Reuben Clark of the First Presidency issued a stern rebuke to those teachers: "On more than one occasion our Church members have gone to other places for special training in particular lines; they have had the training which was supposedly the last word . . . then they have brought it back and dosed it upon us without any thought as to whether we needed it or not."[9]

Years later Elder Packer added, "Happily, though, some of those who went away to study returned magnified by their experience and armed with advanced degrees. They returned firm in their knowledge that a man can be in the world but not of the world."[10]

Among those faithful teachers who returned magnified by their experience were Sidney Sperry, Russel Swensen, and T. Edgar Lyon. These educators published the first scholarly analysis of biblical and Restoration scriptures and produced sophisticated works in defense of the Church. They, in turn, recruited such other scholars as Hugh Nibley, Robert J. Matthews, and David Yarn. Before long, many professional religious and Church history scholars were writing serious scholarly works in defense of the Church.

T. Edgar Lyon, although clearly the most outspoken critic of the Chicago experiment, referred to it as "a landmark in an educational outreach which the Church had never known before, and which has profoundly influenced the teaching in the seminaries and institutes since that day." Lyon also said, "It was a time of an intellectual and spiritual awakening which was the entering wedge that put the Church educational system in contact with the ongoing mainstream of Christian scriptural and historical research. This outlook has aided in the metamorphosis of the LDS Church from a sectionally oriented to a worldwide Church in less than forty years."[11]

Notes

1. Wilkinson, *Brigham Young University*, 2:286.
2. Wilkinson, *Brigham Young University*, 2:286.
3. Merrill to E. J. Call, G. L. Luke, and W. V. Halverson, Apr. 18, 1931, UA 618, box 1, folder 2, Sydney B. Sperry Collection, L. Tom Perry Special Collections, Harold B. Lee Library, Brigham Young University, Provo, Utah.
4. Lyon, *Teacher in Zion*, 132.
5. Swensen to Swen L. Swensen, Sept. 21, 1931, box 2, folder 12, Swensen Collection, Perry Special Collections, Lee Library.
6. Lyon to parents, Aug. 21, 1931, in interview of T. Edgar Lyon Jr., by Frederick S. Buchanan and Marshal B. Poulson, Feb. 7, 1973, 11–15, 28, Thomas Edgar Lyon Jr. Research Collection, MSS 2372, box 2, folder 11, Perry Special Collections, Lee Library.
7. Merrill to Russel B. Swensen, July 21, 1930, Swensen Collection.
8. Packer, *That All May Edified*, 43–44.
9. Clark, "The Charted Course of the Church in Education," in Yarn, *J. Reuben Clark,* 3:251–52.
10. Packer, *That All May Be Edified*, 43–44.
11. Swensen, Collected Statements, in Swensen Collection.

74
The Church Welfare Program Is Launched

1935

Welfare Square is a showcase for the efforts of the Church to assist the poor and needy throughout the world.

A temporal and spiritual responsibility of Latter-day Saints and their families is to be self-reliant. According to general Relief Society president Julie B. Beck, "We become self-reliant through obtaining sufficient knowledge, education, and literacy; by managing money and resources wisely, being spiritually strong, preparing for emergencies and eventualities; and by having physical health and social and emotional well-being."[1]

Marion G. Romney, a counselor in the First Presidency, enjoyed telling of a man who refused to be self-reliant, believing the Church

owed him a living. President Romney said: "He did not have anything to eat and refused to labor to care for himself. Out of desperation and disgust they decided they might as well take him to the cemetery.

"On the way, one man said, 'We can't do this. I have some corn I will give to him.'

"So they explained this to the man, and he said, 'Is it husked?'

"They said, 'No.'

"He said, 'Well, then, drive on.'"[2]

The Church established a welfare program for those experiencing economic difficulties and wanting to become self-reliant. The first welfare program was begun in Jackson County, Missouri, in 1831.[3] At that time, the Saints were asked to consecrate their all to the Lord and were promised an inheritance from the Lord in return. In later years, Latter-day Saints gathering to Kirtland, Far West, and Nauvoo received Church assistance. For example, Luman Shurtliff, a builder on the Nauvoo Temple, wrote, "We labored ten hours a day, and got something to take to our families for supper and breakfast. . . . Thank God that I and my family were thus blessed."[4]

President Brigham Young, following the welfare pattern established by Joseph Smith, taught, "If a Bishop will act to the extent of his calling and office, and magnify it, there will not be an individual in his Ward that is not employed to the best advantage."[5]

President Joseph F. Smith observed, "It has always been a cardinal teaching with the Latter-day Saints, that a religion which has not the power to save the people temporally and make them prosperous and happy here, cannot be depended upon to save them spiritually, to exalt them in the life to come."[6]

During the Great Depression of the 1930s, when employment opportunities had dried up and faithful Latter-day Saints were standing in breadlines and taking the government dole, Church leaders recognized the need for a better welfare system to help Latter-day Saints experiencing economic misfortunes. President Heber J. Grant established the Church Security Plan, today known as Church Welfare Services. He foresaw that under the Church system, "the curse of idleness would be done away with, the evils of a dole abolished, and independence, industry, thrift and self-respect [would] be once more established amongst our people."[7]

President Grant turned to Harold B. Lee, then a stake president in Salt Lake City and a city commissioner, to implement the Church Security Plan.[8] President Lee recalled:

"We had been wrestling with this question of welfare. There were few government work programs; the finances of the Church were low. . . . And here we were with 4,800 of our 7,300 people [in the stake] who were wholly or partially dependent. We had only one place to go, and that was to apply the Lord's program as set forth in the revelations. . . .

"The First Presidency . . . called me one morning [in 1935] asking if I would come to their office. . . . They wished me now to head up the welfare movement to turn the tide from government relief, direct relief, and help to put the Church in a position where it could take care of its own needy.

"After that morning I rode in my car (spring was just breaking) up to the head of City Creek Canyon into what was then called Rotary Park; and there, all by myself, I offered one of the most humble prayers of my life.

"There I was, just a young man in my thirties. My experience had been limited. I was born in a little country town in Idaho. I had hardly been outside the boundaries of the states of Utah and Idaho. And now to put me in a position where I was to reach out to the entire membership of the Church, worldwide, was one of the most staggering contemplations that I could imagine. How could I do it with my limited understanding?

"As I knelt down, my petition was, 'What kind of an organization should be set up in order to accomplish what the Presidency has assigned?' And there came to me on that glorious morning one of the most heavenly realizations of the power of the priesthood of God. It was as though something were saying to me, 'There is no new organization necessary to take care of the needs of this people. All that is necessary is to put the priesthood of God to work. There is nothing else that you need as a substitute.'"[9]

Putting the priesthood to work, Harold B. Lee was able to move the new welfare program forward in ways in which the character of the giver and the receiver were both enlarged. Latter-day Saints with means were encouraged to care for the poor. Employment bureaus were established to help find work for the unemployed. Bishop's storehouses were established to store and distribute products. A Church-sponsored transportation system was created to move products from one location to

DID YOU KNOW?

• Church President Heber J. Grant established the Church welfare program so that "the curse of idleness would be done away with, the evils of a dole abolished."

• A young stake president and city commissioner of Salt Lake City named Harold B. Lee was called to lead the Church's new welfare program.

another. Welfare farms and ranches were purchased and processing plants established near cities with large numbers of Latter-day Saints. Deseret Industries was established as a retail store. At Deseret Industries, Church members were offered employment training to help them reenter the private workplace. Periodic collections of clothing, books, furniture, and glassware were made. The elderly and disabled were employed to sort and repair the collected articles and make them ready for distribution at a minimum cost.

Through the years, this pattern of employment and distribution has continued to be the backbone of the Church's welfare program. Its purpose, to help individuals and families become self-reliant and not only find solutions but also cope with short-term and long-term welfare issues, has remained largely the same. At the October 2011 general conference, Dieter F. Uchtdorf, second counselor in the First Presidency, said:

"The prophetic promises and blessings of Church welfare, of providing in the Lord's way, are some of the most magnificent and sublime the Lord has pronounced upon His children. . . . Whether we are rich or poor, regardless of where we live on this globe, we all need each other, for it is in sacrificing our time, talents, and resources that our spirits mature and become refined. This work of providing in the Lord's way . . . cannot be neglected or set aside. It is central to our doctrine; it is the essence of our religion."[10]

Under the inspired welfare program, hundreds of thousands of individuals and families have been helped on a short-term basis to reach self-reliance and to overcome seemingly insurmountable financial obstacles by implementing the Church welfare program.

NOTES

1. Beck, "The Welfare Responsibilities of the Relief Society President," *Basic Principles of Welfare and Self-Reliance*, 4–5.
2. Romney, "Work and Welfare: A Historical Perspective," *Ensign*, May 1982, 88.
3. Romney, "Work and Welfare," 87–89.
4. Luman Shurtliff Autobiography, 52–53, Church History Library, The Church of Jesus Christ of Latter-day Saints, Salt Lake City, Utah.
5. Young, in *Journal of Discourses*, 8:146.
6. Joseph F. Smith, in Arrington, *Great Basin Kingdom*, 425.
7. Heber J. Grant, in Conference Report, Oct. 1936, 3.
8. Harold B. Lee, in Conference Report, Oct. 1972, 123–24.
9. Lee, in Conference Report, Oct. 1972, 123–24, or *Harold B. Lee* [manual], 165–66.
10. Uchtdorf, "Providing in the Lord's Way," *Ensign*, Nov. 2011, 53–56.

75
The Church Radio, Media, and Publicity Committee

1935

President Heber J. Grant (right) speaking on the first radio broadcast on KZN (now KSL), May 6, 1922. Elder George Albert Smith (middle, left) and Augusta Grant (center) look on.

Since the dawn of the Restoration, the Church has moved quickly to adopt the use of media. Church-sponsored newspapers, pamphlets, and other print media proved invaluable in spreading the gospel in the nineteenth century. Early in the twentieth century, Church leaders were quick to embrace new forms of communication. In 1922, for instance, Church-owned radio station KSL began broadcasting from a tin shack atop the roof of the Deseret News Building. That was the beginning of "the first full time broadcasting operation between the Mississippi Valley and the Pacific Coast."[1]

Historian Leonard J. Arrington noted, "At every stage of our history, the leaders of the Latter-day Saints have sought to use every communication facility that civilization afforded."[2] Church use of broadcast media continued throughout the 1920s and early 1930s.

The beginning of a unified approach to using media, however, can be traced to the visit of returned missionary Gordon B. Hinckley to Church leaders in the summer of 1935.[3]

Before leaving his service in the European Mission, Elder Hinckley was handed a glowing letter of recommendation from mission president Joseph F. Merrill, who commended his "ability as a writer of narratives" and lauded his young friend as "energetic and dependable."[4] President Merrill instructed Elder Hinckley to meet with the First Presidency and ask them to hire him to develop new materials for missionary work.

President Merrill, a member of the Quorum of the Twelve Apostles, had much confidence in young Elder Hinckley and what he could do for the Church. When newspapers in England reprinted an old anti-Mormon book and touted it as an authentic history, President Merrill turned to Hinckley and asked him to meet with the publisher and protest. Through the dogged efforts of the young elder, the publishing house agreed to paste a note in the front of each copy of the book, declaring the work fictional and not history.

Elder Hinckley had also demonstrated his skill as a writer, writing a history of the Church that appeared in a popular London magazine and preparing a series of lantern slides for missionary use. Greatly pleased by Elder Hinckley's work, President Merrill told an acquaintance, "We have come to the conclusion that the lantern lecture for cottages and movie lectures for the larger halls would bring many more contacts than we have been able to make during the last twenty-five years."[5]

Back in Utah, young Gordon Hinckley's first meetings with Church leaders were discouraging. He wrote to President Merrill, "The brethren are anxious to help, but they just haven't quite our viewpoint on some of these things and Europe seems rather remote when there are so many things near at hand to hold their attention," adding forlornly, "I have come to learn that England is not the only place where things move slowly."[6]

After repeated requests over two weeks, Hinckley was granted a meeting with President Heber J. Grant and counselors J. Reuben Clark and David O. McKay. Hinckley wrote to his former mission president, "Brother McKay expressed himself as being heartily in favor of the thing," but added, "The President was non-committal. . . . It's just about taken the heart out of me to have to go pounding on the doors of busy men, one day after another, with no obvious success."[7]

After six weeks with no apparent results, Hinckley dejectedly informed President Merrill that he needed to "get busy at something with which to patch my missionary rags."[8] He accepted an offer from Elder John A. Widtsoe to teach a difficult afternoon seminary class. It was a desperate move to "keep a little butter on my bread," Hinckley wrote.[9] A few weeks later, an enthusiastic Hinckley wrote to President Merrill that the First Presidency had hired him as the first employed publicity professional in the Church.

On October 16, 1935, the First Presidency announced the creation of the Radio, Publicity, and Mission Literature Committee, chaired by Elder Stephen L Richards. Gordon B. Hinckley was asked to be the executive secretary and day-to-day director of the committee. That same day Hinckley enthusiastically wrote to Elder Merrill, "The committee [will] engage me to do the work, perhaps some other work besides."[10]

One of his first productions was a half-hour radio series, *The Fulness of Times,* which ran from 1938 to 1942. At its height, the series was broadcast on 400 radio stations. It attracted a wide audience, providing a new standard for professionalism in Church media. A nonmember producer of the series praised Hinckley's work, writing, "There are no reservations in my endorsement of the show we made this afternoon. . . . It made me cry. . . . Driving back to the office I had that sensation which comes only a few times in a lifetime of spiritual cleansing."[11]

The Radio, Publicity, and Mission Literature Committee made significant strides in nearly every aspect of Church work. For instance, after President David O. McKay announced that a temple would be built in Bern, Switzerland, he asked Hinckley to find a simple way to present the temple endowment in several different languages. With President McKay's approval, Hinckley assembled a team

DID YOU KNOW?

- Extensive media programs of the Church were started in part by Gordon B. Hinckley when he was just twenty-five years old.

- Media programs of the Church have won several prestigious rewards, including back-to-back Emmy Awards in 1997 and 1998.

and produced a film designed to present the endowment dialogue to a multilingual audience. Before many years had passed, it was a standard practice to use films to present the endowment in nearly every temple.

In the ensuing decades, Elder Hinckley, in his role as an apostle, continued to lead Church efforts in innovative media use. With Elder Hinckley spearheading broadcasts on radio and television, media became a keystone in Church missionary work and teaching. Popular media, such as the filmstrip *Tom Trails,* the *Hold to the Rod* series, and a series of public service announcements entitled *Homefront,* became hallmarks of the Latter-day Saints. A milestone was reached when the *Homefront* series won several awards, including back-to-back Emmy Awards in 1997 and 1998.[12]

By the time Gordon B. Hinckley became President of the Church in 1995, he presided over bustling international media ventures owned by the Church. He welcomed a new era of openness, with one scholar describing him as the "standard bearer" in an era of Latter-day Saint publicity.[13] Under his capable leadership, the Church embraced the Internet and other forms of digital media, giving people across the world access to the message of the Restoration.

Recognizing the profound effect of the Internet on missionary work, Elder M. Russell Ballard of the Quorum of the Twelve Apostles, asked Latter-day Saints to become involved:

"There are too many people participating in conversation about the Church for our Church personnel to converse with and respond to individually. We cannot answer every question, satisfy every inquiry, and respond to every inaccuracy that exists. . . . May I ask that you join the conversation by participating on the Internet, particularly the new media, to share the gospel and to explain in simple, clear terms the message of the Restoration."[14]

In a church whose every member is a missionary, the work of the media committee empowered Latter-day Saints to use effective technological tools to spread the gospel message.

NOTES

1. Ashton, *Voice in the West,* 270–72, 407; Sherry Pack Baker and Elizabeth Mott, "From Radio to Internet: Church Use of Electronic Media in the Twentieth Century," in Whittaker and Garr, *Firm Foundation,* 339–60.
2. Leonard J. Arrington, "The Deseret Telegraph," *This People,* Jan. 1989, 53; see Baker and Mott, "From Radio to Internet," 342.
3. Dew, *Go Forward with Faith,* 71–73.
4. Merrill to Hinckley, Sept. 4, 1935, in Joseph F. Merrill Collection, Box 20, Fd. 4, L. Tom Perry Special Collections, Harold B. Lee Library, Brigham Young University, Provo, Utah.
5. Merrill to James H. Douglas, Apr. 2, 1935, in Merrill Collection.
6. Hinckley to Merrill, Aug. 21, 1935, in Merrill Collection.
7. Hinckley to Merrill, Aug. 20, 1935 and Sept. 17, 1935, in Merrill Collection.
8. Hinckley to Merrill, Sept. 19, 1935, in Merrill Collection.
9. Hinckley to Merrill, Sept. 17, 1935, in Merrill Collection.
10. Hinckley to Merrill, Oct. 16, 1935, in Merrill Collection.
11. Dew, *Go Forward with Faith,* 98.
12. Baker and Mott, "From Radio to Internet," 348.
13. Haws, *Mormon Image in the American Mind,* 159.
14. Ballard, "Using New Media to Support the Work of the Church," Mormon Newsroom, lds.org.

76
The First Stake outside North America

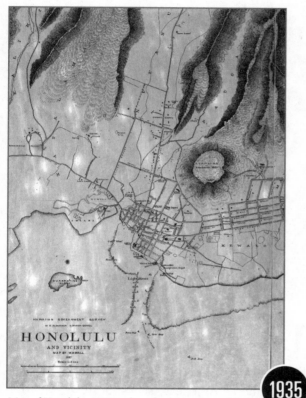

Map of Honolulu, 1887, where the first stake outside North America was organized.

1935

The organization of the first stake outside North America seems now like a relatively inconsequential event, considering the Church's rapid growth in the second half of the twentieth century with the constant creation and division of stakes around the world. "However, in the 1930s it was a matter of some weight and concern in the highest councils of the Church."[1]

Church leaders gave great consideration to organizing the first stake outside of the North American continent in Hawaii, due largely to the presence of the Laie Hawaii Temple. The biggest concern about creating a stake in the Hawaiian Mission was a lack of sufficient local priesthood brethren to provide leadership. But "the Brethren found a precedent in California, where there were both stakes and a mission, and decided to give the proposal support in Hawaii."[2]

Preparations were made at the local level before the Oahu Stake was created. In 1927, boards for all the Church auxiliaries were organized, including Sunday School, Relief Society, Primary, and the Mutual Improvement Association. In 1931, a district council, consisting of representatives of members from throughout the island of Oahu, was created.[3]

President Heber J. Grant, first counselor President J. Reuben Clark Jr., and several other general authorities arrived in Honolulu on June 20, 1935. Ten days later, President Grant organized the Oahu Stake, calling Ralph E. Woolley, a son of former mission president Samuel E. Woolley, as stake president.

"President Grant and President Clark believed that after eighty-five years of experience in the Church, 'the Hawaiians had earned the right to the gift of a greater power and fuller local responsibility in the administration of the Church activities upon the islands.' It was a source of deep satisfaction to Presidents Grant and Clark that the distribution of Church offices in the new stake, between the Hawaiians and other racial groups in the Church, 'was essentially proportionate to their relative numbers.'"[4]

When the Oahu Stake was organized,

President Ralph Woolley and Hawaii Mission president Castle Murphy proposed building a tabernacle, or what is now known as a stake center. President Woolley, one of Honolulu's leading builders, found a suitable location for the tabernacle and negotiated to purchase the land at a price well below market value. Ground was broken on March 16, 1940, with Presiding Bishop LeGrand Richards and Elder Charles A. Callis of the Quorum of the Twelve in attendance.

Nothing similar had been constructed by the Church in Hawaii before. Fundraisers held at the construction site, including Hawaii's largest carnival, helped pay for the structure. In 1941 the impressive Oahu Stake Tabernacle was finished. Now called the Honolulu Stake Tabernacle, it is a beautiful architectural attraction and has often been mistakenly called a temple by visitors to the islands. "The Tabernacle on Beretania Street," as it was generally referred to, did much to enhance the image of the Church among Latter-day Saints and members of other faiths.[5]

Two decades later the First Presidency and the Quorum of the Twelve concluded another stake was needed in the Pacific. Again, the presence of a temple was strategic in selecting the location of the stake. On April 20, 1958, President David O. McKay dedicated the Hamilton New Zealand Temple.

Mission presidents largely paved the way for the New Zealand Saints to have a stake. For example, mission president Gordon Claridge Young reorganized three of the largest New Zealand districts after the pattern of stakes. He also combined the two branches in Auckland into one. Previously, there had been a branch for Maori Church members and another branch for pakehas (members of European descent). President Young said to the members, "We're not Maoris and Samoans and Tongans and Cook Islanders and Europeans, we're Latter-day Saints and we're to be together, not pulling in different directions, having these little family feuds."[6]

Successive mission presidents "train[ed] local leaders through leadership seminars, training classes, and personal teaching sessions with priesthood and auxiliary leaders throughout the country." President Ariel S. Ballif removed "almost all missionaries from branch and district positions and placed the burden of authority on the local people. He organized elders quorums and district councils and did everything else he could to prepare for stakes."[7]

On May 18, 1958, Elder Marion G. Romney organized the Auckland and Waikato districts into the Auckland Stake, the first stake created outside North America and Hawaii. George R. Biesinger was called as stake president; William Roberts and Stanford W. Bird were his counselors. Historian R. Lanier Britsch observed that often foreigners have assumed that a large number of Americans served in stake leadership positions. Britsch explained, "Actually, since the first several stakes were organized, and experienced American leaders were used, the Maoris and other local Saints have assumed a large proportion of the stake presidency, high council, and bishopric assignments. Many Maoris have pakeha names, thus making it difficult to take an accurate census of racial distribution."[8]

The New Zealand stakes organized after the Auckland Stake were at Hamilton (1960), Hawkes Bay (1960), and Wellington (1965).

"By following approximately the same developmental pattern, Church leaders in the

---

DID YOU KNOW?

• The first stake outside North America was organized in Hawaii.

• The Oahu Stake Tabernacle, completed in 1941 in Honolulu, was the last tabernacle built by the Church.

Pacific have created stakes at an almost explosive rate since the early 1960s. The first stake in Australia was organized at Sydney in 1960, the first in Samoa at Apia two years later, the first in Tonga at Nuku'alofa in 1968, and the first in Tahiti by 1972. By April 1980, there were fifty-two stakes in the Pacific. By the early years of the twenty-first century, this total had more than doubled."[9]

Church historians Donald Q. Cannon and Richard O. Cowan surmised "the island peoples are able to adapt well to the highly structured Church [stakes] of the twenty-first century," despite the "generally underdeveloped state of island economies and the limited level of education in many island groups."[10] What started as a local event when the first stake outside of North America was created has now blossomed into hundreds of stakes throughout the world.

Notes

1. Cannon and Cowan, *Unto Every Nation,* 216.
2. Cannon and Cowan, *Unto Every Nation,* 216
3. Britsch, *Mormona,* 147.
4. Britsch, *Mormona,* 217. For a fuller treatment of the growth of the Church in Hawaii, including the organization of the Oahu Stake, see J. Reuben Clark Jr., "The Outpost in Mid-Pacific," *Improvement Era,* Sept. 1935, 535.
5. Comfort Margaret Bock, "The Church of Jesus Christ of Latter Day Saints in the Hawaiian Islands," master's thesis, University of Hawaii (1941), 91.
6. Gordon Claridge Young, in Britsch, *Unto the Islands of the Sea,* 320.
7. Cannon and Cowan, *Unto Every Nation,* 217–18.
8. Britsch, *Unto the Islands of the Sea,* 330.
9. Cannon and Cowan, *Unto Every Nation,* 218.
10. Cannon and Cowan, *Unto Every Nation,* 227.

77
The Hill Cumorah Pageant

1937

The annual Hill Cumorah Pageant, described as "America's Witness for Christ."

In two separate actions, in 1907 and 1928, the Church was able to purchase the Hill Cumorah. Within a few years, a striking monument, a pillar of Vermont granite standing thirty-nine feet, three-inches high (one foot for each year of the Prophet Joseph's life), was built on the brow of the hill. The pillar was topped by a ten-foot, four-inch-tall bronze statue of the angel Moroni.

During the service dedicating the monument in 1935, President Heber J. Grant prayed that the monument and its surroundings would "stand here as a testimony of God, of Jesus Christ, and of the dealings of Jesus Christ with the people that lived anciently upon this continent."[1] In the years since, a series of events brought President Grant's desires to pass, creating one of the most well-known artistic witnesses of the story of the Book of Mormon.

In 1937 Harold I. Hansen, a missionary in the Eastern States Mission, was asked to direct an outdoor play at the Hill Cumorah. Although plays on the history of the Church had been performed in that vicinity since 1917, including one performed at the foot of the hill just the year before, a play that centered on the Book of Mormon had never been performed on the hill.

For Hansen, there were many obstacles to overcome in creating an outdoor production, the most obvious being that the actors could not be heard. To rectify the problem, fourteen-inch-long microphones were hung around the actors' necks. Then there was the problem of actors dragging microphone cables over the grass. The static caused by cables was so loud that the dialogue was almost incomprehensible. Then there was the issue of lighting—car headlights. The audience could barely see the players in the evening productions.

Despite all the technical difficulties, the pageant came together in a way none of its organizers could have imagined. Hansen recalled the opening night of *America's Witness for Christ*:

"When I saw the audience, there were over

13,000 people there. . . . As I stood . . . and watched . . . there were things happening that I just could not believe. I saw things happen on that hill that were never touched by any of us there . . . and we knew it beyond a shadow of a doubt . . . because we had worked with it day by day. . . . [F]or the twelve months after I left that hill, I just kept saying to myself, in the practical sense, 'It could not be. It just could not be.' I heard individuals around me that night say certain things that I did not think could ever come from a human being who knew nothing about Mormonism."[2]

By 1939, there were 18,000 in attendance on opening night, most of whom were not Latter-day Saints. Hansen left his mission for home, believing his responsibility for the pageant was over, and he settled down in Logan, Utah. In 1940 he was working on a master's degree at Iowa State University. He interrupted his schooling to accept an assignment from the president of the Eastern States Mission to return to New York and direct *America's Witness for Christ*. He returned to New York because of his belief that directing the pageant was divinely commissioned. Under his direction, the production at "Mormonism's Mount Sinai," as *Time* magazine called the Hill Cumorah, received much public acclaim.[3]

"Some 100,000 people from the United States and Canada, most of them non-Mormons, and all of them nonpaying guests, crammed themselves into specially constructed seats to watch members of the Mormons' Eastern States Mission dramatize the Book of Mormon. . . . Sound effects were dubbed in by a former disc jockey. The hour-long spectacle called 'America's Witness for Christ' was presented on four stages erected each year on the drumlin hill."[4]

In 1948 a committee headed by Elder Mark E. Peterson of the Council of the Twelve took direct responsibility for the pageant. The committee was very receptive to Hansen's requests. For instance, in 1952 they authorized new stages along with ingenious water curtains to represent the vision scenes. In 1954 they agreed to release Brigham Young University professor Crawford Gates from his university responsibilities for a year to write a musical score for the pageant. In 1959 they authorized the purchase of state-of-the-art speakers with stereophonic sound.

Hansen by now held a professorship at BYU, but he retained responsibility for the pageant. In fact, he envisioned the university becoming part of the pageant experience. "My plan was to invite principally women volunteers [and a few young men to serve as bus drivers] from the west to do as the missionaries do and pay their own way to participate in the pageant," Hansen said.[5]

He anticipated the pageant would bring significant spiritual growth to university students as well as to other faithful Latter-day Saints. BYU President Ernest L. Wilkinson supported his ideas but cautioned Hansen to move forward with care. Looking back, Hansen observed:

"The counsel was wise because as you look at it from the outside, it was insanity. To put a load of college age women on a bus and then send it across the United States without incident was expecting a great deal. But from the inside, I knew the type of youth available in the Church and had seen the missionary sisters

DID YOU KNOW?

- Partly because of the influence of the pageant, *Time* magazine once referred to the Hill Cumorah as the "Mount Sinai of Mormonism."

- Due to the marvelous success of the Hill Cumorah Pageant, other Church-related pageants are now presented in various places in the United States, Canada, and Europe.

function. I knew that if the right spirit was established at the beginning of the trip, the plan would work."[6]

Sixty volunteers were selected the first year to participate in the pageant. By the time Hansen directed his last pageant in 1977, there were almost 250 volunteers. Remarkably, from 1953 to 1977, Hansen never had to send a volunteer home or pull a cast member from a performance. For forty years, Hansen was the heart of the Hill Cumorah Pageant.

In 1977 the First Presidency honored him with a formal written release: "Many have come into the Church as a result of an introduction to the Book of Mormon through the Pageant. Many thousands of our young people have been blessed in their lives through participating in the production. No one can adequately measure the good that has been accomplished as the Pageant has been presented annually over this extended period.

"Your professionalism, matched with your vibrant testimony of the divine origin of the Book of Mormon and its message for the world, have both been evidenced in the quality and spirit of the annual presentation."[7]

Forty years have passed since Hansen's release. Since that time, the pageant has continued to reach out to members and nonmembers alike. "Most converts in the region credit the Hill Cumorah Pageant as one of the significant experiences in their conversion process." The production has changed through the years to include the Palmyra New York Temple as a backdrop and to add new scenes. In the ever-evolving process, one thing has remained the same—constant public interest. Gerald S. Argetsinger, artistic director of the pageant from 1990 to 1997, said, "The Hill Cumorah Pageant has become a major media event, drawing almost as many people of other faiths as Latter-day Saints." Expanded media coverage has included the *New York Times, Philadelphia Inquirer,* and *Good Morning America.*[8]

Due to the success of the Hill Cumorah Pageant, other Church-related pageants are now presented in various places in the United States, Canada, and Europe. The first was the Mesa Pageant, *Jesus the Christ,* begun in 1938. Several began in the 1960s, including *The Nativity,* performed in Calgary, Alberta, and *The Mormon Miracle Pageant,* performed in Manti, Utah. By the 1970s, Nauvoo, Illinois, was presenting *The City of Joseph,* and Clarkston, Utah, *Martin Harris, the Man Who Knew.*[9]

Notes

1. "Dedicatory Prayer," *Improvement Era,* Sept. 1935, 545; Rex C. Reeve Jr. and Richard O. Cowan, "The Hill Called Cumorah," in Backman et al., *New York,* 74–80.
2. Harold I. Hansen, "Cumorah's Lonely Hill," typescript, 1986, 1, private possession, in Mary Jane Woodger, "Harold and the Hill: Harold I. Hansen and the Hill Cumorah Pageant, 1937–1977," in Baugh and Hedges, *New York–Pennsylvania,* 158.
3. "Religion: Cumorah's Pageant," *Time,* Aug. 12, 1940, 42–43.
4. "Witness for Christ," *Newsweek,* Aug. 20, 1951, 79.
5. Hansen, "Cumorah's Lonely Hill," 163.
6. Hansen, "Cumorah's Lonely Hill," 163.
7. First Presidency to Hansen, June 15, 1977, in Baugh and Hedges, *New York–Pennsylvania,* 170–71.
8. Argetsinger, "The Hill Cumorah Pageant: A Historical Perspective," *Journal of Book of Mormon Studies* 13, nos. 1–2 (2004): 69.
9. Albert Jay Blair, "Pageants," in Garr et al., *Encyclopedia of Latter-day Saint History,* 587–88.

78

"The Charted Course of the Church in Education"

1938

The stage at Aspen Grove, Utah, where President J. Reuben Clark delivered the landmark address "The Charted Course of the Church in Education."

The Charted Course of the Church in Education," delivered in 1938 by J. Reuben Clark Jr. of the First Presidency, is still the landmark charge to Church educators. Since 1938 prophets and apostles have held it up as a model for classroom instruction.

President Henry B. Eyring advised religious educators: "The place I would always begin . . . would be to read President J. Reuben Clark Jr.'s talk 'The Charted Course of the Church in Education.' . . . He saw our time and beyond, with prophetic insight. The principles he taught, of how to see our students and thus how to teach them, will always apply in our classrooms."[1]

President Boyd K. Packer said, "'The Charted Course' may comfortably be referred to as scripture."[2]

In 1938 the need for a definitive statement on religious education had become evident to Church leaders. President J. Reuben Clark Jr., a counselor in the First Presidency, "made a thorough review of curriculum materials being used in the Church schools, institutes, and seminaries. Fearing the influence of secularization, he underlined [questionable terms]. . . . In his opinion, the terms were a compromise with secular ideas which asserted that the teachings of Jesus were purely ethical and not divine."[3]

President Clark believed there were "two prime things" that should not be "overlooked, forgotten, shaded, or discarded" in teaching religion: "First—that Jesus Christ is the Son of God, the Only Begotten of the Father in the flesh, the Creator of the world, the Lamb of God, the Sacrifice for the sins of the world, the Atoner for Adam's transgression; that He was crucified. . . . The second of the two things . . . is that the Father and the Son actually and in truth and very deed appeared to the Prophet Joseph in a vision in the woods; that other heavenly visions followed to Joseph and to others; that the gospel and the Holy Priesthood after the Order of the Son of God were in truth and fact restored to the earth."[4]

President Clark accepted an invitation from the Church commissioner of education, Franklin L. West, to address the religion faculty of Church schools at Aspen Grove in Provo Canyon, Utah, on August 8, 1938. At that time, the religion faculty in the Church consisted of 128 seminary teachers, 18 institute of religion instructors, and four Brigham Young University religion teachers. They assembled at Aspen Grove to attend special courses at BYU's six-week Alpine term.

President Clark shared with the faculty the prime importance of teaching about the Savior and the Restoration. He then spoke of his concern that teachers refrain from planting doubt in the hearts of the youth:

"The youth of the Church are hungry for things of the Spirit; they are eager to learn the gospel, and they want it straight, undiluted. They want to know about the fundamentals . . . about our beliefs; they want to gain testimonies of their truth. They are not now doubters but inquirers, seekers after truth. Doubt must not be planted in their hearts."[5]

President Clark instructed the assembled Church educators to plant a "personal testimony of their truth" in the heart of each student. Concerned about the intellectual approach of some teachers, President Clark warned: "No amount of learning, no amount of study, and

no number of scholastic degrees can take the place of this testimony . . . of the teacher in our Church school system." He said that teachers who do "not have a real testimony of the truth of the gospel" do not have a "place in the Church school system." He indicated the need for a "pruning" of the teachers. He was emphatic that educators in the Church system were "not to teach the philosophies of the world, ancient or modern, pagan or Christian, for this is the field of the public schools. Your sole field is the gospel, and that is boundless in its own sphere."[6]

The response to President Clark's milestone address was mixed. Seminary teacher Sterling McMurrin called the address "notorious" and recorded that Church educators, he being one of them, "divided ourselves up pretty quickly into liberal and conservative camps." Newell K. Young said that evening, "'I don't know about the rest of you; but . . . I'm going over to see Lynn Bennion and resign.' He did too."[7] Young's resignation was not accepted.

The main concern of the religious educators was a perceived loss of academic freedom. President Clark, aware of the controversy generated by his declaration, wrote to a friend, "There has been not a little rather severe fault-finding on the part of certain groups because of the things which I said at Aspen Grove. We expect to follow through on this matter and to try to bring our Church education institutions in line herewith."[8]

Excerpts from President Clark's address were published in Utah newspapers the day after it was delivered. The *Deseret News* included this introduction:

"Voicing an official pronouncement of the First Presidency of the Church, President Clark gave direct counsel to teachers of the Church Seminary System who are attending special courses during the university's Alpine term. The policy, he said, was to apply also to other

DID YOU KNOW?

• President J. Reuben Clark Jr. gave the address entitled "The Charted Course of the Church in Education" amid fears that Church education was becoming too secularized.

• The "Charted Course" emphasizes "two prime things" that should not be "overlooked, forgotten, shaded, or discarded" in teaching religion: Jesus Christ is the Son of God, and the gospel was restored to the earth.

institutions of the system, including Brigham Young University, and Church academies and institutions."[9]

In September 1939, the *Improvement Era* ran the full text of Clark's address under its present title, "The Charted Course of the Church in Education." The *Improvement Era* declared, "Its significance pertains to the whole Church, and may well serve as an authoritative guide in all our teaching and all our meetings—auxiliary and otherwise, where there is any possibility of Church facilities and Church time being used to expose Church people to contrary influences."[10]

On February 2, 1939, the BYU board of trustees restructured its religious curriculum to match the curriculum established by the general Church board of education. The three members of the First Presidency and seven members of the Quorum of the Twelve Apostles composed the two boards.

Personnel changes within the religious education system were also made. It was agreed that no person should be employed on the college level who was not in a position spiritually to teach any subject in religion. Moreover, new curriculum was developed according to the guidelines that President Clark had set forth in his address.

Though reaction to "The Charted Course" was immediate, in the decades of the 1940s and 1950s the address was never quoted in general conferences. Not until 1974, beginning with a talk given by Elder Boyd K. Packer of the Quorum of the Twelve, did "The Charted Course" once again rise to prominence. Elder Packer said to religious educators, "Surely you read that every year, every one of you, every year."[11]

"The Charted Course" has been quoted in more than fifteen general authority addresses to religious educators and prospective teachers and continues to rise in importance. It appears in *Teaching the Gospel: A Handbook for CES Teachers and Leaders,* and was reprinted as the first address in a collection of addresses to Church educators entitled *Charge to Religious Educators.*

President Henry B. Eyring said of "The Charted Course": "The great change in our classrooms, as the kingdom goes forth to every nation, kindred, tongue, and people, will only verify the prophetic vision of President Clark. . . . The principles described so many years ago will be a sure guide in the years ahead, both in our classrooms and in the homes of our students and their posterity."[12]

NOTES

1. Eyring, "The Lord Will Multiply the Harvest," in *Teaching Seminary,* 94.
2. Packer, *That All May Be Edified,* 44.
3. Wilkinson, *Brigham Young University,* 2:243; see Casey Paul Griffiths, "The Chicago Experiment: Finding a Voice and Charting the Course of Religious Education in the Church," *BYU Studies* 49, no. 4 (2010): 91–130, especially 107–10.
4. Clark, "The Charted Course of the Church in Education," lds.org.
5. Clark, "Charted Course of the Church in Education."
6. Clark, "Charted Course of the Church in Education."
7. McMurrin and Newell, *Matters of Conscience,* 115.
8. Clark to William E. Tew, Sept. 22, 1938, in Scott C. Esplin, "Charting the Course: President Clark's Charge to Religious Educators," *Religious Educator* 7, no. 1 (2006): 107.
9. "Pres. Clark Sets Forth Church Seminary Policies," 16, in Esplin, "Charting the Course," 103.
10. Clark, "The Charted Course of the Church in Education," *Improvement Era,* Sept. 1938, 520.
11. Packer, "The Great Plan of Happiness," in *Teaching Seminary,* 70. President Clark's "The Charted Course" was cited by President Packer in several published addresses to religious educators: "Seek Learning Even by Study and Also by Faith" (1974), "Equally Yoked" (1975), "Teach the Scriptures" (1977), "The Great Plan of Happiness" (1993), and "The One Pure Defense" (2004).
12. Eyring, "The Lord Will Multiply the Harvest," 95.

79
The Beginning of Church Correlation

1939

The Church Administration Building and the Church Office Building, Salt Lake City, Utah.

In 1963 N. Eldon Tanner of the First Presidency said that the correlation program of the Church is "the closest blueprint yet in mortality to the plan presented in the Grand Council of Heaven before the world was created and is the most effective utilization thus far of special keys given to the Prophet Joseph Smith in the Kirtland Temple."[1]

Yet most Latter-day Saints know little or nothing about correlation and its beginnings. According to historian Michael Goodman, "The formation of correlation provides a powerful witness to how God guides and directs his work through inspired servants using their agency to act to the best of their abilities."[2]

As the Church expanded in the nineteenth century, new programs and auxiliaries were added. The Relief Society was organized in 1842, Sunday School in 1849, Young Women's Mutual Improvement Association (YWMIA) in 1875, and Primary in 1878. These programs helped the work of the Lord's Church move forward, and yet their growth created unique challenges for the Church and its leaders.

According to Goodman, "Each auxiliary was created to help the presiding authorities accomplish the work of the ministry. As each auxiliary grew in size, it also grew in complexity. Though each auxiliary was intended to meet the needs of distinct groups, it soon became evident that much of what they did overlapped and at times complicated the work as a whole."[3]

As the auxiliaries expanded, the need for training and curriculum materials grew as well. Many organizations were writing and publishing their own materials, which led to "inevitable duplication, disparity, and expense." Ultimately, there were "so many organizations often working in so many directions and requiring great amounts of time from individual members, [that] the family unit began to suffer."[4]

Church leaders recognized the pressing need to identify the roles and duties of each auxiliary and to coordinate and unify the auxiliaries to help the family, not burden it.[5]

Early in the twentieth century, the First Presidency began taking steps toward unifying Church curriculum. The Committee of Correlation and Adjustments was established in 1907, followed soon afterward by the Correlation Committee. In 1908 President Joseph F. Smith organized the General Priesthood Committee on Outlines and appointed Elder David O. McKay, a recently called member of the Twelve, as chair. The purpose of the General Priesthood Committee was to create a curriculum for each office in the priesthood. In 1916 the Social Advisory Committee was organized, in 1939 the Committee of Correlation and Coordination was established, and in 1940 the Union Board of the Auxiliaries found its place in the administrative program of the Church. Each committee was to "correlate Church organizations in their structures, curricula, activities, and meetings."[6]

While these committees worked to consolidate efforts and minimize duplication, they did not focus on minimizing the work of the auxiliaries. Thus, while initial correlation efforts were generally successful, the Church still had much to do. This became more evident in the 1950s with unprecedented membership growth. Recognizing the need for change, in 1960 the General Priesthood Committee, with Elder Harold B. Lee at the helm, began a major correlation effort of curriculum materials. In the 1961 general conference, Elder Lee explained the scope of the issue and outlined basic principles that would guide priesthood correlation:

"The repeated necessity for re-examination of the programs, the activities, and the prescribed courses of study has been apparent over the years to make certain that the original concepts relative to each organization were being adhered to, that each in its field was functioning up to its capacity, that one was not usurping the field of activity designed for the other, and that duplications . . . were reduced to a minimum. . . .

"This whole problem of correlation grows and develops, if you will just stop to think for a moment what the rapid expansion and growth of the Church entails. Within each year by . . . convert baptisms and natural increase, there are enough people being added to the Church to make from seventeen to twenty stakes each year."[7]

After presenting various studies that supported the need for correlation, Elder Lee announced the establishment of a Churchwide coordinating council and three coordinating committees: one for children, one for youth, and one for adults. The council and the committees consisted of "representatives of the General Authorities, the executive heads of the auxiliary boards, and representatives of various agencies and auxiliaries of the Church."[8]

Elder Lee explained that the council and the committees would correlate instructional and activity programs of all auxiliaries and priesthood quorums for the entire Church. A consequence of this decision was that auxiliaries would no longer develop their own curricula. The curriculum was to be created in the Church coordinating committees.

In general conference April 1963, Elder Lee asked for "exhaustive, prayerful study and consideration" of Church correlation "so that the Church might reap the maximum harvest from the devotion of the faith, intelligence, skill and knowledge of [the] various Auxiliary Organizations and Priesthood Committees."[9]

As Churchwide correlation moved ahead, attention turned to the stake and ward levels

DID YOU KNOW?

• Before Churchwide correlation, each auxiliary organization printed its own curriculum and magazines.

• Church correlation was part of an effort to streamline Church organizations and strengthen families.

to ensure coordination on a smaller scale. In 1964, the Church established ward priesthood executive committee meetings, monthly ward council meetings, and similar ward and stake meetings to coordinate activities, programs, and the needs of individual Latter-day Saints and their families.

To strengthen gospel teaching in the home, the Church organized home teaching efforts and family home evenings. Church leaders recognized, "If Church organizations do not strengthen the home, there is no justification for their existence."[10] By unifying Church auxiliary organizations and their curriculums under the priesthood, it was believed that families, wards, and stakes would become more unified.

The importance of Church correlation cannot be overstated. President David O. McKay testified that priesthood correlation is "one of the greatest undertakings that have yet been presented to the Priesthood."[11] In 1967 Elder Thomas S. Monson affirmed the significance of correlation: "We are encamped against the greatest array of sin, vice, and evil ever assembled before our eyes. Such formidable enemies may cause lesser hearts to shrink or shun the fight. But the battle plan whereby we fight to save the souls of men is not our own. It was provided to our leader, even President David O. McKay, by the inspiration and revelation of the Lord. Yes, I speak of that plan which will bring us victory, even the Correlation Program of the Church."[12]

Church correlation was not merely a temporal or logistical effort. It strengthened the functions of the Church and in so doing, strengthened families and individuals so that the purposes of the Lord could move forward with greater strength: "In short, the major objective of priesthood correlation is to move Latter-day Saints toward salvation in the celestial kingdom."[13]

NOTES

1. Tanner, Minutes of the Priesthood Genealogy Committee Training Session, Dec. 1963, in Daniel H. Ludlow, "Correlation," in Garr et al., *Encyclopedia of Latter-day Saint History,* 251.
2. Michael A. Goodman, "Correlation: The Early Years," in Whittaker and Garr, *Firm Foundation,* 320.
3. Goodman, "Correlation," 322.
4. Goodman, "Correlation," 322–23; see Frank O. May Jr., "Correlation of the Church Administration," in Ludlow, *Encyclopedia of Mormonism,* 1:324.
5. See Mouritsen, *Defense and a Refuge,* 34.
6. May, "Correlation of the Church Administration," 1:324.
7. Lee, in Conference Report, Oct. 1961, 78.
8. Lee, in Conference Report, Oct. 1961, 79–80.
9. Lee, in Conference Report, Apr. 1963, 83.
10. Mouritsen, *Defense and a Refuge,* 34.
11. McKay, in Conference Report, Oct. 1961, 77.
12. Monson, "Correlation Brings Blessings," *Relief Society Magazine,* Apr. 1967, 247.
13. Mouritsen, *Defense and a Refuge,* 35.

80
The Statement of the First Presidency on War

1942

United States servicemen who answered the call to arms during World War II.

Four months after Japan attacked Pearl Harbor, President J. Reuben Clark Jr. read at the April 1942 general conference the First Presidency's statement on war. This authoritative declaration was widely distributed as a pamphlet during World War II. Its inspired message gave direction and solace to thousands of Latter-day Saints and their family members who were serving in the military.[1]

The 1942 First Presidency declared, "The Church is and must be against war. . . . It cannot regard war as a righteous means of settling international disputes; these should and could be settled—the nations agreeing—by peaceful negotiations and adjustments." The statement defined the Church's stance on war: "The Church itself cannot wage war, unless and until the Lord shall issue new commands. . . . But the Church membership are citizens or subjects of sovereignties over which the Church has no control."[2]

Therefore, when Latter-day Saints are called "into the armed service of any country to which they owe allegiance, their highest civic duty requires that they meet that call. If harkening to that call and obeying those in command over them, they shall take the lives of those who fight against them, that will not make of them murderers. . . . For it would be a cruel God that would punish His children as moral sinners for acts done by them as the innocent instrumentalities of a sovereign whom He had told them to obey and whose will they were powerless to resist."[3]

Later historians observed: "Given the Church's international character, Church members unavoidably found themselves praying to the same God but from the vantage point of opposing camps. Nevertheless, righteous members of the Church who answered the call to arms—as indeed they should in response to their highest civic duty—and who conducted themselves as honorably as they could were absolved from responsibility for the shedding of blood. That responsibility necessarily would reside with those duly empowered to engage the nations in war."[4]

Latter-day Saints were assured that although "hate can have no place in the souls of the righteous," they are "part of the body politic" and must obey those in authority, for there is an "obligation to come to the defense of their country when a call to arms was made."[5]

The 1942 statement contained prophetic promises for Latter-day Saint soldiers who prayed and kept the commandments: "Whatever betides you the Lord will be with you and nothing will happen to you that will not be to the honor and glory of God and to your salvation and exaltation." The First Presidency promised Latter-day Saint soldiers that they would receive "a joy that will pass your powers of expression or understanding." Moreover, they were assured that the Lord will "guard and protect you to the full extent that accords with His all-wise purpose."[6]

They were also promised: "When the conflict is over and you return to your homes, having lived the righteous life, how great will be your happiness—whether you be of the victors or of the vanquished—that you have lived as the Lord commanded. You will return so disciplined in righteousness that thereafter all Satan's wiles and stratagems will leave you untouched. Your faith and testimony will be strong beyond breaking. You will be looked up to and revered as having passed through the fiery furnace of trial and temptation and come forth unharmed. Your brethren will look to you for counsel, support, and guidance. You will be the anchors to which thereafter the youth of Zion will moor their faith in man."[7]

Over the course of World War II, this promise was fulfilled in the lives of Elders David B. Haight, Neal A. Maxwell, Thomas S. Monson, Boyd K. Packer, and L. Tom Perry, all of whom later served in the Quorum of the Twelve Apostles.

The First Presidency's statement on war has defined the Church's stance in subsequent military conflicts. Robert C. Oaks, a Latter-day Saint who was a general in the United States Air Force and later a member of the Seventy, wrote: "The Church considers being loyal citizens to be a duty of its members, irrespective of nationality. Responding to a call for military service is one appropriate manner of fulfilling this duty of citizenship. . . . While any member is free to object to military service because of conscience, Church membership in and of itself is not a justification."[8]

DID YOU KNOW?

- The First Presidency made an official statement in part to assure Latter-day Saint servicemen that they would not be guilty of murder if they were called upon to take a life in the course of their military service.

- During World War II, the First Presidency supported the spiritual life of servicemen on both sides of the conflict.

NOTES

1. First Presidency, in Conference Report, Apr. 1942, 94.
2. First Presidency, in Conference Report, Apr. 1942, 94.
3. First Presidency, in Conference Report, Apr. 1942, 95–96.
4. Mark Henshaw, Valerie M. Hudson, Eric Jensen, Kerry M. Kartchner, and John Mark Mattox, "War and the Gospel: Perspectives from Latter-day Saint National Security Practitioners," *Square Two* 2, no. 2 (2009).
5. First Presidency, in Conference Report, Apr. 1942, 90, 92–93.
6. First Presidency, in Conference Report, Apr. 1942, 96.
7. First Presidency, in Conference Report, Apr. 1942, 96.
8. Oaks, "Military and the Church," in Ludlow, *Encyclopedia of Mormonism,* 2:903.

81
Elder Ezra Taft Benson's Mission to Europe After World War II

1946

Elders Spencer W. Kimball and Ezra Taft Benson, about the time of Elder Benson's 1946 mission to Europe.

In November 1945 Church President George Albert Smith called upon President Harry S Truman of the United States to secure permission to ship food, clothing, and bedding to Europe. "Well, what do you want to ship it over there for?" asked President Truman. "Their money isn't any good." President Smith replied, "We don't want their money. . . . We would give it to them. . . . We will be glad to send it if we can have the co-operation of the government."

Surprised by such generosity, President Truman said, "You are on the right track. . . . We will be glad to help you in any way we can." President Truman was equally surprised when he asked President Smith how long it would take to get the shipment together and learned the shipment was ready.

Reflecting upon his visit with President Truman, President Smith said: "While the administration at Washington were advising the destroying of food, we were building elevators and filling them with grain, and increasing our flocks and our herds, and now what we need is the cars and the ships in order to send considerable food, clothing and bedding to the people of Europe who are in distress. We have an organization in the Church that has over two thousand homemade quilts ready."[1]

When President Smith returned to Salt Lake City, he called a special meeting of the First Presidency and the Quorum of the Twelve Apostles on December 22, 1945. He had determined to call one of the Twelve to go to Europe for an unspecified length of time "to re-establish contact with the Saints in Europe and to distribute much-needed welfare supplies."[2] He called Ezra Taft Benson, the youngest member of the Twelve, to carry out this assignment to distribute supplies to the needy. Frederick W. Babbel was called to serve as Elder Benson's aide.[3]

Elder Benson and Brother Babbel obtained permission for their visit from military officials. Transportation proved a difficult challenge. Airplanes were reserved for military personnel.

Most railway lines had been bombed, and passenger trains were virtually nonexistent. Functioning automobiles were even more scarce. Moreover, most roads, bridges, and wharfs had been destroyed. Nevertheless, Elder Benson and Brother Babble undertook their journey, being among the first civilians to travel throughout the occupied areas of Germany, Czechoslovakia, Poland, and Austria.[4] In getting in and out of these war-ravaged countries, they had to rely on the Lord.

Biographer Sheri Dew describes the miraculous way they entered Germany: "In Paris [Elder Benson] tried to gain access to the occupied areas of Germany, but the U.S. colonel was incredulous: 'Mr. Benson, are you crazy? Don't you realize there has been a war here? No civilian travelers have entered these areas. All travel is restricted to the military.' Elder Benson quietly asked if he could obtain permission to travel into those areas if he could find a car. Finally, the colonel conceded. And much to the colonel's surprise, Elder Benson found a car. Again and again, Elder Benson was told no. No, he couldn't get seats on a plane, but he'd get seats on that plane. No, he couldn't proceed into certain areas, and then those in charge would relent. No, he couldn't buy fuel, and he'd find fuel. And everywhere he went, he found Saints who were suffering."[5]

Food ration cards were in use, but most food was "sold on the black market at exorbitant prices." Starvation was widespread. Few buildings had survived the war, and entire cities were reduced to rubble.[6]

Elder Benson described what he encountered in Berlin: "I witnessed scenes that seemed almost outside this world. . . . I smelled the odor of decaying human bodies. . . . I saw old men and women with small hatchets eagerly digging at tree stumps and roots in an effort to get scraps of fuel and then pulling them home for miles on anything that would roll. . . . Later I faced in a cold half-wrecked auditorium off a bombed street, 480 cold half-starved but faithful Latter-day Saints. . . . I heard their harrowing experiences including murder, rape and starvation of their loved ones."[7]

Yet Elder Benson found, amid such terrible circumstances, that the Saints' testimonies were unshakable. One sister, in particular, touched his heart: "One sister who had walked to Western Germany from East Prussia bore her testimony of the power of prayer and of the gospel. Her husband was killed in a battle near the end of the war. She fled with her four small children, the youngest still a baby. She walked over a thousand miles with them, pulling a small cart with all their belongings. Along the way she lost each of her children, digging graves for them along the way with a tablespoon. Near the end of the unbearable journey, her baby died, and she dug the grave with her bare hands. Despairing and near to suicide, she felt the impression she needed to pray, which she did. She was comforted and strengthened and bore a fervent testimony that she was happy because she knew Jesus is the Christ and that if she continued faithful, she would be rewarded in the next life for all she had suffered in this life."[8]

Elder Benson and Brother Babbel met with Saints "in bombed-out schoolhouses and meetinghouses." They learned of "Saints who

DID YOU KNOW?

- Elder Ezra Taft Benson and Brother Frederick Babbel were among the first American civilians to travel throughout the occupied areas of Germany, Czechoslovakia, Poland, and Austria after World War II.

- Elder Benson helped distribute nearly two thousand tons of supplies to needy Latter-day Saints throughout war-torn Europe.

had lost homes, families, health—everything except their devotion to the gospel."[9] They worked eighteen-hour days or longer, often "without food—either because it was not available or because they gave what they had to the Saints who needed it so much more."[10]

"Elder Benson traveled more than sixty thousand miles to Germany, Poland, Czechoslovakia, and Scandinavia—often in freezing weather in unheated trains and planes." When gaining "permission to enter war-torn countries or to distribute supplies seemed impossible to obtain, Elder Benson appealed to the Lord to open the way."[11]

The service of Elder Benson and Brother Babbel produced amazing results. All previous missions were reestablished, and the Church units that had been broken up in the chaos of the war were reorganized. Missionaries were sent once again to Europe, and Finland was opened for the preaching of the gospel. Ninety-two railway carloads of food, clothing, utensils, medical supplies, totaling about two thousand tons, were distributed. By March 1947 the countries benefiting from the mission included Britain, France, the Netherlands, Denmark, Norway, Finland, Poland, Czechoslovakia, Austria, and Germany.[12]

As Elder Benson prepared to return to Salt Lake City, he wondered if his service had been acceptable to the Lord. The answer came to him: "Last night, in a dream, I was privileged to spend, what seemed about an hour, with Pres. George Albert Smith in Salt Lake. It was a most impressive and soul-satisfying experience. We talked intimately together about the Great Work in which we are engaged and about my devoted family. I felt the warmth of his embrace as we both shed tears of gratitude for the rich blessings of the Lord. . . . The last day or so I have been wondering if my labors in Europe have been acceptable to the [First] Presidency and the Brethren at home and especially to my Heavenly Father. This sweet experience has tended to put my mind completely at ease, for which I am deeply grateful."[13]

Notes

1. Smith, in Conference Report, Oct. 1947, 5–6.
2. Dew, *Ezra Taft Benson,* 197.
3. Dew, *Ezra Taft Benson,* 197.
4. Dew, *Ezra Taft Benson,* 207–8.
5. Dew, "Ezra Taft Benson: 'Serving Church and Country,'" *LDS Church News,* Nov. 28, 2014.
6. "Church's Aid to the European Saints after WWII," *History of Mormonism,* historyofmormonism.com.
7. Dew, "Ezra Taft Benson: 'Serving Church and Country.'"
8. "Church's Aid to the European Saints after WWII"; Babbel, *On Wings of Faith,* 40–42.
9. "President Ezra Taft Benson: A Sure Voice of Faith," *Ensign,* July 1994, 14.
10. "Church's Aid to the European Saints after WWII."
11. "President Ezra Taft Benson," 14.
12. "The Church's Aid to the European Saints after WWII."
13. Dew, *Ezra Taft Benson,* 224.

82
The First Temples outside the United States

1951

The Hamilton New Zealand Temple.

When Elder David O. McKay became president of The Church of Jesus Christ of Latter-day Saints in 1951, six of the eight operating temples were in the western United States.[1] The other two were in Laie, Hawaii, and Cardston, Canada, where enclaves of Latter-day Saints resided outside the main cultural regions of the Church.

In the decades after World War II, a massive migration of Latter-day Saints from traditional centers in the American West led to innovations in temple building that signaled a new policy—temples would serve as anchors for future growth. In October 1951, six months after becoming President of the Church, David O. McKay met with Robert S. Richards, president of the British Mission. Richards reported to President McKay on the state of the Church in Europe. During their meeting, Richards asked if the time was right for a temple to be built in Europe.

A few months later, President McKay told the Quorum of the Twelve Apostles of his meeting with Richards and said: "For years it has been recommended that the branches in Great Britain and Europe be strengthened, but members of the Church in those lands when they get the spirit of the Gospel realize the importance of temple work, and notwithstanding some of them held good positions, they have given those positions up and have come here in order to go through the temple." President McKay restated the basic obstacle to the international growth of the Church: the full program of the gospel, meaning the temple, was not available to faithful Latter-day Saints outside North America and Hawaii. President McKay continued, "The Brethren of the First Presidency considered it carefully and prayerfully and have now come to the conclusion that if we build a temple in Great Britain we should at the same time build one in Switzerland."[2]

President McKay felt the hand of the Lord strongly influencing his decision to build temples closer to members of the Church in Europe. He wrote to one stake president,

"Recently the Lord revealed the fact that temples should be taken to foreign countries, so people unable to come to the temple might have the opportunity of doing work in their own land."[3]

This decision, made in 1951, foreshadowed the pattern of temple building for decades to come. Temples began to be considered and announced in areas of the world where organized stakes did not exist. It should be noted that in 1915, when the temple in Hawaii was announced, the village of Laie had a strong community of Saints, although the creation of a stake was twenty years away. The announcement of temples in Great Britain and Switzerland signaled a new policy in which temples would serve as anchors for future growth.

This approach changed the reason for building temples not only outside North America but also within the United States. The first temple approved within the United States by President McKay was the Los Angeles Temple, which was to be constructed on land formerly owned by Hollywood producer Harold Lloyd. The Los Angeles Temple was to be the largest temple constructed to that time. Completed in 1954, the Los Angeles Temple served as a center of strength for future growth. Its massive size, location, and appearance attracted much local attention. During the temple open house, director Cecil B. DeMille, then in the process of filming *The Ten Commandments,* had a personal tour of the temple with President McKay. According to one account, when DeMille asked if he could visit the temple after its dedication, President McKay simply replied, "We'll take care of that. The first thing we'll do is baptize you!" Both men laughed.[4]

While the Los Angeles Temple was being constructed, President McKay pushed forward work on the London and Swiss temples. He oversaw technological innovations that would allow temple ceremonies to be performed in a number of different languages. As the temples in London and Switzerland neared completion, Church leaders set their sights on the Pacific, where members often had to travel thousands of miles to attend the temple in Laie, Hawaii. With missionaries having enjoyed unusual success among the Maori people of New Zealand and with continuous Church growth on that island, in February 1955 plans to build the New Zealand Temple were announced.

To construct the temple in New Zealand, local supervisors adopted a building program that had been used in Tonga and Samoa with some success. Instead of the Church hiring professional construction crews, young men from New Zealand received calls to labor as work missionaries. They were supervised by a small team of professionals, who provided skill training for the missionaries and the expertise necessary to complete the construction of the temple, a school for Church youth, and a village known as Temple View.

Their success led to other building projects, even though when President McKay visited New Zealand in 1955, he planned to curtail further projects. But he was "not prepared for the surprise that awaited him at the school there." Deeply moved by the sacrifice of the labor missionaries, he "doubted that there is another enterprise in the Church that will compare with [the Church College of New Zealand]."[5]

DID YOU KNOW?

• More than a century after the Church was organized, only eight temples were operating, six of them in the western United States.

• At one point, the First Presidency considered a mobile "temple ship" to make ordinances available to the Saints throughout the Pacific.

Rather than curtailing future projects, President McKay enlarged the projects by extending calls to thousands of labor missionaries. The missionaries built hundreds of new Church structures throughout the Pacific, including chapels, dormitories, houses, and schools. At the height of their success in the 1960s, thirty-seven Church schools operated throughout the region. This number eclipsed the number of Church schools established in the western United States in the nineteenth century.

Throughout the remainder of his life, President McKay continued to look for ways to make temples more accessible to faithful Latter-day Saints. In 1967 he asked Mark Garff, chairman of the Church Building Committee, to "look over the temples and to come back with a recommendation as to what our program should be in the matter of providing new temples and how we could accommodate our people who wish to go to the temples."[6]

Garff traveled extensively throughout the world to research an answer to President McKay's question. He found that 30 percent of Latter-day Saints worldwide did not have access to a temple. He then made an unconventional proposal to President McKay that to solve the problem, "the Church obtain or build a ship sufficient in size to run the oceans and we equip this ship as a temple ship; that we take the ship and outfit it as a temple, then take the ship into the ports and harbors where our people live."[7]

Garff believed his plan could be accomplished with minimal cost and provide access to temple ordinances for Latter-day Saints in Europe, South America, South Africa, and around the Pacific Rim. His plan was not adopted, even though President McKay offered initial approval. When counselors in the First Presidency presented doctrinal concerns with the plan, chiefly lack of scripture support, the proposal was abandoned. Yet, the fact that President McKay would consider such a plan demonstrates the lengths he was willing to go to provide access to temple worship for all Latter-day Saints.

Similarly, President McKay supported the nontraditional design of the Provo Utah Temple and Ogden Utah Temple. In these temples, several endowment rooms were built around a central celestial room, which allowed more endowments to be performed at one time than previous temple designs had permitted. The number of ordinances performed in these temples soon surpassed the number of ordinances performed in other operating temples. Such statistics are a tribute to President David O. McKay, who declared, "Temples have a special place in the Church aside from the ordinances given and performed within. They are lights upon the hill."[8]

Notes

1. Temple Chronology, ldschurchtemples.com.
2. McKay, Prince and Wright, *David O. McKay*, 202–3.
3. Prince and Wright, *David O. McKay*, 263.
4. Prince and Wright, *David O. McKay*, 259.
5. David O. McKay Diary, Jan. 2, 1955, to Feb. 15, 1955, in David O. McKay Papers, Special Collections, Willard J. Marriott Library, University of Utah, Salt Lake City, Utah.
6. Prince and Wright, *David O. McKay*, 273.
7. Prince and Wright, *David O. McKay*, 273.
8. Woodger, *Teachings of David O. McKay*, 179.

83
The First Uniform Missionary Curriculum

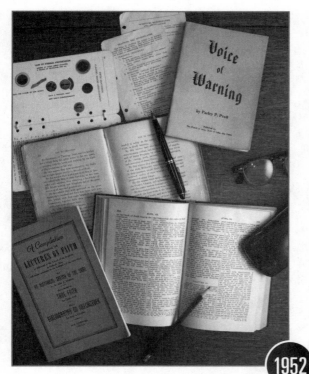

1952

Materials used in the first standard plan for teaching the gospel, introduced in 1952.

Since June 1830, when Samuel H. Smith left on his mission with a knapsack filled with some of the first printed copies of the Book of Mormon, missionary work has played a significant role among the Latter-day Saints. Throughout its history, Church leaders have searched to discover the most effective way to teach the gospel of Jesus Christ. Starting with the printing press and leading up to the latest electronic device, establishing a uniform missionary curriculum has become an integral part of Church history.

Among the earliest instructions given for teaching the gospel is a revelation to Joseph Smith in February 1831 which instructed that "the Elders priests & teachers of this Church shall teach the scriptures which are in the Bible & the Book of Mormon in the which is the fullness of the Gospel."[1]

A later revelation emphasized the importance of using the scriptures, particularly the Book of Mormon, declaring the Church to be under condemnation for neglecting "the new covenant even the book of Mormon and the former commandments which I have given" (D&C 84:57).[2]

Apart from these instructions, there was not a uniform curriculum for missionaries in the nineteenth century. The first material developed specifically for missionaries was *A Voice of Warning* (1837) by Elder Parley P. Pratt.[3] This 225-page tract contains a thoughtful outline of gospel principles and was widely read, though not officially endorsed by the Church as the official guide for missionary work.

Latter-day Saints became prolific producers of missionary tracts in the decades that followed. *A Friendly Discussion* (1906) by Ben E. Rich gained widespread use because of its narrative that was "at once simple and agreeable."[4] It is an imaginary dialogue between Rich, a Mr. Brown, and several others who are not members of the Church. The tract presents biblical passages in a nonargumentative discussion.

Another significant missionary teaching tool came in 1930 when LeGrand Richards, president of the Southern States Mission, wrote *Message of Mormonism,* a systematized approach for teaching the gospel. Richards abandoned the imaginary dialogue of Rich, favoring a straightforward approach for presenting the gospel. Richards's book lays out the message of the Restoration in logical progression, starting with the First Vision and the nature of God, and then leading its readers through a progression of key tenets of gospel living, such as Sabbath Day observance, the Word of Wisdom, and the law of tithing. *Message of Mormonism* was not adopted as an official missionary approach of the Church, but it was popular among Latter-day Saints. It was later published under the title *A Marvelous Work and a Wonder.*

The next important missionary curriculum development followed World War II, when the number of missionaries increased from 400 in 1945 to 2,297 just one year later. The war had disrupted the normal ebb and flow of missionaries in the mission field, resulting in a lack of seasoned missionaries to train new arrivals. At that time, Richard L. Anderson, a young missionary serving in the Northwestern States Mission, created a system for teaching the gospel. The Anderson Plan, as it came to be known, borrowed from earlier approaches and introduced a systematized approach to teaching the gospel. Anderson emphasized using the Book of Mormon as a essential tool of missionary work. Once initial contact was made with the investigators, Anderson urged missionaries to present a series of discussions designed to lead the investigator through the basics of the gospel. Joel Richards, the mission president of Anderson and a brother of LeGrand Richards, enthusiastically adopted the Anderson Plan and printed it under the title *A Plan for Effective Missionary Teaching.* Within two years, the Northwestern States Mission saw extraordinary success using this plan, with baptisms showing an "increase of 255 percent."[5]

As word of Joel Richards's success with the Anderson Plan spread, mission presidents throughout the world requested a copy of *A Plan for Effective Missionary Teaching.* Recognizing the effectiveness of his plan, after his mission Anderson and several other returned missionaries met with Gordon B. Hinckley, then a Church employee and executive secretary of the Missionary Committee. Hinckley interviewed each returned missionary, discussed various teaching approaches with them, and gave a recommendation to the Missionary Department to adopt a uniform curriculum. Under Hinckley's direction, in 1952 the first official set of standard missionary discussions was developed, entitled *A Systematic Program for Teaching the Gospel.*

This approach to effective missionary work featured seven scripted lessons, along with a long list of annotated scriptures to support the gospel topics presented. It featured drawings and illustrations to help investigators better understand basic gospel principles. For example, in the sixth lesson missionaries were told to draw circles to represent the phases of existence—premortal life, mortality, world of spirits, and degrees of glory.[6]

These materials were updated in 1961, 1973, and 1986. Each edition of *A Systematic Program for Teaching the Gospel* added suggestions for innovations, including flannel boards, filmstrips, binders with full color pictures, and so forth. Missionaries were given training

DID YOU KNOW?

• The first material specifically developed for missionary use was *A Voice of Warning* (1837) by Parley P. Pratt.

• The familiar "circles" diagram of the plan of salvation was first introduced through the missionary curriculum in the 1950s.

on how to conduct a discussion that encouraged investigators to interact with them. For instance, in the *Uniform System for Teaching Families* (1973) missionaries received instruction to "keep in mind how you want the family to feel. Do not force them to say what you want them to say—TEACH THEM—help them feel good about the gospel."[7]

The uniform curriculum helped to convert millions of people around the world, including the missionaries who used the curriculum to teach the gospel.

The latest version of the standardized discussions, *Preach My Gospel* (2005), emphasizes the earliest instructions given by the Lord to Joseph Smith in the Doctrine and Covenants. Counseling missionaries to avoid mechanical memorization, *Preach My Gospel* gives instructions to teach by the Spirit and rely on the scriptures for support. *Preach My Gospel* suggests a standard set of lessons but gives missionaries flexibility in teaching the lessons by using "their own words under the guiding influence of the Holy Spirit."[8]

Church leaders continue to urge the use of *Preach My Gospel* by all Latter-day Saints, not just missionaries. Electronic media has made the distribution of this volume more widespread than was possible only a few years ago.

NOTES

1. MacKay et al., *Documents,* 1:251, or josephsmith papers.org.
2. Godfrey et al., *Documents,* 2:298, or josephsmith papers.org.
3. See Givens and Grow, *Parley P. Pratt,* 103–17.
4. Rich, *Mr. Durant of Salt Lake City, "That Mormon"*; Dennis A. Wright and Janine Gallagher Doot, "Missionary Materials and Methods: A Preliminary Study," in Neilson and Woods, *Go Ye into All the World,* 97.
5. Wright and Doot, "Missionary Materials and Methods," 100–102.
6. Wright and Doot, "Missionary Materials and Methods," 100–102.
7. Benjamin White, "A Historical Analysis of How *Preach My Gospel* Came to Be," master's thesis, Brigham Young University (2011), 5.
8. Gordon B. Hinckley, in Richard G. Scott, "The Power of *Preach My Gospel*," *Ensign,* May 2005, 29–31.

84
The Mission of A. Theodore Tuttle to South America

1961

Map of South America, where A. Theodore Tuttle served as supervisory mission president over all the missions on the continent.

Beginning late in 1925, Elder Melvin J. Ballard spent six months in Argentina and experienced only limited success in sharing the gospel. He dedicated the country on December 25 for the preaching of the gospel. Before he departed, Elder Ballard made a remarkable prophecy regarding the spread of the gospel in South America:

"The work of the Lord will grow slowly for a time here just as an oak grows slowly from an acorn. It will not shoot up in a day as does the sunflower that grows quickly and then dies. But thousands will join the Church. It will be divided into more than one mission and will be one of the strongest in the Church."[1]

The prophesied growth did not come until the 1960s, nearly forty years later. It was ushered in when Elder A. Theodore Tuttle, a member of the First Council of the Seventy, was assigned to serve as the supervisory president over all missions in South America. During his five-year mission, Elder Tuttle oversaw thousands of leaders, missionaries, and converts. He was responsible for several structural changes that eventually became the model for the international expansion of the Church.

As early as the 1850s, Church leaders regarded the South American continent as a potentially fruitful field for sharing the gospel. In 1851 Elder Parley P. Pratt arrived in Chile to begin missionary labors there. He departed for the United States four months later without baptizing a single convert. By 1925, when Elder Ballard was in South America, the Church growth had remained relatively anemic. By 1935 there were only 340 members on the entire continent. In 1954 when David O. McKay, the first Church President to visit South America, toured the continent, Church membership totaled 3,250 in four countries: Argentina, Brazil, Uruguay, and Paraguay. Less than ten years later, after Elder Tuttle arrived, Church membership had increased almost fivefold, to 15,475. Under his leadership, the number of Latter-day Saints more than doubled to 37,735, and stakes were created in Brazil, Argentina, and Uruguay.[2]

Before Elder Tuttle was assigned to oversee the work of the Church in South America, he had no special connection to the continent. His interest had been in the religious education program of the Church and serving in the Council of the Seventy. His assignment to South America was part of a Churchwide attempt to create a larger international structure of leadership. In July 1961 Elder Tuttle was one of nine general authorities, including three future Church Presidents—Spencer W. Kimball, Howard W. Hunter, and Gordon B. Hinckley—assigned to supervise "groupings of missions" throughout the world.

Three of the general authorities assigned to preside over these groupings were asked to reside in their assigned fields of labor. Elder Alvin R. Dyer relocated to Frankfurt, Germany, Elder N. Eldon Tanner moved to London, England, and Elder Tuttle was sent to Montevideo, Uruguay, to the newly created South American Mission.[3]

During Elder Tuttle's mission in South America, he invited Church members, who had previously met in homes, to participate in an expansive building program that would raise the profile of the Church. Large, spacious, and beautiful chapels, similar to those being built in Utah, were built throughout the continent. More important even than the chapels, however, was Elder Tuttle's emphasis on training local leadership. Recognizing that American missionaries provided only short-term stability, Elder Tuttle began to train local leaders for long-term structure.[4]

Elder Tuttle set the tone for expansion, and mission presidents serving under his direction followed his lead. In the fall of 1962, Thomas Fyans, president of the Uruguay Mission, made arrangements for three promising leaders—

Juan Echizarto, Vincente Rubio, and Cesar Guerra—to attend the April 1963 general conference. During their stay in Utah, they visited Welfare Square, Brigham Young University, the Language Training Mission, and seminary and institute classes, and they attended all sessions of general conference. They also attended a stake conference in Bountiful, Utah, a high council meeting, and other such meetings. When these three elders returned to South America, they shared their experience and their vision for what the Church could be like in South America. Guerra told one gathering, "We did not visit the United States; we visited the Church."[5]

In the meantime, Elder Tuttle worked behind the scenes to simplify the lines of communication among mission presidents in South America and gave them greater autonomy to function in their callings. Before Elder Tuttle's leadership, mission presidents wrote to the First Presidency for permission to purchase something as simple as a heating unit for their home. Under Elder Tuttle's leadership, decentralization moved the power to make simple decisions to local authorities. The success of Elder Tuttle in South America laid the groundwork for area presidencies, usually consisting of three general authorities, to provide leadership to Church members around the world.

Elder Tuttle also refused to see the number of members in South America as too small for

DID YOU KNOW?

• Despite rapid growth in recent decades, the nations of South America were once seen as one of the most difficult mission fields in the world.

• A. Theodore Tuttle was one of nine general authorities assigned to supervise groupings of missions around the world—a forerunner to the modern system of area presidencies.

any programs offered by the Church. When converts in Chile voiced concerns about their children being refused entry to certain schools because of their religious affiliation, Tuttle organized a system of Church schools similar to that operating in Mexico.[6]

Also under Elder Tuttle's direction, mission presidents gave local leaders a six-step process for creating stakes, a culmination of the Church program.

When Elder Tuttle returned to Church headquarters twice a year for general conference, he spoke enthusiastically about the progress of the Church in South America. All four of his general conference addresses during his South American mission related to that continent and the remarkable growth in membership. In his 1962 conference address, Elder Tuttle said that South America "could best be characterized as a sleeping giant—both giant and sleeping." He added, "There is tremendous potential there."[7]

Elder Tuttle also spoke of the promises in the Book of Mormon concerning the Lamanites, believing the people of South America represented some of the descendants of the Nephites and the Lamanites.

The efforts of Tuttle and the leaders under his direction laid the groundwork for a phenomenal expansion of the Church in South America. By the end of the twentieth century, Latter-day Saints in South America numbered nearly 2.5 million, or 23 percent of the total membership of the Church. Nearly 43 percent of all Latter-day Saints living outside of the United States lived in South America.

By the beginning of the twenty-first century, nearly every country in South America had a temple, except the three small nations of French Guyana, Guyana, and Suriname. Nearly all local Church leaders came from among local members, providing an indigenous perspective to lead the Saints in their stewardships. As prophesied by Elder Ballard some ninety years before, the Latter-day Saints in South America have now "become a power in the Church."[8]

NOTES

1. Ballard, *Sermons and Missionary Services,* 100.
2. Grover, *Land of Promise and Prophecy,* 10–11.
3. "New Program to Intensify Supervision of World-wide Church Missions," *Church News,* July 1, 1961, 6; Kahlile Mehr, "Area Supervision: Administration of the Worldwide Church, 1960–2000," *Journal of Mormon History* 27, no. 1 (Spring 2001): 194.
4. Grover, *Land of Promise and Prophecy,* 14–15.
5. Grover, *Land of Promise and Prophecy,* 177.
6. A. Delbert Palmer, "Church Schools in Chile: Why and How," unpublished paper in private possession; see Casey Paul Griffiths, Scott C. Esplin, Barbara E. Morgan, and E. Vance Randall, "Colegios Chilenos de los Santos de los Ultimos Dias: The History of Latter-day Saint Schools in Chile," *Journal of Mormon History* 40, no. 1 (Winter 2014): 89–134.
7. Tuttle, in Conference Report, Apr. 1962, 120–23.
8. Ballard, *Sermons and Missionary Services,* 100.

85
The Mormon Pavilion at the New York World's Fair

The New York World's Fair, where the Mormon Pavilion influenced millions with its video, Man's Search for Happiness.

1964

As a young missionary in New York City, G. Stanley McAllister "imagined the Church building some impressive edifice that would stir people's interest in the Church." While serving years later as president of the New York Stake, McAllister saw the possibility of his imaginations becoming a reality in 1961, when a World's Fair was announced in New York. President McAllister and Elder Mark E. Petersen of the Quorum of the Twelve were the earliest advocates of Latter-day Saints

participating in the fair. These brethren made a "self-conscious effort [for the Church] to become more integrated into mainstream American culture."[1]

Through their efforts and those of other Church leaders, the Mormon Pavilion at the New York World's Fair permanently reshaped the approach to preaching the gospel. It was a watershed project that moved perceptions of Latter-day Saints into the mainstream and heightened the visibility of the Church in American society.

President David O. McKay assigned Elder Harold B. Lee to be the executive director of the Mormon Pavilion and President McAllister to negotiate with the World's Fair Committee for the best site available for a pavilion. President McAllister negotiated to have an exhibit site that visitors could see as they entered the main entrance. The desired space had been assigned to the World of Food exhibit, but when World of Food went bankrupt in 1963, the Church was offered the vacant lot.

As President McAllister worked to secure the site, David W. Evans, president of Evans Advertising in Salt Lake City and a member of the Church Information Service organization, developed a theme for the pavilion—"Man's Search for Happiness." Evans reasoned that the theme would have "a universal appeal to people of all races, creeds, colors, nationalities."[2]

Elder Lee assigned the Brigham Young University Motion Picture Studio to produce a film titled *Man's Search for Happiness* to address "the three great questions of life: where we came from, our purpose and reason for being here upon the earth, and what happens to us after death."[3]

The First Presidency approved a facade for the pavilion that replicated the three eastern spires of the Salt Lake Temple, a design "readily recognizable and uniquely associated with the Latter-day Saints."[4]

Inside the pavilion were colorful exhibits on the life of Joseph Smith, "the Book of Mormon and Christ in America, a mural of the life of Christ, two theaters, a replica of the *Christus* statue by Bertel Thorvaldsen, and a Church history mural." But no single exhibit or display at the pavilion had as powerful an influence on the six million visitors as the film *Man's Search for Happiness.* Thousands of visitors wrote comments on guest registers about their feelings while watching the film and the "peace they felt there."[5]

A unique aspect of the Mormon Pavilion was the full-time missionaries who served as tour guides. "Our missionaries became our most interesting exhibit," Elder Bernard P. Brockbank, managing director of the pavilion, recalled. "We had the . . . visual aids plus their own spiritual witness and so . . . they became very effective."[6]

Brent L. Top summarized the success of the missionaries: "While no official statistics were kept on missionary lessons taught or baptisms performed as a direct result of the pavilion, David Evans reported that during the year previous to the fair, there had been only six convert baptisms in that area, but he estimated that

there were a thousand baptisms in each of the two years the fair was open and 'in the succeeding several years, there were six to eight hundred per year.'"[7]

Rather than focusing on the number of converts, however, historian Kogan suggested that "a more valid interpretation of its significance is not only how it created a corporate image for the LDS Church based on family, community and wholesome living, but also in how it formed the prototype for the Church's later pavilions and future visitors' centers."[8]

The pavilion produced a "profound influence on individuals and institutions, [and] the Church's innovative involvement in the New York World's Fair was undoubtedly one of the most significant events for Latter-day Saints in the New York City area in the twentieth century." With techniques developed in dozens of visitors' centers and other venues throughout the Church, "the Mormon Pavilion's influence reached far beyond the borders of New York. . . . Its legacy will continue to be realized into the twenty-first century and beyond."[9]

NOTES

1. Nathaniel Smith Kogan, "The Mormon Pavilion: Mainstreaming the Saints at the New York World's Fair, 1964–65," *Journal of Mormon History* 35, no. 4 (Fall 2009): 10.
2. Evans to Irene E. Staples, Oct. 16, 1975, in Brent L. Top, "Legacy of the Mormon Pavilion," *Ensign,* Oct. 1989, 25n10.
3. Whitaker, *Pioneering with Film,* 59–60, in Top, "Legacy of the Mormon Pavilion," 26n13.
4. Top, "Legacy of the Mormon Pavilion," 25.
5. Joel Campbell, "World's Fair in New York Set Stage for LDS Missionary Work," *Deseret News,* Feb. 13, 2010.
6. Top, "Legacy of the Mormon Pavilion," 27.
7. Top, "Legacy of the Mormon Pavilion," 28.
8. Kogan, "Mormon Pavilion," 48; Top, "Legacy of the Mormon Pavilion," 28.
9. Top, "Legacy of the Mormon Pavilion," 28.

86
President Spencer W. Kimball's Charge to Missionaries

1974

Missionary in the Hong Kong Mission with Church Educational System leaders Jeffrey R. Holland, Frank Day, and Sheldon Shiu-Tat Poon, 1978.

Few Churchwide efforts have had greater effect on the growth of the Church than the call in the 1970s for more devout missionaries. When Spencer W. Kimball became Church President in 1973, the sharing of the gospel became a worldwide effort. During his eleven-year presidency, the number of missionaries from outside the United States and Canada grew nine-fold.[1]

President Kimball encouraged every worthy and able young man to serve a mission. Speaking of President Kimball's contribution to modern-day missionary work, President Marion G. Romney said, "I think there has never been a president of the Church who has moved the Church in missionary work as has President Kimball. His statements to 'lengthen your stride' and 'quicken your pace,' and his emphasis that 'every worthy young man should go on a mission,' are quoted and implemented

from Alaska to South Africa, and from . . . Norway to . . . New Zealand."[2]

One hallmark of President Kimball's service was his aggressive approach to expanding the number of missionaries from outside the United States and Canada. He emphasized at a regional representative meeting his prophetic vision that nations then dependent on American missionaries would one day produce their own missionaries and that the doors to the countries then closed to the gospel would open.

As he spoke those words, Elder W. Grant Bangerter of the First Quorum of the Seventy recalled, "We became alert to an astonishing spiritual presence. . . . It was as if, spiritually speaking, our hair began to stand on end. . . . With a new perceptiveness we realized that President Kimball was opening spiritual windows and beckoning to us to come and gaze with him on the plans of eternity."[3]

During the April 1974 general priesthood session, President Kimball presented the Lord's expectations for missionary work:

"The question has been often asked, 'Is the mission program one of compulsion?' And the answer, of course, is no. Everyone is given his free agency. The question is asked: 'Should every young man fill a mission?' And the answer of the Church is yes, and the answer of the Lord is yes. Enlarging this answer we say: Certainly every male member of the Church should fill a mission, like he should pay his tithing, like he should attend his meetings, like he should keep his life clean and free from the ugliness of the world and plan a celestial marriage in the temple of the Lord. . . . And so we repeat it: Every LDS male who is worthy and able should fill a mission."[4]

President Kimball was the first prophet to state clearly and boldly that every able-bodied young man should serve a mission. This new emphasis on missionary work as a priesthood responsibility sparked renewed vigor in Churchwide missionary efforts. The number of full-time missionaries increased steadily as Church leaders embraced President Kimball's vision and passed that vision on to future missionaries.

Even with an unprecedented and increasing number of missionaries and convert baptisms, President Kimball's zeal for the work never slackened. During an April 1974 address, he asked, "How can we be satisfied with 100,000 converts out of nearly four billion people in the world who need the gospel?"[5]

Moreover, upon learning that the number of annual convert baptisms had doubled in a relatively short time, President Kimball recognized there was still more to be done. Slightly modifying his question from four years previous, he asked again, "How can we be satisfied with 200,000 converts in a year out of four billion people in the world who need the gospel?"[6]

Throughout his presidency, Spencer W. Kimball repeatedly urged Latter-day Saints to "lengthen your stride" and to move forward with a "quiet resolve . . . to do a better job."[7] In

what became one of his most well-known addresses on missionary work, President Kimball said:

"The lengthening of our stride suggests urgency instead of hesitancy, now instead of tomorrow. It suggests not only an acceleration, but more efficiency. It suggests, too, that the whole body of the Church move forward in unison with a quickened pace and a pulse, doing our duty with all our heart, instead of half-heartedly. . . . We are not suggesting in the lengthening of our stride that we try to move faster than we are able or than would be wise, but rather a mobilization of our potential in order to move the kingdom forward for the more rapid and deeper benefit of our fellow men everywhere."[8]

The term "lengthen your stride" came to define President Kimball's presidency and is a motto still used by Latter-day Saints.

To accommodate the rapid growth of missionaries, missionary training also grew and adapted. President Kimball dedicated the Language Training Mission (LTM) in 1976 for all missionaries learning a second language. The LTM came to be known by its present name, the Missionary Training Center, two years later. Due to the number of missionaries called from outside the United States and Canada, in 1977 the Church set up its first foreign missionary training center, then known as the Missionary Orientation Center, in São Paulo, Brazil. This center was used to train missionaries from South America.

As missionary work moved forward at an unprecedented pace, greater blessings were received. Few blessings are as noteworthy as the revelation President Kimball received in 1978 to extend the priesthood to all worthy males. From that point, missionary efforts not only became more effective but missionary service opportunities were extended to all worthy

DID YOU KNOW?

• During President Kimball's administration, the number of missionaries called from outside the United States and Canada increased nine-fold.

• President Kimball was the first prophet to declare that every young man who is worthy and able should serve a mission.

priesthood holders. Leaders began to see the greater fulfillment of what the Prophet Joseph Smith declared, and what President Kimball reiterated, "The truth of God will go forth boldly, nobly, and independent, till it has penetrated every continent, visited every clime, swept every county, and sounded in every ear."[9]

Despite rapid growth, President Kimball always felt more could be done. After the number of missionaries grew to 20,000, Elder Carlos E. Asay, former executive director of the Missionary Department, recollected, "I happened to meet President Kimball in an elevator and thought he'd be interested in this information so I told him. He smiled, and without hesitation said, 'Wonderful. Now double it.' Later, when we reached 25,000 missionaries . . . he pulled me down and kissed me on the cheek and said, 'Now double it.'"[10]

President Kimball sought to expand missionary forces on all fronts, valuing efforts by sister missionaries and couple missionaries alike. President Kimball's counsel led to significant increases in the size of the missionary force. For instance, the proportion of sister missionaries grew from 6 percent in 1970 to 13 percent in 1979. Similarly, the number of senior couples increased dramatically. In 1974, about three hundred couples were serving missions. By 1980 the number of couples had more than tripled, to some nine hundred.[11] At the same time, the number of full-time missionaries had doubled. By the end of President Kimball's administration, there were nine missionary training centers, eight of them located outside the United States.[12] These and other strides in missionary work contributed to the ever-growing force of missionaries serving throughout the world.

Of the missionary work of President Kimball, President Ezra Taft Benson said, "No prophet in this dispensation, since the Prophet Joseph Smith, has spoken on missionary work as much or as forcefully as has our beloved prophet, President Spencer W. Kimball. . . . Each of us has a solemn obligation to, first, understand by the Spirit what President Kimball has said . . . about the mission of the Church; second, to catch his prophetic vision of missionary work; and third, to implement completely in our own lives the words of [President Kimball] pertaining to missionary work."[13]

NOTES

1. Kimball, *Lengthen Your Stride,* 119.
2. Romney, in Kimball, *Lengthen Your Stride,* 113.
3. W. Grant Bangerter, "A Special Moment in Church History," *Ensign,* Nov. 1977, 26; see Kimball, *Lengthen Your Stride,* 18–19.
4. Kimball, in Conference Report, Apr. 1974, 125–26.
5. Kimball, in Regional Representatives' Seminar, Apr. 4, 1974.
6. Kimball, in Regional Representatives' Seminar, Sept. 1978; see Ezra Taft Benson, "President Kimball's Vision of Missionary Work," *Ensign,* July 1985, 6–9.
7. Spencer W. Kimball, in David Croft, "Pres. Kimball: Convert World," *LDS Church News,* Mar. 22, 1975, 5.
8. Kimball, in "Historic Conferences End," *LDS Church News,* July 5, 1975, 3.
9. Joseph Smith, in Kimball, "No Unhallowed Hand Can Stop the Work," *Ensign,* May 1980, 6.
10. Kimball, *Lengthen Your Stride,* 117.
11. Kimball, *Lengthen Your Stride,* 120.
12. Kimball, *Lengthen Your Stride,* 116.
13. Benson, "President Kimball's Vision of Missionary Work," *Ensign,* July 1985, 6.

87
The Equal Rights Amendment and the Church

1974

The United States Capitol, where the hotly debated Equal Rights Amendment to the Constitution was proposed.

In March of 1972 the Equal Rights Amendment (ERA) to the United States Constitution was brought to the floor of the Congress, proposing to establish by amendment that "equality of rights under the law shall not be denied or abridged by the United States or by any State on account of sex."[1] With its origins in such feminist movements as the Women's Liberation Movement, the ERA prompted many rallies and caucuses across the nation to bring attention and support against gender-related discrimination that many women felt. Many issues that had once been considered domestic, such as family and other typically personal matters, were brought into the political arena.[2]

Though the ERA was ultimately not included in the United States Constitution, events and responses to the ERA, both leading up to its failure to become law and afterward, caused a maelstrom of strife and division across the United States. Members of The Church of Jesus Christ of Latter-day Saints did not escape this tumult. A wide spectrum of opinions and stances surfaced among the members of the Church in the wake of the ERA.[3]

Barbara B. Smith, who became general Relief Society president in early 1974, came to the forefront in defending womanhood both in and out of the Church. In November 1974, the Special Affairs Committee of the Church invited Sister Smith to take part in discussions regarding possible repercussions if the proposed amendment were to pass. As the Church had not yet made any formal public statement regarding the ERA, the committee determined it was time to deliver one. The committee was concerned that in giving a statement on women's rights, however, the public would misinterpret it to mean that the Church did "not want the women of the Church to achieve, [and] that Mormon men were trying to put women down and have them controlled by men."[4]

On December 13, 1974, Barbara Smith presented the statement at the Latter-day Saint institute of religion near the University of Utah. She indicated her support for improving women's rights:

"In my opinion, many of the concerns are valid, and the efforts being made to correct injustices, and unfair practices, and attitudes are deserving of support. . . . Many of these organizations and many individual citizens, however, are pinning their hopes for betterment upon a single act—the adoption of an amendment to the United States Constitution—popularly called 'The Equal Rights Amendment.' They feel the passage of the amendment will somehow be a panacea for all that remains to be accomplished. It is my considered judgment that the Equal Rights Amendment is not the way."[5]

President Smith explained that passage of the ERA could potentially nullify other protective laws for women, eliminate rights of privacy, mandate military conscription for women, and create a system without allowances for physical, biological, or emotional differences between genders.[6]

This statement created a variety of responses. Many women gratefully accepted the statement as direction. For others, however, the introductory phrasing—"It is my opinion that . . ."—raised the question of whether her position represented the Church or was merely personal opinion. Sister Smith maintained that she had felt guided by the Lord to say what she said.[7]

Almost two years passed after Smith's statement before the First Presidency made their official statement on the issue. Meanwhile, Sister Smith became the target of questions and criticism. She reflected, "I doubt that any previous general Relief Society presidency had ever faced a more constant spotlight than was directed at my counselors and me. Relief Society became the focal point of intense scrutiny. The media tended to pit my associates and me against the proponents of equal rights for women. It was a continuing frustration."[8]

On October 22, 1976, the First Presidency delivered their first official statement regarding the proposed amendment. This statement reiterated Barbara Smith's position, declaring, "There have been injustices to women before the law and in society generally. These we deplore. There are additional rights to which women are entitled. However, we firmly believe that the Equal Rights Amendment is not the answer."[9]

Even with that official Church statement, confusion and questions continued to abound. In 1978 the First Presidency provided further explanation for their position:

"A. Its deceptively simple language deals with practically every aspect of American life, without considering the possible train of unnatural consequences which could result because of its very vagueness—encouragement of those who seek a unisex society, an increase in the practice of homosexual and lesbian activities, and other concepts which could alter the natural, God-given relationship of men and women.

"B. It would strike at the family, the basic institution of society. ERA would bring ambiguity to the family structure which could encourage legal conflict in the relationship of husbands and wives.

"C. ERA would invite legal action on every conceivable point of conflict between men and women. Its sweeping generalizations could challenge almost every legally accepted social custom, as well as every morally accepted behavior pattern in America.

"D. Men and women have differences biologically, emotionally and in other ways. The proposed Equal Rights Amendment does not recognize these differences. For example, present laws protecting the rights of pregnant women in the working force could be challenged if ERA becomes law.

"E. Passage of ERA, with its simplistic approach to complex and vitally important problems, could nullify many accumulated benefits to women in present statutes, such as those protecting mothers and children from fathers who do not accept their legal responsibilities to their families."[10]

Even with prophetic guidance, some Latter-day Saints continued to wrestle with the ideologies pressed upon them. Sister Smith recalled there was a divisive spirit upon many men and women, in and out of the Church, and "an underlying awareness of the unrest that was upsetting the thinking of some of our sisters and causing them much pain as they struggled to find harmony in their hearts and minds."[11]

One Latter-day Saint woman, Sonia Johnson, brought national attention to both Relief Society and the Church as she aggressively advocated for the ERA. In attempting to rally public support for her pro-ERA loyalties, she developed attitudes and behaviors that ultimately led to her excommunication from the Church in December 1979. This action created a significant stir nationwide as media coverage made it appear the Church was a strong patriarchy silencing women who spoke out for woman's rights. Confusion abounded in the nation and within the Church over the reasons for Johnson's excommunication.

"Because the Johnson incident became publically controversial, it caught the attention of national talk show host Phil Donahue."[12] Barbara Smith and Beverly Campbell, the Church's ERA spokesperson, appeared on the *Phil Donahue Show* on February 4, 1980. Donahue led a lively discussion that addressed Johnson's excommunication and why the Church spoke out on the ERA. President Smith and Campbell ably responded to questions and comments from both Donahue and the audience through the duration of the program.

Concerning potential effects of the ERA, Smith shared her unease with a requirement for women to enter into military combat due to the brutalizing effect combat can have on a woman and the effect that could have on a family. Smith conveyed to the audience that central to a woman's role is protecting the family. She received supportive audience applause with her statement: "Women have a different role than men. Women must bear and nurture children, and we can't destroy the life-giving source and then expect civilization to go on."[13]

Perhaps the greatest benefit of Smith and Campbell appearing on the *Phil Donahue Show* was the opportunity to clarify on a national level that the Church did indeed support equality for women and was open to discuss the issues in noncontentious ways. Ultimately, the ERA issue created division and controversy during the 1970s and into the early 1980s, but in 1982 the proposal was three states short for ratification and the time limit expired.

As did President Kimball and other Church leaders, President Smith recognized that the real issue was how Church leaders could help women honor their eternal role as a woman, wife, and mother through the organization of Relief Society.

In October 1979, the First Presidency asked Barbara Smith to speak at the welfare session of

DID YOU KNOW?

- The proposed Equal Rights Amendment to the United States Constitution caused a maelstrom of discussion and division across the United States and in some Latter-day Saint families.

- General Relief Society president Barbara B. Smith publicly expressed views in opposition to the Equal Rights Amendment.

general conference and explain the role Relief Society women would play within Church councils. Sister Smith began her talk by explaining that "a fundamental reason for organizing the Relief Society was so that the sisters could act together to extend the work of the bishop in caring for the Saints and thus help build the kingdom of God on earth."[14]

She felt that all Church members, especially Relief Society members, should understand how the new developments emphasized the essential aspect of Relief Society being involved at every level, adding that those who would be involved in those councils had a vast influence upon the Church.[15]

Sister Smith outlined each council established in the Church—the general welfare services committee, area councils, multiregional councils, regional councils, stake and ward councils, and family councils. In detail she explained the role women should play in each and then provided examples of how women had influenced decisions, types of data they had collected, input women had given that changed decisions, and the compassionate perspective women had provided.[16]

The change to include Relief Society sisters in councils was significant, as it brought visibility to the equality and importance of the work of Relief Society and the work of the priesthood.

NOTES

1. *The Church and the Proposed Equal Rights Amendment: A Moral Issue,* 1–23.
2. Fisanik, *Feminism.*
3. *Church and the Proposed Equal Rights Amendment,* 1.
4. Smith, *Fruitful Season,* 74.
5. Smith, "Receive the Gift Bestowed," address at institute of religion, University of Utah, Salt Lake City, Utah, Dec. 13, 1974, 10; Smith, *Fruitful Season,* 6.
6. Carrie L. Taylor, "The Relief Society and President Spencer W. Kimball's Administration," 16, scholarsarchive.byu,edu.
7. Smith, *Fruitful Season,* 75.
8. Smith, *Fruitful Season,* 77.
9. *Church and the Proposed Equal Rights Amendment,* 21.
10. "First Presidency Reaffirms Opposition to ERA," *Ensign,* Oct. 1978, 63–64.
11. Smith, *Fruitful Season,* 76.
12. Taylor, "Relief Society and President Spencer W. Kimball's Administration," 20, scholarsarchive .byu.edu. The *Phil Donahue Show,* known as *Donahue,* was an American television talk show that ran nationally for twenty-six years.
13. Taylor, "Relief Society and President Spencer W. Kimball's Administration," 20.
14. Smith, "The Relief Society Role in Priesthood Councils," *Ensign,* Nov. 1979, 83.
15. Smith, "Relief Society Role," 83.
16. Smith, "Relief Society Role," 84–85.

88
The Creation of General Authority Seventies

1975

Elder Helvécio Martins, the first priesthood holder of black African descent to be called as a general authority.

On December 30, 1973, Spencer W. Kimball became president of The Church of Jesus Christ of Latter-day Saints. Of his prophetic calling, President Kimball said, "I know that the Lord called me to this position. I know that there are greater prophets, perhaps, than I, but I wish to do all I can to carry forward the work of the Lord as he wants it done."[1] President Kimball directed several vital organizational changes during his administration (1973–85).

After the Church was organized in 1830, during its first century the general authorities consisted principally of the First Presidency, the Quorum of the Twelve Apostles, the presidency of the Seventy, and the Presiding Bishopric. The seven presidents of the Seventy, commonly called the First Council of the Seventy, were general authorities who presided over the hundreds of seventies quorums throughout the stakes of the Church. Historian Richard O. Cowan, for example, recalled the existence of two quorums of the Seventy—the 274th and the 355th, in the Los Angeles, California, stake where he grew up in the 1930s and 1940s.[2]

By the 1930s the administrative duties of the small number of general authorities was enormous. Several administrative changes were introduced to lighten the administrative load, and most general authorities were recalled to serve at Church headquarters. During this time, Church leaders considered organizing a Quorum of the Seventy and designating its members as general authorities.[3] They eventually decided against this change because, according to the Doctrine and Covenants "a majority may form a quorum," meaning that the new organization would require at least thirty-six members.

According to President Spencer W. Kimball, "The scope and demands of the work at that time did not justify the reconstitution of the First Quorum of the Seventy." Instead, Church leaders chose to establish a new office, Assistants to the Twelve, with five leaders forming this group in 1941. During the ensuing decades, the number of Assistants to the Twelve grew as the work expanded. By 1975 the combined total of Assistants to the Twelve and the presidency of the Seventy reached thirty, only six short of the minimum number required to organize a quorum.[4]

At the October 1975 general conference, President Kimball organized the general authority First Quorum of the Seventy. "With this move," President Kimball explained, "the three governing quorums of the Church defined by the revelations,—the First Presidency, the Quorum of the Twelve, and the First Quorum of the Seventy,—have been set in their places as revealed by the Lord. This will make it possible to handle efficiently the present heavy workload and to prepare for the increasing expansion and acceleration of the work, anticipating the day when the Lord will return to take direct charge of His church and kingdom."[5]

Most of the leaders then serving as Assistants to the Twelve were brought into the new quorum. Of the thirty-seven men called to the First Quorum of the Seventy by October 1976, eleven were not Caucasian Americans, and quorum members had "different mother tongues—Navajo, French, Japanese, Dutch, German, English, Spanish, and Portuguese."[6] In 1978, emeritus status was granted to quorum members who turned seventy years old or suffered from ill health.[7]

The number of general authorities called into the First Quorum of the Seventy increased in the years following. By the April 1989 general conference, the total number of Seventies in the quorum reached seventy-eight, leading to the creation of the Second Quorum of the Seventy.

In 1986, after the creation of general authority Quorums of Seventy, the First Presidency discontinued seventies quorums in the stakes of the Church. Priesthood bearers still serving in these quorums could return to their ward elders quorums or be ordained high priests. From that point on, "the office of the Seventy was thus reserved for General Authorities of the Church," according to Elder Dale C. Tingey.[8]

The role and duties of the Seventy changed to meet the needs of the growing number of Latter-day Saints. During the 1980s the First Presidency announced the division of the worldwide Church into thirteen areas, each presided over by three members of the First Quorum of the Seventy designated as area presidencies. These presidencies resided primarily in the areas they served, reducing the need for international travel. During the 1990s, the First Presidency announced the creation of Area Authority Seventies, further increasing the leadership of the Church. For the most part these leaders served in the areas where they lived and met with the general authorities twice a year during general conference.[9]

The new Quorums of the Seventy brought into leadership roles in the Church a number of leaders from widely varied backgrounds. Representative of the new leaders was Elder Helvécio Martins, who was called into the Second Quorum of the Seventy in April 1990. Elder Martins, a native of Brazil, became the first priesthood leader of black African ancestry to serve as a general authority. Elder Martins, along with his wife and family, had joined the Church in 1972, six years before the 1978 revelation granting the priesthood to all worthy men. Reflecting on that time, Elder Martins said, "We had found the truth, and nothing would stop us from living it. . . . When the Spirit tells you the gospel is true, how can you deny it?"

In the years after his baptism, Elder Martins served in the Church as the public communications coordinator for the North Brazil Region, helping to raise funds for the construction of the São Paulo temple. After the 1978 revelation on priesthood, Elder Martins served as a bishop, a counselor to two stake presidents, and president of the Brazil Fortaleza Mission.[10]

The call of Elder Martins to the Second Quorum of the Seventy received widespread publicity because he was the first black general authority. He said, "Perhaps because of the media reports emphasizing my nationality and race, some members mistakenly went on to identify me as the 'Brazilian General Authority' or as a representative for the black race in the councils of the Church." He clarified, "I was not called by the Lord to represent any specific race, nationality, or ethnic group of his children. I was called by prophecy, revelation, and the laying on of hands to represent God's children . . . wherever they live on earth."[11] The calling of Elder Martins is representative of the expanding role of the Seventy, as priesthood holders were called as general authorities from every continent where the Church is organized.

The calling of general authority Seventies is just one example of the extensive organizational changes made during President Kimball's time as president of the Church. During the same era, the Church Patriarch received emeritus status, leaving the office vacant. Area or zone offices under the Presiding Bishopric were organized to handle the temporal affairs of the Church. Stake conferences were held twice a year instead of quarterly. General conference was reduced to two days and no longer needed to include April 6. Leaders of general women's auxiliaries were invited to sit on the stand and to speak in general conference, and women were invited to offer prayers in sacrament meeting. Signs on meetinghouses and letterhead of the Church were altered to present the words JESUS CHRIST in larger letters. The names of wards, stakes, missions, and temples were changed to include geographic information.

Of all the changes made under President Kimball's direction, however, the most far-reaching is the creation of general authority Seventies. The expanding numbers of Quorums of the Seventy represents a maturing of the global Church. Members of these quorums come from throughout the world, enlarging the cultural perspectives of the leaders of the Church. Referring to the original revelation creating the role of the Seventy, Elder L. Aldin Porter, said, "The basics were revealed then, and continuing revelation has brought the Seventy to the present day. . . . We can have 50 quorums of the Seventy, even 70 quorums of the Seventy as they are needed."[12]

As time goes on, the labors of the Seventy in fulfilling their charge in "building up the church and regulating all the affairs of the same in all nations" will continue to grow (D&C 107:34).

DID YOU KNOW?

• Church leaders considered adding a general authority Quorum of the Seventy as early as the 1930s.

• The thirty-seven men called to the first general authority Quorum of the Seventy came from a variety of backgrounds and spoke a variety of languages, including Navajo, French, Japanese, Dutch, German, English, Spanish, and Portuguese.

NOTES

1. *Spencer W. Kimball* [manual], 237–38.
2. Richard O. Cowan, "The Seventies' Role in Worldwide Church Administration," in Whitaker and Garr, *Firm Foundation*, 574.
3. Cowan, "Seventies' Role," 575.
4. Cowan, "Seventies' Role," 575–76.
5. Kimball, in Conference Report, Oct. 1976, 10.

6. Kimball, "Events and Changes during the Administration of Spencer W. Kimball," in Whitaker and Garr, *Firm Foundation*, 527.

7. Cowan, "Seventies' Role," 581–82.

8. Earl C. Tingey, "The Saga of Revelation: The Unfolding Role of the Seventy," *Ensign,* Sept. 2009, 57; Cowan, "Seventies' Role," 584.

9. Cowan, "Seventies' Role," 584–86.

10. "News of the Church: Elder Helvécio Martins of the Seventy," *Ensign,* May 1990.

11. Martins and Grover, *Elder Helvécio Martins*, 116–17.

12. In Greg Hill, "Quorums of Seventy Set in Place," *LDS Church News,* May 1, 1999.

89
The Revelation on Priesthood and Official Declaration 2

1978

An institute class in Africa in the early 2000s.

Few events have had greater effect on the Church's worldwide expansion than the 1978 revelation extending the priesthood to all worthy males. For Latter-day Saints the announcement became a moment of "I remember where I was when I heard."

Elder Dallin H. Oaks recalled, "I sat down on a pile of dirt and beckoned to my boys. . . . This is the scene etched in my memory of this unforgettable event—sitting on a pile of dirt as I told my boys that all worthy male members of the Church could now be ordained to the priesthood, and weeping as I spoke."[1] The announcement created a media frenzy on June 9, 1978: "*Time* and *Newsweek* magazines stopped the presses on their weekend editions to get stories in, and the news made the front page of the *New York Times.*"[2]

Though many, including Latter-day Saints, were surprised at the 1978 announcement, prophets had prayed for years that the priesthood would one day be extended to all worthy

males. In 1852 Brigham Young prophesied that the "time will come when they [persons of black African descent] will have the privilege of all we have the privilege of and more."[3] President Wilford Woodruff recorded in his journal, "The day will come when all that race (the blacks) will be redeemed and possess all the blessings."[4] In January 28, 1928, President Heber J. Grant wrote that men of black African descent could not hold the priesthood "until such time as he (the Lord) shall see fit to withdraw the decree."[5] Two decades later, President David O. McKay wrote, "Sometime in God's eternal plan, the [blacks] will be given the right to hold the priesthood."[6] In October 1972, President Harold B. Lee said, "The [blacks] will achieve full status. We're just waiting for that time."[7]

These prophets and others had looked forward to the day the Lord would extend the priesthood to all worthy males. During Spencer W. Kimball's apostolic ministry, "his heart had gone out to faithful priesthood-denied people wherever they resided in the world."[8]

In 1978, he "began an exhaustive personal study of the scriptures as well as statements of Church leaders since Joseph Smith, and asked other General Authorities to share their personal feelings relative to the longstanding Church policy."[9] Church leaders discussed the subject "at length on numerous occasions in the preceding weeks and months."[10]

President Kimball began to importune the Lord for a revelation. "I prayed with much fervency," he said. "I knew that something was before us that was extremely important to many of the children of God." He went to the "temple alone, and especially on Sundays and Saturdays when . . . [he] could have it alone." He explained, "It went on for some time as I was searching for this, because I wanted to be sure."[11]

Francis M. Gibbons, secretary to the First Presidency recorded, "On Tuesday, May 30, 1978, President Kimball read to his counselors a tentative statement he had written in long-hand removing all priesthood restrictions from blacks except those restrictions as to worthiness that rest upon all alike. He said that he had 'a good, warm feeling' about it."[12]

The following Thursday, President Kimball asked the Twelve to meet at the Salt Lake Temple in the attitude of fasting and prayer. That Thursday, June 1, 1978, the First Presidency and the Twelve counseled for two hours on the subject, each one expressing himself freely. At 2:45 P.M., they formed a prayer circle around the temple altar, and "the Lord confirmed the wishes of the Brethren to rescind the policy that prohibited African blacks from receiving the priesthood."[13]

The feelings shared by the thirteen men present (Elder Delbert L. Stapley was in the hospital, and Elder Mark E. Petersen was in South America) were of a "greater unanimity in the council" than ever experienced before.[14] Elder Gordon B. Hinckley said, "Not one of us who was present on that occasion was ever quite the same after that."[15] The announcement was released to the media the next day and accepted as an official declaration by a sustaining vote of the Church membership on September 30, 1978, at general conference.

Latter-day Saints of black African descent rejoiced at the opportunity to be ordained to the priesthood and receive the blessings of the temple. On June 11, 1978, Joseph Freeman became the first man of black African descent to receive the Melchizedek Priesthood and be ordained an elder after the revelation was received. He and his wife, Toe Isapela Leituala, were sealed in the Salt Lake Temple a few days later, on June 23.[16]

In November 1978, the first missionaries were sent to Nigeria to establish the Church in black Africa. In 1978 there were fewer than one thousand members of black African lineage among the world's four million Latter-day Saints. By 1998, twenty years after the revelation, there were an estimated half million Church members with black African roots among the 10.3 million members of the Church. An estimated 100,000 lived in Africa and the Caribbean, and another 300,000 in Brazil.

The effects of the revelation on Church growth cannot be overstated. Elder Dallin H. Oaks explained, "Whether we look on the revelation as the end of the beginning of the Restoration or as the beginning of the end of what it portends . . . it is difficult to overstate its importance in the fulfillment of divine command that the gospel must go to every nation, kindred and people."[17]

DID YOU KNOW?

• The revelation on priesthood was received by President Spencer W. Kimball after a long period of studying and reflecting on the scriptures and the statements of former Church leaders on the subject.

• On June 11, 1978, Joseph Freeman became the first man of black African descent to be ordained an elder after Official Declaration 2 was received.

NOTES

1. Oaks, in Woodger, "Revelation Attitudes: The Coming Forth of Official Declaration 2," *Religious Educator* 3, no. 2 (2002): 185–200.

2. Haws, *Mormon Image in the American Mind*, 71–72.

3. Brigham Young Papers, Feb. 5, 1852, in Alan Cherry and Jessie L. Embry, "Blacks," in Ludlow, *Encyclopedia of Mormonism*, 1:126.

4. History of Wilford Woodruff, 351, in "Prophets Tell of Promise to All Races," *LDS Church News*, June 17, 1978, 4.

5. Grant, letter to questioner, Jan. 28, 1928, in "Prophets Tell of Promise to All Races," 4.

6. McKay, letter to unknown recipient, Nov. 3, 1947, in "Prophets Tell of Promise to All Races," 4.

7. Lee, in "Prophets Tell of Promise to All Races," 6.

8. Tate, *Boyd K. Packer*, 227.

9. Cook, *Revelations of the Prophet Joseph Smith*, 353.

10. Bruce R. McConkie, "The New Revelation on Priesthood," in *Priesthood*, 127.

11. Lee Warnick, "I Knew That the Time Had Come," *LDS Church News*, June 4, 1988, 7.

12. Gibbons, *Spencer W. Kimball*, 294; Edward L. Kimball, "Spencer W. Kimball and the Revelation on Priesthood," *BYU Studies* 47, no. 2 (2008): 5–78

13. Cook, *Revelations of the Prophet Joseph Smith*, 354; see Edward L. Kimball, "I Sustain Him as a Prophet, I Love Him as an Affectionate Father," *Dialogue*, Winter 1978, 61.

14. Knowles, *Howard W. Hunter*, 235–36.

15. Hinckley, "Priesthood Restoration," *Ensign*, Oct. 1988, 70.

16. Freeman, *In the Lord's Due Time*, 90, 106–10.

17. Oaks, in Stoker, "LDS Blacks Hoping to Become 'Generic' in Growing Church," *LDS Church News*, June 18, 1988, 4.

90
New Editions of the Scriptures

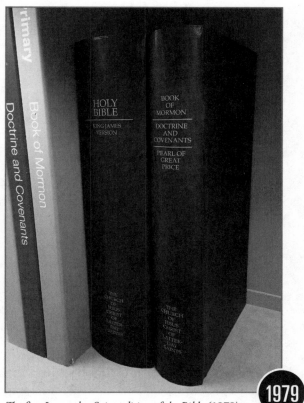

The first Latter-day Saint edition of the Bible (1979) and a new edition of the Book of Mormon, Doctrine and Covenants, and Pearl of Great Price (1981).

1979

President Spencer W. Kimball presided over the Church during a period of constant innovation in Church government, missionary work, and temple building. Assessing the advances of the Kimball administration, Elder Boyd K. Packer identified the publication in 1979 of the Latter-day Saint edition of the Bible as "the crowning achievement in the administration of President Spencer W. Kimball."[1] Another writer declared that "the new Latter-day Saint edition of the King James Version of the Bible has been heralded as one of the most significant resources ever made available for understanding the word of God."[2]

The need for a Latter-day Saint edition of the King James Bible was recognized during the early 1970s, when the standard works were established as the curriculum of the adults in Sunday School. At the time "three different Bibles were in circulation among Church members—one for adults, one for seminary students, and one for Primary children."[3]

The project began when George A. Horton and Grant E. Barton, two religion teachers who carpooled to their work in the Church Office Building, started discussing the advantages of a Latter-day Saint edition of the Bible. Believing such an edition was needed, they decided to survey Latter-day Saints about "what the ideal characteristics/features would be of the ideal Bible that would be used by all."[4]

After distributing their survey and receiving the results, they contacted the director of the Church Correlation Committee, Daniel H. Ludlow. He proposed to the First Presidency and the Quorum of the Twelve that a Latter-day Saint edition of the King James Bible be published. Soon, a Scriptures Publication Committee was formed with three apostles assigned to oversee it. Elder Boyd K. Packer, a member of the Scriptures Publication Committee, described the reasons for the appointment of Elder Thomas S. Monson, Elder Bruce R. McConkie, and himself:

"Elder Monson, he was a printer. And he

was an expert in printing. That's what he did for a living. So he had that pattern. Bruce McConkie was the expert on the doctrine, and I was somewhere in between them on my concern . . . to have them printed in such a way that the ordinary man could afford them and could handle them."[5]

Along with supervising doctrinal accuracy, Elder McConkie was responsible for developing new chapter headings for the Bible. "In reality, these headings constitute a doctrinal commentary of the particular chapter."[6] Elder McConkie's work on the Scriptures Publication Committee was seen by Elder Packer as "one great crowning contribution and achievement in his ministry. . . . If ever there was a man who was raised up unto a very purpose, if ever a man was prepared against a certain need—it was Bruce R. McConkie. It had to do with the scriptures."[7]

President Spencer W. Kimball charged the Scriptures Publication Committee "to assist in improving doctrinal scholarship throughout the Church" from Primary children through adults and to put into the hands of Latter-day Saints tools that would "enable them better to study and understand the Lord's revelations through his prophets."[8]

To meet these prophetic charges, the committee was aided by new computer technology and the work of dedicated technicians. Other help came from Brigham Young University religious educators—Robert J. Matthews, Ellis T. Rasmussen, and Robert C. Patch. They were given the task "to prepare a King James Bible which would include a standardized concordance, dictionary, atlas, and index and . . . have footnotes, ready references, and cross-references related to other L.D.S. scriptures."[9]

The committee met for the first time in January 1973. Professor Robert J. Matthews observed, "For nearly a decade, several of us worked with Elders Thomas S. Monson, Boyd K. Packer, and Bruce R. McConkie in the preparation of the new editions of the standard works. We saw them work with divine inspiration in the day-to-day activities of that Committee, and often marveled at their clarity of vision and quickness of perception in deciding the course to follow."[10]

The work of the Scriptures Publication Committee was double-checked by editors from Deseret Book Company and by Cambridge University Press, the book's publisher.

Not one word of the King James Version text was changed in the Latter-day Saint edition. There is, however, new wording in the headnotes to chapters, new cross-references to all the standard works, more than six hundred quotations from the Joseph Smith Translation, new language notes, a 750-category topical guide, a revised Bible dictionary, and new maps.

The positive response of the Saints to this edition of the Bible convinced Church leaders to proceed with publishing a new edition of the Book of Mormon, the Doctrine and Covenants, and the Pearl of Great Price—the triple combination. In November 1979, the Scriptures Publication Committee submitted plans for a new edition to the First Presidency and the Quorum of the Twelve. The plan indicated "that new footnotes and cross-references would be developed for all three books of

---

DID YOU KNOW?

- The committee for new editions of the scriptures was led by three apostles: Thomas S. Monson, Boyd K. Packer, and Bruce R. McConkie.

- The Latter-day Saint edition of the King James Bible included more than six hundred references to the Joseph Smith Translation, which made significant portions of it widely available to Church members for the first time.

latter-day scriptures, that new chapter and section headings would be prepared, that the typographical features of the triple combination would follow those established in the Bible (thus making the two volumes truly companions), and that the indexes would be revised and expanded without duplicating the topical guide in the Bible."[11]

Due to expertise acquired in preparing and publishing the Latter-day Saint edition of the Bible, the production of the new triple combination was much simpler than it might have been. By 1980 the Doctrine and Covenants was finished, and by 1981, work on the Book of Mormon had commenced. A "Pronouncing Vocabulary" (now called "Pronunciation Guide") for the Book of Mormon was revised for consistency and simplicity, and an index for all three books of scripture was prepared. The footnote system adopted in the Latter-day Saint edition of the Bible was applied in the triple combination.

In the April 1976 conference, President N. Eldon Tanner of the First Presidency had proposed that the record of Joseph Smith's vision of the celestial kingdom and Joseph F. Smith's vision of the redemption of the dead be accepted by the Saints as scripture and added to the Pearl of Great Price. The First Presidency later decided to include them in the Doctrine and Covenants, and they were printed in the 1981 edition as sections 137 and 138, respectively.

The work to create the 1979 Latter-day Saint edition of the Bible and the 1981 edition of the Book of Mormon, Doctrine and Covenants, and the Pearl of Great Price was groundbreaking. Not until 2013, more than thirty years later, were adjustments made to chapter and section headings and study aids. New photos and updated maps were also provided. Elder Neil L. Andersen of the Quorum of the Twelve Apostles said that the new edition of the scriptures in English "incorporates adjustments that will be a blessing to Church members in years to come, but members should not feel that they need to purchase a new set of scriptures, particularly since all of the adjustments are available in digital formats at no cost. Changes to the scriptural text include spelling, minor typographical, and punctuation corrections."[12]

President Boyd K. Packer had envisioned that the new editions of the scriptures would enable future generations to "develop a gospel scholarship beyond that which their forebears could achieve." These publications, he declared, are "the most comprehensive compilation of scriptural information on the mission and teachings of the Lord Jesus Christ that has ever been assembled in the history of the world."[13]

NOTES

1. Packer, "Scriptures," *Ensign,* Nov. 1982, 53.
2. Bruce T. Harper, "The Church Publishes a New Triple Combination," *Ensign,* Oct. 1981, 9.
3. Fred E. Woods, "The Latter-day Saint Edition of the King James Bible," in Jackson, *King James Bible and the Restoration*, 260.
4. Woods, "Latter-day Saint Edition of the King James Bible," in Jackson, *King James Bible and the Restoration,* 260–61.
5. Packer, interview by Martin Andersen, Salt Lake City, May 15, 2009, in Jackson, *King James Bible and the Restoration,* 262–63.
6. McConkie, *Bruce R. McConkie Story,* 384.
7. McConkie, *Bruce R. McConkie Story,* 383, 427.
8. Harper, "Church Publishes a New Triple Combination," 9.
9. Lavina Fielding Anderson, "Church Publishes First LDS Edition of the Bible," *Ensign*, Oct. 1979, 12.
10. McConkie, *Bruce R. McConkie Story,* 383–84.
11. Harper, "Church Publishes a New Triple Combination," 10.
12. "Church Releases New Edition of English Scriptures in Digital Formats," lds.org.
13. Packer, "Scriptures," 53.

91
The First Great Expansion of Temple Building

1980

The angel Moroni atop a temple spire, a practice that became standard during the presidency of Spencer W. Kimball.

Before the presidency of Spencer W. Kimball, construction and dedication of a temple was an infrequent event. For the first 140 years after the organization of the Church, only fifteen temples were dedicated. After the departure of the Saints from Kirtland, Ohio, and Nauvoo, Illinois, most temples were constructed in the western United States, where most of the Saints lived. The exceptions were Hawaii, New Zealand, Switzerland, and England. During the twelve years of President Kimball's

administration, the number of temples in operation more than doubled from fifteen to thirty-six, with construction begun on five temples and another six announced.

Just as important as the number of temples was the diverse nature of their locations. Temples were built in Latin America, Asia, Africa, Australia, and in areas throughout the Pacific. President Kimball was determined to build temples wherever faithful Latter-day Saints lived. In explaining his plan for temple expansion, President Kimball said, "It isn't a matter of just saying, 'Well, we'll build one here and one there.' . . . It's a matter of bringing temple work to the people that want it."[1]

The first temple dedicated by President Kimball was the Washington D.C. Temple in November 1974. The first Latter-day Saint temple built on the eastern seaboard of the United States is an architectural masterpiece that towers above the trees on the outskirts of the American capital. During the temple's open house, three-quarters of a million people visited the structure, setting a new record for temple open house attendance. When President Kimball dedicated the temple, his prayer reflected his earnest desire to take the gospel to all nations:

"There are national gates which seemingly need to be unlocked and doors that need to be opened," he prayed, requesting that the "hearts of kings, presidents, emperors, and ministers . . . be softened, that they may permit the gospel to be taken to their people."[2]

Early in 1975 President Kimball announced

a temple to be built in São Paulo, Brazil—the first temple to be built outside the United States since the London England Temple in 1958. Beginning with the São Paulo Temple, President Kimball immersed himself in architectural temple drawings. For instance, he directed Church architect Emil Fetzer to design a baptismal font with the symbolic oxen instead of the basic font used in stake centers. He also insisted that plans for the temple be relatively small, for he wanted to build temples all over the South American continent.

In October 1975 the First Presidency began to encourage Latter-day Saints to contribute to the construction of new temples rather than donating funds to allow members to travel great distances to receive their temple ordinances. The statement represented a tectonic shift in temple policy. Previously, some Latter-day Saints in distant lands had made great sacrifices to go to a temple to receive their ordinances. Now, temples would be built nearer to them. This perspective, combined with the development of construction techniques, opened the door for a rapid expansion in the rate of temple building.[3]

When the São Paulo Brazil Temple was completed, it served faithful Latter-day Saints throughout South America. Previously, the nearest temple was in Washington, D.C. Even though the new São Paulo Temple was considerably closer geographically, many Saints still had to make huge sacrifices in means and time to receive their temple ordinances. One example of such sacrifice was a family from Paraguay who had saved enough money to travel to São Paulo but not enough for transportation to the temple. After arriving in São Paulo, they walked seventeen miles to reach the temple. Every family member was barefoot, except for the father, who wore homemade sandals. When local members heard of their

situation, they collected clothes and shoes for the family to take home.

At the April 1980 sesquicentennial conference, President Kimball announced seven new temples to be constructed, an unprecedented number at that time. Before that conference, the largest number of temples announced simultaneously was two—the Provo Utah Temple and the Ogden Utah Temple in August 1967. Of those seven temples announced in 1980, only the Atlanta Georgia Temple was located in the United States. The other temples were to be constructed in Buenos Aires, Argentina; Sydney, Australia; Santiago, Chile; Nuku'alofa, Tonga; Apia, Samoa; and Papeete, Tahiti.

The temple most representative of President Kimball's earnest desire to build temples closer to the people was in Freiberg, East Germany—the first temple built in a Communist nation. Only a few years before the Freiberg Temple was announced, the German Democratic Republic (GDR) had no wards, stakes, patriarchs, or opportunities for traditional missionary work. Even the possibility of building a chapel was dubious. Working primarily through Elder Thomas S. Monson, President Kimball urged Church members to develop better relations with the communist government. A thawing in relationships led to the astounding announcement of a small, beautiful temple in 1982 and its dedication in 1985.

Temple policy during the Kimball years changed not only where the Church built temples but how they were built. Under

DID YOU KNOW?

• President Spencer W. Kimball implemented a plan to build smaller temples to put them within a shorter distance of more Church members.

• A statue of the angel Moroni was not generally used on Latter-day Saint temples before 1980.

President Kimball's direction, a statue of the angel Moroni was to be placed atop the temples as the recognizable symbol of the Restoration. Before 1975, only the temples in Nauvoo, Salt Lake, Los Angeles, and Washington, D.C., had a representation of an angelic messenger on their spires. After 1975, everywhere local building ordinances would allow, a representation of Moroni adorned a temple spire. The statues became such a recognized symbol of the Church in the following decades that several temples built without a statue added one.[4]

An even more important innovation came in the size of temples. As early as March 1974, the First Presidency began discussing the possibility of building smaller, less expensive temples in areas remote from Salt Lake City. For example, almost all the temples built in the Pacific had only half the floor space of many stake centers in the United States, and only one or two ordinance rooms and two or three sealing rooms. The Papeete Tahiti Temple, for example, contained only 10,000 square feet, compared to the 253,000 square feet in the Salt Lake Temple and annex. New temples rewarded faithful Latter-day Saints throughout the Pacific by saving them the exorbitant cost of traveling to New Zealand or Hawaii to receive their temple ordinances. "The [smaller] temples will be of a quality that will be pleasing to all and at a cost that will not be burdensome for members to bear," President Kimball assured Church members in April 1980.[5]

Even as President Kimball's health declined in 1981, the rising wave of temple building continued. His counselor President Gordon B. Hinckley dedicated twenty-two of the thirty-two temples announced during the Kimball administration. The work begun by President Kimball and continued by Presidents Hinckley and Monson and others was the beginning of an even greater era of temple building in the future.

NOTES

1. Kimball, *Teachings of Spencer W. Kimball*, 540.
2. Kimball, *Lengthen Your Stride* (2005), 361–62.
3. Kimball, *Lengthen Your Stride* (2005), 358–59.
4. ldschurchtemples.com.
5. Kimball, *Lengthen Your Stride, Working Draft* (2009), 548.

92
The Establishment of LDS Humanitarian Services

1985

A water system like those funded by LDS Humanitarian Services, an organization established in response to a famine in Ethiopia in the early 1980s.

In 1984 it was estimated that 7.7 million Ethiopians were suffering from starvation.[1] On January 27, 1985, the First Presidency asked members of the Church worldwide to participate in a fast for those starving in Ethiopia. The $6.4 million contributed in fast offerings from that fast was dedicated to assisting the Ethiopians.

That event marked the beginning of what has become Latter-day Saint Charities, or Humanitarian Services. Elder Glen L. Pace of the First Quorum of the Seventy explained, "While the Church has always responded to the suffering caused by various disasters, the Ethiopian famine triggered a more methodical and organized effort than had been experienced before."[2]

Previously, surplus from the Welfare Services system was contributed to other charitable organizations in the form of food, clothing, and other in-kind household goods throughout the world. After the fast for Ethiopia, the Church created a separate unit to assist with ongoing humanitarian projects. Today, Humanitarian Services is a branch of the Welfare Services Department. Its mission is "to relieve suffering, to foster self-reliance for families of all nationalities and religions, and to provide opportunities for service."[3]

The fast for the victims of the Ethiopian famine marked a burgeoning in the humanitarian work of the Latter-day Saints. After the executive secretary of the Church Humanitarian Services Committee visited Ngorika, Kenya, Church leaders detailed the need for clean water in that region of Africa. Church members donated $300,000 to assist in building a water system in Ngorika, making safe drinking water available to an entire region of Kenya. At the dedication of the water system, one woman remarked, "For the past 40 years, I have walked eight miles one way every day to get water for my family." Pointing to the water flowing from the spigot, she said, "This is like a dream."[4]

In the years that followed, the Church

honed its approach towards disaster and relief efforts. Responses were launched when a series of violent storms afflicted the islands of Western and American Samoa and parts of Tonga in 1990. In 1992, the Church launched efforts to clear debris and assist in rebuilding after Hurricane Andrew ravaged the tip of southern Florida. Some 1,800 volunteers went to the affected region from stakes throughout the southeastern United States to assist. The president of the South Miami Florida Stake distributed to workers several thousand yellow t-shirts printed with "Mormon Helping Hands" on one side and "LDS Emergency Relief Services" on the other.

At one point, a non-member helicopter pilot and friend of the one of the local stake presidents flew President George H. W. Bush and presidential candidates Bill Clinton and Ross Perot over the area. When the men inquired about the identity of the workers in the yellow shirts, the pilot responded, "Those are my friends, Mormon volunteer rescue workers who have come here to help." Responses from the three dignitaries included "wonderful," "marvelous," and "God bless the Mormons."[5]

With only a few exceptions—such as the Churchwide fast for Southeast Asia tsunami victims in 2005—fast offering donations are used to assist Latter-day Saints with welfare needs. Humanitarian donations, on the other hand, are used to assist anyone regardless of religion, race, or nationality. In giving this service, the Church absorbs all overhead and administrative costs and guarantees that every penny donated to the humanitarian fund will be used to assist the poor and needy throughout the world. When a disaster strikes, Humanitarian Services coordinates its efforts with government and nonprofit agencies, such as the Red Cross and Catholic Charities, to provide needed food, water, and other supplies.

The list of Church humanitarian projects is lengthy, ranging from such natural disasters as tsunamis, earthquakes, and hurricanes to war relief efforts. From 2008 to 2011, "the Church joined in more than 200 major disaster assistance efforts, including the recent 2011 Japan earthquake and tsunami, the 2010 Haiti earthquake, the 2010 Chile earthquake, the 2010 Pakistan flooding, the 2009 Samoa tsunami, the 2009 Philippines typhoon, the 2009 Indonesia earthquake, the 2008 Ethiopia famine and many others."[6]

The Church's emergency response to major disasters has drawn much media attention. Receiving less media notice are other initiatives that rely on monetary donations, time, expertise and other resources of Latter-day Saint volunteers. Such initiatives include providing training for neonatal resuscitation, food production, and nutrition; providing clean water, wheelchairs to the disabled, and vision care; and administering immunizations.[7]

To coordinate these initiatives, the Church established the Humanitarian Center in Salt Lake City where supplies are prepared for worldwide use. The center houses humanitarian supplies, including clothing, hygiene kits, school kits, emergency medical modules, and quilts. These items are processed and prepared for shipment to wherever they are needed most. In a typical year, the Latter-day Saint

DID YOU KNOW?

- Latter-day Saint Humanitarian Services came into existence to respond to a severe famine affecting Ethiopia in the 1980s.

- In a typical year, the Latter-day Saints Humanitarian Center will ship 8 million pounds of shoes and clothing, 300,000 hygiene and school kits, and 12,000 quilts to relieve suffering in more than 50 countries.

Humanitarian Center ships about 8 million pounds of shoes and clothing, 300,000 hygiene kits and school kits, and 12,000 quilts to relieve suffering in more than 50 countries.[8]

Since 1985, Humanitarian Services has provided assistance to millions of people in 185 countries.[9] In the thirty years since the fast for the victims of the Ethiopian famine, the Church has sent $1.2 billion in assistance to those in need.[10] As Humanitarian Services has grown, the Church has earned a reputation for caring for the poor and needy and those suffering from natural and manmade disasters throughout the world.

Recently, Church leaders announced another focus, spearheaded by the women of the Church, to assist the rapidly increasing number of refugees from around the globe. Called "'I Was Stranger': Refugee Relief," the new effort was launched by a letter from the First Presidency, along with the general presidencies of the Relief Society, Young Women, and Primary, to "invite women of all ages to join together to help refugees in their local communities."[11]

While assisting the poor and needy has been a part of the work of the Latter-day Saints since the beginning of the Restoration, the organization provided by Latter-day Saint Humanitarian Services, begun with the Ethiopian famine in 1985, is one of the most compelling extensions of Church efforts to fulfill the Savior's charge to "impart of your substance to the poor, every man according to that which he hath, . . . administering to their relief, both spiritually and temporally, according to their wants" (Mosiah 4:26) and will continue to grow in importance.

NOTES

1. Rahmato, *Famine and Survival Strategies.*
2. Sarah Jane Weaver, "Fast for Ethiopia Accelerated Work," *LDS Church News,* Feb. 6, 2010.
3. "Overview of Humanitarian Services," *Welfare Operations Training,* providentliving.lds.org.
4. Rudd, *Pure Religion,* 268.
5. Rudd, *Pure Religion,* 274.
6. "Humanitarian Aid and Welfare Services Basics: How Donations and Resources Are Used," mormonnewsroom.lds.org.
7. "Humanitarian Aid and Welfare Services Basics."
8. "Latter-day Saint Humanitarian Center," lds.org.
9. LDSCharities.org.
10. "Viewpoint: 1985 Fast Marked Beginning of LDS Charities," *LDS Church News,* lds.org.
11. First Presidency Letter, Mar. 26, 2016; "'I Was a Stranger,'" lds.org.

93
Flooding the Earth with the Book of Mormon

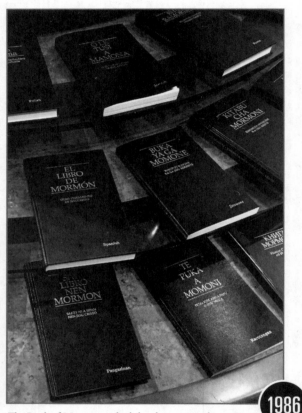

The Book of Mormon, which has been printed in 110 different languages

1986

Elder Howard W. Hunter declared at the funeral of President Ezra Taft Benson, "No president of the church since the Prophet Joseph Smith himself has done more to teach the truths of the Book of Mormon, to make it a daily course of study for the entire membership of the church, and to 'flood the earth' with its distribution."[1]

Clearly, the defining characteristic of President Benson's nine years as President was his vision to elevate the importance of the Book of Mormon in the lives of Latter-day Saints.[2] Six years after his death, the Book of Mormon held "center stage in Latter-day Saint scriptural study and appreciation. Congregations, the Church Educational System, individuals, and families . . . focus[ed] on the Book of Mormon with unprecedented enthusiasm."[3]

Before Ezra Taft Benson became President of the Church, many Latter-day Saints had no idea they were guilty of failing to use the Book of Mormon enough in their studies. Historian Grant Underwood analyzed early Latter-day Saint literature and found that the Book of Mormon was infrequently cited in comparison with the Bible. Richard Galbraith studied scriptural references cited in general conference and found that only 12 percent of all scriptural references were to the Book of Mormon.

During the groundbreaking April 1986 conference, President Benson cited a verse from the Doctrine and Covenants: "Your minds in times past have been darkened because of unbelief, and because you have treated lightly the things you have received—which vanity and unbelief have brought the whole church under condemnation" (D&C 84:54–55).[4]

After stating that the Church was under condemnation for viewing the Book of Mormon so lightly, he powerfully declared, "The Lord inspired His servant Lorenzo Snow to reemphasize the principle of tithing to redeem the Church from financial bondage. . . . Now, in our day, the Lord has revealed the need to reemphasize the Book of Mormon to get the Church and all the children of Zion out from under condemnation—the scourge and judgment."[5]

President Benson further declared, "The Book of Mormon has not been, nor is it yet, the center of our personal study, family teaching, preaching, and missionary work. Of this we must repent."[6]

From that April 1986 conference until the end of his ministry in 1994, President Benson was adamant that his message about the Book of Mormon be conveyed to all throughout the world. He promised blessings to Latter-day Saints and "good people everywhere" if they adhered to his counsel:

"I bless you with increased discernment to judge between Christ and anti-Christ. I bless you with increased power to do good and to resist evil. I bless you with increased understanding of the Book of Mormon. I promise you that from this moment forward, if we will daily sup from its pages and abide by its precepts, God will pour out upon each child of Zion and the Church a blessing hitherto unknown."[7]

Wherever President Benson traveled while he was President of the Church, he testified of the Book of Mormon. Latter-day Saints never wondered about what topic President Benson would address. His messages always related to the Book of Mormon.

In 1988, President Benson again warned Latter-day Saints that they were taking the Book of Mormon too lightly:

"We have not been using the Book of Mormon as we should. Our homes are not as strong unless we are using it to bring our children to Christ. Our families may be corrupted by worldly trends and teachings unless we know how to use the book to expose and combat falsehoods in socialism, rationalism, etc. Our missionaries are not as effective unless they are [teaching] with it. Social, ethical, cultural, or educational converts will not survive under the heat of the day unless their taproots go down to the fullness of the gospel which the Book of Mormon contains. Our Church classes are not as spirit-filled unless we hold it up as a standard."[8]

President Benson wondered in 1988 if he would live to see the Saints fulfill his vision of flooding their lives with Book of Mormon teachings. "Moses never entered the promised land," President Benson recalled. "Joseph Smith never saw Zion redeemed. Some of us may not live long enough to see the day when the Book of Mormon floods the earth and when the Lord lifts His condemnation." Nonetheless, President Benson was emphatic that the remainder of his life was to be spent in what he called "that glorious effort."

To President Benson, the time to move forward was now:

"In this age of electronic media and mass distribution of the printed word, God will hold us accountable if we do not now move the Book of Mormon in a monumental way."[9]

He then described his vision of flooding the earth with the Book of Mormon: "I have a vision of homes alerted, of classes alive, and of pulpits aflame with the spirit of Book of Mormon messages. . . .

"I have a vision of artists putting into film, drama, literature, music, and paintings great themes and great characters from the Book of Mormon.

DID YOU KNOW?

• The defining characteristic of President Ezra Taft Benson's nine years as Church President, from 1985 to 1994, was his vision to elevate the importance of the Book of Mormon in the lives of Latter-day Saints.

• President Benson played a key role in moving the Book of Mormon to the center of Latter-day Saint teaching and beliefs.

"I have a vision of thousands of missionaries going into the mission field with hundreds of passages memorized from the Book of Mormon so that they might feed the needs of a spiritually famished world. I have a vision of the whole Church getting nearer to God by abiding by the precepts of the Book of Mormon. Indeed, I have a vision of flooding the earth with the Book of Mormon."[10]

President Benson promised blessings for studying the Book of Mormon, including "increased love and harmony in the home, greater respect between parent and child, and increased spirituality and righteousness." He was emphatic in declaring that these were "not idle promises, but exactly what the Prophet Joseph Smith meant when he said the Book of Mormon will help us draw nearer to God." President Benson asked, "Can anyone doubt that this book was meant for us and that in it we find great power, great comfort, and great protection?"[11]

President Benson also asked Latter-day Saints to "imagine what would happen with an increasing number of copies of the Book of Mormon in the hands of an increasing number of missionaries who know how to use it and who have been born of God." He assured the Saints, "When this happens we will get the bounteous harvest of souls that the Lord promised."[12]

Scholar Noel B. Reynolds observed that with each new admonition and promise from President Benson, "Latter-day Saints responded with an enormous and passionate effort to fully utilize the Nephite record."[13] By the April conference of 1989, President Benson had written to the children of the Church: "I know you are reading the Book of Mormon, for I have received hundreds of personal letters from you telling me that you are reading this sacred book. It makes me weep for joy when I hear this."[14] Evidence suggests that there was increased use of the Book of Mormon not only by children but youth, young adults, and adult Church members.

The scriptural flood that President Benson envisioned soon followed. In 2003, *Book Magazine* named the Book of Mormon one of "20 Books That Changed America." Editor Jerome Kramer wrote, "The book provides the theological underpinnings for one of the world's most vibrant religions."[15]

President Benson's "counsel stimulated an enthusiastic wave of Book of Mormon study and focus that continues to this day" in Sunday Schools, seminaries, institutes of religion, Brigham Young University, and individual homes.[16] The increased use of the Book of Mormon became a modern event unparalleled in Church history.

NOTES

1. Lynn Arave, "Pres. Benson Receives a Fond Farewell," *Deseret News,* June 5, 1994.
2. Dew, *Ezra Taft Benson,* 493–95.
3. Noel B. Reynolds, "The Coming Forth of the Book of Mormon in the Twentieth Century," *BYU Studies* 38, no. 2 (1999): 7.
4. Reynolds, "Coming Forth," 7.
5. Benson, "A Sacred Responsibility," *Ensign,* May 1986, 78.
6. Benson, "Cleansing the Inner Vessel," *Ensign,* May 1986, 5–6
7. Benson, "Sacred Responsibility," 78.
8. Benson, "The Book of Mormon Is the Word of God," *Ensign,* Jan. 1988, 5.
9. Benson, "Flooding the Earth," *Ensign,* Nov. 1988, 5.
10. Benson, "Flooding the Earth," 6.
11. Benson, "The Book of Mormon—Keystone of Our Religion," *Ensign,* Nov. 1986, 7.
12. Benson, "Born of God," *Ensign,* July 1989, 4.
13. Reynolds, "Coming Forth," 7.
14. Benson, "To the Children of the Church," *Ensign,* May 1989, 81.
15. Kramer, "20 Books That Changed America," *Book Magazine,* July/Aug. 2003, in "In the News," *Ensign,* Dec. 2003, 69.
16. Reynolds, "Coming Forth," 30–31.

94
The BYU Jerusalem Center Is Dedicated

The Brigham Young University Jerusalem Center.

1989

On May 16, 1989, a handful of people gathered in the auditorium of the newly finished Brigham Young University Jerusalem Center for the dedication of the building by Howard W. Hunter, president of the Quorum of the Twelve Apostles. The dedication was quiet, peaceful, and private, the exact opposite of the previous decade of public opposition and controversy that surrounded the construction of the BYU Jerusalem Center. Planning, hard work, and miracles led to the completion and

dedication of what President James E. Faust of the First Presidency called "a veritable jewel . . . worthy of the Holy City."[1]

In 1968, the first BYU students arrived in Jerusalem to study. They were housed in hotel rooms throughout the city, including dormitory facilities at Kibbutz Ramat Rachel. By 1973 Church leaders and BYU administrators were talking about building a university facility in Jerusalem. Six years later, in the fall of 1979, when President Spencer W. Kimball went to Jerusalem to dedicate the Orson Hyde Memorial Garden, approval was given to acquire land on Mount Scopus, near the Mount of Olives, for the BYU Jerusalem Center.[2]

As soon as President Kimball announced plans for the center, difficulties arose. David B. Galbraith, former director of the Jerusalem Study Abroad Program, said, "We were not surprised when all our friends in high places told us, 'Forget it! There have been far more powerful and influential people than you who have sought to obtain that land . . . and all have failed.'"[3]

Between 1980 and 1984, lengthy negotiations took place to secure land and building permits for the center. The First Presidency appointed Elders Howard W. Hunter, James E. Faust, and BYU president Jeffrey R. Holland to serve as an executive committee responsible for overseeing development of the Jerusalem Center. Assisted by administrators from BYU, Church leaders persisted and eventually were granted a forty-nine-year lease on the specified land, as well as an option to renew.[4] Brother

Galbraith later commented, "Certainly it was a miracle that the government would even entertain our desire to build on that site. We'd been told over and over again that it was hopeless."[5]

It took another three years of submitting plans and securing permits before construction could begin. But those obstacles paled in comparison to the controversies that erupted in August 1984 when the public saw bulldozers cutting into Mount Scopus. Galbraith recorded, "In almost every case, the issue is 'missionary work among the Jews' and the primary reason the Center has become a target is due to the fear that it will become a 'center for proselyting the Jews' in Israel."[6]

The controversy continued for four years. Opposition groups demonstrated outside of government offices and held a protest at the Wailing Wall in Jerusalem. Inked stamps on Israeli currency read, "Mormon go home." "Concerts were held to raise money in order to buy out the Mormons."[7]

Demonstrators picketed near the construction site, at Mayor Teddy Kollek's office in Jerusalem, and even at the homes of BYU administrators David Galbraith and D. Kelly Ogden. "They harassed us, our children at school, and threatened violence against us. They tapped our telephones," Galbraith recalled.[8]

There was also opposition from the Israeli media and around the world. The story of the Mormons in Jerusalem was covered on television networks and in major publications, including the *New York Times* and *Los Angeles*

DID YOU KNOW?

- It took three years to secure permits and licenses before the Israeli government allowed construction to begin on the BYU Jerusalem Center.

- The students and professors who first lived in the BYU Jerusalem Center moved into the center in a single day because of local opposition.

Times. The Knesset, the legislative branch of the Israeli government, threatened to shut down if building on the Mormon center continued.

In August 1985, BYU President Jeffrey R. Holland visited Jerusalem to meet with Israeli government leaders to dispel concerns over building of the BYU Jerusalem Center. President Holland assured Israelis that the center was not intended to be a missionary center. "We have been active here for seventeen years and have never conducted missionary work or proselyting," he reported. "We know of no Jew who has been converted to Mormonism through the activities of students or faculty."[9]

Despite protests and controversies mixed with support for the center as a way to celebrate diversity and religious freedom, construction moved forward. One proponent of the BYU Center was Mayor Kollek, who gave a "strong and positive endorsement," personally attending or sending a representative to each center meeting.[10]

Other support came from the United States. On May 8, 1986, a letter signed by 154 members of Congress was sent to members of the Knesset, encouraging the completion of the center. The letter stated, "We believe that rather than hinder[ing] U.S.–Israeli ties, the BYU Center will be a further source of understanding and cooperation between our two countries. Those students who study there will be uniquely able to teach the rest of us about your society, your culture and your rich and fascinating history."[11]

Support from highly placed people and high-profile organizations proved a turning point in favor of the BYU Jerusalem Center. But difficulties were not over. The Israeli Department of Antiquities declared that if any relics or ruins were discovered in excavating the property, the project must stop immediately. This was potentially a problem, for the entire area near Mount Scopus and the Mount of Olives was "peppered with tombs and antiquities." Yet, against all odds, neither antiquities nor burial sites were uncovered. Galbraith said, "It was another miracle as though the hand of the Lord had preserved that entire site for us through the centuries."[12]

On March 8, 1987, BYU students moved from lodgings at the Kibbutz Ramat Rachel to their new quarters at the center. Although the center was not completely finished, BYU administrators advised students and administrators to move quickly to avoid opponents who did not want BYU to take possession of the building. Galbraith recalled, "We moved into the center unannounced in one day."[13]

About a decade after President Kimball announced plans to build a BYU Jerusalem Center, President Howard W. Hunter of the Quorum of the Twelve Apostles and President Holland signed legal documents stating that the center would not be used for missionary activity in Israel. These documents were the last step before dedicating the center. Because of the incessant turmoil and controversy surrounding the center, the dedication took place on May 16, 1989, in a private ceremony in the center's auditorium. Though the dedication was a private affair, it was a powerful moment for expressing gratitude for the opportunity to have the center.

Almost overnight, the center "moved from being an issue of discussion and argument to being a contributor to the cultural, social, and economic climate of the city."[14] Galbraith reflected, "In the end, strong friendships were forged through the opposition and adversity we faced. Today we have a good reputation and are well regarded by both Israelis and Palestinians. We've made our peace with most everyone."[15]

Thousands visit the BYU Jerusalem Center to tour the building, view art exhibits, and attend weekly concerts in the auditorium. D. Kelly Ogden, the first associate director of the BYU Center, recorded President James E. Faust's comments when visiting the center: "Some have wondered if the Center hasn't required too much time, too much energy, too much money. . . . We make no apologies for this Center—how big it is, how lovely it is. . . . This is the jewel of the Holy City."[16]

The center is set on a hill that overlooks the Old City. The location of the building makes the center physically visible, and events surrounding its planning, building, dedication, and use have elevated the image of the Church to the world, or as Galbraith said, "Because of the Jerusalem Center, everyone in Jerusalem—and even Israel—has heard of the Mormons in a positive light."[17] The BYU Jerusalem Center has expanded the Church's educational programs, demonstrated loyalty and commitment to promises, and established a positive Latter-day Saint presence in the Holy Land.

Notes

1. James E. Faust, "Where Is the Church?" Brigham Young University devotional address, Sept. 24, 1989, 2.
2. "BYU Continuing Education: Jerusalem Center," jerusalemcenter.ce.byu.edu/
3. David B. Galbraith and Blair Van Dyke, "The Jerusalem Center for Near Eastern Studies: Reflections of a Modern Pioneer," *Religious Educator* 9, no. 1 (2008): 41.
4. Galbraith et al., *Jerusalem,* 457–58.
5. Jamie Lawson, "A Jewel of Jerusalem," *LDS Living,* May 15, 2009.
6. Galbraith, "A Survey and Analysis of Recent Anti-Mormon Materials Collected in Israel," June 1, 1985, L. Tom Perry Special Collections, Harold B. Lee Library, Brigham Young University, Provo, Utah.
7. S. Kent Brown, "History of BYU Students in Jerusalem As Remembered and Recorded by

S. Kent Brown," 1995, fred-schwendiman.tripod
.com.

8. Lawson, "Jewel of Jerusalem."

9. "BYU President Defends School's Jerusalem
   Center," *Ensign*, Oct. 1985, 73–74.

10. Galbraith and Van Dyke, "Jerusalem Center," 43.

11. Letter from the Congress of the United States, May
    8, 1986, in Galbraith et al., *Jerusalem*, 465–66.

12. Galbraith and Van Dyke, "Jerusalem Center," 44.

13. Galbraith and Van Dyke, "Jerusalem Center," 50.
    According to Israeli law, even one occupant in a
    building cannot be evicted.

14. Brown, "History of BYU Students in Jerusalem."

15. Lawson, "Jewel of Jerusalem."

16. "Excerpts from the Journal of D. Kelly Ogden,"
    Oct. 19, 1987, in Lawson, "Jewel of Jerusalem."

17. Galbraith and Van Dyke, "Jerusalem Center," 52.

95
The Church Enters Formerly Communist Countries

1989

The Berlin Wall, whose destruction opened the door for the Church to enter the countries of eastern Europe.

On September 16, 1959, Soviet Premier Nikita S. Khrushchev visited Washington, D.C., where he was hosted by Ezra Taft Benson, United States Secretary of Agriculture. During his tour of the Beltsville Agricultural Center, Khrushchev told Elder Benson that his grandchildren would live under Communism. His statement was unacceptable to Benson, who in 1946 had "witnessed the ebbing away of freedom resulting in the total loss of liberty

to a wonderful people" in eastern Europe. Elder Benson assured Khrushchev "that his and all other grandchildren [would] live under freedom."[1]

In part because of his experiences serving in the Eisenhower administration at the height of the Cold War, Elder Benson became a vocal opponent of Communism. It was fitting that during his service as president of the Church, the Communist governments in eastern Europe collapsed, and the first proselyting missionaries entered those formerly Communist nations. In addition to President Benson, several leaders, including Elder Thomas S. Monson and Elder Russell M. Nelson of the Quorum of the Twelve, played key roles in opening this region of the world to the restored gospel.

At the end of World War II, the Saints in eastern Europe found themselves largely cut off from contact with western Europe and the United States. Like Germany itself, the former capital of Berlin was divided into a Soviet Zone, which became part of the German Democratic Republic (GDR), and the Western Zone, which became part of the German Federal Republic (GFR). In 1961, the Berlin Wall was constructed by the Soviets to prevent emigration and defection from East Germany. The wall was a symbol of the Iron Curtain that separated Western Europe from the Eastern Bloc. During this era, often referred to as the Cold War, Latter-day Saints in the Soviet Zone, or the GDR, had very little contact with Latter-day Saint leaders in the West.

In 1968, Elder Thomas S. Monson was

assigned to visit Latter-day Saints behind the Iron Curtain. While speaking to an LDS congregation in the town of Görlitz in the GDR, Elder Monson prophesied, "If you will remain true and faithful to the commandments of God, every blessing any member of the Church enjoys in any other country will be yours." Elder Monson returned to his hotel room, very concerned about the prophecy he had made, for there were "no patriarch, no wards or stakes—just branches [in the GDR]. They could not receive temple blessings—either endowment or sealing." He dropped to his knees and pleaded, "Father, I'm on Thy errand; this is Thy Church. I have spoken words that came not from me but from Thee and Thy Son. Wilt Thou fulfill the promise in the lives of this noble people."[2]

With the hope of witnessing the prophecy fulfilled, the East German Saints quietly and faithfully lived the gospel. In 1978, when the GDR refused to issue visas to Latter-day Saints to travel to Switzerland to attend the temple, Elder Monson traveled to meet with GDR government leaders. Much to his surprise, GDR officials proposed a solution: "Rather than having your people go to Switzerland to visit a temple, why don't you build a temple here in the German Democratic Republic?"[3]

In fulfillment of Elder Monson's promise, the Freiberg Germany Temple—the only temple built behind the Iron Curtain—was constructed and dedicated in 1985. Elder Russell M. Nelson declared, "This house of the Lord was the pivot point around which all good things subsequently seemed to turn."[4]

After the temple dedication, Elders Monson and Nelson met with government representatives in the GDR to discuss sending missionaries to preach the gospel of Jesus Christ in that country. Because of the government's positive experience with Latter-day Saints and the temple dedication, their request was granted. On March 31, 1989, Latter-day Saint missionaries entered the GDR. In November of that year, the Berlin Wall was torn down.

This action set in motion a domino effect in convert baptisms, construction of Church buildings, and dedication of new lands for the preaching of the gospel. Historian Kahlile Mehr reported, "After the Freiberg Germany Temple was dedicated in 1985, the baptismal rate in Czechoslovakia jumped from several a year to 20 a year. This first temple in eastern Europe symbolized the emergence of the gospel into a world controlled by communism."[5] Five years later, on July 1, 1990, the Czechoslovakia Mission was reopened.

Concerts of the Mormon Tabernacle Choir greatly assisted in opening nations in the former Soviet Zone to missionary work. Questions were raised about the wisdom of the Choir's planned European tour with the outbreak of the Gulf War in August 1990. When Choir president Wendell M. Smoot discussed concerns with President Gordon B. Hinckley, he was told, "The Choir will go to Europe this coming summer. The war will be over."[6] Elder Russell M. Nelson described the choir's tour of Eastern Europe as "part of the Lord's plan to preach the gospel to the people of the world. . . . The Lord is hastening His work in its time."[7]

The Mormon Tabernacle Choir performed in Frankfurt, Zurich, Vienna, Dresden, Berlin,

DID YOU KNOW?

- Elder Ezra Taft Benson, while serving as the United States Secretary of Agriculture, met with Nikita Khrushchev, the Soviet premier, at the height of the Cold War.

- Leaders of the Communist German Democratic Republic suggested to Elder Thomas S. Monson that the Church build a temple in their country.

Strasbourg, Budapest, Prague, Warsaw, and Leningrad. In 1991, just six days after the first election in Russia in a thousand years, the choir sang in Moscow. Special dinners and receptions were held so that choir members and local church leaders could meet with government leaders and other prominent figures. Relationships were formed, and the reputation of the Church soared in the eastern European cities they visited. On June 24, 1991, at a banquet following the choir's concert in Moscow, the vice president of the Russian Soviet Federal Socialist Republic announced that the Church was officially recognized in his country.

During the 1990s, other formerly Communist nations were dedicated for the preaching of the gospel—Albania, Armenia, Belarus, Bulgaria, Estonia, Hungary, Latvia, Lithuania, Romania, Russia, and Ukraine. By 2016 there were more than twenty-two thousand members and ninety-five congregations in Russia alone. The crowning achievement in the former Soviet Union took place on August 29, 2010, when the Kyiv Ukraine Temple was dedicated in a country once controlled by the Soviet regime. The Saints in eastern Europe and surrounding areas still face challenges, but the miracles that have already brought the light of the restored gospel to their lands provide hope.

NOTES

1. Benson, "Our Immediate Responsibility," address at Brigham Young University, Oct. 25, 1966, speeches.byu.edu.
2. Monson, "Thanks Be to God," *Ensign*, May 1989, 51.
3. Monson, "Thanks Be to God," 51.
4. Nelson, "Drama on the European Stage," *Ensign*, Dec. 1991, 9.
5. Kahlile Mehr, "Czech Saints: A Brighter Day," *Ensign*, Aug. 1994, 52.
6. Jay M. Todd, "An Encore of the Spirit," *Ensign*, Oct. 1991, 43.
7. Gerry Avant, "Choir Leaves Trail of Joyful Tears," *LDS Church News*, 6 July 1991, 3.

96
The Family: A Proclamation to the World

1995

The Family: A Proclamation to the World, *first read by President Gordon B. Hinckley in a general Relief Society meeting, September 1995.*

In the 1990s, the United Nations sponsored world conferences on the family in Beijing, China, and Cairo, Egypt. The Church sent representatives to attend the conferences.[1] "It was not pleasant what they heard," President Boyd K. Packer later remarked. "It was at a conference on the family, but marriage was not even mentioned. It was then announced that they were going to have such a conference here in Salt Lake City." Members of the Quorum of the Twelve recommended, "They are coming here. We had better proclaim our position."[2]

Their recommendation was the impetus for the First Presidency and Quorum of the Twelve

to issue *The Family: A Proclamation to the World* (1995). All of the leadership quorums of the Church helped prepare the proclamation in "the hope that Latter-day Saints will recognize the transcendent importance of the family and live in such a spiritually attentive way that the adversary cannot steal into the home and carry away the children."[3]

In 2008, during a worldwide leadership training broadcast, President Packer said, "A proclamation in the Church is a significant, major announcement. Very few of them have been issued from the beginning of the Church. They are significant; they are revelatory."[4] Over the entire history of the Church, only five proclamations had been issued to that time.[5]

Introduced on September 23, 1995, at a general Relief Society meeting by President Gordon B. Hinckley, this prophetic proclamation defines the official position of the Church on family, marriage, gender roles, and human sexuality. President Hinckley explained:

"With so much of sophistry that is passed off as truth, with so much of deception concerning standards and values, with so much of allurement and enticement to take on the slow stain of the world, we have felt to warn and forewarn. In furtherance of this we of the First Presidency and the Council of the Twelve Apostles now issue a proclamation to the Church and to the world as a declaration and reaffirmation of standards, doctrines, and practices relative to the family, which the prophets, seers, and revelators of this church have repeatedly stated throughout its history."[6]

Although the proclamation is not canonized scripture, President Packer declared, "It is scripture-like in its power."[7]

He explained, "When you wonder why we are the way we are and why we do the things we do and why we will not do some of the things that we will not do, you can find the authority for that in this Proclamation on the Family. There are times when we are accused of being intolerant because we won't accept and do the things that are supposed to be the norm in society." Noting the value of a clear set of principles in the murky moral atmosphere of the world, President Packer taught that as we examine this proclamation more closely, "see if you don't see in it the things that are foremost in society, in politics, in government, in religion now that are causing the most concern and difficulty. And you'll find answers there. And the answers that are there are the answers of the Church."[8]

Elder David B. Haight defined the proclamation on the family as relevant to all dispensations and one of the chief guides for modern Latter-day Saints. He instructed, "That marvelous document brings together the scriptural direction that we have received that has guided the lives of God's children from the time of Adam and Eve and will continue to guide us until the final winding-up scene."[9]

In 2015, during the twentieth anniversary of the proclamation, a number of Church leaders commented on its importance in articulating the position of the Church on many vital issues of our time. General Young Women president Bonnie L. Oscarson observed that when President Gordon B. Hinckley first read *The Family: A Proclamation to the World,* the Saints were "grateful for and valued the clarity, simplicity, and truth of this revelatory document." Sister Oscarson said further, "Little did we realize then how very desperately we would need these basic declarations in today's world as

the criteria by which we could judge each new wind of worldly dogma coming at us from the media, the Internet, scholars, TV and films, and even legislators. The proclamation on the family has become our benchmark for judging the philosophies of the world."[10]

The Church has published copies of the proclamation in many languages and distributed them worldwide. Many Latter-day Saints, in response to counsel given in general conference, have framed the proclamation for display in their homes. It has been discussed and referenced in general conferences and other Church meetings throughout the world. Lastly, as Elder M. Russell Ballard taught, Latter-day Saints are asked to "commit themselves to live by its precepts."[11] Indeed, as Elder Dallin H. Oaks said, Latter-day Saints are "responsible to teach and practice its truth."[12]

DID YOU KNOW?

- The First Presidency and the Quorum of the Twelve Apostles prepared a proclamation on the doctrine of the family after the United Nations world conferences on the family failed to mention marriage.

- *The Family: A Proclamation to the World* was first presented in a general Relief Society meeting in September 1995.

NOTES

1. Packer, "The Instrument of Your Mind and the Foundation of Your Character," address at Brigham Young University, Feb. 2, 2003, speeches.byu.edu.
2. Packer, "Instrument of Your Mind."
3. Packer, "Fledgling Finches and Family Life," address at Brigham Young University, Aug. 28, 2009, speeches.byu.edu.
4. Packer, "Proclamation on the Family," in *Worldwide Leadership Training Meeting*, 5.

5. Henry B. Eyring, "The Family," address at Brigham Young University, Nov. 5, 1995, speeches.byu.edu.

6. Gordon B. Hinckley, "Stand Strong against the Wiles of the World," *Ensign*, Nov. 1995, 100.

7. Packer, "Proclamation on the Family," 5.

8. Packer, "Proclamation on the Family," 5–6.

9. Haight, "Be a Strong Link," *Ensign*, Nov. 2000, 20.

10. Oscarson, "Defenders of the Family Proclamation," *Ensign*, May 2015, 14–15.

11. Ballard, "What Matters Most Is What Lasts Longest," *Ensign*, Nov. 2005, 42.

12. Oaks, "As He Thinketh in His Heart," address to religious educators, Feb. 8, 2013, lds.org.

97
The Second Great Expansion of Temple Building

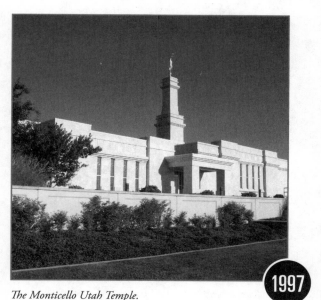

The Monticello Utah Temple.

1997

In June 1997 President Gordon B. Hinckley traveled to northern Mexico to attend a celebration marking the centennial of Academia Juárez, a school operated by the Church in the heart of the Mormon colonies in Mexico. Meredith I. Romney, president of the Juárez Stake, met President Hinckley at the El Paso International Airport and drove him to the colonies for the celebration. During the three-hour drive, President Hinckley talked "quite a bit about temples," President Romney said. "One of his concerns for the people here was the distance they traveled to attend the temple." Their closest temple, the Mesa Arizona Temple, was a seven-hour drive to the north and included a difficult border crossing into the United States. During his meetings with approximately five thousand Latter-day Saints, President Hinckley said, "This is the greatest era in the history of the Church and in the world for temple building. I would like to see the time come when all of our people throughout the world could get to a temple without too much inconvenience." He then remarked, "There aren't enough of you to justify a temple. Now, if you'd multiply the membership here and get about twenty thousand members of the Church here, or thirty thousand, we'd build a beautiful temple."[1]

President Hinckley's remarks reflected the temple policy of the Church at the time, but he was troubled. Later that evening, he spoke of the many contributions to the growth of the Church by the Saints living in Colonia Juárez and Colonia Dublán.

The next day as President Hinckley was being driven to the El Paso airport, he was uncharacteristically quiet.

"I reflected on what we could do to help these people in the Church colonies in Mexico," President Hinckley said. "They've been so faithful over the years. They've kept the faith. They've gone on missions in large numbers. . . . They've been the very epitome of faithfulness. And yet they've had to travel all the way to Mesa, Arizona, to go the temple." He continued, "I thought of these things and what could be done. The concept of . . . smaller temples came into my mind. I concluded we didn't need the laundry. We didn't need to rent temple clothing. We didn't need eating facilities. These have been added for convenience of the people but are not necessary [for the temple ordinances]."[2]

Once on the plane, President Hinckley sketched on a piece of paper his conception of small temples. When he arrived home, he handed the sketch to Church architects to refine.

At the October 1997 priesthood session of general conference, President Hinckley announced three small temples planned for Anchorage, Alaska, the Mormon colonies in northern Mexico, and Monticello, Utah. Emphasizing the advantages of this strategic shift in temple building, he outlined the new temple plan:

"One of these small temples can be constructed for about the same cost it takes just to maintain a large temple for a single year. It can be constructed in a relatively short time, several months. I repeat that none of the essentials would be missing. Every ordinance performed in the House of the Lord would be available."[3]

President Hinckley was right in his assessment. The Monticello Utah Temple was dedicated eight months after ground was broken. Construction of the Anchorage Alaska Temple was even faster—six months. The Colonia Juárez Mexico Temple took about a year. These small temples, with only 7,000 square feet, had an ordinance room, a celestial room, a sealing room, and a font for baptisms.

Encouraged by these successes, President Hinckley announced at the April 1998 general conference, "I take this opportunity to announce to the entire Church a program to construct some 30 smaller temples immediately. They will be in Europe, in Asia, in Australia, and Fiji, in Mexico and Central and South America and Africa, as well as in the United States and Canada." Acknowledging the fifty-one temples in operation, the seventeen under construction, and the thirty just announced, he concluded, "I think we had better add 2 more and make it an even 100 by the end of this century."[4]

President Hinckley's announcement escalated temple building to a scale never before seen. The years 1998, 1999, and 2000 were the most prolific era of temple building in the history of the Church. When President Hinckley discussed with Presiding Bishop H. David Burton his plan to build a hundred temples, the bishop wryly joked, "President, I pray the Lord will bless you with great longevity."[5]

The Boston Massachusetts Temple, which was dedicated on October 1, 2000, by President Hinckley, became the one-hundredth operating temple in the Church.

After the year 2000, a standard plan of 11,000 square feet was inaugurated for small temples. These temples included additional endowment and sealing rooms. The first temple to be built using the revised standard plan was in Columbus, Ohio. Similar temples built in St. Paul, Spokane, Detroit, and Edmonton made it clear that smaller temples were intended not only for Latter-day Saints living in remote areas but also for those who living in larger centers of population.

Soon the size of the standard plan for small temples was enlarged to 16,000 square feet. Temples of this size were constructed in Montana and Texas.

By the end of the year 2000, there were 102 operating temples.

Perhaps the high point of this wave of temple building came with the reconstruction of the Nauvoo Temple as the Nauvoo Illinois Temple. At 47,000 square feet, it had the same footprint and stood on the same spot as the

DID YOU KNOW?

- The greatest era of temple building in the Church began with a visit to the Mormon colonies in northern Mexico.

- More temples were dedicated in the three years of 1998, 1999, and 2000 than in the previous 167 years.

original Nauvoo Temple. The Nauvoo Illinois Temple was dedicated June 27, 2002.

The last temple dedicated by President Hinckley was in Helsinki, Finland, in October 2006. At the time of his passing in January 2008, President Hinckley had dedicated or re-dedicated 90 of the 124 operating temples in the Church.

"Why build so many temples in such a short time?" President Hinckley was asked. He replied, "The Church is not complete without temples. The doctrine is not fulfilled without these sacred ordinances. . . . This is the greatest era of temple building in all the history of the world. But it is not enough. We must continue to pursue it until we have a dedicated temple within reach of our faithful people everywhere."[6]

Notes

1. Romney and Cowan, *Colonia Juárez Temple,* 19.
2. Romney and Cowan, *Colonia Juárez Temple,* 20; "Colonia Juárez Temple Dedication," *LDS Church News,* Mar. 13, 1999.
3. Hinckley, "Some Thoughts on Temples, Retention of Converts, and Missionary Service," *Ensign,* Nov. 1997, 59–52.
4. Hinckley, "New Temples to Provide 'Crowning Blessings' of the Gospel," *Ensign,* May 1998, 87–88.
5. Burton, "A Season of Opportunity," *Ensign,* Nov. 1998, 100.
6. *Teachings of Gordon B. Hinckley,* 629.

98
"The Living Christ"

The Christus *in the North Visitors' Center on Temple* Square, Salt Lake City, Utah.

In July 1838 the Prophet Joseph Smith stated, "The fundamental principles of our religion are the testimony of the Apostles and Prophets concerning Jesus Christ, 'that He died, was buried, and rose again the third day, and ascended into heaven;' and all other things are only appendages to these, which pertain to our religion."[1]

In the year 2000, to commemorate the birth of Jesus Christ two millennia before, the First Presidency and the Quorum of the Twelve issued "The Living Christ: The Testimony of the Apostles," a one-page declaration that affirms the truthfulness of the fundamental principles, doctrines, and teachings of Jesus Christ.

The declaration states without equivocation that Jesus is "the Living Christ, the immortal Son of God."[2] It contains scriptural passages from the standard works and a testimony of the restoration of the priesthood and the Lord's Church upon the earth. It bears witness of the reality of the Second Coming of the Savior.

"The First Presidency and Quorum of the Twelve Apostles have boldly declared where they stand," said Sharon Larsen of the general Young Women presidency. "Their testimony of 'The Living Christ,' validated by each one of their signatures, is for all the world to see and know of their conviction."[3]

Elder Dallin H. Oaks proclaimed that in "The Living Christ," apostles and prophets "testify that His [Jesus'] life, which is central to all human history, neither began in Bethlehem nor concluded on Calvary. . . . [They] bear testimony, as His duly ordained Apostles—that Jesus is the Living Christ, the immortal Son of God. . . . He is the light, the life, and the hope of the world. His way is the path that leads to happiness in this life and eternal life in the world to come."[4]

At the first general conference after "The Living Christ" was issued, Elder M. Russell Ballard stated: "Our hope and faith are rooted in the profound understanding that He lives today and that He continues to lead and guide His Church and His people. We rejoice in the knowledge of the living Christ, and we reverently acknowledge the miracles that He continues to work today in the lives of those who have faith in Him."[5]

More recently, Elder Robert D. Hales emphasized the importance of "The Living Christ" as a firmly stated set of key doctrines and beliefs testifying of the divinity of the Savior:

"In recent decades the Church has largely been spared the terrible misunderstandings and persecutions experienced by the early Saints. It will not always be so. The world is moving away from the Lord faster and farther than ever before. The adversary has been loosed upon the earth. We watch, hear, read, study, and share the words of prophets to be forewarned and protected. . . . 'The Living Christ: The Testimony of the Apostles' was prepared in advance of when we will need it most."[6]

From the date of its issuance, the declaration has frequently been featured and quoted in Church magazines and other publications. It has influenced the lives of numerous Latter-day Saints. In 2014, Sister Neill F. Marriott of the Young Women general presidency told of nine hundred sisters in Young Women in Alaska memorizing "The Living Christ." They stood together and recited the entire document word for word from memory.[7]

"The Living Christ: The Testimony of the Apostles" is a twenty-first-century witness of Jesus Christ and has become a standard-bearer of testimony.

Elder John M. Madsen of the First Quorum of the Seventy stated, "I know of no more wonderful summary of the identity and role of the Lord Jesus Christ than the declaration of the First Presidency and the Quorum of the Twelve entitled "The Living Christ: The Testimony of the Apostles."[8]

Elder Keith Crockett of the Second Quorum of the Seventy assured Latter-day Saints that they could "stand steadfast in the testimony of 'The Living Christ,' as given by living Apostles."[9]

DID YOU KNOW?

• "The Living Christ" was issued by the First Presidency and the Quorum of the Twelve in 2000 to commemorate the birth of Jesus Christ two millennia before.

• Elder Robert D. Hales declared that "The Living Christ" was written to prepare Latter-day Saints to withstand future trials.

Notes

1. *Elders' Journal,* July 1838, 44, josephsmith papers.org.
2. Dennis B. Neuenschwander, "Living Prophets, Seers, and Revelators," *Ensign,* Nov. 2000, 41.
3. Larsen, "Standing with God," *Ensign,* May 2000, 90.
4. Oaks, "Resurrection," *Ensign,* May 2000, 16.
5. Ballard, "How Is It with Us?" *Ensign,* May 2000, 32–33.
6. Hales, "General Conference: Strengthening Faith and Testimony," *Ensign,* Nov. 2013, 7.
7. Marriott, "Sharing Your Light," *Ensign,* November 2014.
8. Madsen, "Eternal Life through Jesus Christ," *Ensign,* May 2002, 78.
9. Crockett, "Retaining a Remission of Sin," *Ensign,* Nov. 2000, 78.

99
The Perpetual Education Fund Is Established

Educational materials like those financed by the Perpetual Education Fund to help members in dozens of countries receive greater opportunities.

2001

Knowledge of the challenges faced by past leaders and the solutions they discovered had a direct bearing on President Gordon B. Hinckley's ability to find solutions to challenges he faced in his administration.

One was the growth of the Church. When a reporter asked in 1995 about issues surrounding growth, President Hinckley responded, "Growth is a serious problem for us, of course. But it is wonderful problem."[1]

Most of the growth of the Church in the 1990s was occurring outside the United States in the developing nations of the world. The issue of providing a path to a better life for Latter-day Saints living in impoverished conditions in these countries was a serious concern to President Hinckley. He looked to his predecessors in the nineteenth century to find the solution.

In the April 2001 general conference, President Hinckley spoke of the time when thousands of needy Latter-day Saints longed to gather to Utah. "Under the inspiration of the Lord, a plan was devised," he noted. "What was known as the Perpetual Emigration Fund was established. . . . Money was loaned to those members who had little or nothing. The money repaid would then be loaned to others to make possible to emigrate."

He then announced, "Now, my brethren, we face another problem in the Church. We have many missionaries, both young men and young women, who are called locally and who serve with honor in Mexico, Central America, South America, the Philippines, and other places. They have very little money, but they make a contribution with what they have."

He expressed concern that when those promising young missionaries returned home, they "sink right back into the pit of poverty from which they came." In response, President Hinckley announced "a plan which we believe is inspired by the Lord. . . . Based on similar principles to those underlying the Perpetual Emigration Fund, we shall call it the Perpetual Education Fund."[2]

Two months before President Hinckley's monumental announcement, Elder John K. Carmack of the Seventy was asked to serve as the managing director of the new program. "Surprised and shocked," Elder Carmack later recalled, "I nevertheless found words to respond." After the announcement, Elder Carmack, along with others, launched the Perpetual Education Fund. Rex J. Allen, one of the primary organizers of the Perpetual Education Fund, recalled, "President Hinckley's inaugural speech became our constitution, by-laws, and plan for operations and training. We pored over it dozens of times, gaining insight as we grew."[3]

By September 2001, the Perpetual Education Fund was ready to offer loans. "At first we wondered if anyone would apply," Elder Carmack recalled. "But by December we had 300 applications."[4] The median age of the applicants was twenty-four years old. Within the first two years, nearly ten thousand loans were approved. By the end of the first decade, the Perpetual Education Fund had assisted more than 46,000 Latter-day Saints in forty-five nations.[5] Recipients of a Perpetual Education Fund loan had a 70 percent graduation rate from their programs, compared to a 35 to 55 percent graduation rate for colleges in the United States. Nearly 90 percent of Perpetual Education Fund graduates found gainful employment and enjoyed an increase of three to five times their previous income.[6]

The impressive numbers of the Perpetual Education Fund tell part of the story. Thousands of young Latter-day Saints helped by this program saw tremendous changes in their lives. One young member in Colombia named Claudia had received some college training before her mission, but family opposition to her newfound faith blocked her path to graduation. Claudia recalled:

"Before my graduation, the opposition reached a point where I was unable to attend Sunday Church meetings because my family would not allow it. My Church books vanished, and my participation became limited to secretly attending institute, where we were studying the Old Testament. Some of the lessons that impacted me the most were the lessons about Job. I learned about patience and perseverance. I had a loving and dedicated teacher who was going through some very painful trials. He taught us the doctrine, but he mainly taught through his example."[7]

After much fasting and prayer, Claudia decided to move to Cartagena, Colombia, to seek other opportunities. There she fell in love with a righteous Latter-day Saint man, and they were sealed in the temple. After her marriage, Claudia continued to express a desire to finish her college education. She recalled that her mother "offered me ways to pay for graduate school and to improve my financial standing if I would sacrifice my membership in the Church and my sealing. My answer was always no, and these exchanges were a source of anger for my mother and tears for me. Even so, I still had the desire to continue my schooling."

Claudia applied for a Perpetual Education Fund loan and was approved. She wrote, "The hearts of my parents and my brother softened toward me, and so I enrolled at the university with the help of my father, my brother, and the

DID YOU KNOW?

- Within the first decade of the founding of the Perpetual Education Fund, more than 46,000 Latter-day Saints in forty-five nations received assistance.

- The Perpetual Education Fund was incorporated into a larger plan to launch self-reliance centers around the globe.

Perpetual Education Fund. My mother also helped me with money, paying a percentage of the third-semester tuition. I graduated on November 2, 2011. This degree started improving my quality of life even before I completed it: I have managed to increase my earnings with activities related to my graduate studies by working as a teacher at a technical school and as a welfare coordinator at an educational institute. All of this is thanks to the support of the Perpetual Education Fund during this period."[8]

Stories like Claudia's repeat themselves thousands of times in diverse locations around the world as the Perpetual Education Fund is now incorporated into a larger plan of self-reliance centers around the globe.[9] These centers provide funds and trainings for members to start their own businesses, find better employment, and receive education through loans from the Perpetual Education Fund.

Along with the already established Church welfare programs, President Hinckley's vision of raising Latter-day Saints out of poverty and into a new life continues to be realized. "Long ago, Moses stretched his staff over the Red Sea and the waters divided," said Rex Allen. "President Hinckley mirrored this same faith when he figuratively held his prophetic mantle over the dark sea of poverty and initiated [the Perpetual Education Fund]."[10]

While the relatively recent initiation of the Perpetual Education Fund makes it difficult to determine the long-term effect of the program, the foundational concepts have produced a compelling change within the Church. But President Hinckley hoped for more. He admonished Church members, "We must do all we can to help them lift themselves, to establish their lives upon a foundation of self-reliance that can come of training. Education is the key to opportunity."[11]

NOTES

1. Interview with Phil Riesen, May 12, 1995, in Dew, *Go Forward with Faith,* 576.
2. Hinckley, "The Perpetual Education Fund," *Ensign,* May 2001, 52.
3. Carmack, *Bright Ray of Hope,* 58–59.
4. "The Perpetual Education Fund: A Decade of Changing Lives," mormonnewsroom.org.
5. "Perpetual Education Fund."
6. "Perpetual Education Fund."
7. pef.lds.org.
8. pef.lds.org.
9. "Perpetual Education Fund."
10. "Perpetual Education Fund."
11. Hinckley, "Perpetual Education Fund," 53.

100
Ages Lowered for Missionary Service

2012

Part of the Church's missionary force, which was greatly altered by the missionary age change.

In the April 2013 general conference, Elder Russell M. Nelson spoke of an "unprecedented wave of enthusiasm for missionary work."[1] That wave had started with President Thomas S. Monson's announcement six months earlier:

"Effective immediately, all worthy and able young men who have graduated from high school or its equivalent, regardless of where they live, will have the option of being recommended

for missionary service beginning at the age of 18, instead of age 19 . . . [and] able, worthy young women who have the desire to serve may be recommended for missionary service beginning at age 19, instead of age 21. . . .

"We affirm that missionary work is a priesthood duty—and we encourage all young men who are worthy and who are physically able and mentally capable to respond to the call to serve. Many young women also serve, but they are not under the same mandate to serve, as are the young men. We assure the young sisters of the Church, however, that they make a valuable contribution as missionaries, and we welcome their service."[2]

Elder Quentin L. Cook, speaking after President Monson's announcement, said, "I am confident that an even greater harvest will be achieved now as righteous, committed missionaries fulfill the Savior's commandment to preach His gospel."[3]

A year later, "the number of full-time missionaries serving had increased from 58,500 in October 2012 to 80,333." President Monson called the response "tremendous and inspiring."[4]

The executive director of the Missionary Department, Elder David F. Evans, observed, "There are significantly more sister missionaries serving now than there were before. It's gone from about 15 percent of the missionary force to about 24 percent during this past year. There's about 11,000 more sister missionaries serving than there was a year ago."[5]

With the age change and faithful youth putting their education on hold to serve missions, the Utah System of Higher Education felt a pinch. One spokesperson noted, "Utah's public colleges and universities saw a slight drop in enrollment between fall 2012 and fall 2013 due to the impact of the missionary age change."[6] Brigham Young University and Utah Valley University experienced the sharpest declines in 2013, but enrollments returned to normal in the fall 2015.

Another entity to experience challenges from the volume of missionaries leaving and returning home from missions was the Salt Lake City International Airport. Bianca Shreeve, airport public relations manager, spoke of the issues posed when groups of thirty or more well-wishers blocked the way to the baggage claim for other passengers. To better serve passengers, airport officials announced a construction at the airport "to include a special greeting area for loved ones—including families of returning LDS missionaries—in the major renovation underway at the airport."[7] That construction and other renovations are scheduled to be completed in 2020.

Other adjustments had to be made by mission presidents around the world. They were pleased to have many additional missionaries but scrambled to find appropriate housing for them. Yong-in Shin, president of the Korea Daejeon Mission, said that the additional sisters in his mission reported more baptisms than the elders. He explained the reason: "Korean women usually do not want male strangers, some barely past adolescence, visiting them when they are alone, but two cheerful young American women are another story."[8]

Elder Jeffrey R. Holland said of the young sister missionaries, "We enthusiastically welcome your service. . . . Personally, I am absolutely delighted if this change in policy allows many, many more young women to serve."[9]

With so many young people and senior couples catching the wave of missionary work and volunteering their time and talents to serve the Lord, the work of salvation began to move forward at a quicker pace. Elder Russell M. Nelson said: "Since President Monson's historic announcement last October, thousands of elders, sisters, and couples have been called, and many more are preparing. Now we get questions like 'What are you going to do with all these missionaries?' The answer is simple. They will do what missionaries have always done. They will preach the gospel! They will bless the children of Almighty God! More of you young men and women will catch this wave as you strive to be worthy of mission calls. You see this as a wave of truth and righteousness. You see your opportunity to be on the crest of that wave."[10]

It is too soon to fully measure the effects of the missionary age change, but there is no doubt it has already made a significant impact on the missionary work of the Church. The change has made missionary service an even more deeply embedded rite of passage for the young men and women of the Church.

In the years immediately following the change, it has become clear that the age change has begun a new phase in missionary work, not just for the youth of the Church but for all members. Church leaders began calling for a hastening of the work. President Henry B. Eyring was among those sounding the call,

DID YOU KNOW?

- One year after the announcement lowering the age for the beginning of missionary service, "the number of full-time missionaries serving had increased from 58,500 . . . to 80,333."

- The proportion of young sister missionaries serving in October 2012 was 15 percent of the missionary force. Six months later, it was 24 percent.

declaring, "Whatever our age, capacity, Church calling, or location, we are as one called to the work to help Him in His harvest of souls."[11]

Notes

1. Nelson, "Catch the Wave," *Ensign,* May 2013, 45.
2. Monson, "Welcome to Conference," 4–5.
3. Cook, "Can Ye Feel So Now?" *Ensign,* Nov. 2012, 6.
4. Monson, "Welcome to Conference," *Ensign,* Nov. 2012, 4.
5. "The Impact of Missionary Service Age Change— One Year Later: A Conversation with Elder David F. Evans, Executive Director, Missionary Department," lds.org.
6. "What Is the Impact of the LDS Missionary Age Change at Utah Colleges and Universities?" higheredutah.org.
7. Amy McDonald, "Are Mormon Missionary Arrivals at Salt Lake City's Airport Getting Out of Hand?" *Salt Lake Tribune,* Dec. 10, 2015.
8. "Missions Signal a Growing Role for Mormon Women," *New York Times,* Mar. 1, 2014.
9. "Church Lowers Missionary Service Age," lds.org.
10. Nelson, "Catch the Wave," 45.
11. Eyring, "We Are One," *Ensign,* May 2013, 62.

Epilogue
The Next 100 Events

After we finished compiling our initial list and began the research and writing phase of this book, we were offered an opportunity to present our early results during Education Week at BYU in 2015. Over the course of four days, we made presentations on the events we had chosen and received enthusiastic feedback from attendees, who varied widely in age, geographic distribution, and Church experience.

We were gratified that over the course of the week, the crowds grew larger each day, and many participants asked for a copy of our list before leaving. At the end of each class we opened the floor for questions, and on the last day one attendee asked a question we were not quite prepared for. That question was, "What do you think the next 100 events will be?"

Ours is a Church led by apostles and prophets, and the scriptures testify that those given these sacred callings are often given the gift to know "of things which are to come" (Mosiah 8:17). The Prophet Joseph Smith himself predicted events up to our time and beyond. According to Wilford Woodruff, on one occasion the Prophet told a small group of priesthood holders, "Brethren, I have been very much edified and instructed in your testimonies here tonight, but I want to say to you before the Lord, that you know no more concerning the destinies of this Church and kingdom than a babe upon its mother's lap. You don't comprehend it. . . . It is only a little handful of Priesthood you see here tonight, but this Church will fill North and South America—it will fill the world."[1]

Throughout our history, inspired Church leaders have provided assurance of its millennial destiny, but they have wisely avoided making any declarations that are too specific, allowing the "marvelous work and wonder" to gradually unfold (2 Nephi 27:26; Isaiah 29:14). We too will avoid making any specific predictions, but we believe we can identify several trends likely to continue within the Church as it moves towards the third century of the Restoration.

First, though the doctrines of the Church will remain constant, the programs, policies, and practices of the Church will likely change. President Boyd K. Packer taught, "There will be changes made in the future as in the past. Whether the Brethren make changes or resist them depends entirely upon the channels of revelation which were established in the beginning. *The doctrines will remain fixed, eternal; the organization, programs, and procedures will be altered as directed by Him whose church this is.*"[2]

The Church is a living, changing organization. If the changes of the last century alone are any indication, in another few decades the programs of the Church may look quite different.

Second, the Church will become more diverse as it spreads and grows deeper roots in other countries and cultures. Church doctrine is universal, but until the last few decades the culture of the Latter-day Saints has possessed a strong correlation to American culture. With the most significant increases in membership occurring outside of the United States, the culture of the Church will likely change to more fully transcend national boundaries and cultures.

In 2012 Elder Dallin H. Oaks taught, "As a way to help us keep the commandments of God, members of The Church of Jesus Christ of Latter-day Saints have what we call a gospel culture. It is a distinctive way of life, a set of values and expectations and practices common to all members. This gospel culture comes from the plan of salvation, the commandments of God, and the teachings of the living prophets. It guides us in the way we raise our families and live our individual lives." Elder Oaks continued, "To help its members all over the world, the Church teaches us to give up any personal or family traditions or practices that are contrary to the teachings of the Church of Jesus Christ and to this gospel culture. . . . We ask all to climb to the higher ground of the gospel culture, to practices and traditions that are rooted in the restored gospel of Jesus Christ."[3]

As the Church matures worldwide, we will undoubtedly see changes in the cultural backgrounds of the general leadership of the Church, a phenomenon we are even now witnessing. Unity will remain a trademark of Church members, and the roles of men and women within different cultures, backgrounds, and experiences will continue to diversify and enrich the kingdom.

Finally, more than two thousand years ago, our Savior Jesus Christ taught his disciples, "In the world ye shall have tribulation: but be of good cheer, I have overcome the world" (John 16:33). Throughout its history, the restored Church has often experienced a degree of tension and opposition from the environment surrounding it, no matter what the context. This is an expectation and condition for the kingdom of God in the latter days and is not necessarily a negative in the growth and progress of the work. Some of most momentous periods in Church history also corresponded with times of extreme persecution and duress. The character of our religion has often been purified by the refiner's fire. In the years to come the Latter-day Saints will be seen as a "peculiar" people, a characteristic that has always defined us (Deuteronomy 14:2).

Our history will remain vital to us. For the Latter-day Saints, history is more than just memory—it is theology, our record of God's dealings with us. Many of what are now considered the 100 most important events may be eclipsed by even more important developments as the Church moves closer to the grand millennial day.

NOTES

1. *Joseph Smith* [manual], 137.
2. Boyd K. Packer, "Revelation in a Changing World," *Ensign,* Nov. 1989, 16; emphasis added.
3. Oaks, "The Gospel Culture," *Ensign,* Mar. 2012, 42–43.

Books Cited

Alexander, Thomas G. *Mormonism in Transition: A History of the Latter-day Saints, 1890–1930.* Urbana: University of Illinois Press, 1996.

———. *Things in Heaven and in Earth: The Life and Times of Wilford Woodruff, a Mormon Prophet.* Salt Lake City: Signature Books, 1993.

Allen, James B., and Glen M. Leonard. *The Story of the Latter-day Saints.* 2d ed. Salt Lake City: Deseret Book, 1992.

Allen, James B., Ronald K. Esplin, and David J. Whitaker. *Men with a Mission: The Quorum of the Twelve Apostles in the British Isles, 1837–1841.* Salt Lake City: Deseret Book, 1992.

Anderson, Karl Ricks. *Joseph Smith's Kirtland: Eyewitness Accounts.* Salt Lake City: Deseret Book, 1996.

Anderson, Lavina Fielding. *Lucy's Book: A Critical Edition of Lucy Mack Smith's Family Memoir.* Salt Lake City: Signature Books, 2001.

Anesaki, Masaharu. *History of Japanese Religion.* Rutland, Vt.: Charles E. Tuttle Company, 1971.

Arrington, Leonard J. *Brigham Young, American Moses.* New York: Alfred A. Knopf, 1985.

———. *Great Basin Kingdom: Economic History of the Latter-day Saints, 1830–1900.* Lincoln: University of Nebraska Press, 1958.

Arrington, Leonard J., and Davis Bitton. *The Mormon Experience: A History of the Latter-day Saints.* New York: Vintage Books, 1979.

Arrington, Leonard J., Feramorz Y. Fox, and Dean L. May. *Building the City of God: Community and Cooperation among the Mormons.* Urbana: University of Illinois Press, 1992.

Ashton, Wendell J. *Voice in the West: Biography of a Pioneer Newspaper.* New York: Duell, Sloan, & Pearce, 1950.

Babbel, Frederick W. *On Wings of Faith.* Salt Lake City: Bookcraft, 1972.

Backman, Milton V., Jr. *Eyewitness Accounts of the Restoration.* Orem, Utah: Grandin Book, 1983.

———. *Heavens Resound: A History of Latter-day Saints in Ohio, 1830–1838.* Salt Lake City: Deseret Book, 1983.

Backman, Milton V., Jr., Susan Easton Black, and Larry C. Porter, eds. *New York.* Regional Studies in Latter-day Saint Church History series. Provo, Utah: Brigham Young University, Department of Church History and Doctrine, 1992.

Baker, LeGrand K. *Murder of the Mormon Prophet: The Political Prelude to the Death of Joseph Smith.* Salt Lake City: Eborn Books, 2006.

Ballard, Melvin J. *Sermons and Missionary Services of Melvin Joseph Ballard.* Comp. Bryant S. Hinckley, Salt Lake City: Deseret Book, 1949.

Barrett, Ivan J. *Young Joseph.* RCI Publishing, 1981.

Basic Principles of Welfare and Self-Reliance [pamphlet]. The Church of Jesus Christ of Latter-day Saints, 2009.

Baugh, Alexander L., and Andrew H. Hedges, eds. *New York–Pennsylvania.* Regional Studies in Latter-day Saint Church History series. Provo, Utah: Brigham Young University, Department of Church History and Doctrine, 2002.

Beebe, Fred G. *The Cluff Missionaries in the Sandwich Islands.* Iosepa Colony: Family History Publishers, 1987.

Beers, Paul B. *Pennsylvania Politics Today and Yesterday.* University Park: Pennsylvania State University Psress, 1980.

Bennett, Richard E. *Mormons at the Missouri, 1846–1852: "And Should We Die . . ."* Norman: University of Oklahoma Press, 1987.

———. *We'll Find the Place: The Mormon Exodus, 1846–1848.* Salt Lake City: Deseret Book, 1997.

Berrett, William E. *A Miracle in Weekday Religious Education.* Salt Lake City: Salt Lake Printing Center, 1986.

Bieber, Ralph P. *Exploring Southwestern Trails, 1846–1854.* Chatham, Mich.: Porcupine Press, 1974.

Bitton, Davis. *George Q. Cannon, a Biography.* Salt Lake City: Deseret Book, 1999.

Bjork, Kenneth O. *West of the Great Divide.*

Northfield, Minn.: Norwegian-American Historical Association, 1985.

Black, Susan Easton, and Larry C. Porter, eds. *The Lion of the Lord: Essays on the Life and Service of Brigham Young.* Salt Lake City: Deseret Book, 1995.

Black, Susan Easton, Randy L. Bott, Dee R. Darling, and Fred W. Woods. *Out of Obscurity: The Church in the Twentieth Century.* Sidney B. Sperry Symposium series. Salt Lake City: Deseret Book, 2000.

Bloxham, Ben V., James R. Moss, and Larry C. Porter, eds. *Truth Will Prevail: The Rise of the Church of Jesus Christ of Latter-day Saints in the British Isles, 1837–1987.* Salt Lake City: The Church of Jesus Christ of Latter-day Saints, 1987.Bock, Comfort Margaret. *The Church of Jesus Christ of Latter-day Saints in the Hawaiian Islands.* Honolulu: University of Hawaii, 1941.

Britsch, R. Lanier. *Moramona.* Laie, Hawaii: Institute for Polynesian Studies, 1989.

———. *From the East: The History of the Latter-day Saints in Asia, 1851–1996.* Salt Lake City: Deseret Book, 1998.

———. *Unto the Islands of the Sea: A History of the Latter-day Saints.* Salt Lake City: Deseret Book, 1986.

Brooks, Juanita. *On the Mormon Frontier: The Diary of Hosea Stout, 1844–1889.* Salt Lake City: University of Utah Press, 2009.

Bushman, Richard L. *Joseph Smith, Rough Stone Rolling.* New York: Alfred A. Knopf, 2005.

Cannon, Donald Q., and Lyndon W. Cook. *Far West Record: Minutes of The Church of Jesus Christ of Latter-day Saints, 1830–1844.* Salt Lake City: Deseret Book, 1983.

Cannon, Donald Q., and Richard O. Cowan. *Unto Every Nation: Gospel Light Reaches Every Land.* Salt Lake City: Deseret Book, 2003.

Cannon, Donald Q., and David J. Whittaker. *Supporting Saints: Life Stories of Nineteenth-Century Mormons.* Provo, Utah: Brigham Young University Religious Studies Center, 1986.

Cannon, George Q. *Life of Joseph Smith.* 1888. Salt Lake City: Deseret Book, 1986.

———. *My First Mission.* Salt Lake City: Juvenile Instructor Office, 1879.

Carmack, John K. *A Bright Ray of Hope: The Perpetual Education Fund.* Salt Lake City: Deseret Book, 2004.

Carter, Kate B. *Heartthrobs of the West.* 12 vols. Salt Lake City: Daughters of the Utah Pioneers, 1947–51.

Charge to Religious Educators. Salt Lake City: The Church of Jesus Christ of Latter-day Saints, 1981.

Church History in the Fulness of Times. 2d ed. Salt Lake City: The Church of Jesus Christ of Latter-day Saints, 2003.

Clark, J. Reuben, Jr. *J. Reuben Clark: Selected Papers.* 5 vols. Edited by David H. Yarn Jr. Provo, Utah: Brigham Young University Press, 1984.

Classic Experiences and Adventures: Labors in the Vineyard—Eventful Narratives—Scraps of Biography—Helpful Visions. Salt Lake City: Bookcraft, 1969.

Clayton, William. *William Clayton's Journal.* Salt Lake City: Deseret News, 1921.

A Collection of Sacred Hymns for the Church of the Latter Day Saints. Kirtland, Ohio: F. G. Williams & Co., 1835.

Cook, Lyndon W. *The Revelations of the Prophet Joseph Smith.* Provo, Utah: Seventy's Mission Bookstore, 1981.

Cowan, Richard O. *Answers to Your Questions about the Doctrine and Covenants.* Salt Lake City: Deseret Book, 1996.

———. *Doctrine and Covenants: Our Modern Scripture.* Provo, Utah: Brigham Young University Press, 1978.

———. *Temples to Dot the Earth.* Salt Lake City: Bookcraft, 1989.

Cowley, Matthias F. *Wilford Woodruff, Fourth President of The Church of Jesus Christ of Latter-day Saints.* Salt Lake City: Bookcraft, 1964.

Cornwall, J. Spencer. *Stories of Our Mormon Hymns.* Salt Lake City: Deseret Book, 1980.

Cowley, Matthias F. *Wilford Woodruff, Fourth President of The Church of Jesus Christ of Latter-day Saints.* Salt Lake City: Bookcraft, 1964.

Crawley, Peter. *A Descriptive Bibliography of the Mormon Church.* 3 vols. Provo, Utah: Brigham Young University Religious Studies Center.

Daughters in My Kingdom: The History and Work of Relief Society. Salt Lake City: The Church of Jesus Christ of Latter-day Saints, 2011.

Davidson, Karen Lynn. *Our Latter-day Hymns: The Stories and the Messages.* 2d ed. Salt Lake City: Deseret Book, 2009.

Davidson, Karen Lynn, David J. Whittaker, Mark Ashurst-McGee, and Richard L. Jensen, eds. *Histories, Volume 1: Joseph Smith Histories, 1832–1844.* Vol. 1 of the Histories series of *The Joseph*

Smith Papers, edited by Dean C. Jessee, Ronald K. Esplin, and Richard Lyman Bushman. Salt Lake City: Church Historian's Press, 2012.

Davidson, Karen Lynn, Richard L. Jensen, and David J. Whittaker. *Histories, Volume 2: Assigned Histories, 1831–1847.* Vol. 2 of the Histories series of *The Joseph Smith Papers,* edited by Dean C. Jessee, Ronald K. Esplin, and Richard Lyman Bushman. Salt Lake City: Church Historian's Press, 2012.

Daynes, Kathryn M. *More Wives Than One: Transformation of the Mormon Marriage System, 1840–1910.* Urbana: University of Illinois Press, 2008.

Derr, Jill Mulvay, Carol Cornwall Madsen, Kate Holbrook, and Matthew J. Grow, eds. *The First Fifty Years of Relief Society: Key Documents in Latter-day Saint Women's History.* Salt Lake City: Church Historian's Press, 2016.

Dew, Sheri L. *Ezra Taft Benson: A Biography.* Salt Lake City: Deseret Book, 1987.

———. *Go Forward with Faith: The Biography of Gordon B. Hinckley.* Salt Lake City: Deseret Book, 1996.

Dirkmaat, Gerrit J., Brent M. Rogers, Grant Underwood, Robert J. Woodford, and William G. Hartley, eds. *Documents, Volume 3: February 1833–March 1834.* Vol. 3 of the Documents series of The Joseph Smith Papers, edited by Ronald K. Esplin and Matthew J. Grow. Salt Lake City: Church Historian's Press, 2014.

Draper, Richard D., Brown, S. Kent, and Michael D. Rhodes. *The Pearl of Great Price: A Verse-by-Verse Commentary.* Salt Lake City: Deseret Book, 2005.

Durham, G. Homer. *The Discourses of Wilford Woodruff.* Salt Lake City: Bookcraft, 1946.

Early Scenes in Church History. Salt Lake City: Juvenile Instructor Office, 1882.

Ehat, Andrew F., and Lyndon W. Cook. *Words of Joseph Smith.* Provo, Utah: Brigham Young University Religious Studies Center, 1980.

England, Breck. *The Life and Thought of Orson Pratt.* Salt Lake City: University of Utah Press, 1985.

Evans, Richard L. *A Century of "Mormonism" in Great Britain.* Salt Lake City: Publisher's Press, 1937.

Faldmo, Norman W., Sr., ed. *Church College of Hawaii and Its Builders.* Laie, Hawaii: Continuing Committee, 1958.

Family Home Evenings, 1970–71. Salt Lake City: The Church of Jesus Christ of Latter-day Saints, 1970.

Firmage, Edwin Brown, and Richard Collin Mangrum. *Zion in the Courts.* Urbana: University of Illinois Press, 1988.

Fisanik, Christina, ed. *Feminism: Opposing Viewpoints.* Farmington Hills, Mich.: Greenhaven Press, 2008.

Flake, Kathleen. *The Politics of American Religious Identity: The Seating of Senator Reed Smoot, Mormon Apostle.* Chapel Hill: University of North Carolina Press, 2004.

Flanders, Robert Bruce. *Nauvoo: Kingdom on the Mississippi.* Urbana: University of Illinois Press, 1965.

Fleek, Sherman L. *History May Be Searched in Vain: A Military History of the Mormon Battalion.* Spokane, Wa.: Arthur H. Clark Company, 2008.

Francis, Nettie H., ed. *Century of Honor: 100 Years of Scouting in the Church of Jesus Christ of Latter-day Saints.* Salt Lake City: LDS-BSA Relationships Office, 2013.

Freeman, Joseph, Jr. *In the Lord's Due Time.* Salt Lake City: Bookcraft, 1979.

Galbraith, David B., D. Kelly Ogden, and Andrew C. Skinner. *Jerusalem, the Eternal City.* Salt Lake City: Deseret Book, 1996.

Garr, Arnold K., Donald Q. Cannon, and Richard O. Cowan, eds. *Encyclopedia of Latter-day Saint History.* Salt Lake City: Deseret Book, 2000.

Garr, Arnold K., and Clark D. Johnson, eds. *Missouri.* Regional Studies in Latter-day Saint Church History series. Provo, Utah: Brigham Young University, Department of Church History and Doctrine, 1994.

Garrett, Dean H., ed. *Illinois.* Regional Studies in Latter-day Saint Church History series. Provo, Utah: Brigham Young University Church History and Doctrine, 1995.

Gates, Susa Young. *History of the Young Ladies' Mutual Improvement Association of the Church of Jesus Christ of Latter-day Saints.* Salt Lake City: General Board of the YLMIA, 1911.

Gates, Susa Young, and Leah D. Widtsoe. *The Life Story of Brigham Young.* New York: Macmillan, 1930.

Gibbons, Francis M. *Spencer W. Kimball: Resolute Disciple, Prophet of God.* Salt Lake City: Deseret Book, 1995.

Givens, George W. *In Old Nauvoo: Everyday Life in the City of Joseph.* Salt Lake City: Deseret Book, 1990.

Givens, Terryl L. *By the Hand of Mormon.* New York: Oxford University Press, 2002.

Givens, Terryl L., and Matthew J. Grow. *Parley P.*

Pratt: The Apostle Paul of Mormonism. New York: Oxford University Press, 2011.

Godfrey, Matthew C., Mark Ashurst-McGee, Grant Underwood, Robert J. Woodford, and William G. Hartley., eds. *Documents, Volume 2: July 1831–January 1833.* Vol. 2 of the Documents series of The Joseph Smith Papers, edited by Dean C. Jessee, Ronald K. Esplin, Richard Lyman Bushman, and Matthew J. Grow. Salt Lake City: Church Historian's Press, 2013.

Gordon, Sarah Barringer. *The Mormon Question: Polygamy and Constitutional Conflict in Nineteenth-Century America.* Chapel Hill: University of North Carolina Press, 2002.

Grover, Mark L. *A Land of Prophecy and Promise: Elder A. Theodore Tuttle in South America, 1960–65.* Provo, Utah: Brigham Young University Religious Studies Center, 2008.

Grow, Matthew J. *"Liberty to the Downtrodden": Thomas L. Kane, Romantic Reformer.* New Haven: Yale University Press, 2009.

Hafen, LeRoy R., and Ann W. Hafen. *Handcarts to Zion: The Story of a Unique Western Migration, 1856–60.* Lincoln: University of Nebraska Press, 1992.

———, eds. *Mormon Resistance: A Documentary Account of the Utah Expedition, 1857–1858.* Lincoln: University of Nebraska Press, 1958.

Hales, Brian C. *Joseph Smith's Polygamy: History.* 2 vols. Salt Lake City: Greg Kofford Books, 2013.

Hardy, B. Carmon. *Solemn Covenant: The Mormon Polygamous Passage.* Urbana: University of Illinois Press, 1992.

Haws, J. B. *The Mormon Image in the American Mind.* New York: Oxford University Press, 2013.

Hearken, O Ye People: Discourses on the Doctrine and Covenants. Sperry Symposium series. Sandy, Utah: Randall Book, 1984.

Hedges, Andrew H., J. Spencer Fluhman, and Alonzo L. Gaskill, eds. *The Doctrine and Covenants: Revelations in Context.* Provo, Utah: Brigham Young University Religious Studies Center, 2008.

Hedges, Andrew H., Alex D. Smith, and Richard Lloyd Anderson, eds. *Journals, Volume 2: December 1841–April 1843.* Vol. 2 of the Journals series of The Joseph Smith Papers, edited by Dean C. Jessee, Ronald K. Esplin, and Richard Lyman Bushman. Salt Lake City: Church Historian's Press, 2011.

Hedges, Andrew H., Alex D. Smith, and Brent M. Rogers, eds. *Journals, Volume 3: May 1843–June 1844.* Vol. 3 of the Journals series of The Joseph Smith Papers, edited by Ronald K. Esplin and Matthew J. Grow. Salt Lake City: Church Historian's Press, 2015.

Hicks, Michael. *Mormonism and Music: A History.* Urbana: University of Illinois Press, 2003.

———. *The Mormon Tabernacle Choir: A Biography.* Urbana: University of Illinois Press, 2015.

Hillcourt, William, with Lady Olave Baden-Powell. *Baden-Powell: The Two Lives of a Hero.* New York: G. P. Putnam's Sons, 1964.

Hinckley, Gordon B. *Teachings of Gordon B. Hinckley.* Salt Lake City: Deseret Book, 1997.

The History of the Reorganized Church of Jesus Christ of Latter Day Saints. 8 vols. Independence, Mo.: Herald House, 1896.

Holzapfel, Richard Neitzel, and Kent P. Jackson, eds. *Joseph Smith, the Prophet and Seer.* Provo and Salt Lake City, Utah: Brigham Young University Religious Studies Center and Deseret Book, 2010.

Howlett, David J. *Kirtland Temple: The Biography of a Shared Mormon Sacred Space.* Urbana: University of Illinois Press, 2014.

Hymns of The Church of Jesus Christ of Latter-day Saints. Salt Lake City: The Church of Jesus Christ of Latter-day Saints, 1985.

Jackson, Kent P. *The King James Bible and the Restoration.* Salt Lake City: Deseret Book, 2011.

Jacob, Norton. *The Mormon Vanguard Brigade of 1847.* Edited by Ronald O. Barney. Logan, Utah: Utah State University Press, 2005.

Jenson, Andrew, ed. *The Historical Record.* Salt Lake City: Andrew Lenson, 1886.

Jenson, Andrew. *L.D.S. Biographical Encyclopedia: A Compilation of Biographical Sketches of Prominent Men and Women in the Church of Jesus Christ of Latter-day Saints.* 4 vols. Salt Lake City: Andrew Jenson History Co., 1901.

———, ed. *The Historical Record.* Salt Lake City: Andrew Jenson, 1886.

Jessee, Dean C., ed. *Personal Writings of Joseph Smith.* Salt Lake City: Deseret Book, 2002.

Jessee, Dean C., Mark Ashurst-McGee, and Richard L. Jensen, eds. *Journals, Volume 1: 1832–1839.* Vol. 1 of the Journals series of The Joseph Smith Papers, edited by Dean C. Jessee, Ronald K. Esplin, and Richard Lyman Bushman. Salt Lake City: Church Historian's Press, 2008.

Johnson, Annie Richardson. *Heartbeats of Colonia Diaz.* Salt Lake City: Publishers Press, 1972.

Johnson, Benjamin F. *My Life's Review: Autobiography of Benjamin F. Johnson.* Orem, Utah: Grandin Press, 1997.

Johnson, Clark V. *Mormon Redress Petitions: Documents of the 1833–1838 Missouri Conflict.* Monograph Series, vol. 16. Provo, Utah: Brigham Young University Religious Studies Center, 1992.

Journal of Discourses. 26 vols. Liverpool: Latter-day Saints' Book Depot, 1854–86.

Jubilee History of Latter-day Saints Sunday Schools. Salt Lake City: Deseret Sunday School Union, 1900.

Kenney, Scott G. *Wilford Woodruff's Journals: 1833–1898.* 9 vols. Midvale, Utah: Signature Books, 1983–1985.

Kimball, Edward L. *Lengthen Your Stride: The Presidency of Spencer W. Kimball.* Salt Lake City: Deseret Book, 2005.

———. *Lengthen Your Stride: The Presidency of Spencer W. Kimball, Working Draft.* Salt Lake City: Benchmark Books, 2009.

Kimball, Spencer W. *Spencer W. Kimball* [manual]. Teachings of Presidents of the Church series. Salt Lake City: The Church of Jesus Christ of Latter-day Saints, 2006.

———. *The Teachings of Spencer W. Kimball.* Edited by Edward L. Kimball. Salt Lake City, Utah: Bookcraft, 1982.

Knowles, Eleanor. *Howard W. Hunter.* Salt Lake City: Deseret Book, 1994.

Largey, Dennis L., ed. *Book of Mormon Reference Companion.* Salt Lake City: Deseret Book, 2003.

Launius, Roger D. *Alexander William Doniphan: Portrait of a Missouri Moderate.* Columbia: University of Missouri, 1997.

Law, Reuben D. *The Founding and Early Development of the Church College of Hawaii.* St. George, Utah: Dixie College Press, 1972.

Lee, Harold B. *Harold B. Lee* [manual]. Teachings of Presidents of the Church series. Salt Lake City: The Church of Jesus Christ of Latter-day Saints, 2000.

Leonard, Glen M. *Nauvoo: A Place of Peace, a People of Promise.* Salt Lake: Deseret Book, 2002.

Ludlow, Daniel H., et al., eds. *Encyclopedia of Mormonism.* 4 vols. New York: Macmillian, 1992.

Lyon, T. Edgar, Jr. *T. Edgar Lyon, a Teacher in Zion.* Provo, Utah: Brigham Young University Press, 2002.

MacKay, Michael Hubbard, and Gerritt J. Dirkmaat.

From Darkness unto Light: Joseph Smith's Translation and Publication of the Book of Mormon. Salt Lake City and Provo, Utah: Deseret Book and Brigham Young University Religious Studies Center, 2015.

MacKay, Michael Hubbard, Gerrit J. Dirkmaat, Grant Underwood, Robert J. Woodford, William G. Hartley, eds. *Documents, Volume 1: July 1828–June 1831.* Vol. 1 of the Documents series of The Joseph Smith Papers, edited by Dean C. Jessee, Ronald K. Esplin, Richard Lyman Bushman, and Matthew J. Grow. Salt Lake City: Church Historian's Press, 2013.

MacKinnon, William P., ed. *At Sword's Point, Part 1: A Documentary History of the Utah War to 1858.* Norman, Okla.: Arthur H. Clark Company, 2008.

Madsen, Truman G. *Joseph Smith the Prophet.* Salt Lake City: Bookcraft, 1989.

Martins, Helvécio, and Mark L. Grover. *The Autobiography of Elder Helvécio Martins.* Salt Lake City: Aspen Books, 1994.

Matthews, Robert J. *"A Plainer Translation," Joseph Smith's Translation of the Bible: A History and Commentary.* Provo, Utah: Brigham Young University Press, 1985.

McConkie, Joseph Fielding. *The Bruce R. McConkie Story: Reflections of a Son.* Salt Lake City: Shadow Mountain, 2003.

McConkie, Mark L. *Remembering Joseph: Personal Recollections of Those Who Knew the Prophet Joseph Smith.* Salt Lake City: Deseret Book, 2003.

McCulloch, J. E. *Home, the Savior of Civilization.* Washington, D.C.: The Southern Co-operative League, 1924.

McGavin, E. Cecil. *The Historical Background of the Doctrine and Covenants.* Salt Lake City: Paragon Printing, 1949.

McGavin, E. Cecil. *The Mormon Pioneers.* Salt Lake City: Stevens and Wallis, 1947.

McKay, David O. *The Teachings of David O. McKay.* Edited by Mary Jane Woodger. Salt Lake City: Deseret Book, 2003.

McMurrin, Sterling M., and L. Jackson Newell. *Matters of Conscience: Conversations with Sterling M. McMurrin on Philosophy, Education, and Religion.* Salt Lake City: Signature Books, 1996.

Messages of the First Presidency of The Church of Jesus Christ of Latter-day Saints. Compiled by James R. Clark. 6 vols. Salt Lake City: Bookcraft, 1965.

Millet, Robert L., and Kent P. Jackson, eds. *The*

Doctrine and Covenants. Vol. 1 in Studies in Scripture series. Sandy, Utah: Randall Book, 1984.

———. *The Pearl of Great Price*. Vol. 2 in Studies in Scripture series. Sandy, Utah: Randall Book, 1985.

Moffat, Riley M., Fred E. Woods, and Jeffrey N. Walker. *Gathering to La'ie*. Laie, Hawaii: Brigham Young University–Hawaii Jonathan Napela Center for Hawaiian and Pacific Island Studies, 2011.

Moorman, Donald R. *Camp Floyd and the Mormons: The Utah War*. Salt Lake City: University of Utah Press, 2005.

Mouritsen, Dale C. *A Defense and a Refuge: Priesthood Correlation and the Establishment of Zion*. Provo, Utah: Brigham Young University Publications, 1972.

Mulder, William. *Homeward to Zion: The Mormon Migration from Scandinavia*. Minneapolis: University of Minnesota Press, 1985.

My Fellow Servants: Essays on the History of the Priesthood. Provo, Utah: BYU Studies, 2010.

Neilson, Reid L. *Early Mormon Missionary Activities in Japan, 1901–1924*. Salt Lake City: University of Utah Press, 2010.

———. *To the Peripheries of Mormondom: The Apostolic Around-the-World Journey of David O. McKay, 1920–1921*. Salt Lake City: University of Utah Press, 2011.

———, ed. *The Japanese Missionary Journals of Elder Alma O. Taylor, 1901–10*. Provo, Utah: BYU Studies, 2001. Deseret Bookshelf, eBook.

Neilson, Reid L., and Van C. Gessel, eds. *Taking the Gospel to the Japanese, 1901 to 2001*. Provo, Utah: Brigham Young University Press, 2006.

Neilson, Reid L., Steven C. Harper, Craig K. Manscill, and Mary Jane Woodger, eds. *The Pacific Isles*. Regional Studies in Latter-day Saint Church History series. Provo, Utah: Brigham Young University Religious Studies Center, 2008.

Neilson, Reid L., and Fred E. Woods, eds. *"Go Ye into All the World": The Growth and Development of Mormon Missionary Work*. Provo and Salt Lake City, Utah: Brigham Young University Religious Studies Center and Deseret Book, 2012.

Nevins, Allan. *Polk: Diary of a President, 1845–1849*. New York City: Longmans Green, 1952.

Nibley, Preston. *The Presidents of the Church*. Salt Lake City: Deseret Book, 1971.

———. *The Witnesses of the Book of Mormon*. Salt Lake City: Deseret Book, 1953.

Nyman, Monte S., and Robert L. Millet, eds. *The*

Joseph Smith Translation: The Restoration of Plain and Precious Things. Provo, Utah: Brigham Young University Religious Studies Center, 1985.

O'Driscoll, Jeffrey S. *Hyrum Smith: A Life of Integrity*. Salt Lake City: Deseret Book, 2003.

Olsen, Andrew D. *The Price We Paid: The Extraordinary Story of the Willie and Martin Handcart Pioneers*. Salt Lake City: Deseret Book, 2006.

Orton, Chad M., and William W. Slaughter. *40 Ways to Look at Brigham Young*. Salt Lake City: Deseret Book, 2008.

Pack, Alice C. *Building Missionaries in Hawaii, 1960–1963*. Laie, Hawaii: Church College of Hawaii, 1963.

Packer, Boyd K. *That All May Be Edified*. Salt Lake City: Bookcraft, 1982.

The Pearl of Great Price, Being a Choice Selection from the Revelations, Translations, and Narrations of Latter Day Saints. Liverpool: Franklin D. Richards, 1851.

Petersen, Gerald A. *The Mormon Tabernacle Choir: More Than Music*. Provo, Utah: Brigham Young University Press, 1979.

Peterson, H. Donl. *Moroni: Ancient Prophet, Modern Messenger*. Bountiful, Utah: Horizon Publishers, 1983.

Peterson, Janet, and Larene Gaunt. *Keepers of the Flame*. Salt Lake City: Deseret Book, 1993.

Peterson, Levi S. *Juanita Brooks: Mormon Woman Historian*. Salt Lake City: University of Utah Press, 1996.

Plewe, Brandon S. *Mapping Mormonism*. Provo, Utah: Brigham Young University Press, 2012.

Powell, Allan Kent. *Utah History Encyclopedia*. Salt Lake City: University of Utah Press, 1994.

Pratt, Orson. *An Interesting Account of Several Remarkable Visions of the Late Discovery of Ancient American Records*. Edinburgh: Ballantyne and Hughes, 1840.

———. *The Bible and Polygamy*. Salt Lake City: Deseret News Publishing Company, 1892.

Pratt, Parley P. *Autobiography of Parley P. Pratt, Revised and Enhanced Edition*. Edited by Parley P. Pratt Jr., 1874. Edited by Scott Facer Proctor and Maurine Jensen Proctor. Salt Lake City: Deseret Book, 2000.

Priesthood. Salt Lake City: Deseret Book, 1981.

Prince, Gregory A., and William Robert Wright. *David O. McKay and the Rise of Modern Mormonism*. Salt Lake City: University of Utah Press, 2005.

Rahmato, Dessalegn. *Famine and Survival Strategies: A Case Study from Northeast Ethiopia*. Sweden: Nordic Africa Institute, 1991.

Rich, Ben E. *Mr. Durant of Salt Lake City, That Mormon.* Salt Lake City: George Q. Cannon and Sons, 1893.

Rich, Russell R. *Ensign to the Nations: A History of the LDS Church from 1846 to 1972.* Provo, Utah: Brigham Young University Publications, 1972.

Roberts, B. H. *A Comprehensive History of The Church of Jesus Christ of Latter-day Saints.* 6 vols. Provo, Utah: Brigham Young University Press, 1965.

———. *The Missouri Persecutions.* Salt Lake City: George Q. Cannon and Sons, 1900.

Robinson, Stephen E., and H. Dean Garrett. *A Commentary on the Doctrine and Covenants.* 4 vols. Salt Lake City: Deseret Book, 2000–2005.

Rogers, Aurelia Read Spencer. *Life Sketches of Orson Spencer and Others and History of Primary Work.* Salt Lake City: Geo. Q. Cannon & Sons, 1898.

Romney, Thomas Cottam. *The Mormon Colonies in Mexico.* Salt Lake City: Deseret Book, 2005.

Romney, Virginia Hatch, and Richard O. Cowan. *The Colonia Juarez Temple: A Prophet's Inspiration.* Provo, Utah: Brigham Young University Religious Studies Center, 2009.

Rudd, Glen L. *Pure Religion: The Story of Church Welfare.* Salt Lake City: The Church of Jesus Christ of Latter-day Saints, 1995.

Scraps of Biography, Designed for the Instruction and Encouragement of Young Latter-day Saints. Salt Lake City: Juvenile Instruction Office, 1883.

Sessions, Gene A. *Mormon Thunder: A Documentary History of Jedediah Morgan Grant.* Salt Lake City: Greg Kofford Books, 2008.

Shepard, William, and H. Michael Marquardt. *Lost Apostles: Forgotten Members of Mormonism's Original Quorum of the Twelve.* Salt Lake City: Signature Books, 2014.

Skousen, Royal, and Robin Scott Jensen, eds. *Revelations and Translations, Volume 3: Printer's Manuscript of the Book of Mormon, Part 1: 1 Nephi 1–Alma 35.* Vol. 3, part 1, of the Revelations and Translations series of The Joseph Smith Papers, edited by Dean C. Jessee, Ronald K. Esplin, and Richard Lyman Bushman. Salt Lake City: Church Historian's Press, 2011.

Smith, Barbara B. *A Fruitful Season.* Salt Lake City: Bookcraft, 1988.

Smith, Joseph. *History of The Church of Jesus Christ of Latter-day Saints.* Edited by B. H. Roberts. 7 vols. 2d ed. rev. Salt Lake City: The Church of Jesus Christ of Latter-day Saints, 1938–51.

———. *Joseph Smith* [manual]. Teachings of Presidents of the Church series. Salt Lake City: The Church of Jesus Christ of Latter-day Saints, 2007.

Smith, Joseph Fielding. *Life of Joseph F. Smith.* Salt Lake City: Deseret Book, 1969.

Sonne, Conway B. *Knight of the Kingdom: The Story of Richard Ballantyne.* Salt Lake City: Deseret Book, 1989.

Staker, Mark L. *Hearken, O Ye People: The Historical Setting of Joseph Smith's Ohio Revelations.* Salt Lake City: Greg Kofford Books, 2009.

Stenhouse, T. B. H. *Rocky Mountain Saints: A Full and Complete History of the Mormons.* New York: Appleton, 1878.

Sterne, Harold E. *Catalogue of Nineteenth-Century Printing Presses.* New Castle, Del.: Oak Knoll Press, 2001.

Stout, Hosea. *On the Mormon Frontier: The Diary of Hosea Stout.* Edited by Juanita Brooks. 2 vols. Salt Lake City: University of Utah Press, 1964.

Swinton, Heidi S. *America's Choir: A Commemorative Portrait of the Mormon Tabernacle Choir.* Menomonee Falls, Wis.: Inland Press, 2004.

Tate, Lucile C. *Boyd K. Packer: A Watchman on the Tower.* Salt Lake City: Bookcraft, 1995.

Taylor, Mark H. *Witness to the Martyrdom: John Taylor's Personal Account of the Last Days of the Prophet Joseph Smith.* Salt Lake City: Deseret Book, 1999.

Taylor, Samuel W. *The Last Pioneer: John Taylor, a Mormon Prophet.* Salt Lake City: Signature Books, 1999.

Teaching Seminary: Preservice Readings. Prepared by the Church Educational System. Salt Lake City: The Church of Jesus Christ of Latter-day Saints, 2004.

Tucker, Pomeroy. *The Origin, Rise, and Progress of Mormonism.* New York: Appleton, 1867.

Tullidge, Edward W. *The Women of Mormondom.* New York: Tullidge and Crandall, 1877.

Turley, Richard E., Jr., and William W. Slaughter. *How We Got the Doctrine and Covenants.* Salt Lake City: Deseret Book, 2015.

Tyler, Daniel. *A Concise History of the Mormon Battalion, 1846–1847.* Glorieta, New Mexico: Rio Grande Press, 1969.

Van Orden, Bruce A. *Prisoner for Conscience' Sake: The Life of George Reynolds.* Salt Lake City: Deseret Book, 1992.

Van Wagoner, Richard S. *Complete Discourses of*

Brigham Young. 5 vols. Salt Lake City: Signature Books, 2009.

———. *Sidney Rigdon: A Portrait of Religious Excess.* Salt Lake City: Signature Books, 1994.

Vogel, Dan, ed. *History of Joseph Smith and the Church of Jesus Christ of Latter-day Saints: A Source- and Text-Critical Edition.* 6 vols. Salt Lake City: Smith-Petit Foundation, 2015.

Walker, Ronald W., Richard E. Turley Jr., and Glen M. Leonard. *Massacre at Mountain Meadows: An American Tragedy.* Oxford: Oxford University Press, 2008.

Watson, Elden Jay. *Manuscript History of Brigham Young, 1801–1844.* Salt Lake City: Smith Secretarial Service, 1968.

Welch, John W., and Erick B. Carlson, eds. *Opening the Heavens: Accounts of Divine Manifestations, 1820–1844.* Provo, Utah: Brigham Young University Press, 2005.

Whetten, LaVon Brown. *Colonia Juarez: Commemorating 125 years of the Mormon Colonies in Mexico.* Bloomington, Ida.: Authorhouse, 2010.

Whitaker, David J., and Arnold K. Garr, eds. *A Firm Foundation: Church Organization and Administration.* Provo and Salt Lake City, Utah: Brigham Young University Religious Studies Center and Deseret Book, 2011.

Whitaker, Wetzel O. *Pioneering with Film: A History of Church and Brigham Young University Films.* Provo, Utah: [n.p.], 1982.

Whitmer, David. *An Address to All Believers in Christ.* Richmond, Mo. 1886.

Whitney, Orson F. *History of Utah.* 4 vols. Salt Lake City: George Q. Cannon and Sons, 1904.

———. *Life of Heber C. Kimball, an Apostle, the Father and Founder of the British Mission.* Salt Lake City: Kimball Family, 1888.

Widtsoe, John A., and Leah D. Widtsoe. *Word of Wisdom: A Modern Interpretation.* Salt Lake City: Deseret Book, 1937.

Wilkinson, Ernest L., ed. *Brigham Young University: The First One Hundred Years.* 4 vols. Provo, Utah: Brigham Young University Press, 1975.

Winder, Michael K. *Presidents and Prophets: The Story of America's Presidents and the LDS Church.* American Fork, Utah: Covenant Communications, 2007.

Woodger, Mary Jane, ed. *Champion of Liberty: John Taylor.* Provo and Salt Lake City, Utah: Brigham Young University Religious Studies Center and Deseret Book, 2009.

Woodruff, Wilford. *Leaves from My Journal, Third Book of Faith-Promoting Stories.* Salt Lake City: Juvenile Instructor Office, 1882.

———. *Waiting for the World's End: The Diaries of Wilford Woodruff.* Edited by Susan L. Staker. Salt Lake City: Signature Books, 1993.

———. *Wilford Woodruff* [manual]. Teachings of Presidents of the Church series. Salt Lake City: The Church of Jesus Christ of Latter-day Saints, 2011.

Worldwide Leadership Training Meeting: Building Up a Righteous Posterity. Salt Lake City: The Church of Jesus Christ of Latter-day Saints, 2008.

Yorgason, Blaine M., Richard A. Schmutz, and Douglas D. Alder. *All That Was Promised: The St. George Temple and the Unfolding of the Restoration.* Salt Lake City: Deseret Book, 2013.

Image Credits

Photos courtesy Casey Paul Griffiths, except as indicated below. All photos used by permission.

Chapters 4, 11, 16, 43, 45, 49, 53, 54, 56, 61, 62, 63, 65, 66, 69, 71, 72, 75, 81. Courtesy Intellectual Reserve, Inc.

Chapter 10. Oliver Cowdery. Unidentified man, half-length portrait, with arm resting on table with tablecloth, by James Presley Ball. Courtesy Library of Congress.

Chapter 15. *Bird's-eye View of the City of Independence, Jackson Co., Missouri, 1868,* by A. Ruger. Courtesy Library of Congress.

Chapters 19, 31, 33, 40, 59, 83, 91. Courtesy Malina Grigg.

Chapters 20, 21, 29, 35, 46. © Everett Historical/ shutterstock.com.

Chapter 25. © Slava Gerj/shutterstock.com.

Chapter 32. *Joseph Smith's Original Temple, Nauvoo, Ills.* Courtesy Library of Congress.

Chapters 38, 39, 51, 52. Courtesy Kenneth Mays.

Chapter 42. Richard Ballantyne. Image via Wikimedia.

Chapter 44. Orson Pratt, bust portrait, 1875, by C. R. Savage. Courtesy L. Tom Perry Special Collections, Harold B. Lee Library, Brigham Young University, Provo, Utah.

Chapter 47. Confederate general Albert Sidney Johnston. Image via Wikimedia.

Chapter 50. George Reynolds. Image via Wikimedia.

Chapter 55. Capstone laying on Cardston Alberta Temple, ca. 1917. Courtesy Library of Congress.

Chapter 58. Salt Lake City, Utah, ca. 1896, by William Henry Jackson. Courtesy Library of Congress.

Chapter 60. Moses Thatcher bust portrait, 1883, by C. R. Savage. Courtesy L. Tom Perry Special Collections, Harold B. Lee Library, Brigham Young University, Provo, Utah.

Chapter 64. Reed Smoot, ca. 1898. Courtesy L. Tom Perry Special Collections, Harold B. Lee Library, Brigham Young University, Provo, Utah.

Chapter 67. *Boy Scouts and Scoutmasters, 1926,* by George Edward Anderson. Courtesy L. Tom Perry Special Collections, Harold B. Lee Library, Brigham Young University, Provo, Utah.

Chapter 68. *Still There's No Place like Home.* Courtesy Library of Congress.

Chapter 70. Joseph F. Smith, ca. 1901. Courtesy L. Tom Perry Special Collections, Harold B. Lee Library, Brigham Young University, Provo, Utah.

Chapter 73. Russel B. Swensen and Sidney B. Sperry of the Division of Religion, Brigham Young University, 1943. Courtesy L. Tom Perry Special Collections, Harold B. Lee Library, Brigham Young University, Provo, Utah.

Chapter 76. Honolulu and vicinity, 1887. Courtesy Library of Congress.

Chapter 77. Courtesy Edwin Griggs.

Chapter 78. Rustic stone stage at Aspen Grove, 1929. Courtesy L. Tom Perry Special Collections, Harold B. Lee Library, Brigham Young University, Provo, Utah.

Chapter 80. © jmboix/shutterstock.com.

Chapter 84. © Olga Rutko/shutterstock.com.

Chapter 85. © itoodmuk/shutterstock.com.

Chapter 86. Courtesy Frank Day.

Chapter 87. United States Capitol, Washington, D.C., by Carol M. Highsmith. Courtesy Library of Congress.

Chapter 88. Courtesy Marcus Martins.

Chapter 89. Courtesy Randall L. Hall.

Chapter 92. © Riccardo Mayer/shutterstock.com.

Chapter 94. Courtesy Dan Belnap.

Chapter 95. © Antilo/shutterstock.com.

Chapter 97. Courtesy Rick Satterfield.

Chapter 99. © alexkich/shutterstock.com.

Chapter 100. Elders in Mozambique. Photo by Todd Williams. Courtesy Cameron Biddulph.